DATE DUE			
DEC 0 2 2005			
GAYLORD			PRINTED IN U.S.A.

Timber, Tourists, and Temples

Conservation and Development in the Maya Forest of Belize, Guatemala, and Mexico

Edited by
Richard B. Primack, David Barton Bray,
Hugo A. Galletti, and Ismael Ponciano

ISLAND PRESS
Washington, D.C. • Covelo, California

No copyright claim is made in chapters 15, 17, and 22, work produced in part by employees of the U.S. government.

Library of Congress Cataloging-in-Publication Data

Timber, tourists, and temples: conservation and development in the
   Maya Forest of Belize, Guatemala, and Mexico/edited by Richard B.
   Primack
        p.   cm.
     Includes bibliographical references and index.
     ISBN 1-55963-541-X (cloth). — ISBN 1-55963-542-8 (paper)
     1. Forest conservation—Maya Forest. 2. Maya Forest. 3. Forest
   policy—Maya Forest. 4. Non-timber forest resources—Maya Forest.
   5. Ecotourism—Maya Forest.   I. Primack, Richard B., 1950–
   SD414.M47T55   1998
   333.75′0972—dc21   97-34519
                                                           CIP

Printed on recycled, acid-free paper ⊕

Manufactured in the United States of America

10   9   8   7   6   5   4   3   2   1

Contents

Chapter 23
Community-Based Development As a Conservation Tool: The Community
Baboon Sanctuary and the Gales Point Manatee Reserve   343
Robert H. Horwich and Jonathan Lyon

Chapter 24
Illuminating the Petén's Throne of Gold:
The ProPetén Experiment in Conservation-Based Development   365
Conrad Reining and Carlos Soza Manzanero

Chapter 25
The Belize Zoo: Grassroots Efforts in Education and Outreach   389
Rafael Coc, Laura Marsh, and Elizabeth Platt

Acknowledgments

Special thanks are extended to Twig Johnson, formerly with the U.S. Agency for International Development and now with the World Wildlife Fund, whose initial vision of a comparison among Belize, Guatemala, and Mexico started this project. We also would like to thank some of the institutions and people that made possible the conference on which this volume is based. The conference "Conservation and Community Development in the Maya Forest of Belize, Guatemala, and Mexico" was held in Chetumal, Quintana Roo, Mexico, November 8–11, 1995, and was sponsored by the Secretaría de Medio Ambiente, Recursos Naturales, y Pesca (SEMARNAP) of Mexico; the Tropical Ecosystems Directorate of the U.S. Man and the Biosphere Program (TED/USMAB); the Patronato por la Ecología y el Desarrollo Forestal de Quintana Roo, A.C.; the Sociedad de Ejidos Productores Forestales de Quintana Roo, S.C.; and the Inter-American Foundation. The Museo de la Cultura Maya in Chetumal provided optimal surroundings for the successful development of the conference. Current and past members of the TED/USMAB, David Bray, Francisco Dallmeier, Gary Hartshorn, James D. Nations, Richard B. Primack, Anthony Stocks, Kristiina Ann Vogt, Aaron Zazueta, Tom Ankersen, Laura Snook, Margaret Symington, Kathy Moser, and Archie Carr III; its two chairs during this period, Twig Johnson and John Wilson; and Roger Soles of the U.S. MAB national office provided steadfast support for the conference and this publication.

Chapter authors, the book editors, and the TED/USMAB members reviewed individual chapters. Outside reviews were also provided by I. Olmsted, D. Clark, G. Fonseca, S. Jacobson, C. Miller, A. Blundel, B. Miller, C. Munn, C. R. Carroll, T. Synnott, J. Ewel, D. Ackerly, A. Gomez-Pompa, A. L. Hudson, E. Mallory, B. Loiselle, R. Bierregard, G. Wilkes, K. Redford, A. B. Jorgenson, J. Lynch, J. Denslow, and F. E. Putz. Carlisle J. Levine, currently Program Staff Assistant for Mexico and Bolivia at the Inter-American Foundation, has provided a constant thread of efficient and thoughtful support throughout the organization of the conference and its implementation in Chetumal and in the preparation of this volume. Elizabeth Platt has lent her considerable editing skills to the project, and her work has improved every aspect and every chapter in this volume; her familiarity with the Maya Forest region has been crucial to this volume and the TED/USMAB project from the beginning. Barbara Dean, Barbara Youngblood, and Cecilia González of Island Press have shown the skills that have helped make Island Press the leading environmental publisher that it is, and we thank them.

Introduction: The Maya Forest

James D. Nations, Richard B. Primack, and David Bray

Every 16 days, a LANDSAT satellite passes silently and swiftly over the Maya Forest of Mexico, Guatemala, and Belize (Map 1). Viewed from the vantage point of space, this combination of forests, rivers, and savannahs is a single swath of green spread across the midriff of Mesoamerica. It stretches from the Mexican state of Chiapas across northern Guatemala, into the southern Yucatán Peninsula, and across the Central American nation of Belize.

On the ground, human history has divided the Maya Forest, or Selva Maya, into three sovereign nations. As if in defiance of political borders, though, the flora and fauna of this mosaic of ecosystems are remarkably similar. The natural biological systems of the region include montane and lowland tropical moist forest, large, seasonally flooded scrub forests called *bajos*, oxbow lakes, and the largest freshwater wetland in Central America. Wildlife is rich and varied, with jaguars, pumas, tapirs, monkeys, potos, and peccaries among the larger mammals, and macaws, toucans, harpy eagles, and jabiru storks among the hundreds of species of birds. Every year, the region also becomes home to up to 1 billion migratory birds escaping winter in Canada and the United States.

The three nations that share the Maya Forest are also tied together by the rich cultural roots of the Maya peoples who have lived in the forest for millennia. The ancient Maya turned this seemingly intractable wilderness into the biological foundation for a society that flourished for more than 1,000

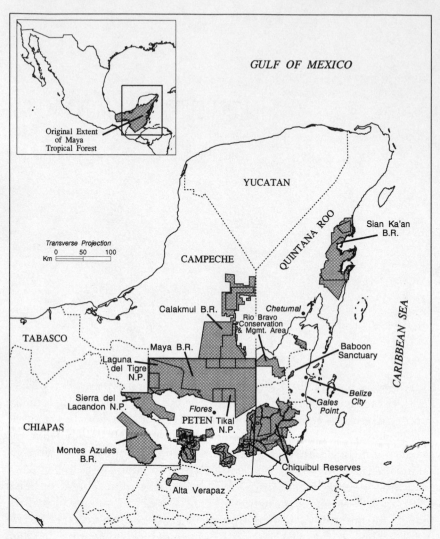

Map 1

Map of areas mentioned in the text, in particular Biosphere Reserves (B.R.) and National Parks (N.P.). National boundaries are solid lines and state boundaries are dashed. The inset shows the original extent of the Maya Forest.

years. The Maya Forest provided the ecological fuel for one of the most developed civilizations of its time—the classical Maya period of A.D. 250 to 900; the Maya practiced mathematics, astronomy, water control, sophisticated writing, and a calendric system that measured time more accurately than the modern Gregorian calendar.

Figure 1

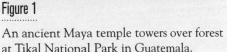

An ancient Maya temple towers over forest
at Tikal National Park in Guatemala.

Today, the modern descendants of the ancient Maya mix the traditions of
the past with contemporary technology to forge new adaptations in a rapidly
changing environment. But the ancient Maya also left their modern descendants two other valuable legacies: a forest filled with species useful to human
beings and one of the world's premier ecotourism destinations. Within the
Maya Forest grows the raw material for one of Latin America's most promising systems of extractive reserves: a rich mixture of renewable species, such as
xate palms, chicle resin, and allspice, that produces employment for thousands of local families and millions of dollars in income for the governments
of Mexico, Guatemala, and Belize.

The region's income from tourism is even greater. The Maya Forest is one
of the few places on earth where visitors can look up from a stone city ten centuries old to watch spider monkeys turning somersaults through a tropical
forest canopy. This combination of tropical wildlands and ancient ruins brings
hundreds of thousands of tourists to the Maya Forest each year, providing the
basis for a multimillion-dollar tourism industry that could well be one of the
chief elements in the Maya Forest's survival.

The Maya Forest's cornucopia of biodiversity, cultural heritage, and economic benefits is countered by the immediate, real-world threats the region faces. A 1995 satellite image of the Maya Forest shows huge blotches of deforestation spreading out from human settlements in concentric rings of destruction. In Mexico's Selva Lacandóna, PEMEX oil roads spread across the forest like spider webs, multiplying the number of cattle ranchers and *ejidatarios* (cooperative members) clearing land for beef production and corn farming. Population in the Guatemalan Petén is growing at 7% to 10% per year, bringing new influxes of land-hungry colonists into the region's national parks and biosphere reserves. In Belize, Salvadoran refugee farmers and Guatemalan Kekchi Indians are clearing forest for subsistence agriculture, while Mennonite farmers rip hectare after hectare of trees from the ground using giant anchor chains dragged between two bulldozers. The current rate of forest destruction in the Maya Forest surpasses 80,000 hectares (ha) per year.

At times, efforts to ease ecological threats in one country are hindered by environmental damage in another. Mexicans from deforested areas of Tabasco, Chiapas, and Campeche are poaching timber and wildlife in core areas of the Maya Biosphere Reserve of adjoining Guatemala. Deforested slopes in southern Belize are creating flash floods in communities of the southern Petén. And acid rain from Mexico's Coatzacoalcos oil refineries is threatening ancient Maya ruins in the Guatemalan Petén and in Mexico's own Yucatán Peninsula.

Just as the national economies of the Maya region are increasingly tied into a larger, regional economy, so also are their national environments inextricably bound to those of their neighbors. Increasingly, the threats to the Maya Forest are being recognized as regional problems that demand regional solutions. Nonetheless, one of the primary tools in maintaining the biological integrity of the Maya Forest is the creation of biosphere reserves, national parks, and other protected areas within the individual countries. In Chiapas, the government of Mexico established the 3,300-square-kilometer (km^2) Montes Azules Biosphere Reserve in the Lacandón rainforest in 1978. In 1992, President Carlos Salinas added 550 km^2 to the reserve, and the indigenous inhabitants of Chiapas recently created a community reserve, La Cojolita, that connects the Montes Azules Biosphere Reserve to a similar reserve in Guatemala.

On the Guatemalan side of the Usumacinta River, which serves as the border between Mexico and Guatemala, lies the 16,000 km^2 Maya Biosphere Reserve, a protected area the size of the country of El Salvador. Guatemala's Maya Biosphere Reserve connects in the north with the Calakmul Biosphere Reserve of Quintana Roo, Mexico, and to the east with the Río Bravo protected area operated by the Programme for Belize.

Just south of this connection, two frontier parks focus on the watershed of the Chiquibul River. The Chiquibul is born in the Maya Mountains of Belize, but passes almost immediately into the Guatemalan Petén, where it runs for 75% of its length before crossing back into Belize as the Río Mopan. In Belize, it merges with the Belize River and travels through the San Ignacio Valley, Belize's breadbasket, then on through the two largest cities of the country, Belmopan and Belize City. In 1991, Belize created the Chiquibul National Park and Chiquibul Forest Reserve to protect this vital watershed. In 1995, Guatemala followed suit by declaring the Chiquibul Biosphere Reserve on its side of the border, creating a mirror-image frontier protected area. Today, 80% of the common border between Belize and Guatemala's Petén lies under protected status.

Together, this complex of protected areas in Belize, Guatemala, and Mexico creates what conservationists call the Maya Arch, providing legal, if not actual, protection for more than 25,000 km^2 of tropical forest and related natural ecosystems.

The building blocks of the Maya Arch and of the Maya Forest itself are the region's five biosphere reserves: Montes Azules, Maya, Calakmul, Sian Ka'an, and Chiquibul. This remarkable constellation of protected areas makes the Maya Forest the second largest complex of biosphere reserves in the Western Hemisphere, second only to the Rocky Mountain complex of biosphere reserves along the border between the United States and Canada.

Like biosphere reserves throughout the world, those of the Maya Forest were created with the combined goals of conservation, scientific investigation, and sustainable economic development. The purpose of a biosphere reserve is not to exclude people from the protected area, but to identify ways in which people and nature can coexist to the benefit of both. All biosphere reserves have core areas that are designed to remain inviolate except for visits by scientists and, sometimes, ecotourists. Many reserves have multiple-use areas inhabited by indigenous peoples and other communities that, ideally, practice sustainable harvesting of natural resources. And all biosphere reserves have buffer zones intended to provide a transition zone between the protected reserve and activities of the outside world.

Conservationists know that the nuclear zones of the biosphere reserves of the Maya Forest must be protected from destruction if the region's wealth of biodiversity is to survive. But the most important step in preventing this destruction may well be what happens in the lives and communities of the families who live outside the reserves' boundaries.

At its peak of population around the year A.D. 700, the Maya Forest was probably home to as many as 5 million Maya people. Today, there are fewer than 1 million people in the region—only a small percentage of them Maya—yet the area is being transformed from forest to pastures and wasteland. This transformation is bringing little benefit to the people of the Maya Forest, many of whom continue to live lives of poverty and desperation. Solutions to this situation have been suggested, but too few politicians and decision makers are focused on implementing them.

The most serious challenge the Maya Forest faces is caused by poverty. Poverty impels individuals with no other options to clear the forest for pasture and croplands, simply to keep their families alive. Because many of the region's traditional, and sustainable, systems of agriculture have been eradicated, the expansion of extensive *milpas* (fields used in shifting agriculture) and pastures across the forest is jeopardizing the ecological systems that sustain human life, wiping out the economic future of generations of Mexicans, Guatemalans, and Belizeans yet unborn.

The expansion of the agricultural frontier is abetted by the construction of roads through forested areas and, sometimes, national parks and biosphere reserves as well. In many cases, these roads benefit only a few individuals who make large profits selling petroleum or timber on international markets. As the profits flow out, the roads bring in families who have nowhere else to go and no economic alternatives to turn to beyond destroying the natural resources on which their own lives depend. Identifying viable economic alternatives to this pattern of destruction has become the single most important action for the survival of the Maya Forest and the people who call it home. Our strategy must be to keep alive as much of the biological foundation of the Maya Forest as possible, for the benefit of the three countries that share it, the people who live within it, and the other species of animals and plants that create its web of life.

The chapters contained in this volume are an outgrowth of efforts on the part of many people to achieve this goal. The origins of this book took shape in 1991, when the U.S. Man and the Biosphere Program's Tropical Ecosystem Directorate first contemplated supporting projects in the region. As they investigated possible means of encouraging conservation in this region, Directorate members discovered that this prospect was very complicated. Not only were there intricate social and political issues among the three countries of the region, there were also complex scientific and management problems to be worked out.

As a region rich in biological and historical treasures, the Maya Forest has attracted attention from researchers of many disciplines from many nations. The sheer quantity of information generated by these researchers staggers the imagination, yet they have barely begun to scratch the surface. Directorate members, sifting through the available information, realized that one vital piece was missing: a method by which the various people who needed the data—researchers, managers, conservation advocates, and policy makers—could pool resources and exchange information. Researchers studying the natural and cultural history of the Maya Forest work in three separate countries—each with its own procedures for acquiring permits, all having occasional disputes with one another as neighbors always do, and each possessing distinctive linguistic and cultural traditions. These factors contribute to insularity: information tends to stay within national boundaries, where, even if it is put to good use, it is by definition limited in its impact. But to conserve an ecosystem of the size and complexity of the Maya Forest, it is imperative that this information be available to all of the parties contributing to the conservation effort.

Realizing that few avenues existed to encourage communication across borders, the Tropical Ecosystems Directorate initiated the processes that eventually led to the workshops from which the chapters in this volume are drawn. Along the way, the Directorate sought to create lines of communication to promote information exchange, not only across borders, but between researchers of different disciplines, management personnel, and policy makers. The workshops led to fruitful and spirited discussions among individuals who addressed the conservation issues at hand from a multitude of perspectives; thus, the chapters that follow reflect a broad range of ideas and viewpoints.

Despite the international boundaries that divide the Maya Forest, the region shares many features; thus, Part I of this volume discusses data collected using Geographical Information Systems (GIS) and remote sensing technologies—methods that allow us to erase the lines on the map and see the forest as a unified entity. Yet the reality of national boundaries—and the distinctions between nations—cannot be denied, as each nation has its own perspective on how best to manage forest resources. Thus, Part II of this volume contains chapters that introduce these perspectives to readers who may be unfamiliar with the policies of one or more of the three nations. In addition to general introductions to each nation's forestry and conservation policies, several chapters focus upon specific projects examining techniques of forest management and sustainable resource use that are being developed by all three countries. In particular, several chapters highlight efforts by communities to manage their forest resources for conservation and sustainable timber harvest.

Part III takes up an issue that has generated great excitement and heated debate in the conservation community. Nontimber forest products are considered by some to be a promising source of sustainable alternative income for local people—a way in which standing forests can become profitable enough to discourage forest residents from cutting them down for farmland and pastures. These chapters, drawn from examples in all three nations, show just how closely tied is the conservation of species and ecosystems to the behavior of the people who make use of their products. Part IV highlights research projects that seek to integrate baseline biological research—sorely needed for both timber and nontimber species—with assessment of impacts of resource extraction and human activities upon forest species.

The last part of the volume focuses upon what is perhaps the most crucial aspect of conservation in the Maya Forest: the need to involve local people in the conservation of resources. Past experience has taught a sharp lesson about ignoring the needs of local inhabitants, informing us in no uncertain terms that it does no good to designate an area as off-limits to human use or habitation when there are people in need of land, housing, and food. Local inhabitants may be quite well educated on the issues and problems of tropical forest conservation, but may be unable to act upon this knowledge because their economic circumstances dictate otherwise. But this situation is hopeful: it is far easier to preserve a forest with the cooperation of those who live in it than to try to police it against the depredations of people who, disregarding external mandates that ignore their day-to-day well-being, have no alternative but to use the land as the source of their sustenance, albeit only for a short time. By assisting grassroots efforts at forest preservation, creating alternative sources of income for communities, and increasing the economic and social value of the forest itself, it may be possible to halt the ongoing destruction of the Maya Forest.

We can keep alive this unique and wonderful ecosystem by ensuring the stability of the region's protected areas, by intensifying agricultural production in areas that have already been deforested, and by creating economic alternatives through microenterprises, ecotourism, and the sustainable harvesting of renewable forest products. Some of these alternatives are described in the chapters that follow. As the reports indicate, confronting the challenges we face in the Maya Forest will not be easy, but for the future of the forest's biological diversity, and for the future of the families who depend on it for survival, there is no task that is more important.

Part I

A Regional Approach to the Maya Forest

Scientists working in the Maya Forest generally limit their research to sites within the boundaries of one country. The reasons for this practice are mainly pragmatic: it is difficult enough to obtain permission for research from one government without looking for additional headaches. Crossing international borders requires obtaining additional permits, paying additional fees, and completing additional time-consuming forms such as passport applications, customs documents, and inventory forms. When two nations are involved in political conflict, as happens from time to time in the region, these difficulties increase exponentially, particularly for scientists who are citizens of the quarreling countries.

In short, working across national borders is arduous, demanding work, so it is not surprising that few have attempted it. What is surprising is that some multinational projects have been attempted and have produced far-reaching results. Two examples are highlighted in this part. The first, a series of workshops sponsored by Conservation International, brought together specialists from all three countries as well as international experts to produce a regional assessment of the Maya Forest's characteristics. As reported by Rodstrom and colleagues, this project pooled Geographic Information Systems (GIS) data for all three countries to develop a perspective that encompassed the Maya Forest as a whole, freed from the limitations imposed by national boundaries.

The second example illustrates the ways that national governments can work together to achieve conservation goals in a shared ecosystem, even under circumstances of international conflict. Belize and Guatemala, historically not the friendliest of neighbors, created mirror-image reserves in the

Chiquibul River basin to preserve the unique species that live in this area. The discussion by Matola and Platt suggests ways in which this cooperative venture might be further extended to benefit both nations as well as the greater Maya Forest region.

Chapter 1

A Regional Approach to Conservation in the Maya Forest

Chris Rodstrom, Silvio Olivieri, and Laura Tangley

Stretching over southern Mexico, northern Guatemala, and Belize, the Maya Forest, or Selva Maya, constitutes one of the last large blocks of tropical forest remaining in North and Central America. Home to Mayan-speaking people for over 5,000 years, the region is also uncommonly rich in cultural and archaeological resources. Yet the survival of this vast bioregion, which at the peak of Maya civilization supported more than 5 million people, is endangered by fewer than 1 million people today.

Major threats to the Maya Forest include illegal logging, cattle ranching, and unsustainable forms of subsistence agriculture. These destructive practices wreak havoc on natural habitats while bringing little long-term benefit to the region's human inhabitants, many of whom live in poverty. To combat these related problems, several local, national, and international organizations are working to promote conservation and sustainable development in different portions of the Maya Forest. These efforts so far have failed to stem the loss of natural habitat in the region as a whole, in part because the projects do not communicate or coordinate their activities, particularly among different countries. As part of a single ecosystem, the Maya Forest's plant and animal species and biological processes do not recognize national borders. Similarly, threats to species and their habitat in one country are intimately connected with events in others. Yet until now, research and management activities within the region have been restricted to single nations. Unless scientists and conservationists begin sharing information and coordinating efforts across borders, they will be unable to stop the powerful forces of destruction facing the Maya Forest today.

In an effort to overcome obstacles to information sharing and coordination, four organizations currently working in the Maya Forest—the U.S. Man and the Biosphere Program (USMAB), Conservation International (CI), El Colegio de la Frontera Sur (ECOSUR), and the U.S. Agency for International Development (USAID)—sponsored a workshop in San Cristobal de las Casas, Chiapas, Mexico, in August 1995. The workshop brought together the leading biologists, social scientists, and conservationists working in this region to produce a consensus on conservation priorities and actions; it left behind a database combining relevant information from all three countries. Equally important, the gathering was the start of a process of collaboration among those who, together, have the power to stop the Maya Forest's destruction.

Conservation Priorities: The Need for Consensus

Lack of coordination among conservation professionals in Mexico, Guatemala, and Belize has been a problem because there has been no broad consensus on conservation priorities within the region. Why is such consensus important? With limited time and funding, the first logical step in any regional conservation plan is to decide precisely where to work and what to do. Although international funding organizations including USMAB, CI, and USAID have been willing to invest in conservation in the Maya Forest, so far they have had limited guidance from regional experts as to which parts of the region are the most biologically important—and, equally important, which are most threatened.

To achieve this consensus, workshop organizers adapted a methodology developed by CI six years ago (Olivieri et al. 1995). First used to set conservation priorities for the Amazon Basin at a workshop in 1990 (IBAMA/ INPA/CI 1991), this methodology has been employed in Papua New Guinea (Swartzendruber 1993), Madagascar (Hannah and Hough 1995), and the endangered Atlantic Forest of Brazil (Conservation International et al. 1995). The methodology involves bringing together the world's leading experts on a given geographic region's species, ecosystems, and biological and social processes. Each scientist may be an expert only on a few species or a small portion of the entire ecosystem, but the knowledge and experience of these experts taken together provide the best possible understanding of the region as a whole. To quickly capture the information the experts offer, the workshop model focuses their attention on Geographic Information System (GIS) maps, onto which they transmit and synthesize their diverse knowledge. As with the previous exercises, the consensus reached by participants at the Maya Forest workshop has provided a valuable resource for targeting scarce conservation dollars where they are needed most (Johnson 1995).

Information Sharing and Coordination

Fragmented efforts to conserve the Maya Forest also have meant that conservation professionals lack the considerable advantages provided by information sharing. This statement is especially true with respect to information on the rate and type of changes happening to the landscape, such as conversion of forest to agriculture. If organizations in Mexico, Guatemala, and Belize want to make a case for conserving their bioregion to attract international funding, they must be able to determine how much forest once existed in the region, how much is left, the condition of the remaining forest, and the current deforestation rate. Thus far, however, conservationists have been unable to make these arguments because they lack comparative data across national boundaries.

Regional information exchange also allows conservation funding agencies to keep track of how well their projects are doing relative to others that are tackling similar problems. Such monitoring and evaluation of ongoing work is essential to continually fine-tune rapidly evolving methodologies. In addition, it ensures that scarce resources go to the projects that are making the greatest contribution to conservation and sustainable development.

At the local level, information sharing allows conservation organizations to build upon the experience of others, avoiding wasteful duplication of effort. Because the cost of building a conservation database from scratch is too high for most groups in developing countries and even for many international organizations, such collaboration is essential for any group to get enough information to launch a successful conservation strategy. Although still at an early stage, the Maya Forest project has launched a process to bring together the vast amount of disparate information housed in the three countries and to build, eventually, a regional conservation database.

The Workshop's Contributions

Preparation for the Maya Forest workshop began many months before its participants convened. One essential step was to compile a "metadatabase" that summarized what relevant data already existed and what institutions and individuals were responsible for collecting them. To do this, the groups sent out information request forms to more than 200 organizations. The results were compiled, published, and distributed through a booklet and electronically on CI's World Wide Web page (http://www.conservation.org).

Another project that helped lay the groundwork for the workshop was creation of the Digital Geographic Database for the Maya Forest Region. Undertaken by the Paseo Pantera Consortium—a collaboration of the Wildlife Conservation Society and the Caribbean Conservation Corporation—and the University of Florida, it is the first standardized GIS database ever put together for the entire Maya Forest region (University of Florida et al. 1995). While its creators hope that the database will be continually updated and augmented by others, it currently consists of more than a dozen data layers, including protected areas, archaeological sites, and population centers. The database is available both on diskette and on the Internet.

Immediate workshop preparations began in March 1995. Organizers convened panels of experts on five topics: (1) biological resources, (2) landscape processes, (3) biological corridors, (4) cultural and economic resources, and (5) conservation law. Made up of approximately equal numbers of experts from Mexico, Guatemala, and Belize, each panel was charged with compiling and synthesizing as much information as possible before the August exercise, a step designed to make the workshop itself operate more efficiently.

To integrate the diversity of data provided by the experts on each panel, GIS technology was essential. Because scientists in the three countries had never before worked together, their geographic data sets were all at different scales and projections, which meant they could not be analyzed together or even combined onto a single map. To solve this problem, the GIS stretched or compressed data sets so that they fit together in one projection. This provided one comprehensive picture showing all relevant data and relationships among different data at any given location.

The database was designed to provide representative samples of information for each discussion group. For the Landscape Processes Panel, this included land-use maps from SEGEPLAN (Plan for the Integrated Development of the Petén) of northern Guatemala. The boundaries and names of protected areas were included for the Biological Resources Panel. Maps of linguistic groups provided background to the discussions of the Cultural and Economic Resources Panel. Together this information was stored and documented in a GIS, and presented as hard-copy maps at the workshop. The Corridors Panel also provided comprehensive base maps of the region for each working group that identified protected areas, archaeological sites, population centers, and roads (University of Florida et al. 1995).

At the workshop itself, the 40 panel members were joined by 25 additional invited participants: scientists, conservationists, members of funding organizations, and others who work on projects in the Maya Forest. The newly formed working groups met concurrently during the first two days. Their tasks were to evaluate the data gathered before the workshop, revising these data according to participants' own experiences; to identify gaps and areas of overlap in the type and geographical coverage of the data; and to draw up plans for future data sharing and coordination. In addition, the Biological Resources, Corridors, and Landscape Processes Panels identified and mapped high conservation priorities within the region. The Cultural and Economic Resources Panel and the Conservation Law Panel recommended actions for promoting conservation and sustainable development within these priority areas.

Biological Resources

The working group on biological resources pooled diverse information and reached a consensus on priority areas based upon relative biological importance. After considerable debate and negotiation, a list of six criteria for priority status was drawn from an original list of 12: (1) level of threat, (2) distribution/extension, (3) ecological importance, (4) biodiversity, (5) ecological processes/critical habitat, and (6) level of endemism (the number of species found only in that location). The definition for each criterion is shown in Table 1.1. Using these criteria, 20 areas with the highest biological importance in the region were defined, as shown in Figure 1.1. Table 1.2 lists each area by code and name.

High priority areas include lowland tropical moist forests, montane systems, and coastal ecosystems. Area RB3 in Mexico, with palms and flooded riparian zones, ranked high in ecological importance, biodiversity, critical habitat, and endemism. The coastal northern and southern lagoons in Belize, Area RB10, contain red mangrove and a population of West Indian manatee (*Trichechus manatus*). Both the manatee and hawksbill turtles (*Eretmochelys imbricata*) are believed to rely on these areas for breeding and nesting areas, respectively. Several areas span political or legal boundaries. For instance, Area RB6, Tikal–Southern Calakmul–Río Bravo, covers three types of protected area within three countries. However, the group distinguished areas by the similarity of their biological characteristics rather than by their legal status. Finally, Area RB8, the Maya Mountains, included two separate areas, but only the area located along the Guatemala–Belize border was fully described.

Landscape Processes

Focusing on deforestation, land-use changes such as agricultural conversion, and degradation of protected areas, the landscape processes working group identified priority areas based upon the extent of threats to these areas compared to others. Making such comparisons is difficult because all prior estimates of forest cover and deforestation rates have generally focused on selected areas within the three countries of the Maya region (Calleros and Brauer 1983; Sader et al. 1994). As a gathering that brought together experts who have contributed to these previous studies along with many others with knowledge of landscape changes occurring throughout the region, the workshop provided the first opportunity to achieve a broad consensus on how different portions of the Maya Forest are faring relative to one another. It was

Table 1.1. Biological importance criteria for determining priority areas.

Criteria	Score/Value	Definition of the score
Level of Threat (LT)	HIGH	a. Deforestation >20% of original extent b. Population growth ≥5% per year
	MEDIUM	a. Does not satisfy the requirements of HIGH
Distribution/Extension (DE)	HIGH	a. Continuous distribution of habitat
	MEDIUM	a. Habitat fragmented into 3 or more sections b. Area reduced by more than 50%
Ecologic Importance (EI)	HIGH	a. Serves as a carbon reserve (tree density >500/ha; tallest vegetation >20 m high) b. Protects important aquifers c. Integrates important ecological functions
	MEDIUM	a. Does not satisfy the requirements of HIGH
Biodiversity (B)	HIGH	a. Contains at least 5 distinct ecosystems b. Local flora contains ≥20% total species in region
	MEDIUM	a. Contains fewer than 5 distinct ecosystems b. Local flora contains <20% total species in region
Critical Habitat (CH)	HIGH	a. Presence of migratory species b. Site of specialized ecological interactions
	MEDIUM	a. Does not satisfy the requirements of HIGH
Endemism (E)	HIGH	a. Number of endemic species ≥5% of total species b. Contains species with unique evolutionary lineage c. Center of diversity
	MEDIUM	a. Does not satisfy the requirements of HIGH

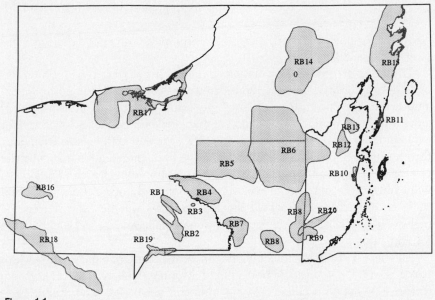

Figure 1.1

Biological priority areas identified by the Biological Resources Panel.

Table 1.2. Biological priority areas (see Figure 1.1).

Code	Name
RB1	Ocotal Mesa
RB2	Slope of the Ocotal Mesa
RB3	Palms and dispersed flooded zones and riparian vegetation
RB4	Sierra Lacandón
RB5	Wetlands of Laguna del Tigre
RB6	Tikal–Southern Calakmul–Río Bravo
RB7	Wetlands of the La Pasión River
RB8	Machaquilá–Maya Mountains
RB9	Colombia River
RB10	Northern and Southern Lagoon
RB11	Bacalar Chico
RB12	Crooked Tree
RB13	Freshwater Creek Forest
RB14	Calakmul–Bala'am K'aax
RB15	Siaan Ka'an–Uaymil
RB16	El Ocote–Benito Juárez
RB17	Wetlands of Centla–Términos
RB18	La Sepultura–La Frailescana–El Triunfo (Sierra Madre of Chiapas)
RB19	Monte Bello–Yolnabaj
RB20	Maya Mountains (High)

also an opportunity to identify existing information sources and projects mapping land-use change.

The group debated and finally agreed upon a list of 16 criteria for high priority status. Forested areas are considered particularly threatened if, for example, they are currently experiencing colonization, they border populated areas with little available land, they are managed poorly, they are targeted for exploitation for oil and minerals, they are occupied by illegal settlements, they host poorly planned tourism, they have been targeted for hydroelectric projects, or they are located along international borders, which makes them vulnerable to illegal resource exploitation from neighboring countries. Using these criteria, the panel agreed that 61 areas within the Maya Forest are highly threatened: 27 in Mexico, 17 in Guatemala, and 17 in Belize (Figure 1.2 and Table 1.3).

An area experiencing the dramatic landscape changes typical of the Maya Forest is M5, located in the north of the Montes Azules Biosphere Reserve (Figure 1.3) between 600 and 900 meters (m) above sea level. Rapid colonization and loss of native vegetation from human activities has led to soil erosion and forest fragmentation. Area M5 also overlaps Area RB1, a critical area identified by the biological working group. The landscape group also

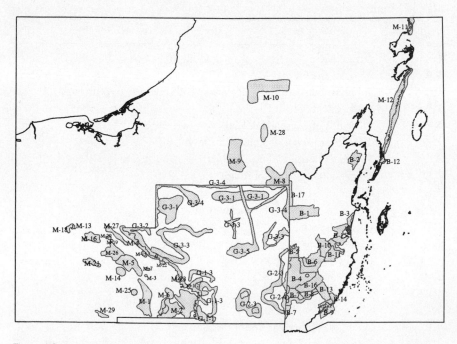

Figure 1.2

Highly threatened areas identified by the Landscape Processes Panel.

Table 1.3. List of highly threatened areas identified by the Landscape Processes Panel, shown in Figure 1.2.

Code	Name
B1	Yalbac, south of Gallon Jug
B2	Area between Shipstern and Fresh Water Creek
B3	Northern and Southern Lagoon
B4, 7, 8	Chiquibul NP, FR Columbia River, and FR Mountain Pine Ridge
B5	Vaca FR
B6	Chiquibul FR
B9, 13, 14	Paynes Creek NP, area proposed as Marine Reserve (Port Honduras)
B10, 11, 15	Areas the length of the Colibrí road (Hummingbird Highway) in Stann Creek Valley
B12	Section north of Ambergris Caye
B16	Bladen
B17	Gallon Jug
G1	Compex I and II/PROSELVA
G2	Complex III and IV/PROSELVA
G3	Maya BR
G4	Central section of the Department of El Petén (Cerro Cahuí–Lago Petén Itzá)
M1	Sector west of the Montes Azules BR
M2	Marqués de Comillas
M3	Locality Indio Pedro (in the Montes Azules BR)
M4	Diverse areas and canyons of the Río Usumacinta
M5	North of the Montes Azules BR
M6	Banks of the Río Lacantún
M7	Natural Monument Bonampak
M8	Calakmul–Dos Naciones (Tres Banderas)
M9	Calakmul–Conhuás
M10	Section north of the Calakmul BR
M11	Peninsula to the south of Tulum
M12	Littoral coast to the north of Xcalac to Punta Herrera
M13	Special BR Agua Azul
M14	Meseta Agua Escondida
M15	Sector north of the Sierra La Cojolita
M16	Nudo Diamante (between the towns of Chilón and Ocosingo)
M18	Watershed of the Río Tulijá that feeds the Agua Azul waterfalls
M19, 20, 21, 22	Localities of Menzabok and Nahá; Cañada de Patihuitz, Frontera Corozal
M23,25	Benemérito of the Américas; Lago Miramar and surroundings
M26	El Tumbo
M27	Sierra of St. Domingo
M28	Xpujil Corridor
M29	Lagos of Montebello NP

NP = National Park; FR = Forest Reserve; BR = Biosphere Reserve highlighted those areas likely to experience changes in the near future, but that lacked any definitive studies to assess the impact. One area, B2, located in southwest of Shipstern Nature Reserve in northeastern Belize, is not covered by any legal protected status and is surrounded by sugar cane plantations. This area is an important link between two small reserves, but future land-use plans are unknown, with strong potential for conversion to agriculture.

Past projects have tracked landscape changes over time in each of the three countries. An outgrowth of these projects is an inventory of over 80 data sources, including satellite images (Figure 1.4), aerial photography, digital data, and maps that describe the region. This simple inventory is useful both to understand the region as a whole and to indicate what coordination is needed for similar future projects. These types of data are important not only for answering discrete questions, but also for modeling the interactions between humans and the environment, which is a rapidly growing research field (Groffman and Likens 1994).

A sample of databases describing the region is given in Appendix 1 at the end of this chapter. Among these are several unique databases that may be of interest to researchers and planners alike. These include site-specific databases, such as the Conservation International/ProPetén database used for the management of the Bethel Cooperative in Guatemala. GIS data includes ecological communities, forest inventories, elevation, and water features. Other

Figure 1.3

Forest in the Montes Azules Biosphere Reserve.

databases have a regional scope, such as the ECOSUR Chiapas regional database containing base maps, hydrology, population centers and political boundaries, protected areas, and communication networks.

The greatest challenge to disseminating information is encouraging agencies and individuals to share data with those who need it. The reluctance to provide data stems from many valid concerns: how the information will be used; whether the recipient will duplicate the custodian's own efforts or publish the data without attributing proper credit; how to pay for the cost of making the information available; and whether caveats on data quality will be considered responsibly (Heywood 1995). However, the data generated collectively to describe the region as a whole, as was done for the workshop, provide a shared vision of critical areas and a list of data sources and contacts. These facilitate individual exchange agreements and form a basis for a broader data-sharing process.

Corridors

Like international boundaries, the borders of protected areas often do not correspond with ecological reality. Animal species may migrate in and out of an area depending on the season. A forested watershed located outside a park

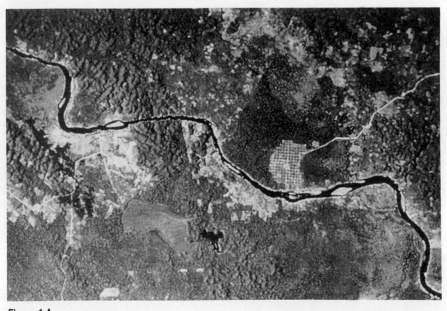

Figure 1.4

Landsat image of the Selva Lacandóna. Lighter patches near the river and roads are cleared areas.

may determine whether the park's streams and rivers continue to flow. Because its protected areas are divided among three different countries, such problems are particularly common within the Maya Forest. In most cases, protected areas end abruptly at national borders.

To combat this problem, the working group on biological corridors pooled its members' knowledge and came to a consensus on priority areas that would function as ecological links between established protected areas (as well as between other zones of high biological significance). While acknowledging complex issues and often heated debate over corridors (Simberloff and Cox 1987; Noss 1987), the group identified and mapped five types of corridors warranting protection: (1) extensions of protected areas necessary to protect complete habitats; (2) biological corridors, such as migration routes; (3) cooperative management zones, where different groups have claims to the resources affected; (4) riparian zones; and (5) ecological units under fragmented management, requiring administrative coordination (Figure 1.5 and Table 1.4). Panel members noted that protecting these corridors does not necessarily mean establishing new reserves but could be accomplished by management practices that ensure they maintain their special ecological function.

Examples of corridors include the protected area extension across the Belize River Valley–Beaver Dam–Castillo Manatee Reserve (B2), identified in the National Protected Area Management Plan (Belize) as containing im-

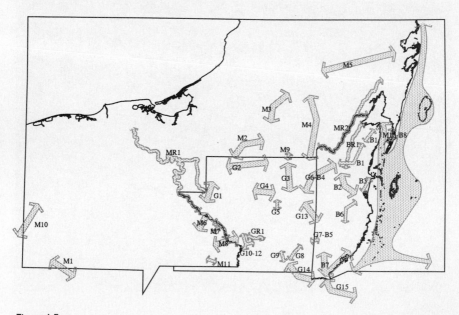

Figure 1.5

Biological linkages map identified by the Corridors Panel.

Table 1.4. Corridors shown in Figure 1.5.

Code	Name
B1	Shipstern Nature Reserve–Freshwater Creek FR
B2	BZE River Valley–Beaver Dam–Castillo Manatee FR
B3	Burdon Canal Park South–Northern and Southern Lagoon Manatee Area
B4	Río Bravo Conservation Management Area/Gallon Jug with Park Yaxha
B5	Chiquibul NP–Chiquibul Montaement Area/Gallon
B6	Sibun–Manatee
B7	Temash–Sarstoon: Sartstun NP, Paynes Creek, and Deep River with Colombia FR
B8	Bacalar Chico and Xcalak
G1	Biotopo Río Escondido/Sierra Lacandón NP
G2	Laguna del Tigre/Mirador NP
G3	Biotopo Dos Lagunas/Tikal NP–Calakmul México
G4	Paso Caballo/Biotopo El Zotz
G5	San José–El Zotz
G6	Nakum/Yaxha (Guatemala)/Chan Chich (Belize)
G7	Chiquibul–Maya Mountains
G8, G9	Areas of Central–South of the Petén
G10, 11, 12	Southeast of the Petén
M1	La Frailescana between the BR El Triunfo and La Sepultura Reserve
M2	Zone west of the Conección Reserve and Guatemala
M3	Calakmul
M4	Bosque Modelo Calakmul
M5	Sian Ka'an–Calakmul
M6	Montes Azules BR–Sierra Lacandón NP
M7	Chan-Kin Refuge–Lacantún BR
M8	Lacantún BR–Complex II of the Protected Areas System South of the Petén
M9	Bosque Modelo Calakmul
M10	Chimalapas–Ecocote Reserve with La Sepultura Reserve
M11	Montes Azules BR with Zona Marqués de Comillas
M12	Bacalar Chico–Xcalak

NP = National Park; FR = Forest Reserve; BR = Biosphere Reserve

portant vegetation types not under other forms of protection. The riparian corridor MR2 links the protected areas in Bacalar and Aguas Turbias along the Río Hondo. Others, such as Chiquibul–Montañas Mayas (G7-B5) link areas across an international border where transmigration and intensive agriculture occur in a landscape marked by ravines and rugged terrain. In all cases implementation of a corridor requires a political and legal strategy unique to the area.

Conservation Strategies Based on Political Reality

While it is essential that conservation priorities be based on biological and ecological criteria, deciding what actions are needed to protect priority areas depends largely upon political and socioeconomic realities. Recommending such actions was the responsibility of the workshop's final two panels, one focusing on socioeconomic and cultural issues and the other on conservation law.

Composed of experts from all three countries, the first of these working groups took a long, hard look at the forces that underlie deforestation in the Maya Forest. Primary among these forces are poverty, lack of land tenure, and an influx of immigrants including overseas immigrants (Taiwan), migrants from urban areas, and refugees (CARE/CI 1995). Because people facing such problems rarely can afford to think about conservation, any conservation strategy for the region should include efforts to improve local health and education, clarify land tenure, and, especially, promote economic activities that improve human well-being without harming the environment. These activities could include multiple crop and forestry systems, sustainable commercialization of forest products, and ecotourism.

A number of organizations already have begun sponsoring such activities throughout the Maya Forest. As with current research efforts, however, these widely scattered projects often do not share information or coordinate their efforts. Such lack of coordination represents a missed opportunity. While groups throughout the region promote ecotourism, for example, their product might be more attractive to potential travelers if offered as a package. Similarly, Conservation International has helped local people in Guatemala's Petén region find international markets for nontimber forest products such as chicle, allspice, and xate palm (Flynn 1995). These local enterprises could be made stronger by joining forces with other groups working in the Maya Forest to forge a regional forest-product marketing strategy. By continuing to meet and share information, conservationists from all three countries are beginning to take steps in this important direction.

Even with improved cooperation among conservationists, basic legal and political barriers to integrated management remain. A single biogeographic region, the Maya Forest is nonetheless divided among three sovereign nations, each having distinct legal and political systems as well as different languages and cultural traditions. To promote more integrated conservation efforts despite such barriers, the Conservation Law Panel looked at the possibilities offered by existing legal structures.

While a new trinational treaty would be one attractive way to promote a regional conservation vision, working group participants agreed that such a step is not necessary. There are already two treaties that could be used for the same purpose: the Central American Convention on Environment and Development and the Central American Convention on Biodiversity and Priority Protected Areas. Although Mexico is not a party to either treaty, the country could be included through cooperative agreements specifically related to the Maya Forest at the executive and ministerial levels.

Another option would be a presidential declaration similar to the Copán Declaration, an agreement in which the presidents of Mexico and Guatemala and the prime minister of Belize (along with the governments of Honduras and El Salvador) agreed to cooperate on a regional tourism development program called El Mundo Maya. Central American nations also have entered into an agreement, known as CONCAUSA (CONCAUSA Declaration 1994), to cooperate on sustainable development issues with the United States. While not currently a party, Mexico could sign on to this agreement as well.

Building on an Integrated Picture

In the end, the Maya Forest workshop was a step forward in the fight to protect this biologically rich and endangered ecosystem. By bringing together many of the region's major conservation players, organizers were able to obtain a first-cut consensus among these experts on where funding organizations should target their resources and what specific strategies they should pursue. Participants also pledged to stay in touch and continue the process, fine tuning their recommendations and amassing the collective data needed to achieve effective conservation and sustainable development.

To fuel this process, several products from the workshop have been made available. These include a published volume of proceedings; a large, two-sided map in Spanish and English; and a regional database containing information collected during the workshop as well as from other sources. These data include a bibliography of biological studies done within the Maya Forest; maps and recommendations from the five working groups; and even slides and videos of animals, plants, and other attributes of the Maya Forest. The data are to be presented using an innovative new computer tool, called PRISMA, that combines raw data and the more user-friendly, storytelling features of a Windows-based program (Fernandes 1996). By widely distributing the database through the Internet and CD-ROM, sharing data with colleagues throughout the region will be encouraged.

Workshop participants formed two working groups made up of members from all three countries. With one focusing on biological processes and the other on land-use changes, these groups are beginning to fill in the information gaps identified during the meeting. The ultimate goal is to transform the workshop's first-cut picture into a complete conservation database for the Maya Forest region. Even an incomplete picture has given policy makers enough to act on, however. As the only category of protected area that crosses national borders, biosphere reserves offer particular promise for immediate action. Created by UNESCO in 1976, biosphere reserves are special kinds of protected areas that combine conservation, scientific research, and sustainable economic development. There are currently four biosphere reserves within the Maya Forest, with a fifth in the planning stage. The biosphere reserves of the region, along with the organizations and researchers working within them, offer a promising model for regional conservation efforts.

Over the past ten years, teams of conservationists have pointed to the need for greater coordination and cooperation between organizations working in rapidly vanishing ecosystems like the Maya Forest (McNeely et al. 1990; U.S. Department of State 1993). Working together in fora to identify the areas and issues identified by the participants in the workshop offers a concise strategy of where to work and what to focus on. To conserve the Maya Forest, however, the organizations and individuals must implement projects jointly, broadly share the results and information, and periodically reassess the progress they have made.

Appendix. Maya Forest Metadata Survey Responses (sample)

Organization	Country	Database Name and Use
Belize Center for Environmental Studies	Belize	Port Honduras (GIS)—ecological assessment for development of a management plan
Belize Center for Environmental Studies	Belize	Belize Country Database (GIS)—land use planning, redefining bounds of forest reserves
Belize Center for Environmental Studies	Belize	Vegetation of Belize (GIS)—protected area system design
Wildlife Conservation Society	Belize	Belize Country Database (GIS)— protected areas planning and management, habitat modeling
Centro de Datos para la Conservación	Guatemala	Protected areas (tabular)—support protection strategies and management decision making
Centro de Datos para la Conservación	Guatemala	Fauna (tabular)—national inventory of species and habitat

Appendix (*continued*)

Organization	Country	Database Name and Use
Centro de Estudios Conservacionista	Guatemala	Butterflies (tabular)—analysis of distribution and population trends in relation to land use
Conservation International	Guatemala	Bethel community cooperative (GIS)— for management plan for forest reserve
Conservation International	Guatemala	Las Guacamayas Biological Station (GIS)—base map information, vegetation, selected species locations
SEGEPLAN (Plan for the Integrated Development of the Petén)	Guatemala	Petén Regional Database (GIS)— monitoring changes and impact assessment
Amigos de Sian Ka'an	Mexico	Protected areas in the Yucatán (GIS)
Centro de Ecologia, Universidad Nacional Autonoma de México	Mexico	Diversity of tropical flora (GIS)— analysis of critical sites
Conservation International	Mexico	Selva Lacandona base maps (GIS)— monitoring conservation strategies
ECOSUR (El Colegio de la Frontera Sur)	Mexico	Geographic base maps of the coast of Chiapas (GIS)
ECOSUR (El Colegio de la Frontera Sur)	Mexico	Geographic base maps of the state of Chiapas (GIS)
ECOSUR (El Colegio de la Frontera Sur)	Mexico	Climatic base maps of Chiapas (GIS)
ECOSUR (El Colegio de la Frontera Sur)	Mexico	Geographic base maps of northern Quintana Roo (GIS)
Universidad Nacional Autonoma de Mexico	Mexico	Bibliography of birds in Mexico
World Conservation Monitoring Centre	UK	Protected Areas (GIS) of Maya region
Center for Conservation Biology	USA	butterflies (tabular)—analysis of distribution and population trends in relation to land use
Conservation International	USA	Chiapas Regional Database (GIS)— analysis of demographic trends in relation to development financing
Conservation International	USA	Mexico Wetlands and Protected Areas (GIS)—national wetlands map, priority wetlands, and protected areas

(continues)

Appendix (*continued*)

Organization	Country	Database Name and Use
Smithsonian Institution	USA	U.S. National Collection of Amphibian (tabular)—systematic and taxonomic research
Smithsonian Institution	USA	National Dinoflagellate Collection (tabular)—ecological, morphological, and physiological research collection
The Nature Conservancy	USA	Ecological characterization of the Petén (GIS)—completed as part of a Rapid Ecological Assessment
United States Forest Service	USA	Percent Forest Area and Forest Type Map (satellite imagery)—model percent forest area with 1km imagery

References

Calleros, G., and F. A. Brauer. 1983. Problemática regional de la Selva Lacandona. Dirección General de Desarrollo Forestal, Secretaría de Agricultura y Recursos Hidráulicos. Coordinación Ejecutiva del Programa Ecológico de la Selva Lacandona. Palenque, Chiapas, México.

CARE/CI. 1995. Analisis de los Impactos Ambientales Actuales y Potenciales del Proceso de Reintegración de los Retornados a Guatemala y Recomendaciones para su Mitigación. Care-Guatemala/Conservation International.

CONCAUSA Declaration. 1994. Joint Declaration of the Governments of the United States and Central America, Summit of the Americas. Miami, Fla., December 10, 1994.

Conservation International, Fundação Biodiversitas, Sociedade de Nordestina de Ecologia. 1995. Prioridades para Conservação da Mata Atlântica do Nordeste. Map prepared from December 1994 Workshop held in Recife, Brazil. Conservation International, Washington, D.C.

Fernandes, Nivaldo. 1996. Multimedia presentations. *Visual Developer* 7(3): 32–39.

Flynn, Sharon. 1995. Building Markets for NTFP's: Challenges and a Few Lessons Learned. Presented at Yale University School of Forestry and Environmental Studies Conference on Non-Timber Forest Products. Yale University, New Haven, Conn.

Groffman, Peter M., and Gene E. Likens, editors. 1994. *Integrated Regional Models: Interactions between Humans and their Environment.* Chapman & Hall, New York.

Hannah, Lee, and John Hough, editors. 1995. GEF Design Assistance to PE2: Summary of Findings. Draft. Conservation International, Washington, D.C.

Heywood, V. H., editor. 1995. *Global Biodiversity Assessment.* Cambridge University Press, Cambridge, U.K.

IBAMA/INPA/CI. 1991. Workshop 90: Biological Priorities for Conservation in

Amazonia. Map prepared from January 1990 conference by IBAMA, INPA, Conservation International, the New York Botanical Graden, and the Royal Botanic Gardens. Conservation International, Washington, D.C.

Johnson, Nels C. 1995. Biodiversity in the Balance: Approaches to Setting Geographic Conservation Priorities. Biodiversity Support Program, Washington, D.C.

McNeely, Jeffrey A., K. R. Miller, W. V. Reid, R. A. Mittermeier, T. B. Werner. 1990. Conserving the World's Biological Diversity. IUCN, Gland Switzerland; WRI, CI, WWF–US, and the World Bank, Washington, D.C.

Noss, R. F. 1987. Corridors in real landscapes: A reply to Simberloff and Cox. *Conservation Biology* 1: 159–164.

Olivieri, S., I. A. Bowles, R. B. Cavalcanti, G. A. B. da Fonseca, R. A. Mittermeier, and C. B. Rodstrom. 1995. A Participatory Approach to Biodiversity Conservation: The Regional Priority Setting Workshop. Discussion Paper. Conservation International, Washington, D.C.

Sader, S. A., T. Sever, J. C. Smoot, and M. Richards. 1994. Forest change estimates for the northern Petén region of Guatemala—1986–1990. *Human Ecology* 22: 317–332.

Simberloff, D., and J. Cox. 1987. Consequences and costs of conservation corridors. *Conservation Biology* 1: 63–71.

Swartzendruber, J. F. 1993. Papua New Guinea Conservation Needs Assessment: Synopsis Report. Biodiversity Support Program, Washington, D.C.

University of Florida, Gainesville/Paseo Pantera Consortium/Wildlife Conservation Society/Caribbean Conservation Corporation. 1995. Digital Geographic Database Maya Forest Region of Mexico, Guatemala, Belize, Version 1. University of Florida, Gainesville.

U.S. Department of State. 1993. The Maya Forest: Key Issues and Recommendations for Action (A Workshop Report). Department of State Publication 10082, Bureau of Oceans and International Environmental and Scientific Affairs, Washington, D.C.

Chapter 2

One Forest, Two Nations:
The Chiquibul Forest of Belize and Guatemala

Sharon Matola and Elizabeth Platt

In the southeastern Yucatán Peninsula, on the fringes of the limestone mountains that mark the transition from the karst plateau to the volcanic highlands of Central America, two great and ancient cities lie hidden amid the towering canopy of the Maya Forest. Caracol and Tikal, located in modern-day Belize and Guatemala, respectively, flourished during the height of ancient Maya civilization. From the writings left behind by the former occupants, it is clear that the two cities did not coexist peacefully (Martin and Grube 1994). Stone monuments at Caracol recount a bloody war in which Caracol's rulers defeated their mighty western rivals, establishing their city's supremacy in no uncertain (and usually immodest) terms. How much of this account is truth and how much is exaggeration—or even sheer invention—we may never know. Yet such quarrels were not unique to the ancient inhabitants of the region; until the national sovereignty of Belize was formally recognized by Guatemala in 1991, these two countries and their colonial predecessors, Britain and Spain, were constantly at odds over territorial rights (Setzekorn 1981). If nothing else, the ancient monuments tell us merely that the Maya Forest has never been a stranger to cross-border conflicts.

As tangled and argumentative as the region's history may be, there is one factor that unifies it: in biological terms, its flora and fauna compose a single ecosystem. The political frictions of the day, whether they be ancient Maya lords warring for personal aggrandizement or modern nations negotiating boundary lines, do not deter movements of birds, mammals, and reptiles, nor can they stop the dispersal of seeds and pollen, borne by wind, water, and migrating animals. With nearly 80% of the Belize–Guatemala border forming an active corridor for species migration, it would be next to impossible to prevent the movement of species from one country into another. Yet it is not strictly accurate to say that ecosystems are independent of political boundaries; the policies a nation holds toward its natural resources can have a profound impact upon a species or community. Thus, there is great interest in—and concern about—the different ways in which Guatemala and Belize manage the resources of the region. Different policies and attitudes toward natural resources may indeed cause changes in communities on either side of the border—a development that may be detrimental to some species in both countries.

This possibility has the strongest implications for one region in particular: the Chiquibul Forest, a segment of land in southern Belize and the southeastern Petén named for the Chiquibul River, which flows from Belize into Guatemala and back into Belize, forming the headwaters of the Belize River. Both countries took separate measures to set aside large portions of the region as nature reserves due to its abundant plant and animal life and, in part, because of the presence of ancient Maya remains (Caracol, the Maya city described earlier, is located at the heart of the Chiquibul Forest in Belize, just east of the Guatemalan border). Its importance in these respects has been recognized for decades by all concerned: an international reserve complex was first proposed for the region as early as 1974, when the concept of international biosphere reserves was still fairly new. Belizean efforts to protect their portion of the Chiquibul ecosystem have been underway for several decades (Barborak, pers. comm.). Though no formal UNESCO-sponsored biosphere reserve has been created as yet, Guatemala formed its own reserve—the Maya Mountains/Chiquibul Biosphere Reserve—adjacent to the established Chiquibul National Park and Chiquibul Forest Reserve in Belize. Thus, the two countries created mirror-image protected areas for this forest, despite their then active disputes over territorial rights.

These steps are important, considering the region's rich natural resources. Two principal types of forest are found in the region: Zapotal, which is the dominant type in karstic limestone soils throughout the northern Petén, and Caobal-Corozal, a less common type named for the caoba or mahogany tree (*Swietenia macrophylla*). Forest species common to both sites include breadnut (*Brosimum alicastrum*), nargusta (*Terminalia amazonia*), fiddlewood (*Vitex gaumeri*), ironwood (*Dialium guianense*), hogplum (*Spondias mombin*), and commercially valuable species such as sapodilla or chicle (*Manilkara zapota*), allspice (*Pimenta dioica*), xate (*Chamadorea elegans* and *C. oblongata*), mahogany, and cedar (*Cedrela odorata*), although the latter two have become depleted through logging (Johnson and Chaffey 1973). However, the floristic composition of the Maya Mountains is not well known. To illustrate this fact, take the following example: in a 1993 expedition to Doyle's Delight, a mountain peak near the southern border of Chiquibul National Park that at 1,124 meters is the highest point in Belize, a botanist from the Missouri Botanical Gardens collected more than 130 species never before reported in Belize, three of which were previously unknown in Central America (Matola et al. 1995). If so many new species could be recorded in a single expedition, the potential number of species still unrecorded staggers the imagination.

Endangered, rare, and unique species of animals and birds are found within the Chiquibul Forest on both sides of the international border; their sustenance depends upon healthy maintenance of the forest. The keel-billed motmot (*Electron carinatum*), one of the rarest bird species in Central America, inhabits this region, as do the scarlet macaw (*Ara macao*), ocellated turkey (*Agriocharis ocellata*), great curassow (*Crax rubra*), crested guan (*Penelope purpurascens*), and king vulture (*Sarcoramphus papa*), all of which exist in depleted populations throughout much of their original Central American ranges. There are indications that this area also may support globally significant numbers of Neotropical migratory birds (Parker et al. 1993). Endangered mammals found within these forests include the Central American or Baird's tapir (*Tapirus bairdii*), spider monkey (*Ateles geoffroyi*), and howler monkey (*Alouatta pigra*), as well as four highly threatened cat species: the jaguar (*Panthera onca*), ocelot (*Felis pardalis*), margay (*Felis wiedii*), and jaguaroundi (*Felis yaguaroundi*).

Given the diversity of species, particularly the rare and endangered species noted above, the fact that both Guatemala and Belize have seen fit to set aside this land for conservation might be regarded as a welcome example of foresight on the part of both nations. However, the fact that the reserves exist does not mean that the resources they are meant to protect are safe from harmful human activities. Pressures for development of the forest in each country have far-reaching impacts on the Chiquibul Forest as a whole. Of principal concern, according to a study by the Centro de Estudios Conservacionistas (CECON), are land tenure policies in Guatemala that have wrought tremendous changes both on the Chiquibul Forest and on the Petén as a whole. As a result of these policies, many subsistence farmers are unable to acquire farmland in their village of origin. These farmers, primarily Kekchi families from Alta Verapaz and Izabal as well as others from western Guatemala, continually immigrate into the Petén in search of unoccupied land. Some 1,200 people have settled in the Chiquibul Biosphere Reserve to farm small plots of corn and beans using slash-and-burn methods. With poor housing, little or no education or health care (Ponciano 1995), and no familiarity with the local soil conditions, these settlers are poorly equipped to create an enterprise that might be sustainable, much less one that would have minimal impacts upon forest life. Furthermore, though settlers at present live only within the Guatemalan reserve, the impact of their presence is also felt in the Chiquibul National Park in Belize. As documented in satellite images (King 1995), illegal incursions into the park to pursue agricultural development have increased sixfold from 1987 up to the present. Illegal poaching of wild-life has also increased.

Such incursions point to the need for increased international cooperation to protect the region's biological diversity. Development opportunities that utilize forest resources and provide alternative sources of income for local people should be created as cooperative ventures to maximize benefits, not merely for one nation's people over the other, but for the Chiquibul region as a whole. One possible cooperative venture involves the creation of a joint ecotourism project for the whole Chiquibul region. The potential benefits of such a project can be observed by noting the impact of ecotourism in Tikal National Park in Guatemala, an important attraction for both its spectacular ancient monuments and its natural history. Tikal National Park earns millions of dollars annually and supports approximately 15% of tourists visiting Guatemala (INGUAT 1990). Tikal therefore might serve as a model for the development of its erstwhile rival city, Caracol. As the premier archaeologi-cal site in the Chiquibul Forest, Caracol already attracts increasing numbers of visitors; satellite sites throughout the forest on both sides of the border could be developed as part of this attraction. Moreover, adventure ecotourism activities have already been developed within the Chiquibul Biosphere Re-serve; for instance, at least two Guatemalan adventure tour agencies are run-ning rafting trips down the Chiquibul River. Linking such ventures by estab-lishing a border crossing leading from Caracol into the Chiquibul Biosphere Reserve would allow travelers to take advantage of attractions on both sides of the border and perhaps increase the overall attractiveness of the region to international tourists. People living in nearby communities could then be employed for this industry, possibly as forest guides and interpreters of the area's flora and fauna. Further development of ecotourism programs in the Chiquibul Forest would contribute to the economic base of the communities located in the area.

Development of complementary forest management strategies must coin-cide with such plans, however. In Guatemala, the nongovernmental organi-zation PROSELVA is developing a strategy for the Chiquibul Biosphere Re-serve that focuses on the extraction of key timber and nontimber products. In the Petén, harvesting of nontimber forest products (NTFPs) is already at an advanced state. Extraction of allspice fruit, the leaves of xate for the North American and European floral industries, as well as extraction of chicle resin from the sapodilla tree are carried out throughout the year in these forests (Reining et al. 1992). These three products are a major source of income for many Petén residents: some 4,000 people are employed harvesting xate in the Petén, while another 1,600 to 1,900 are engaged in chicle latex collection (Dugelby, this volume), the demand for which has been rising steadily since the 1980s. Extraction of NTFPs has been suggested as a means of preventing conversion of forests to agriculture because it provides alternative employment without unduly harming the ecosystem. Harvesting of xate leaves, for instance, brings millions of dollars in revenue to Guatemala each year, yet takes minimal skill or equipment and, if done carefully, does not interfere with the ability of the plant to regenerate quickly. However, NTFP extraction is not the cure-all to the problems facing the Chiquibul Forest: marketing and pricing of these products must be supported by the international community and, above all, the number of individuals engaged in harvesting in the reserves must be strictly monitored. Overharvesting of NTFPs is a serious concern; if allowed to occur, it could have serious consequences for some species. Chicle latex, for example, can be gathered only during the rainy season when the increased humidity and soil moisture allow the sap to flow freely. Trees that have been tapped must be allowed time to recover; a tree that is tapped too soon (that is, before at least three years have passed; see Dugelby, this volume) may die. A mature sapodilla tree is a resource that is not quickly replaced, so most professional tappers are careful to avoid overtapping. Nevertheless, the temptation to take a quick profit regardless of the long-term consequences is surely always present, particularly for migrant workers with no perceived stake in maintaining the health of local resources. Extraction of NTFPs requires low worker densities, stable species densities, and respected land and resource tenure if it is to be successful. At present, no mechanisms exist in either the Belizean or Guatemalan reserves to ensure these qualifications are met.

"Poaching" of forest resources is also a significant threat, as has already been seen in Guatemala's Maya Biosphere Reserve, which has contended with rampant illegal logging to an extent visible in satellite images. It can cause considerable harm to fragile communities. To prevent such activities, forest management plans must mutually reinforce their terms: if, for instance, Guatemala sets a limit of 40 cm diameter at breast height (dbh) for mahogany logs while Belize's limit is 30 cm, a canny logger will cross into bordering Guatemalan forests—which, if previously logged, may have no trees above 40 cm dbh but should still have plenty between 30 to 40 cm—and sell his take on the Belizean side to avoid fines for cutting below the minimum size.

The problem of squatters in the forest using the land for agriculture is also one that must be addressed, and quickly. Although it is possible that some of these farming communities could be employed in alternative industries, no reserve survives very long with a rapidly growing population of subsistence agriculturalists living in its boundaries. If the reserve is to survive, some of these settlers will have to be relocated to more suitable lands, and others must be trained to care for the reserve and take part in its programs, while further immigration into the region must be strictly forbidden.

The real hope for the region, however, lies in the rapprochement of the Belizean and Guatemalan governments. Since the formal recognition of Belize in 1991, the two nations have begun to discuss many common problems, particularly with regard to their shared natural resources. These conversations may ultimately result in a joint management plan for the Chiquibul Forest.

Acknowledgments

Some of this material was originally presented by Sharon Matola as "One Forest, Two Nations: The Importance of Sustaining a Shared Forest Ecosystem: The Chiquibul Forest Reserve/National Park in Belize, and the Chiquibul Biosphere Reserve in Guatemala" at the Workshop on Conservation and Community Development in the Selva Maya of Belize, Guatemala, and Mexico; Chetumal, Mexico, November 8–10, 1995.

References

Instituto Guatemalteco de Turismo (INGUAT). 1990. Estadisticas de turismo 1989. Boletin No. 18. Guatemala City, Guatemala.

Johnson, M. S., and D. R. Chaffey. 1973. An inventory of the Chiquibul Forest Reserve, Belize. Land Resource Study No. 14. ODA, Land Resources Division, London, U.K.

King, B. 1995. Cross-border agricultural incursion into Chiquibul National Park and Columbia River Forest Reserve. Forest Planning and Management Project, Ministry of Natural Resources, Belmopan, Belize.

Martin, S., and N. Grube. 1994. Evidence for macro-political organization amongst Classic Maya lowland states. Mimeograph.

Matola, S., editor. 1995. Expedition to Doyle's Delight, Southern Maya Mountains, Belize. FPMP Occasional Series No. 5.

Parker, D. et al. 1993. A biological assessment of the Columbia River Forest Reserve, Toledo District, Belize. Conservation International, Washington, D.C.

Ponciano, I. et al. 1995. A socioeconomic and cultural study of the rural communities settled in the proposed Chiquibul Biosphere Reserve, Petén, Guatemala. Summary report, n.d.

Reining, C. et al. 1992. Nontimber forest products of the Maya Biosphere Reserve, Petén, Guatemala. Conservation International, Washington, D.C.

Setzekorn, W. 1981. A Profile of the New Nation of Belize. Ohio University Press, Athens.

Part II

Forest Policy and Management and the Emergence of Community Forestry

The introductory chapters to this volume spoke of the Maya Forest in terms of its unity as a landscape—a fact of ecology. The chapters that follow serve to highlight the distinctions between the regions of the Maya Forest that are controlled by Mexico, Guatemala, and Belize—a geopolitical situation that has had strong historical influences on forest policies, rates and periods of deforestation, and overall health of each section of the Maya Forest. The most dramatic evidence of this influence is highly visible in the satellite images described in the Introduction: at the western border of the Petén, there is a stark contrast between the luxuriant forests of the Maya Biosphere Reserve and the farmlands of the neighboring Mexican states of Tabasco and Campeche, stripped virtually bare of their original forests (Garrett 1989). Each of the three nations has different historical, political, social, and cultural circumstances dictating how it manages its forests—circumstances that have led to persistent differences in logging practices, silvicultural techniques, and land use and land tenure policies.

Chapters on Mexico predominate in this section, for good reasons. Significantly more of the Maya Forest is in Mexico than in the other two countries. In addition, Mexico's federal system has allowed individual states considerable sway over forest policy. Indeed, the four Mexican Maya Forest states of Quintana Roo, Campeche, Tabasco, and Chiapas have sometimes taken dramatically different forest policy paths. As a result, Mexico has experienced a wide range of forest policies and practices in its southeastern tropical forests, including concessions to private and parastatal industries (true in most of the region before the 1980s), draconian restrictions on logging in Chiapas (1989–1996), and some of the most advanced experiences in community forest management anywhere in the Third World (in Quintana Roo, since the 1980s, and more recently in Campeche).

The longevity of forest management in Quintana Roo, embracing both concession and community management periods dating to the early 1950s, makes it a particularly rich field of study in forest management. Thus, the first three chapters in this section focus on the social and silvicultural history of forest exploitation in southern Quintana Roo, and particularly the experience of the so-called Forest Pilot Plan (*Plan Piloto Forestal*). Hugo A. Galletti details the impressive and historic accomplishments of the Society of Forest Production Ejidos of Quintana Roo, which has developed one of the most advanced community tropical forest management experiences anywhere in the world. The following two chapters delve more deeply into the crucial area of silvicultural management and sustainability as practiced in southern Quintana Roo. Henning Flaschenberg and Hugo A. Galletti sketch in the forest management plan of the Society, including their management practices of the most commercially and ecologically precious timber in the forest: mahogany. The chapter by Laura K. Snook further targets some of the crucial issues of mahogany management. These two chapters taken together are chapters in a vigorous and important debate on the most appropriate management practices to assure the long-term presence of mahogany as the most prominent emergent species in the canopies of Quintana Roo and throughout the Maya Forest. In the final chapter focusing on Mexico in this section, Deocundo Acopa and Eckart Boege describe another community forest management experience inspired by the Plan Piloto Forestal, in the Calakmul region of Campeche, a state that has provided a basically favorable policy framework for community forest management. This chapter shows the range of forest management issues that well-organized communities can tackle.

The next two chapters focus on the very different forest policy and management issues in Guatemala. Guatemala has experienced some of the same problems as Mexico within a more compressed time period. Still experiencing the colonization pressures that are relatively diminished in Mexico, Guatemala sees only the barest beginning of the strong community forest management alternative present in Mexico. Social and political convulsions and poverty in other parts of Guatemala have created a flood of landless peasant farmers migrating into the Petén, an area historically regarded by Guatemala's government as marginal, worthless swampland and forest. As a result of this sudden influx of immigrants—and of the realization both by Guatemalans and international actors that the Petén's forest is an incomparable biological treasure—Guatemala has had to play "catch-up," trying to design policies and practices that can meet the enormous and conflicting demands for conservation and development that are assailing the region. Unfortunately, changes to the forest have occurred much more rapidly than changes in practices; it is still too soon to say whether equilibrium can be reached. Ismael Ponciano provides an overview of forest policy in Guatemala and the challenges that it faces from events in the forests themselves. Steven P. Gretzinger then discusses the emergence of one of the more promising events in Guatemalan forest policy and practices in recent years, the establishment of community forest concessions in the Petén. This policy, similar to the extractive reserves policy in Brazil, also gives Guatemalan communities secure access to forest lands, the foundation for the successful community experiences in Mexico. It is a practice that must be encouraged and closely monitored.

Belize is a dramatically different case from either Mexico or Guatemala. Large-scale clearing for farmland and pasture is still a recent phenomenon—it has taken place only within the past few decades—and is still nowhere near the scale that has occurred in Mexico and is occurring in Guatemala. Moreover, as a British colony until 1981, Belize has been able to take advantage of forestry lessons learned in other tropical colonies in developing its policies. Belize is therefore in the enviable position of being able to create policies aimed at preventing deforestation and degradation in relatively intact forests, while studying methods for repairing past damage to stocks of timber species and slowing ongoing destruction. But some of the pressures affecting Guatemala and Mexico are beginning to be felt in Belize; immigrants from Honduras, El Salvador, and other parts of Central America are contributing to a rapidly increasing population in this mostly rural country, and, just as in the Petén, many of these new settlers are beginning to clear land for crops and pasture. Elizabeth Platt provides an overview of the policies and problems of forest management in this unique country.

The chapters in this section show the forests of the region to be under intense pressure, but they also demonstrate that alternatives that generate income for local people and preserve hundreds of thousands of hectares of forest cover are not just dreams; they are happening on the ground in several different areas of the Maya Forest.

Reference

Garrett, W. E. 1989. La Ruta Maya. *National Geographic* 176: 424–479.

Chapter 3

The Maya Forest of Quintana Roo: Thirteen Years of Conservation and Community Development

Hugo A. Galletti

At the beginning of this century, Quintana Roo was practically depopulated and covered almost entirely with forests. Most of this land was state owned. In the 1930s and early 1940s, however, ownership and control of the land were transferred to peasants, organized in communal groups called *ejidos*. To each *ejidatario* was allotted 420 ha, an area sufficient to support a family from chicle extraction, which at the time was the most important source of income. The ejido was obligated by law to conserve the forests and manage them rationally in communal form. In the 1960s and 1970s still-available forest lands were settled for agriculture, and 20 ha were given to each ejidatario with no obligation for conservation or rational use of the forests. In this manner the state subsidized the clearing of the land and the destruction of much forest; nevertheless, the existence of the first type of ejido conserved important blocks of forest.

From 1953 through 1983 Maderas Industrializadas de Quintana Roo (MIQRO), a concession dedicated to the harvest of quality timbers such as Spanish cedar (*Cedrela odorata*) and mahogany (*Swietenia macrophylla*) for the production of plywood, operated in the region (Galletti 1993). The company had direct access to the forests; the local farmers did not participate in or benefit from the timber harvests from their forests, being subject to an alliance among the state, the forest service, and the concessionaire. This situation caused resentment in the local population, which looked on the end of the concession as a liberation from a powerful, dictatorial monopoly.

The state government sought to resolve this conflict between the company and the farmers. At the same time, federal government policies encouraged the participation of the owners in the management and harvesting of their forests. The end of the 30-year concession in 1983 opened a strategic opportunity for such participation. The response to this opportunity emerged as the Plan Piloto Forestal (PPF) (Galletti and Acopa 1982; Janka et al. 1983), a joint federal and state effort to work with local forest communities in central and southern Quintana Roo. The plan received the personal support of both the state governor and the subsecretary of forestry of the Secretary of Agriculture and Hydraulic Resources (SARH), important elements in its success.

The PPF used strategic planning techniques and set up institutional arrangements of "shared power," with no single actor making all of the decisions. Methodologically, this meant that a series of consensuses had to be reached between the distinct social actors and the participating institutions (Matus 1981). It also meant that no actor could define objectives a priori on any but the most general level. The process started with concrete possibilities and conditions, building on social trends and existing organizations. It was accepted that there would be confrontations between economic interests and institutional ones, that there would be struggles and steps backward as well as forward. The goal was the rapid emergence of a new social institution capable of standing up for its rights. The exceptional opportunity arising from the end of the concession had to be taken advantage of quickly to occupy the political space left vacant, as well as to generate new relationships between the social groups participating in forestry. If it did not happen fast, the space would be occupied by traditional logging interests. This process also had to happen by 1986, in three years, the end of the term in office of the supportive governor of Quintana Roo. Beyond that, the situation became politically unpredictable.

The PPF was based on two hypotheses: first, that the forest must provide an economic alternative for the local population in order not to be destroyed, and second, that forest owners are the social actors most interested in the conservation of the forest for economic reasons (Janka 1985), as their principal capital is the forest itself and not a speculative, short-term investment in forest products. The plan sought to demonstrate that an economically viable form of community forestry was possible.

The initial steps in the program were as follows. First, ejidatarios set aside part of their land as *permanent forest areas*. Next, farmers began to administer the forestry activities. In the forest, extraction activities continued much as they had before, but now the activities were being done by the local farmers. This step was significant because in only three years the ejidos had gained administrative control—some more, some less—of their own forests. Shortly afterward, farmers stopped selling their wood as standing timber and began to develop the capability of processing timber up through the delivery of logs to the factory. In the beginning they had to rent the harvesting and transportation equipment, but they also learned how to calculate production costs.

Once the high costs of renting were apparent, the farmers decided to buy equipment. They negotiated the first forest credits granted to any farmers' associations in the region. In three years the most important ejidos had their own equipment yards. The ejidos participating in the PPF eventually formed a commercial union to negotiate together the price and conditions of delivery for their wood.

The effects of these steps were enormous. The ejidatarios' incomes increased severalfold. The commercial union consolidated and evolved into a regional organization, the Society of Ejidal Forest Producers of Quintana Roo (SPFEQR), founded in 1986. The first phase of the project achieved its principal goal: within three years a new actor in social forestry has risen in the region, composed of the owners of the forests themselves.

Creation of Local Structures

The traditional forms of ejidal government were developed more for political control than for efficient production. By law, the ejido is administered by an ejidal committee (president, secretary, and treasurer) and an oversight council. The ultimate authority is held by the ejidal assembly. This structure works in conditions of minimal social differences, but becomes insufficient when faced with activities requiring more specialized levels of organization. Additionally, the state authorities historically have discouraged the hiring of professionals by the ejidos and offer poor quality services that come with political "strings" or conditions attached. Before the PPF was formed, the farmers sold their wood as standing timber, which required no specialized institutions. From 1983 to 1986, the ejidos focused on the production of logs. In 1986, the first ejidal sawmill was installed; three more soon followed. These advances required the rise of new organizational forms and professional profiles, as well as an industrial schedule and planning and management techniques.

Technical advances depended on the ability of the ejido to advance organizationally. Important steps were taken in the management of the forest production process and in the sawmill, but the traditional ejido mechanism still made business decisions. The assembly decided the contracts, negotiated prices, approved the budget, appointed personnel for positions, and controlled the operations. To further complicate matters, in various ejidos in the region there is an intermediary figure between the assembly and the ejidal authority: the ejidal advisory board, formed of respected members of the community.

These organizational limitations led to difficulties in developing planning and control functions. The ejido is not a form of organization that facilitates the making of business decisions, but no business organization arose parallel to the communal organization. The traditional pattern of leadership in the ejido reflects the custom of changing personnel at the beginning of each period, which, though democratically permitting all members to serve, also prohibits the rise of a stable and experienced management staff. Moreover, the political (communal management and local justice) and economic (business management) dimensions became intermingled, a circumstance that brought about the mixing of functions, positions, and personnel, and created a continuous process of trial and error with little administrative continuity or ability to anticipate problems. This type of administration created permanent problems of liquidity, caused by a policy of distributing all profits without any reinvestment. The business could not maintain capital and thus continued to depend on external funding sources (Argüelles and Armijo 1995). Currently, the ejidos are attempting to separate community functions and business functions. It seems clear that, once this separation of functions on an organizational level has been achieved, the problems of technical capabilities will easily be resolved, but the community still has not been able to take the necessary steps to achieve this separation.

Despite these limitations, there have been clear improvements in two aspects: first, individuals with appropriate technical profiles are more likely to occupy key positions, and second, the ejidal committees are beginning to evolve into executive boards, although there are still issues to be resolved in this regard. For example, the traditional pattern of ejido leadership makes it difficult to find appropriate people for technical positions. The leaders represent interest groups within the ejido, usually united by family ties. Each group tries to take power in its turn and fill positions with its people. Although the ejidos have begun developing more professional types of leadership, they have not been able to create a niche for such positions within their social organization.

The form of government based on favoritism rooted in friendships, which leads to impunity, political pardons, and reserves of power with no social counterbalances, is a poor example for the ejido. However, it must be made clear that, despite all the obstacles discussed, significant advances toward a more democratic and entrepreneurial culture have been made in the community, in contrast to the prevailing political culture. The community forest industry forms a stable and predictable base for the development of other local industries and family carpentry workshops, the number of which is currently growing.

The advances achieved thus far would not have been possible if the actions had been limited to the community level. Thus, the creators of the PPF sought to occupy the empty political space created by the termination of the concession with an informal regional farmers' group. This group became a kind of marketing cooperative, which permitted the ejidos to negotiate as a group the sale of their wood and at the same time allowed them to defend their interests before the government. Faced with the imminent change of government in 1986, this group formalized their status and founded the SPFEQR. By doing so they consolidated the marketing and political functions and added a third: becoming a vehicle for the provision of the technical services required for logging by Mexican law, which were normally provided by the government or exclusive technical assistance concessionaires, both of whom provided very poor quality services (Galletti and Argüelles 1987b). The Society has been able to provide higher quality services itself while successfully defending the right of small timber producers and farmers to manage their own natural resources against many elements that would like to deny them the opportunity.

Nontimber Products

The nontimber benefit of the greatest economic importance in Quintana Roo is chicle extraction. Since 1940, marketing of this resource has been dominated by state-controlled marketing cooperatives such as the Federation of Cooperatives of Quintana Roo, which brought together the ejido-based cooperatives. This organization was later joined by an official chicle export enterprise called IMPEXNAL (a subdivision of the Mexican Bank of Export Trade), which had a legal export monopoly.

Starting in 1989, as the harvest volume of mahogany and cedar began to diminish, the need to diversify forest harvests in order to maintain or increase incomes became clear. One solution was the more efficient organization of chicle extraction, but the web of pre-existing interests made this effort difficult. In 1992, with the installation of a new state government, two factors helped to create an opportunity for change: first, several chicle cooperatives were highly dissatisfied with the Federation, and second, IMPEXNAL privatized national policies. The second factor opened an empty space similar to that which had led to the foundation of the PPF in 1983. The Pilot Chicle-Tapping Plan (PPCh) was proposed as an alternative, with a philosophy similar to that of the PPF. Its goals were to rebuild the community cooperatives as production units, promote its own administrative organization, and create the capacity to make independent marketing arrangements.

As with the PPF, the plan enjoyed solid political support at the federal level (Aldrete 1994). The cooperatives had no money of their own, and the Federation had annually given them production advances. To replace this source of credit, the National Fund of Union Businesses established a revolving fund for each cooperative, permitting them to buy chicle and store it. Direct and stable commercial relationships were developed with Japanese and Italian chicle buyers, replacing IMPEXNAL. Each cooperative contracted its own sale and the price was set in dollars, constituting protection against inflation for the tappers.

The PPF's experience was drawn upon to avoid repeating the same errors. The PPCh established a more businesslike form of administration and better money management, adopting from the beginning a policy of savings. Each tapper donated a percentage of his production to a cooperative fund for capital and reserves, social security, health insurance, and technical assistance. Through joint banking mechanisms they were able to ensure a continuous flow of cash and coordination with the needs of production, while avoiding pressures from members for profit distribution. These mechanisms allowed the cooperatives to capitalize, giving them power to negotiate the price and conditions of sale of their chicle.

The PPCh has been so successful that it has been able to resist efforts by the state government and the Federation to weaken and disorganize it. From pilot experience in nine cooperatives, activities were extended to cover almost all the chicle production of Quintana Roo and Campeche. The economic benefits have started a revitalization of the chicle tapping industry. New cooperatives have been organized, the number of chicle tappers has risen, and the volume of production has tripled. Chicle has even surpassed mahogany as the most important source of income from the forest in the state, a historic event created by the organized small producers. The increased profits have also led to technical advances. In one cooperative, a pilot coagulating plant was installed, replacing the traditional process of cooking individually. The results were very encouraging: the output increased by 30%, contaminants were eliminated, and the quality of the chicle was superior. This technique is now being adopted by other cooperatives.

The Role of the NGOs and Development Groups

The development of economically viable community-managed forests has depended upon the development of participatory, politically autonomous, democratic organizations with the ability to develop and hire their own technical assistance. Nongovernmental organizations (NGOs) and external funders can play an important role in consolidating these processes if they are willing to commit to longer-term (at least ten years) projects and to working as partners with the local organizations. The principal source of external support for this process has come from the Mexican–German Accord, an agreement between the Mexican Secretary of Agriculture and Hydraulic Resources (SARH) and the German Association of Technical Cooperation (GTZ), present in the region since the initiation of the PPF. From the beginning, the Accord supported a second-level peasant organization as the means for forming local community organizers. The Accord professional staff in Quintana Roo were members of a joint team with local organizers. The principal administrators of the Accord stayed in Mexico City, far from the project, reducing the bureaucracy on the ground. Methodologically, the local team of the Accord forged a close alliance with the ejidos and promoted democratic decision making regarding natural resource use. Some tensions developed between the local team of the Accord, who gave greater importance to the development of the farmers' groups as a political force, and the administrators in Mexico City, who preferred to try to exercise political influence directly in the Quintana Roo state bureaucracy. More recently, the Mexico City administrators and part of the local team have set up rival technical assistance offices, deepening the intra-bureaucratic tensions.

Other support came in a more technical form, and with fewer conflicts. The British Overseas Development Agency (ODA) assisted in the development of new methods of logging and transport, and strongly supported collaborative efforts with the Society. The John D. and Catherine T. MacArthur Foundation also supported in a timely manner forest inventories, wildlife management courses, and other activities, with the Society contributing the equipment necessary for the projects. In the beginning, this support was channeled through Conservation International, with funding coming directly to the Society in the second stage. Further, institutions that certify sustainably harvested timber for export markets, such as the Smart Wood program of Rainforest Alliance and the Mexican Civil Council for Sustainable Silviculture, have helped to develop more ecological criteria for forest management.

Industrialization, Commercialization, and Social Action

At the beginning of the PPF in 1983, it was shown that selective logging based primarily on Spanish cedar and mahogany was not feasible for the long term. Economic feasibility required the logging of other lesser-known tropical species. This meant that thinning had to be used as a silvicultural tool, producing the gaps necessary to regenerate heliophytic (sun-loving) species like mahogany (Stöger and Galletti 1987). For this to work, new markets had to be sought for the lesser-known species. Negotiations with MIQRO produced an agreement wherein it would buy these lesser-known species, but the company made no serious effort to actually saw and market them. In order to overcome their dependence on MIQRO, the ejidos built their own sawmills, which allowed them to increase both their profits and their direct access to the national market. This maneuver provoked local sawmills and MIQRO to pressure the state government to force the farmers to sell them their wood. The Society was able to thwart these efforts and resolve the situation in their favor: the government ruled that milling would stay in the hands of the ejidos and private industry would focus its efforts on more advanced processing (Galletti 1992).

In 1988, Mexico reduced import tariffs and local industry began to obtain large supplies of mahogany from Central America. In response to this crisis, the Society developed new markets for the lesser-known species, such as toothpicks, ice cream sticks, and pencils, but the high-value mahogany and cedar sales suffered. Beginning in the late 1980s, the Society began to develop "green" markets in the United States and Europe. These markets were willing to pay a higher price for timber coming from sustainably managed tropical forests. Several of the Society's ejidos won this "green seal" from certifying agencies.

The Society also benefited as producers by the devaluation of the Mexican peso in late 1994, which drove up the cost of imported timber but also exerted political pressure on the Society to sell exclusively to Quintana Roo industries. Thus, although there has been some progress in government policy, the Society continually has to fight political favoritism. Some local industries have adapted to new market opportunities and are working well with the Society. Since 1992, Pisos Industrializados de Quintana Roo (PIQRO), manufacturers of flooring and parquet, entered the international market with an aggressive promotional campaign using local species with high aesthetic value. The industry requires only moderate quantities of timber, pays well, and coordinates its inventory policies with ejido production schedules. With this market, the production of hardwoods once again became profitable. This healthy development suggests that real markets, free from political influence, are beginning to develop in Quintana Roo. Additional marketing assistance has also come from a national federation of community forestry organizations, the Union Nacional de Organizaciones Forestales Comunitarias (UNOFOC), which has developed a marketing program that has increased ejido response to market demands.

Organizations at the Regional Level

The PPF had begun its activities in 1983 with only six ejidos, but later expanded the number of member ejidos to ten at the time the Society was established. In 1986, a second organization, the Organización de Ejidos Productores Forestales de la Zona Maya de Quintana Roo (OEPFZMQR), was established in a part of central Quintana Roo dominated by Maya Indians, with members from nearly twenty ejidos. Between them the two organizations include the principal forest ejidos and the bulk of the mahogany production in the state. Even so, there were still some important timber-producing areas of the state that were unorganized, and when the PPF formally ended, the state government created the Plan Forestal Estatal (PFE) in 1989 with the objective of expanding organizing efforts to other areas of the state, continuing to use the methodology of the PPF (Argüelles et al. 1989). In 1991 and 1992, two new forest societies of ejidos and one organization of small individual producers were established, making the PFE the major actor in state forestry issues and resulting in the delineation of nearly 500,000 ha of permanent forest areas, almost the entirety of the productive forest area in the state. This change meant that, by agreement of the communities, these areas would never be converted to any other use than forestry, preserving these forests for the future. In 1992, however, when the state government changed again, the PFE was dismantled. Each forest society was left to its own devices and had to operate without the unifying strategy provided by the PPF and the PFE, weakening their capacity for political negotiation and cooperative activities.

Nonetheless, the model of the PPF is beginning to spread: farmers' organizations in the Calakmul Biosphere Reserve and Escárcega areas of neighboring Campeche state have used it to develop their own organizational and natural resource use strategies. It has also become the model for some environmental organizations of how forest management can be compatible with both production and conservation goals. The local societies have also played an increasingly prominent role at the national level and, with the support of elements in the federal government, were instrumental in founding UNO-FOC in 1993. UNOFOC has constituted itself as a national organization of community forestry organizations in order to develop a community of ideas and actions, influence public opinion on community forest management, and support the member organizations in technical, organizational, and marketing issues. Another national organization, the National Union of Autonomous Regional Farmers' Associations (UNORCA), focuses more on political justice issues.

The Policy Environment

Eighty percent of Mexican forests are in the hands of ejidos or indigenous communities, two separate land tenure categories in Mexico. This circumstance has created issues both around how forests should be used for production and how forests should be conserved, as most declared protected areas have peasant communities in and around them. In production, interests of the communities have usually been subordinated to private and parastatal industrial interests. In conservation, protected areas have almost always been declared without taking into account pre-existing claims or occupation by peasant communities. But there have been some exceptions to the indifference or hostility of official government policy toward community forest management. For example, efforts in the mid-1980s by elements within the forestry sub-secretary of SARH encouraged community participation in forest management. These elements also supported the right of forest community organizations to manage the technical services required under Mexican law themselves. In most cases, these had been provided by inefficient and expensive government concessionaires. A persistent problem has remained however. Sustainable forest management can be expensive, and no subsidies have been provided for the community efforts to improve their forest management. Nonetheless, these government policies marked an important strategic alliance between the state and the owners of the forests.

In contrast, environmental policy has been largely closed to participation by farmers. In many regions, the unilateral declaration of biosphere reserves, without consultation of the communities directly affected, has led to long and tangled histories of social and political conflict, in which both conservation and development lose. At the state level, after the initial support in the PPF and PFE periods, support has been much less trustworthy. Nonetheless, the state government took advantage of the declaration of permanent forest areas by the communities to establish the concept of the *strategic forestry reserve* (Gobierno de Quintana Roo 1987), integrating all of these areas for the planning of forestry development for the long term. In effect, the permanent forest area concept was the alternative to biosphere reserves, proposed by the local inhabitants as a means of preserving forest cover and significant biodiversity while at the same time guaranteeing their livelihood from the forest resource.

The period of significant government support for community participation ended around 1986, and by 1988 government forest policy veered toward total deregulation. In a new forestry law passed in 1992, the responsibility for forest technical services passed from the government concessionaires into the hands of private forestry firms, creating competitive pressures on the technical services provided by the forest societies. The 1992 law was passed principally to encourage the development of forest plantations in Mexico. For natural forests, it encouraged joint ventures between forest industries and ejidos, with the former providing capital, expertise, and marketing, and the ejidos providing the trees. However, the law did not recognize the accomplishments of ejidos and indigenous communities in natural forest management.

To counterbalance this market-oriented approach, the government also initiated the National Solidarity Program (PRONASOL), a social program aimed at covering up the gigantic process of concentrating capital in the hands of a few individuals that was occurring in the country at the time. However, the primary source of public funding for community forestry activities during Carlos Salinas de Gortari's presidency (1988–1994) was the National Reforestation Program (PRONARE), which, despite severe conceptual and technical limitations, did arrange for the available support to go directly to the communities. Interest-free loans also became available through another government program, the Fondo Nacional para Empresas Sociales (FONAES). Additionally, the Secretaría de Desarrollo Social (SEDESOL) has budgeted funds for the formation of a trust fund through UNOFOC to finance efforts supporting forestry organizations.

However, a more recent shift in state and federal government policy, which began in 1994, has ignored the presence of the forest societies and has encouraged the establishment of forest technical services by local governments at the municipal level. Further, the funds that SEDESOL dispersed to the organizations in a direct form are going to be channeled through local governments, showing a new governmental hostility to autonomous peasant organizations. The local level of government has little technical capacity and is even more subject to political pressure than the old federal technical services. During the last 13 years, the societies have had to restart the process of obtaining official recognition several times. Their survival has depended on their ability to maintain their central mission of community management of natural resources with a flexible strategy responsive to constantly changing scenarios. They have been able to confront frequent and arbitrary changes in external policies and institutions with a degree of institutional and strategic consistency on their part. This fact shows that autonomous, democratic, and technically trained local natural resource organizations can facilitate progress in conservation and development within the Mexican context. But it should be made clear that these organizations have a larger significance. Democratic natural resource management in Mexico has also produced an important new element in civil society, and environmental and development organizations need to take this into account.

Mexico is characterized by the poverty of the autonomous civil institutions facing the state apparatus, and this element has contributed to the degradation of the environment. Until recently there has been no separate civil society with the power to make the government accountable (Bobbio 1978). In this context, the forest societies and the process through which they were created is an experiment in democratic development that can also lead to better and more sustainable environmental management. It can also lead to greater equity in rural development. In a country where the number of billionaires rose from one to twenty between 1988 and 1994, while the percentage of people living in extreme poverty grew even more sharply, this feature is of the greatest importance. It is within this situation, after all, that the Zapatista uprising occurred in Chiapas, which is part of the same Maya Forest region of southern Mexico occupied by the forest societies of Quintana Roo. It is quite possible that the development of the societies in this part of the Maya Forest is what has created a climate of relative social and political stability compared to the situation in Chiapas. The current political climate in Mexico is dangerous for the autonomous community forest organizations.

Currently, the government is once again limiting autonomous spaces, rendering the future uncertain. It is too early to know if the proven skill of the forestry organizations will be adequate to the new situation.

Conclusions

In 1983 in Quintana Roo, a process of development of community forestry began that continues up to the present. A total of five forestry societies were formed, encompassing more than one-third of the rural population in the state, that have delineated approximately 500,000 ha to remain as permanent forest areas. This move secured a local protected area of comparable size to the Sian Ka'an Biosphere Reserve in central Quintana Roo. But these are areas protected by community action and management, not by federal government decree. The decision of the technical teams linked to the Mexican–German Accord to build up the local organizations created a strong motivational element, and the team also benefited from being able to work in different institutional refuges provided by different levels of government. Nevertheless, the lack of personnel and capabilities remains a significant problem in the whole process. Internal organizational problems are both a serious factor that limits further advances and the stimulus for new paths to follow. It is necessary to separate out the functions of both the technical and farmer work teams, and to encourage their technical development. Technical sustainability is key to economic, organizational, and financial sustainability. But here the problem of external support arises: the federal government is not disposed to subsidize these costs, and the financing offered by development and environmental organizations is for short-term projects rather than technical assistance subsidies. At this stage it is clear that trying to make sustainable forest management self-financing is not viable. Management cannot be financed by the farmers alone. However, new income for small producers has been key for the creation of the forest societies. A system of public and private support must be designed around the income needs of the producers and the conservation needs of the ecosystems. Subsidizing strict conservation alone will not give farmers a stake in preserving the rainforest. The experience shows that constructive alliances among the state, forest owners, and NGOs that acknowledge the role of farmers in conservation are the institutional basis for success in community forestry development.

The historic developments discussed in this chapter exemplify the problems encountered by forest owners when they try to take the management of these resources into their own hands. The problems exist and will continue to exist, and the process has been slow, difficult, and contradictory. However, the societies have spearheaded a transformation from a forest economy based on the mining of forest resources to one that is moving toward the sustainable harvest of multiple products from the rainforest.

References

Aldrete, M. 1994. Propuesta de reestructuración de la actividad chiclera en Quintana Roo. Chetumal, México, n.d.

Argüelles, A., and N. Armijo. 1995. Utilización y conservación de los recursos forestales en Quintana Roo. Problemática y perspectivas del manejo forestal. Chetumal, México, n.d.

Argüelles, A., H. Galletti, and H. Flachsenberg. 1989. Lineamientos para la implementación del Plan Forestal Estatal de Quintana Roo. Chetumal, México, n.d.

Fort, O. 1979. La colonización ejidal de Quintana Roo. Instituto Nacional Indigenista, Mexico, D.F., México.

Galletti, H. 1989. Economía política de la planificación comunal del uso del suelo en áreas forestales tropicales. Una experiencia de caso en Quintana Roo, México. Pages 707–734 in *Simposio Agroforestal en México: Sistemas y Métodos de Uso Múltiple del Suelo*, Vol. 2. Universidad Autónoma de Nuevo León-GTZ, Linares, Nuevo León, México.

———. 1992. Aprovechamientos e industrialización forestal. Desarrollo y perspectivas. Pages 101–153 in *Quintana Roo, los Retos del Fin del Siglo*. Centro de Investigaciones de Quintana Roo, Chetumal, México.

———. 1993. Las actividades forestales y su desarrollo histórico. Pages 131–198 in *Estudio Integral de la Frontera México–Belice*. CIQRO, Chetumal, México.

Galletti, H., and A. Argüelles. 1987a. Strategic plan for rural development: The case of the Plan Piloto Forestal de Quintana Roo. Pages 317–325 in *Land and Resource Evaluation for National Planning in the Tropics*. USDA Forest Service Publication No. GTR WO-39.

———. 1987b. La experiencia en el aprovechamiento de las selvas en el estado de Quintana Roo, México. Del modelo forestal clásico a un modelo forestal alternativeo. Taller Internacional sobre Silvicultural y Manejo de Selvas. SARH-COFAN-FAO, Chetumal, México, 11–20 de mayo de 1987.

Galletti, H., D. Acopa, and H. Janka. 1982. Bases para la formulación de una política forestal para el estado de Quintana Roo, con referencia especial a los aprovechamientos forestales. Proposal for the Government of the State of Quintana Roo, Chetumal, México.

Gobierno del Estado Libre y Soberano de Quintana Roo. 1987. Declaratorio de Política Forestal. Chetumal, México, n.d.

Gutiérrez, C., H. Larios Santillán, V. M. Díaz, and C. Abascal. Entrevista al término de la reunión de la Alianza para la Recuperación Económica. 22 de junio de 1996.

Habermas, J. 1973. Problemas de legitimación del capitalsmo tardio. Amorrortu, Buenos Aires, Argentina.

Instituto Mexicano de la Doctrina Social Cristiana et al. 1996. *El problema de empleo en México*. IMDSC, Ciudad de México, México.

Janka, H. 1985. Algunas consideraciones acerca de una nueva política forestal. Reunión Nacional sobre Economía Forestal, Guadalajara, 23 de enero de 1985. SARH-INIF, Publ. Esp. No. 47.

Janka, H., M. Berger, B. Dewars, and B. Neubegauer. 1981. Bases metodológicos para la formulación de un programa de investigación de uso múltiple en el trópical húmedo. Pages 33–53 in *Alternativas para el uso del suelo en áreas forestales del trópcio húmedo*. SARH-INIF, Publ. Esp. No. 26, T.I., Ciudad de México, México.

Janka, H., J. M. Zapata, H. Galletti, and E. Peralta Porras. 1983. Lineamientos de política forestal y propuestas de acción para el estado de Quintana Roo. Chetumal, México.

Lobato, R., and H. Janka. 1984. El surgimiento de una alternativa forestal campesina. Ciudad de México, México.

Lozano, L. et al. 1996. *Estudio Sobre la Situación Económica de México*. UNAM, Facultad de Economia. Ciudad de México, México.

Matus, C. 1981. Política y planificación en situaciones de poder compartido. CEN-DES, Ciudad de México, México.

Steinlin, H. 1981. Contribución de la economía forestal al mejoramiento de la situación económica y las condiciones de vida en las áreas forestales tropicales y subtropicales. Pages 9–33 in *Alternativas para el uso del suelo en áreas forestales tropicales* SARH-INIF, Publ. Esp. No. 26. T.I.

Stöger, K., and H. Galletti. 1987. Adaptación de la industria a las posibilidades del monte. Posibles pasos para el desarrollo industrial forestal. Chetumal, México. n.d.

Torelli, N. 1983. Breve evaluación technológica del bosque de Quintana Roo con énfasis especial en la sustitución de caoba y cedro con especies corrientes menos utilizadas y el desarrollo de un procesamiento de la madera más eficiente e integral. Chetumal, México.

———. 1984. Forest management and integrated utilization in Quintana Roo (first stage). Chetumal, México.

Chapter 4

Forest Management in Quintana Roo, Mexico

Henning Flachsenberg and Hugo A. Galletti

In this chapter we will focus on silvicultural issues in forest management in southern Quintana Roo, the zone of influence of the Sociedad de Ejidos Productores Forestales de Quintana Roo. As the preceding chapter by Galletti notes, the principal goal of this society and the Plan Piloto Forestal (PPF) was to halt forest destruction by making the rational use of forestry resources a secure and attractive source of income for the local population.

The rational ordering of forest exploitation cannot be obtained by mandate in the context of Quintana Roo; it arises instead from a process of negotiation among many different parties. Mechanical applications of management criteria drawn from the accumulated knowledge on tropical forests (Finegan 1991) are insufficient. In Quintana Roo, the methodological problem becomes determining the means to make knowledge operational for local conditions, so that it can be used by the local inhabitants to help prevent them from exceeding the production capacity of the forest resources (Flachsenberg 1993). The communities in Quintana Roo have struggled with the concept of sustainability and have understood it as successive approximations (Argüelles et al. 1993) as they move from a situation of clearly unsustainable resource use that resulted in rapid forest loss. The development of community forest enterprises was central to this process.

The Traditional Silvicultural Model

Until 1953, the forests of Quintana Roo were logged without any management plan and in a completely disorganized fashion (Galletti 1993). From 1953 until 1983, forests were exploited under a government concession to a parastatal forest industry, Maderas Industrializadas de Quintana Roo (MIQRO), which had a clear management plan. These forests were on both national lands and the lands of six ejidos. MIQRO logged the marketable trees of best quality and size, equal or greater than 60 centimeters (cm) around, of only two species, mahogany and Spanish cedar, which represented only about 2% of the production potential of the forest. The result was an extraordinarily extensive use of the forest. In order to harvest 200,000 cubic meters (m^3) of timber, MIQRO logged in more than 500,000 ha of forest. After this era, management plans were established for the six ejidos, with annual logging taking place in each one, which allowed the community members to gain forest management experience as loggers.

MIQRO applied a polycyclic management system, with the logging cycle adjusted to the 30-year period of the concession. All marketable trees were to be cut in 25 years. Reforestation would depend on natural regeneration and forest plantations (UIEF-MIQRO 1968). These policies had two problems: first, selective logging opened the canopy insufficiently to create optimal conditions for the regeneration of heliophytic species such as mahogany, and second, in conditions of accelerated colonization of the region there was no security for forest plantations. Despite these problems, it must be noted that MIQRO's silvicultural plan was considered pioneering in Latin America at the time.

Beginning in the 1960s, a process of colonization of public lands and advancement of the agricultural frontier was official policy, aimed at the major portion of the national forests. As a consequence of this policy, most of the forest capital in Mexico was destroyed. The policy created a new division of forest land that was superimposed over the planned logging areas' concession management plan. In the new ejido colonies there was no orderly exploitation of forests: in one ejido, for example, all marketable species were cut in just one year, instead of in the sequence planned under the MIQRO concession. The new colonists perceived no value in the forest, so they proceeded to cut it down (Galletti and Argüelles 1987). The MIQRO exploitation plan continued in theory, but it no longer corresponded to reality: the annual volume logged was maintained on a surface that was being reduced yearly by the spread of agriculture. It should be noted, however, that the timber would have been otherwise wasted, since the colonists were cutting the forests regardless of whether they intended to sell the wood.

Nonetheless, by the time the concession ended in 1983 there were still important forest areas left. This result stemmed from the fact that management plans still existed in the six ejidos, and was also due to the economic importance of the chicle industry, which depended on the standing forest and was thus essentially conservationist (Galletti 1989). In addition, the construction of forestry roads by MIQRO was an important investment in community forest management, as this initial infrastructure was an important capital asset for the rapid advancement of the ejido enterprises.

Development of Ejido Management Plans after 1983

Under the circumstances described above, it was impractical to drastically modify the traditional system of logging because it would endanger the process of participation by the farmers. Beginning with MIQRO's management plan, which was already familiar to the farmers, a minimum number of silvicultural measures were adopted to provide basic technical adequacy. The first such measure was to designate in each ejido a permanent forest area, with its location decided by an ejido assembly. There were forested areas outside the permanent forest areas reserved for future agricultural use, but in the permanent forest areas themselves agriculture was prohibited. This step signified the historic emergence of spatially delimited forests with a defined land-use regime, a basic precondition for the development of forest management (Galletti 1989).

The second step was to adopt provisional measures to assure minimally adequate forest management while forest inventories were undertaken. MIQRO's original logging cycle was maintained. The permanent forest area was subdivided into 25 annual logging areas of equal size. The areas were then subdivided into 100 ha quadrants, re-adopting a forest management technique originally used by MIQRO but later abandoned. Within each quadrant trees suitable for logging were measured, maintaining MIQRO's minimum diameter criterion. This method did not assure a stable annual production, but it was easily grasped by the farmers. In addition, MIQRO's forest inventories were revised and adjusted for the new forest areas.

In contrast to the previous period, increased productivity of the rainforest through more intensive but rational exploitation was sought from the beginning, incorporating new species and, as much as possible, going beyond logging oriented exclusively toward the precious tropical woods, mahogany and cedar. For example, for each cubic meter of precious wood, MIQRO, still in operation as a state timber intermediary, was required to buy two cubic meters of the lesser-known species. This feature marked an important break between MIQRO's forest management practices and community practices.

The division of forest labor within the ejido began to evolve, with assignments becoming more specialized as the process evolved. In the first stage, the ejidos organized themselves for the production of logs only, taking on the administration of the forest enterprise and organizing extraction on the basis of the adopted minimum criteria. This laid the organizational bases to begin to develop a more sophisticated and sensitive management plan. Although some progress was made toward the specialized labor requirements needed in the forest exploitation process, traditional patterns of labor allocations by the eji-dos presented a challenge. The ejidos with the most forest resources advanced most quickly to specialized functions, but in many others the permanent ro-tation of personnel called for by ejido custom limited the development of spe-cialized skills (Flachsenberg 1994a).

The development of more comprehensive management plans for each ejido began in 1986. To assure that the producers understood the importance of inventories and management plans, it was essential to include them in every aspect of the process, and not just have it be carried out by professional foresters (Stöger and Galletti 1987a). However, participatory inventories had some limitations. For example, it was difficult to maintain rigor in the collec-tion of the data (Carter et al. 1995). The farmers organized the data collec-tion in the traditional way, by rotating the personnel periodically, resulting in a permanent process of trial and error. In spite of the problems, the invento-ries had the advantage of being "neutral," i.e., not adjusted to the interests of any buyer, and still enjoyed a technical level superior to any other inventories in the region.

At the same time, a Geographical Information System (GIS) was devel-oped that permitted the numerical and graphical analysis of the forest (num-ber of trees, basal area, and volume in hectares) by species and diameter. This system permitted analysis of the composition of the forest mass in areas of a size and shape that could be selected by the user, also permitting the annual incorporation of the utilization data (Sánchez Román 1987).

Species Management

Cedar and mahogany, the most economically important species, depend upon disturbances, whether natural or man-made, for their regeneration. These species require adequate sunlight from the time of establishment until they grow to canopy level. Within mahogany's natural distribution area in the Maya Forest, these conditions occur in an ideal fashion in southern Quintana Roo (Lamb 1966). In the rest of the Yucatán Peninsula, with its poor soils and marked dry season, forests have diameters considerably smaller and with a lower canopy than those located in southern latitudes. Relatively small dis-turbances can produce sufficient sunlight for the regeneration of mahogany trees, and competition from vines is also relatively reduced. The forest is adapted to frequent hurricanes and fires, so the forest mass is in most cases in a pre-climax state (Huguet and Verduzco 1952). Forest management seeks to reproduce the types of disturbance that regenerate mahogany, using logging as a silvicultural tool.

Mahogany was selected as the lead species for various reasons: it has high commercial value and stable markets, and it is ecologically a dominant species (Flachsenberg 1995a). Because there were no data available on the growth of any tropical species, as a first approximation a logging rotation of 75 years was established on the basis of bibliographic information from the National Institute of Forestry Investigation and from studies of the clearings made by logyards in the forest, which have trees of known age and abundant natural regeneration (Rodríguez 1944; Álvarez 1987; Olmsted 1987). The probable maximum cycle was determined by the natural dynamics of succession, linked to the frequency of disturbances (hurricanes or fires), estimated at 105 to 115 years (Sarukhán 1984). Using these data, the estimated target growth of mahogany was 0.8 cm per year.

Two minimum diameters for logging were fixed: 55 cm for species with larger dimensions (*Swietenia macrophylla*, *Cedrela odorata*, *Pseudobombax ellipticum*, *Enterolobium cyclocarpum*, and *Manilkara zapota*) and 35 cm for the other species, but applied flexibly to allow intermediate cuts for enhancement. The 75-year rotation was divided into three 25-year logging cycles, beginning with comparisons between the new inventory and MIQRO's inventory. The tree population was divided into categories—established regeneration, recruits (*repoblado*), reserve, and available for logging—estimating that after a cycle each category would move up to the next level. The tree population was divided into groups of species, making sure that each group would be managed together. The minimum-diameter criterion implies a negative selection that favors slow-growing species and individuals, but the criterion was necessary to allow continued logging while more accurate data were generated.

Because of the lack of data, calculations of timber availability were done using conservative criteria: first, the existing trees available for logging were divided into 25-year cycles, without considering volume growth during the cycle, and second, despite the fact that the forests were mostly in a preclimax state, a net increase was not taken as an assumption. The departure point was a zero increase model, in which the current increase and the mortality rate would balance each other out. Regeneration was promoted in the logging areas, in locations where conditions were adequate or where adequate conditions could be created. Three different cases were identified: esciophytic (shade-loving) species, heliophytic species with long seed viability and/or high potential for reproduction (the majority of the softwoods), and heliophytic species with short seed viability (mahogany and cedar). The regeneration of esciophytic species is virtually guaranteed so long as large areas are not clear-cut, an unlikely possibility. Foreseeing an increase in the number of utilized species, basal and surface area limits of 30% forest clearance were adopted. In the latter two cases regeneration depends on the occurrence of disturbances of the right size and characteristics. Various softwoods have long-lived seed banks, and when an appropriate disturbance is created these seeds germinate. In these cases, adequate management of disturbance from logging seems sufficient to assure repopulation.

The types of disturbances that logging produces are the logyards, the log-ging roads, and the gaps produced by the actual felling of trees. The first kind of disturbance is particularly favorable for the regeneration of mahogany and cedar, because of the relatively large size of the area (Álvarez 1987; Hoffmann 1991). Logging roads have been shown to be inadequate in the majority of cases, and the treefall gaps are too small, further reduced by the slash left on the forest floor. However, the last situation could be improved by combining gaps produced by several adjacent trees to create a larger disturbance area and by cleaning up the logging slash (Stöger and Galletti 1987b; Schulz 1990; Hernández 1992). These disturbances could be the basis for a system of *selec-ción por bosquete* (i.e., selective cutting that favors natural regeneration). In any event, with the exception of the staging areas, other logging disturbances are too small for natural regeneration. Further, the reproductive strategy of mahogany and cedar is high risk. The seeds are short-lived and there is a large annual variation in their production. Thus, natural regeneration must be complemented with enrichment plantings in disturbed areas.

Although catastrophic disturbances do indeed favor the regeneration of mahogany (Snook 1993), in practice it is not feasible to destroy large surfaces in order to promote regeneration of this favored species. A more acceptable path is to increase logging intensity (intervening in larger areas in order to regulate the size and distribution of the gaps) and concentrate mahogany stocks through enrichment plantings in the gaps (Stöger and Galletti 1987b). The management plan foresaw the development of a silviculture adapted to site conditions (Stöger 1988; SPFEQR 1990). The goal was to move from generic and extensive silviculture to a more differentiated stand management. The MIQRO inventory, despite its defects, had shown there was enormous variability in forest composition, both in species and diameter, in Quintana Roo. This variability does not appear to correspond to any single obvious el-ement such as soil type, but seemed to depend more on the history of the par-ticular stand. This feature demands the development of a silvicultural system that is flexible and finely tuned to the reality of a given area.

Evolution of Management from 1989 to the Present

From 1989 on, management activities concentrated in two areas: enrichment and revision of the silvicultural model based on new data, and improvement of inventory management (*ordenación*) and logging practices. These areas did not develop at the same time or in all of the ejidos, resulting in a great deal of variability in management practices from ejido to ejido. The lack of data on growth rates was recognized as a critical element in the management plan, but any monitoring system also had to take into account the great spatial vari-ability in species composition. Thus, in 1989 circular sites began to be tested as units in a network of permanent sampling plots formulated according to the Swiss control method in its modern statistical version (Biolley 1920). This method is based on the division of the forest into stands on the basis of their production potential. For each stand a representative number of sampling plots is established. The objective is not to obtain information about the individual growth, but to measure the total net growth of the stand (Flachsenberg 1995b).

The design and statistical treatment of the sample was refined to achieve an adequate representation of the spatial variation (Sánchez 1993). The model permits the evaluation of individual increments, incorporation, mortality, and regeneration. The GIS was perfected to incorporate the data from the permanent sampling plots (Sánchez 1993). The collection of data was standardized to make it accessible to technicians and farmers (Flachsenberg 1992). In recent years, further advances have been made toward establishing a network of permanent sampling plots that is one of the most intensive in the tropics, adding sampling plots focusing exclusively on studying mahogany growth.

It is too soon to evaluate results from the permanent sampling plots. The initial remeasurements show results that vary greatly by site, with increases in volume that are both greater and less than the average growth forecast (Sánchez and Ramírez 1992; Sánchez, manuscript in preparation; Whigham et al. in press). Given the enormous variation of annual increases, primarily due to variability in precipitation, it is important to carry out remeasurements that permit the calculation of the current growth increment. Current results show a net increase in the forest mass. A proposal under consideration that would increase the logging cycle for mahogany to 120 years is based on data from one 75-year-old stand, dated on the basis of local memory (Snook 1991 and 1992). It generalizes to the entire region data that involve oral transmission through two generations. It is necessary to broaden the database with direct measurements sampling different rotations under the conditions of the different sites, and to consider that hasty decisions could slow down the forest economy of the region, which is the real engine of conservation.

The management plan allowed calculations of production potential at a general level, but the variability in spatial distribution strongly conditioned the results. To date, the location of the area to be logged within the permanent forest area is a decision taken by the general assembly of each ejido. It is necessary to try to influence this decision to achieve more predictable steps toward rational spatial ordering of the exploitation. As a step in this direction, the division of the total exploitable stocks of each group of species into five 5-year blocks of equal volume was proposed, making each block as close to the same size as possible. Within each block the annual volume of mahogany is kept constant, but variability is allowed in the other species. Since the species composition of the forest varies with each cycle, the distribution of each block is valid for only one 25-year cycle. Once the cycle ends, the distribution needs to be revised (Stöger and Galletti 1989). This revision enables advancing from long-term (25-years) volumetric planning to medium-term (5 years) spatial planning (Argüelles 1990). It was a question of finding a medium ground that would be acceptable to the community. The stratification by blocks is an important first step toward the concept of spatial organization of the forest in smaller management units (Flachsenberg 1991).

The Noh-Bec ejido took logical steps in its logging areas. As a result, it has been considered a pilot ejido, and silvicultural efforts have been concentrated there. Annual logging areas had been determined there, but the ejidatarios observed that the areas actually logged went beyond the set limits and verified that the inventory results did not coincide with the actual stocks. Thus, circular sample sites were adopted as a quality control on the inventory data, in addition to the permanent sampling plots. The inventory control sites revealed two problems: first, the original field data contained errors, and second, there was little control over the logging. A considerable volume of usable timber was left in the forest, even though logging was distributed over a larger surface than anticipated. These findings led to a reduction in logging volume, but also forced reorganization of field data collection and the design of a more controllable forestry inventory model. One of the most important tasks in recent years has also been the application of the concept of 5-year blocks for extraction planning in many of the ejidos, with variations between ejidos that had completed their inventories and those that had not. For the smaller ejidos, the system of blocks was not applicable, and for them a more intensive model of logging in successive strips was proposed (Flachsenberg 1995c).

Problems in the Application of the Silvicultural Model

The silvicultural model anticipated an increase in species utilization to create larger gaps as a silvicultural tool. However, what seemed theoretically logical was problematic in the field. The industry did not adapt rapidly to the new species, it did not develop alternative markets, and the farmers could not respond to changes in the market. The demand for new species was quite random, making difficult the management by species group proposed in the model (Flachsenberg 1991b).

The application of the silvicultural model varied greatly because of the variations between the ejidos. Because it is important for understanding the challenges of applying a finely tuned silvicultural model, in the following section we would like to briefly sketch in some of the problems that were encountered in individual cases.

Case 1: Noh-Bec

Noh-Bec has a highly organized exploitation system. The annual logging areas are manageable and limited, allowing for good control. Different species were utilized within the same logging area. As in the case mentioned above, both the community and the technical team could quickly detect and correct errors, facilitated by the installation of an office with a computer in the ejido. Currently, logging is carried out using the corrected inventory. The ejido is also displaying increased ability to plan for the future. For example, the current logging area has proven to have more productive potential than anticipated, but the ejido has decided to conserve the volume as a buffer until the closing of the 25-year cycle. The forest's income is very important in this community, and a favorable combination of socioeconomic and silvicultural elements has laid the basis for the development of rational management practices.

Case 2: Petcacab

The ejido Petcacab is an example of excellence in silviculture, but with many social complications. It is a Maya ejido that has had difficulty, due to deficiencies in the local educational system, in achieving necessary levels of professional specialization. It has an enormous forest reserve, giving it a great margin for trial and error. Petcacab has had problems with forest management, but it has improved over the years. The defining of the permanent forest area was chaotic for several years, with different species taken from different logging areas, but now logging is concentrated in a single annual area. This transition was aided by the fact that various community members were long-time chiefs of inventory teams, acquiring a strong knowledge of local forestry. The economic demonstration effect caused the ejido to expand its permanent forest area; despite this expansion, logging volume did not increase. Thus, the forest has always been underutilized. It also has abundant reserves for the next logging cycle. This ejido is a case where the luxury of high volume and the future composition of the forest have provided a cushion to overcome initial deficiencies.

Case 3: Tres Garantías and Caoba

These two large ejidos have relatively dispersed forests in separate areas. In contrast to the two ejidos previously described, agriculture and cattle raising are important sources of income in Tres Garantías and Caoba. A considerable part of the population receives income from the forest without actively participating in the forest labors. In the first few years the forests were overexploited, in the hope that local development based on processing and the use of new species would permit a later reduction of the volume, but this result did not occur. The location of the annual logging areas did not have a clear rationale, and the inventories were not completed in a timely fashion. The five-year block criterion was inapplicable as a long-term planning tool because of a lack of reference points. Since 1993 an attempt has been made to organize the situation, beginning with the location and inventory of areas that have not been utilized. In the next cycle, the logging of machiche (*Lon-*

chocarpus castilloi) and mahogany will need to be reduced. These ejidos illustrate the difficulties that arise in a situation where the conditions are moderately favorable, with little margin for error, yet the internal politics are difficult and the technical aspects are inadequately controlled.

Case 4: Small Ejidos

In these ejidos, forest production represents at most 20% of income (Flachsenberg 1994; Hess 1996). Forest activities have not produced much social improvement or the acquisition of technical skills. Under these conditions the community organization has not matured. In retrospect, the appropriation of the forest by small cooperative groups should have been favored to encourage family agroforestry and forest plantations. Chicle exploitation provides a model here, but internal interests make its application to timber exploitation difficult. Given the reduced size of the permanent forest areas, the margin for trial and error is small and the 5-year blocks inapplicable.

Two types of small ejidos exist: ejidos with marked deterioration of the forest resources (Manuel Avila Camacho, Plan de la Noria, and Los Divorciados) and ejidos in which relatively economically attractive forests persist (Botes and Chacchoben), where current activities could be redirected into more sustainable forms. In the first type of small ejido, extraction of logs with no subsequent processing had developed as the major form of forestry. The lack of income alternatives created a lack of internal social control. Ejido members logged individually, and their forests' continued existence is threatened. In the second type, internal divisions exist, but these are not significant and do not present a danger to the forest. In the case of Botes, the ejido did not even log for several years, sparing their forest entirely. The present situation is probably the last opportunity to develop a forestry alternative that could correct previous mistakes. Finally, it is clear that these small and poor ejidos require constant technical presence, which is expensive.

Technical Assistance, Forestry Organization, and Silviculture

Keeping community forestry viable depends on the emergence and development of two agents of change: forest groups within the community and a technical team with the capacity to communicate with the farmers, negotiate with the government, and teach technical aspects of forest management. The government forest service has never had a presence in the communities. The technical team, in contrast, went to the forests and incorporated the farmer from the beginning. Each technician was assigned to several ejidos and had to deal with multiple technical problems as well as act as community organizer.

In 1986, the forest society received the concession to administer its own forest technical services. However, the quotas established to pay for the services were insufficient to pay for adequate services, and the management plan called for a level of technical assistance too expensive for the farmers. The situation was particularly critical for overpopulated ejidos with small forests. Each technician had to cover up to 20,000 ha of forests. By comparison, in Germany the norm is one forester for every 500 ha.

At the same time, the government demanded the application of forestry and ecological criteria determined without practical knowledge of the situation—criteria that were generally inapplicable. This situation created a posture of defensiveness toward the government on the part of the technical team, which made it difficult to draw on the experiences of government agencies. Constant economic insecurity also inhibited long-range planning. The team also had difficulties coping when the forest activities reached a high level of complexity. The team had to collect inventory data, monitor the logging process, and design management plans for each ejido. The result was that management decisions were frequently made spontaneously by the ejidos, producing a wide range of silvicultural practices. As more external support from foreign assistance became available, the technical team was able to specialize in inventories or logging control. However, the number of technicians did not increase, and the situation became even more demanding when sawmills were installed in several of the ejidos, requiring even greater levels of specialized technical assistance. In recent years, the original technical team has been replaced by the children of ejido members who have received technical training. These new technicians are progressively showing a greater capacity to administer logging, but are still weak in community organizing skills.

Learning from Experience

In comparison with other tropical forests in Quintana Roo, considerable improvement has been made, but sustainable tropical forest management by communities still faces many issues. These issues are so pressing that it will not be possible to wait for science to produce the relevant information. It is crucial that the internal mechanisms of decisionmaking in the ejidos adapt in order to guarantee the continuity of the forest enterprises. The most viable alternative is to restructure forest management entirely as a cooperative enterprise. But this alternative will require significant amounts of training, technical assistance, and community organization. A more entrepreneurial focus has also been inhibited by the practice of distributing profits to the members rather than reinvesting them in the enterprise, impeding capitalization. Except in the wealthier ejidos, forest income is not sufficient for the livelihood of the ejido population. In these cases, the situation demands new ways of appropriating the resources that are not always accepted by the local population. As a complement to the forest activity, it is necessary to develop small businesses and family workshops, as well as agroforestry and forest plantations.

Experience shows that it is not possible to develop a standard, one-size-fits-all management plan. Within the general criteria, local conditions need local solutions. Permanent sampling plots are a basic tool for decision making, and there has to be a systematic relationship between the data produced by the plots and forest exploitation. Communities' capacity to conduct their own forest affairs must be supported and reinforced. Despite the ups and downs of community forestry management, it is still the best alternative for the conservation of tropical forests, but the conditions that favor its development must be clearly understood by external agents.

References

Álvarez, A. 1987. Perspectivas de la regeneración natural y de plantaciones de enriquecimiento en las áreas de aprovechamiento de los ejidos del Plan Piloto Forestal de Quintana Roo, México. Taller Internacional sobre Silvicultura y Manejo de Selvas, SARH-COFAN-FAO, Chetumal, México.

Argüelles, L. A. 1990. Plan de manejo forestal para el bosque tropical de la empresa ejidal Noh-Bec. Thesis, Universidad Autónoma Chapingo, Chapingo, México.

Argüelles, A., H. A. Galletti, and F. Sánchez Román. 1993. Manejo forestal tropical. El caso del Plan Piloto Forestal de Quintana Roo. In *Primer Foro Nacional sobre Manejo Integral Forestal*. Chapingo, México.

Biolley, H. 1920. L'aménagement des forêts par la méthode éxperimentale et specialment la méthode de controle. Attinger Frères, Paris.

Carter, J., M. Stockdale, F. Sánchez Román, and A. Lawrence. 1995. Local people's participation in forest resource assessment: An analysis of recent experience, with case studies from Indonesia and Mexico. *Commonwealth Forestry Review* 74: 282–287.

Finegan, B. 1991. Manejo y conservación de los bosques naturales ¿es posible manejarlos económicamente? Asamblea Conmemorativa del III Aniversario de REDSA, San José, Costa Rica.

Flachsenberg, H. 1991a. Aprovechamiento, regeneración y silvicultura. Una contribución al monitoreo de la sostenibilidad de la producción biológico-forestal. Acuerdo México–Alemania, Chetumal, México (manuscript).

———. 1991b. Reflexión sobre la utilización de los recursos forestales de las áreas forestales permanentes de los ejidos integrantes de organizaciones campesinas. Acuerdo México–Alemania, Chetumal, México (manuscript).

———. 1992. Instructivo para el establecimiento de parcelas permanentes de muestreo en áreas forestales. Acuerdo México–Alemania, Chetumal, México (manuscript).

———. 1993. Aspectos socioculturales, técnicos, económicos y financieros en el manejo de selva. I Congreso Forestal Centroamericano, III Congreso Forestal de Guatemala, Flores, Guatemala.

———. 1994a. Problemas de transferencia tecnológica. Acuerdo México–Alemania, Chetumal, México (manuscript).

———. 1994b. Manejo de Recurso Forestal. Indices económicos de las anualidades entre 1991 y 1993. Fundación MacArthur/Acuerdo México–Alemania/Sociedad de Productores Forestales Ejidales de Quintana Roo, Chetumal, México (manuscript).

————. 1995a. Grupos de las especies comerciales con su uso principal. Acuerdo México–Alemania, Chetumal, México (manuscript).

————. 1995b. Consideraciones sobre el cálculo de la posibilidad volumétrica de la caoba. Acuerdo México–Alemania, Chetumal, México (manuscript).

————. 1995c. Tratamientos silviculturales por medio de la organización de aprovechamiento de la madera en el ejido Guadalupe Victoria. Acuerdo México–Alemania, Chetumal, México (manuscript).

Flachsenberg, H., A. Álvarez, C. Moreno, and C. Gutiérrez, Salvador y Juárez. 1992. Evaluación de la regeneración natural y de plantaciones en la región Sureste de México. Acuerdo México–Alemania, Chetumal, México (manuscript).

Galletti, H. 1989. Economía política de la planificación comunal del uso del suelo en áreas forestales tropicales. Una experiencia de caso en Quintana Roo, México. Pages 707–734 in *Simposio Agroforestal en México: Sistemas y métodos de uso múltiple del suelo*. Universidad de Nuevo León-GTZ, Linares, México, Tomo 2.

Galletti, H. 1993. ¿Dónde quedó el concepto de frontera forestal? La delimitación espacial como elemento central para el manejo de bosques tropicales. Foro Internacional sobre los Aprovechamientos Forestales en Selvas y su Relación con el Ambiente, SARH-COFAN-FAO, Chetumal, noviembre 1993.

Galletti, H., and A. Argüelles. 1987. La experiencia en el aprovechamiento de las selvas en Quintana Roo, México. Del modelo forestal clásico a un modelo forestal alternativo. Taller Internacional sobre Silvicultura y Manejo de Selvas, SARH-COFAN-FAO, Chetumal, 11–20 mayo.

Galletti, H., K. Stöger, A. Argüelles, and F. Sánchez Román. 1990. Plan de manejo integral de los bosques de los ejidos integrantes de la Sociedad de Productores Forestales Ejidales de Quintana Roo, S. C. Chetumal, México, 12 tomos.

Hernández, J. 1992. Estudio de regeneración de caoba en función de la superficie de perturbaciones provocadas por medio del aprovechamiento forestal. Thesis, Universidad Autónoma de Nuevo León, Linares, México.

Hess, J. 1996. Kommunale Bewirtschaftung feuchttropischer Naturwälder—eine leistungsfähige und stabile Landnutzungsform als Garant für den Walderhalt? Sozioökonomische Untersuchungen in Waldbauerngemeinden von Quintana Roo, Mexiko. Universität Dresden, Germany.

Hoffmann, S. 1991. Naturverjüngung der witschaftsbaumarten im Bereich des Plan Piloto Forestal, Quintana Roo. Thesis, Fachhochschule Hildesheim/Holzminden, Germany.

Huguet, L., and J. Verduzco 1952. Economía forestal de Yucatán. In *Aprovechamiento de los recursos forestales*. IMRNR, Ciudad de México, México.

Lamb, F. B. 1966. *Mahogany of Tropical America: Its Ecology and Management*. University of Michigan, Ann Arbor.

López, J. C. 1994. Diagnóstico de especies forestales comerciales de la empresa forestal ejidal Tres Garantías, Quintana Roo. Thesis, Universidad Autónoma Chapingo, Chapingo, México.

Medina, B., A. Cuevas, and M. de los Santos. 1968. Ajuste al proyecto de ordenación. UIEF-MIQRO, Chetumal, México, 7 tomos.

Olmsted, I. 1987. Bericht über ein Arbeitsprogramm in Bezug auf Verjüngungsaktivitäten im Plan Piloto Forestal de Quintana Roo. Acuerdo México–Alemania (manuscript).

Rodríguez Caballero, R. 1944. La explotación de los montes de caoba en el territorio de Quintana Roo. Thesis, Escuela Nacional de Agricultura, Chapingo, México.

Sánchez Román, F. 1987. Procesamiento de datos de los inventarios del Plan Piloto Forestal de Quintana Roo, México. Taller Internacional sobre Silvicultura y Manejo de Selvas, SARH-COFAN-FAO, Chetumal, Mexico, 11–20 de mayo de 1987.

————. 1993. *Sistema de parcelas permanentes de muestreo (PPM)*. Acuerdo México–Alemania, Chetumal, Mexico (manuscript).

Sánchez Román, F., and Ramírez, E. 1992 y 1995. Crecimiento de los árboles de caoba en la parcela del Pozo Comenzado, ejido de Noh-Bec. Acuerdo México–Alemania, Chetumal (manuscript).

Sarukhán, J. 1984. Requerimientos de información en los inventarios para selvas. In Encuentro Nacional sobre Inventarios Forestales, Chihuahua, INIF, Publ. Esp. No. 45.

Schulz, C. 1990. Untersuchung der natürlichen Verjüngung der Caoba (*Swietenia macrophylla* King) auf Hiebslöchern. Acuerdo México-Alemania (manuscript).

Snook, L. 1991. Opportunities and constraints for sustainable tropical forestry: Lessons from the Plan Piloto Forestal, Quintana Roo, Mexico. Proceedings, Humid Tropical Lowlands Conference, Panama, DESFIL Project, TR/D and U.S. Forest Service Tropical Forestry Program.

————. 1992. Regeneración y crecimiento de la caoba (*Swietenia macrophylla*) en las selvas naturales de Quintana Roo, México. In *Madera, caza y milpa. Contribuciones al manejo integral de las selvas de Quintana Roo, México*. PROAFT-INIFAP-USAID-WWF US.

————. 1993. Stand dynamics of mahogany (*Swietenia macrophylla* K.) and associated species after fire and hurricane in the tropical forests of the Yucatán Peninsula, Mexico. Ph.D. dissertation, Yale School of Forestry and Environmental Studies, New Haven.

Stöger, K. 1988. *Schlussbericht* (Final report to GTZ).

————. 1989. Observaciones y discusiones personales sobre la metodología de parcelas permanentes (manuscript).

Stöger, K., and H. Galletti. 1987a. Evaluación de recursos forestales en selvas tropicales y su relación con comunidades rurales. Pages 343–347 in *Land and Resource Evaluation for National Planning in the Tropics*. U.S.D.A. Forest Service, Publication Nr. GTR WO-39.

————. 1987b. El efecto silvicultural del sistema de aprovechamiento actual en el sur de Quintana Roo. Taller Internacional sobre Silvicultura y Manejo de Selvas, SARH-COFAN-FAO, Chetumal, México, 11–20 de mayo.

————. 1989. Aplicación de los datos del inventario y propuesta de planificación a largo y mediano plazo. Acuerdo México–Alemania, Chetumal, México (manuscript).

Whigham D., J. Lynch, and M. Dickinson. Integrated approach to forest management and wildlife conservation in Quintana Roo, Mexico (this volume).

Chapter 5

Sustaining Harvests of Mahogany (*Swietenia macrophylla* King) from Mexico's Yucatán Forests: Past, Present, and Future

Laura K. Snook

In the past decade, it has become widely accepted that one incentive for con-serving tropical forests is the potential to obtain economic benefits from them. Although harvesting nontimber forest products (NTFPs) is perceived to be less destructive than timber harvesting, timber is among the most valu-able resources of the tropical forest. Like rattan stems or palm leaves, Brazil nuts or chicle latex, timber can be a renewable resource if it is harvested and managed in a sustainable manner.

To assure sustained yields of a timber resource (or any other biotic re-source), harvesting rates must not exceed growth rates, and care must be taken to assure that new individuals of the desired species become estab-lished to replace those that are extracted. Species differ in their patterns of growth and regeneration, so guidelines for sustainable harvesting must be developed on the basis of an understanding of the ecology of the resource species, preferably in the geographical area where it is being exploited.

Mahogany (*Swietenia macrophylla*) has been the most valuable timber species of the Neotropical forests since the arrival of the Europeans (Record 1924; Lamb 1966; Verissimo et al. 1995). To this day, mahogany represents a major source of timber-derived revenue among 62 forest communities in Quintana Roo that control 1,303,000 ha of land, of which 500,000 ha are in commercial forest (Argüelles 1993). These communities and the foresters that work with them have been grappling with the challenges of implement-ing sustainable forestry practices. However, only recently have baseline studies of mahogany regeneration and growth been carried out in this area (Juarez 1988; Negreros 1991; Snook 1993a; Whigham et al., this volume).

This chapter will present a historical overview of the patterns of exploitation of the mahogany timber resource, along with information about mahogany ecology as a foundation for discussing the opportunities and constraints for implementing silvicultural systems to provide for the sustainable production of this valuable timber into the future.

The History of Mahogany Logging in Quintana Roo

Big-leaf or Honduras mahogany (*Swietenia macrophylla*) has been harvested from the forests of Mexico's Yucatán Peninsula for centuries. The Maya hollowed out enormous mahogany canoes for long-distance trading expeditions (Hammond 1982). Historical records date Spanish use of West Indian mahogany (*Swietenia mahogoni*) for construction, shipbuilding, and furniture to the early sixteenth century. In 1629, the Spanish Navy established its principal shipyard on the mainland in what is now the state of Veracruz, Mexico, in order to take advantage of the big-leaf mahogany (*Swietenia macrophylla*) resource. Other European explorers also came to appreciate the qualities of mahogany wood for ship repairs and construction (Lloyds 1850; Mell 1917; Lamb 1966). As early as 1683, the British were harvesting mahogany from the Central American mainland (Record 1924). English logging settlements were the reason for the founding of the colony of British Honduras, now Belize (Edwards 1957, 1986; Napier 1973).

The Maya of present-day Quintana Roo were not conquered by the Spaniards, and after Mexico became independent from Spain in 1821, the Maya continued to resist attempts by the central government to take control of their lands. During the eighteenth and nineteenth centuries, the Maya of Quintana Roo were supported in their struggles by the English colony of British Honduras, which provided them with arms and other supplies in return for access to the forest resources, including mahogany, in the Maya Forest. By the late nineteenth century, logging was carried out in Quintana Roo as far north as Tulum by descendants of African slaves from British Honduras (Konrad 1988). As early as 1846, 85 million board feet (bf) of mahogany were shipped from British Honduras to English ports for shipbuilding (Figure 5.1). It is likely that much of this mahogany had been harvested from the Mexican side of the Río Hondo, the river that is currently the border between Quintana Roo and Belize (Mell 1917). The Mexican government finally defeated the Mayas in 1901, after which President Porfirio Díaz granted concessions for mahogany harvesting on Maya lands to British and American timber companies (Konrad 1988).

Mahogany logging by Europeans in Quintana Roo began along the Río Hondo, which was used to transport the logs to Chetumal Bay. Trees were

Figure 5.1

During the nineteenth and early twentieth centuries, massive ancient mahogonies were logged from Mexican forests by British and American companies and sawn into enormous boards like these.

felled above their buttresses, squared, hauled to the river, and floated in rafts to the bay for loading on ships (Lloyds 1850; Mell 1917; Rey 1983). After 1805, when oxen were brought to British Honduras to replace manpower provided by slaves for hauling, logs could be brought to the river from 8 km or more inland. Mules were used for hauling on the Mexican side of the river. Hauling was done at night, when temperatures were lower (Record 1924; Lamb 1966; Napier 1973).

Logs could be hauled during the dry season over longer and longer distances as mules and oxen were replaced by narrow-gauge railroad and crawler tractors. Using these machines, it became economical to drag logs from 30 or even 60 km deep in the forest to the Río Hondo, the Laguna de Bacalar, or the New River and New River Lagoon in Belize. Once waterborne, the logs were chained in booms and towed by tugboats to the Bay of Chetumal, where they were loaded onto ships (Rodríguez 1944; Medina 1948; Villaseñor 1958; Lamb 1966; Medina et al. 1968; Galletti 1994).

British and American concessionaires controlled mahogany harvesting in Quintana Roo from headquarters in British Honduras until the mid-twentieth century (Mell 1917; Villaseñor 1958; Edwards 1986; Galletti 1994). Recorded exports of mahogany from Quintana Roo peaked in 1943–44, when 29,000 logs (50,000 m³) were registered as having been shipped out from Chetumal (Medina 1948). After 1947, the activities of foreign timber companies in Quintana Roo were suspended. Mahogany harvests from 1948 to 1957 averaged about 7,000 logs, or 16,000 m³, per year. Eighty percent or more of the timber was exported as logs, and another 15% as sawn boards (Villaseñor 1958).

Although Mexican foresters decried the system of concessions and log exports, they also acknowledged that high quality standards for export logs— which had to be completely sound, straight, a minimum of 14 feet (4.2 m) long, and at least 16 inches (40 cm) in diameter at the top—saved the species from being depleted in the forests. Overharvesting already had occurred with cedar (Cedrela odorata), which had been harvested down to very small diameters in northern Quintana Roo to supply local processing industries (Rodríguez 1944; Medina 1948; Villaseñor 1958).

In the 1950s, to obtain greater benefits from the forest resources of Quintana Roo, a federal veneer and plywood industry called Maderas Industrializadas de Quintana Roo (MIQRO) was authorized by presidential decree and established on the banks of the Río Hondo near Chetumal. In 1957, MIQRO was granted a 25-year concession to 550,000 ha of forests in the central and southern part of the state, including six ejidos, as its source of mahogany and cedar, the so-called precious woods (Galletti 1994).

Under the MIQRO concession, a network of logging roads was built, permitting exploitation of all but the furthest reaches of the forest. Rubber-tired skidders and chainsaws were introduced at this time. The first complete forest inventories were done and harvesting plans were developed that controlled the rate of extraction by defining the maximum allowable cut and the minimum cutting diameter. Since growth rates could not be determined because mahogany rings were found not to be annual, the allowable cut for each year was determined by dividing the volume of commercial timber on the concessioned area by the 25 years of the concession period (Rodríguez 1944; Medina et al. 1968). Selective harvesting of the best mahogany trees continued, but trees down to a diameter of 60 cm, the minimum size required by processing machinery, were felled. Many trees that had been left standing during earlier timber concessions because they did not meet the standards of the export market were felled as veneer logs during this phase of exploitation (Medina et al. 1968).

At the end of the MIQRO concession in 1983, forest ejidos in Quintana Roo were reorganized into forest management and marketing cooperatives under a community forestry initiative called the Plan Piloto Forestal (PPF). The PPF began by organizing ten ejidos with the largest and most valuable forests, with support from the forestry agreement funded by the German development agency GTZ, the governor of Quintana Roo at that time, Pedro Joaquin Coldwell, and the then sub-secretary for forestry, Leon Jorge Castaños (Snook 1991). By 1992, this model had been expanded to four associations of forestry ejidos with a combined allowable cut of 10,580 m³ per year of mahogany and cedar from a total of 774,734 ha of land, of which 393,481 ha are forest reserve (Flachsenberg 1993b).

The organization of forestry activities under the PPF model differs in two significant ways from the MIQRO concession. First, during the concession period MIQRO had exclusive rights to purchase and process mahogany timber harvested from the ejidos at a price set by the government. Thus MIQRO obtained the profits derived from transforming raw timber, purchased cheaply, into veneer, a high-value end product. The ejidos obtained a relatively low stumpage fee (*derecho de monte*), of which a portion was put into a trust fund for socially beneficial undertakings. Under the PPF model, the ejidos themselves are free to determine, with guidance from forestry professionals, whether to extract, sell, or process the timber from their forests, and to obtain the full financial benefit from the sale of their forest products. Secondly, whereas MIQRO managed a 550,000 ha concession area, which supplied about 16,000 m³ per year of mahogany and cedar, under the PPF model the unit of forest management is the ejido. Ejido forest reserves vary greatly in size, from 1,000 ha to 30,000 ha. Forests also vary in calculated annual yields of mahogany, ranging from 0 m³ to 1,588 m³ (Flachsenberg 1993b). Organizing forestry at the ejido level thus greatly reduces the range of processing options available and the potential to maximize timber value, because high-value end products require capital-intensive installations and a consistent, high volume of raw timber.

Management of the ejido forests today is based on the same guidelines applied under the MIQRO concession. Although mahogany logs are now being sawn into boards rather than being peeled for veneer, annual harvests are still determined on the basis of a minimum diameter of 55 to 60 cm and the 25-year cutting cycle derived by MIQRO from its concession period. However, efforts are being made to harvest more species than mahogany. Ejidos also have been planting mahogany seedlings in cutting areas after harvesting.

Sustaining Mahogany Harvests in the Past: Three Centuries of Fortuitous Conservation

The fact that mahogany timber has been harvested in commercial quantities from the forests of Quintana Roo since the late 1600s would appear to indicate that harvesting has been sustainable. However, it is important to look more closely at the patterns of mahogany exploitation over the years to understand how these harvests were sustained. First, changes in markets and technology have gradually redefined the mahogany reserve. From the seventeenth century to the 1940s, only select mahogany trees were harvested for the international log export market. Many huge trees were left behind because they were imperfect. From the 1950s to the 1980s, many of these imperfect trees were harvested for the MIQRO veneer mill. Now that mahogany timber is being sawn into boards (a lower-value end product than veneer), standards have dropped still further, and trees of lower quality and even smaller diameters can be processed. These changes in markets and transformation technologies have redefined the mahogany reserve such that trees left behind in earlier logging operations because they were not considered commercial are providing the bulk of today's harvests.

The mahogany reserve has also been redefined by changes in timber extraction technology, which have provided access to more and more previously unlogged forest. Between the seventeenth century and 1920, the successive replacement of manpower by draft animals and a combination of narrow-gauge railroads and crawler tractors increased the forest resource from a fringe of less than 100 m to a band 60 km wide along the Río Hondo, the perimeter of the Laguna de Bacalar, and other bodies of water in the region. Since then, the construction of roads and the introduction of rubber-tired skidders have made it possible to log mahogany trees from almost every area of the forest.

Over the past centuries and decades, mahogany trees have also regenerated and grown into commercial-size classes. Because much of the forest was inaccessible to loggers and many mahogany trees were left behind in logged areas because they were imperfect, mahogany seeds were available to colonize areas where conditions were favorable for regeneration. Trees left behind because they were smaller than the commercial diameter limit have also grown to commercial size.

Nonetheless, the framework for sustaining mahogany harvests has changed significantly over the past decades. First, there is no longer an untapped forest frontier. Second, under the Plan Piloto Forestal the ancient trees that had been left behind in earlier eras have been harvested from the first 12 cutting areas of each ejido's forest reserve, accounting for much of the volume harvested and providing a one-time windfall. The long-term economic viability of forestry among the communities of the Plan Piloto Forestal depends on assuring sustainable mahogany harvests by providing for mahogany regeneration and balancing harvests with growth. This requires an understanding of the ecology of mahogany in these forests, and the design and implementation of silvicultural management systems based on this knowledge.

The Ecology of Mahogany in the Forests of Quintana Roo

The forests of Quintana Roo are seasonal, or dry tropical forests (Holdridge et al. 1971) that experience a dry season when rainfall is less than 100 mm per month. Seasonal tropical forests like this have been described as the most important forest type in Central America (Murphy and Lugo 1986). Annual rainfall in the mahogany forests of central Quintana Roo is 1,200 to 1,500 mm/year and falls mostly between May and October. During the dry season, which becomes most extreme in March and April (SARH in Snook 1993), many tree species drop their leaves for a short time (Pennington and Sarukhan 1968).

Although mahogany is more common in seasonal tropical forests than in any other forest type in Mexico (Pennington and Sarukhan 1968), mahogany trees occur at an average density of only 1 commercial-size individual/ha (≥ 55 cm dbh), and up to 7 individuals/ha ≥ 15 cm dbh within a matrix of 200 to 400 other trees/ha (≥ 15 cm dbh) of 60 or more different species (Argüelles 1991; Flachsenberg 1993a; Snook 1993). The most abundant species in these forests, occurring at densities of 15 to 60 trees/ha or more, is sapodilla or chicozapote (*Manilkara zapota*), source of the chicle latex used to make chewing gum (Medina et al. 1968; Barrera de Jorgenson 1993; Flachsenberg 1993a; Dugelby, this volume).

For millennia the forests of Quintana Roo have been affected by a wide spectrum of drastic disturbances, both natural and anthropogenic. Tropical cyclones measuring about 600 km in diameter occur in August or September almost every year, bringing heavy rains and winds as high as 300 km per hour from the south, southeast, or east (Jauregui et al. 1980; Wilson 1980; Escobar 1981; Whigham et al. 1991). Periodically, they defoliate or knock down thousands of hectares of forest, as occurred in 1942, 1955 ("Janet"), 1974 ("Carmen"), 1988 ("Gilbert"), and 1995 ("Opal" and "Roxanne") (López-Portillo et al. 1990; pers. obs.). The impact of a sixteenth-century hurricane on the Yucatán forests was described as follows: "There came a storm that grew into a hurricane. The storm blew down all the high trees. . . . The land was left so treeless that those of today look as if planted together and thus all grown of one size. . . . To look at the country from heights, it looks as if all trimmed with a pair of shears" (de Landa 1566).

Forest fires also have occurred frequently in Quintana Roo. Typically spreading from agricultural fields, during particularly dry years forest fires have also been caused by lightning (Wolffsohn 1967). Extensive fires typically occur in the years following hurricanes, when fallen foliage, branches, and trees provide an abundant fuel load, and such fires may burn hundreds of thousands of hectares of forest. Extensive forest fires occurred in the post-hurricane years 1945, 1975, and 1990 (Lundell 1938; Lamb 1966; López-Portillo et al. 1990). Shifting agriculture probably has been practiced in the forests of Quintana Roo since around 2,000 B.C., (Hammond 1982). In this system, patches of forest of .5 to 3 ha or more (Murphy 1993) are cleared and burned, planted, and cultivated for one or more years, then abandoned and recolonized by forest species. Within today's forest, the density of crumbling pyramids and other Maya structures, currently overgrown by trees, reveals that much of what is the Maya Forest today grew up on abandoned agricultural lands and urban centers after the collapse of Maya civilization. The process of depopulation began about 1,000 years ago and continued through the period of the Spanish conquest and the establishment of Mexican control (de Landa 1566; Gates 1937; Turner 1976; Hammond 1982; Edwards 1986).

Mahogany is adapted to capitalize on disturbances that periodically destroy patches of forest. Mahogany trees are emergents, the tallest trees in the forest. However, their large crowns are aerodynamic, sustained by a very few thick, strong branches. Mahogany is also unusual among the tree species in Quintana Roo in having large buttresses that reach 2 to 3 m up the bole, and can extend out 10 m or more from the stem. These characteristics contribute to their successful survival through hurricanes that knock down most large trees of other species. Mahogany trees in Quintana Roo also survive intense fires better than any other species in the forest, probably due to their thick bark (Snook 1993).

Mahogany trees produce winged, wind-dispersed seeds that are shed during the dry season, when the tree is leafless (in Quintana Roo, between March and April). Mahogany seeds have been observed to land 60 m downwind from the mother tree (Rodríguez et al. 1994), and probably fly much farther. Seeds germinate during the rains (between July and October), whether in full sun or shade (Gerhardt 1996; pers. obs.). However, even when stored in cool, dry conditions, mahogany seeds do not maintain their viability beyond a few months (Rodríguez and Barrio 1979; Parraguirre 1994), so there is no mahogany seed bank.

Furthermore, mahogany seedlings do not survive long in the forest understory. The lack of mahogany regeneration in primary or selectively logged forests has been observed over and over again, not only in Quintana Roo (Snook 1993), but in Belize (Stevenson 1927; Lamb 1966; Johnson and Chaffey 1973) and elsewhere in Central and South America (Snook 1996). Mahogany seedlings and saplings are also rare, and seem not to survive, in canopy gaps produced by treefalls or single-tree harvesting (Miranda 1958; Wolffsohn 1961; Lamb 1966; Snook 1993, 1996). However, where seed sources are available in the vicinity, mahogany seedlings become successfully established, along with those of 40 to 60 associated tree species, in clearings ranging from abandoned agricultural fields to roadsides, logyards, and areas affected by intense fires. These areas may be as small as a few thousand square meters or as large as hundreds or even thousands of hectares. Post-disturbance, mixed-species stands several decades old have been found to include as many as 50 mahogany trees/ha at 30 to 40 cm diameter (Snook 1993).

A consequence of this regeneration strategy is that mahogany typically occurs in even-aged aggregations that date back to a catastrophic disturbance. New individuals do not become established in the shady understory and rarely survive in gaps produced by treefalls. As a result, young mahogany trees are seldom found intermixed among older trees, except where a few adults that survived the stand-initiating disturbance are found sprinkled among a stand of younger trees. Typically, discrete, essentially even-aged patches of trees of different ages are found scattered across the landscape (Snook 1993, 1996).

Sustaining Mahogany Harvests in the Present: Current Management

When the Plan Piloto Forestal began organizing ejidos to undertake timber harvesting activities, their first step toward forest management was to define permanent forest reserves where agriculture was off-limits. These forests are set aside for timber harvesting, although they are also used for chicle tapping, hunting, cutting railroad ties from hardwooded species, and collection of poles and palm thatch for construction.

The forest management plan for each ejido is designed to assure continuous yields of mahogany from its forest by controlling the rate and spatial distribution of harvesting, based on a polycyclic system (in which trees are selectively removed from a stand more than once over the course of a rotation) with a 25-year cutting cycle and a minimum diameter limit. Whatever the size of the ejido or the standing volume of commercial-size mahogany trees calculated from forest inventories, these figures are divided by 25 to determine how much area and how much volume can be harvested each year. All mahogany trees larger than the minimum diameter are harvested from one of the 25 cutting areas each year. Harvests on a particular area are scheduled to reoccur at 25-year intervals.

This system effectively paces the harvest of existing commercial trees. For each year of the first 25 years of the cutting cycle, $\frac{1}{25}$ of the existing stock of mahogany trees larger than the diameter limit is harvested. This usually translates into about one tree per hectare, including many ancient mahogany giants that were left behind during previous harvests because they did not meet the requirements of MIQRO's veneer plant or earlier export markets (Argüelles 1991; pers. obs.). According to current harvesting guidelines, all of these trees will be logged during the first cutting cycle, although many have been felled and left in the woods in the past because of poor wood quality (Argüelles 1991). This system will alter the age/size structure of the forest, in ways likely to have negative implications for wildlife and biodiversity.

Beginning with the second cutting cycle, in year 26, the forest reserve will be cut over again, one parcel each year. The trees harvested on this second cut will be the mahogany trees currently in the 35 to 54 cm size classes, the so-called reserve. During the 25 years of the first cutting cycle, they are expected to have grown to commercial diameters. By the second cutting cycle, there will be no more gigantic mahogany trees, centuries old, so in some places the annual volumes harvested will be significantly lower than current volumes. However, the proportion of different size/age classes of mahogany in any area is a function of the timing and characteristics of catastrophic disturbances in the past. In some areas the number of trees in pre-commercial-size classes may be greater than the number in commercial-size classes. The third cutting cycle, beginning in year 51, will cut over the 25 annual cutting areas, one by one, for the third time. Harvesting will focus on trees currently in the 15 to 34 cm size classes, the so-called recruits, or *repoblado*, which will have had 50 years to grow into commercial-size classes (Argüelles 1991).

If inventories of trees in commercial-size classes are accurate, this selective, diameter-limit harvesting system will assure continuous and relatively consistent yields of mahogany and other timbers over the 25 years of the first cutting cycle (of which 12 years remain for the first ejidos organized under the PPF). Yields for the second and third cutting cycles will depend on the presence and abundance of mahogany trees currently in pre-commercial-size classes (a function of chance historical disturbances), and the growth rates of these trees.

Inventories of pre-commercial-size classes provide information on the abundance and distribution of these trees on different forest reserves, permitting planning of future harvests (Figure 5.2). However, three recent studies using different methods indicate that average diameter growth rates for mahogany are approximately 0.4 cm per year (Juarez 1988; Snook 1993; Whigham et al., this volume), about half of the rate that would be required for a tree to grow through the three size categories over the course of three cutting cycles (75 years). Although some trees grow faster than this, 90% of the trees are growing more slowly than the projected rate of harvest (Snook 1993). This means that both minimum diameters and total volumes of harvests in the second and third cutting cycles will be considerably lower than projected.

Sustaining Yields from New Trees

The long-term sustainability of mahogany harvests, beyond the first three cutting cycles that focus on existing trees, depends on the establishment of mahogany regeneration on each parcel after each harvest. Regeneration requires seeds or seedlings and a favorable ecological environment for their survival and growth. The opportunities for regeneration depend on the ecology of the species, the calendar and characteristics of harvesting operations, and the design and implementation of silvicultural management techniques.

The practices of mahogany logging in Quintana Roo are defined by both ecological and economic parameters. A key ecological factor is the fact that mahogany occurs at very low densities in stands made up of dozens of other

Figure 5.2
....
Abel Rodríguez Tun, ejidatorio, measures a mahogony tree in a mixed-species,
even-aged stand that regenerated after an intense fire 15 years earlier.

species. The economic context for logging is that mahogany is by far the most
valuable species, with unlimited market demand. Few associated species have
commercial value, and those that do have limited demand and low value
(Flachsenberg 1993b). As a consequence of these combined factors, mahogany is selectively logged, while associated tree species are left standing.
Whereas mahogany typically regenerates in clearings produced by the destruction of most trees of other species, selective harvesting of mahogany in-
verts these conditions. This change impedes the regeneration of mahogany
in two ways: by reducing the availability of mahogany seed and by perpetuat-
ing conditions unfavorable to the establishment and growth of mahogany
seedlings.

Because mahogany seeds do not retain their viability beyond one season,
natural regeneration requires that seed sources be retained within dispersal
distance of an appropriate clearing. Mahogany trees fruit quite young (Lamb
1966; pers. obs.), so pre-commercial trees in the smaller diameter classes could
serve as seed sources. However, since mahogany regenerates in essentially
even-aged aggregations, all mahogany trees on a particular area are likely to
reach commercial size at the same time. If they are all harvested during a single cut, a relatively large area can be depleted of seed sources.

The current harvesting schedule, whereby mahogany trees are felled during

January and February, just before their seeds are dispersed (March and April), does not permit the seeds from harvested trees to contribute to natural regeneration. Furthermore, if the less valuable species are harvested, they are normally felled and extracted after the mahogany trees have been felled, and after the period of mahogany seed dispersal. This means that the felling gaps are not available for colonization by mahogany seeds during that year.

The lack of seeds can be overcome, at some cost, by sowing or planting (see below). A more difficult challenge is the fact that conditions are inhospitable for the survival of mahogany seedlings because of their intolerance of shade and competition. Selective harvesting creates relatively minor impacts on the forest—an average of one treefall gap/ha, the largest averaging between 10 and 20 m in diameter, plus skid trails 5 m wide or less and one 0.5 to 1 ha logyard per 100 ha. This is problematic for a species that requires sunlight and typically regenerates after catastrophic disturbance. Even if all individuals of the 15 species currently harvested for commercial use were extracted from this forest, it has been estimated that only about 12% of the cutting area would be opened up with each harvest (Argüelles 1991). With the exception of logyards—areas cleared by bulldozers so that logs may be stacked and loaded onto trucks—very little of the disturbed area would provide conditions favorable to mahogany regeneration. Several studies of logyards found natural regeneration of mahogany and other species to be dense on those areas as long as seed sources were located nearby (Olmsted pers. comm. 1987; Alvarez 1987 in Argüelles 1991; Snook 1993). However, logyards cover only 1% (Snook 1993) to 5% (Argüelles 1991) of each cutting area, so regeneration on logyards will not sustain the forest's potential for mahogany production.

Mahogany has been observed to regenerate most successfully on the bare soils produced by mechanical clearing or intense fire. In contrast, felling gaps and skid trails do not provide favorable conditions for the establishment of mahogany regeneration. In addition to being so small that the forest canopy recloses long before any seedling has the chance to emerge into the sun, felling gaps and skid trails are densely populated with pre-existing individuals of species other than mahogany. Of the 100,000 seedlings and 8,000 saplings of other species on each hectare, most survive the effects of felling or skidding, resprouting if damaged. Although mahogany regenerates successfully in mixtures with other species when all the seedlings become established on a clearing at the same time, mahogany seedlings do not compete well with pre-existing individuals of any size (Snook 1993, 1996).

Given the low intensity and calendar of harvesting and the characteristic stand structures and regeneration dynamics of mahogany, it is apparent that natural regeneration will not sustain mahogany in these forests. Silvicultural management is necessary. To date, the only silvicultural activities have consisted of planting to compensate for the lack of mahogany seed sources. Seeds are collected from felled or standing mahogany trees, and sown either directly in the forest or in nurseries from whence seedlings are later transplanted into

the forest. Most PPF communities have been carrying out post-harvest enrichment plantings in felling gaps, skid trails, and logyards. However, initial
evaluations of planting one to three years later revealed that only 22% of mahogany seedlings had survived, due in part to poor seedling quality and poor
planting technique (Negreros 1995), but probably also to the level of competition from individuals of other species, in both the overstory and the understory. An evaluation of plantings in logyards revealed a survivorship of only
25% to 75% after five to six years, but the stocking of survivors was considered adequate (Synnott 1995).

Long-Term Sustainability of Harvests: Opportunities and Constraints

If the objective of forest management in Quintana Roo is to sustain yields of
mahogany over time, it will be necessary to modify current practices to take
into account the current base of knowledge about growth and regeneration of
this species. In the short term, it should be recognized that the 25-year cutting
cycle and its implicit 75-year rotation are shorter than the time required for
trees to grow to the 55 cm commercial diameter. Diameter limits and annual
harvests should be reevaluated so that harvests are balanced with the rate of
growth. This is likely to require a reduction in the annual harvest, which
would have important economic implications for the communities that depend on mahogany harvests for a significant portion of their income. The relatively small scale of ejido forestry operations represents a significant con-
straint to making adjustments to increase the value of each meter harvested.
Total volumes of mahogany per ejido are typically too low to provide a constant supply of logs to any kind of transformation industry. Secondly, at the
scale of the ejido it is not cost-effective to invest in the technology necessary
to process mahogany into the products having the highest value per unit of
volume (such as veneer, the product of the former MIQRO mill). The richest
and most organized ejidos have invested in simple sawmills that produce
rough sawn boards during a few months of the year. In a few ejidos, ejido carpentry shops transform some of this production into furniture. Nonetheless,
the return per unit volume of timber harvested is much less than what it
might be with a different industrial capacity.

Over the longer term, efforts to sustain or enhance mahogany production
will have to focus on improving the opportunities and conditions for the establishment of mahogany regeneration by increasing the number of openings
created by harvesting and reducing competition for mahogany seedlings.
However, at a minimum, two relatively minor modifications in the calendar
of harvesting could enhance the potential for natural regeneration of mahogany: (1) harvesting mahogany after its seeds are dispersed and (2) harvesting other species first, before mahogany seeds fall. Such a change would
require that markets be further developed for species other than mahogany. In

addition to providing a greater range of silvicultural options, this would greatly increase the yield from each hectare. It would also be desirable to incorporate into the management plan the harvesting of nontimber products including railroad ties and poles and thatch for construction, in order to concentrate these currently haphazard activities in time (before mahogany seed fall) and space (each year's cutting area) to maximize the openings available for mahogany regeneration and minimize competition for seedlings from mid-canopy and understory species.

Additional treatments would probably increase the success of regeneration. During the 1920s, in Belize (then British Honduras), silvicultural practices including the poisoning and girdling of undesirable species to open up the canopy and understory cleaning, were implemented to encourage the establishment of mahogany regeneration before logging and foster its subsequent development. These methods led to the establishment of about 100 mahogany seedlings/ha (Stevenson 1927). While these treatments were abandoned in Belize during the depression of the 1930s (Johnson and Chaffey 1973), experiments with canopy opening combined with understory cleaning have been initiated in Quintana Roo (Negreros 1991). Three years after treatment, the density of mahogany seedlings of natural origin was 1,000/ha (Negreros and Mize 1994). It seems likely that these seedlings will require periodic cleanings to successfully compete with the sprouts of understory seedlings and saplings of other species. In another experiment, line plantings of mahogany seedlings were widely established in the forests of Quintana Roo in the 1950s (Miranda 1958; Medina et al. 1968; Weaver 1987). They were unsuccessful, probably due to canopy shade, root competition, and understory sprouts (Miranda 1958; Negreros 1996). However, line planting of mahogany has been considered successful in Puerto Rico, where careful tending has been applied (Bauer 1991).

More intensive silviculture would be required to duplicate the conditions that have favored the establishment of high-density stands of mahogany in the past. Probably the most common disturbance pattern to have given rise to high-density mahogany stands in Quintana Roo in the past has been hurricanes followed by fire. Very similar ecological conditions are produced by slash-and-burn agriculture (Figure 5.3), still the mainstay of the subsistence farmers who make up the rural and forest-dwelling population of Quintana Roo (Murphy 1990). It seems likely that the regeneration of mahogany and associated tree species was favored in the past by shifting agriculture, yet, ironically, the first step in establishing the Plan Piloto Forestal was to create permanent forest reserves where agriculture is prohibited. There were logical reasons for doing so: where population densities are high, fallow periods become so short that forests never grow beyond a scrubby stage; there are also significant logistical difficulties and risks associated with having agricultural activities, and their associated fires, in a commercial forest.

Nonetheless, farmers have noticed that where mahogany seed trees occur

Figure 5.3

Slash-and-burn agriculture, in which forest trees are felled and burned and the clearing is cultivated for a year or two and then abandoned, provides ideal regeneration conditions for mahogany, almost identical to those produced naturally by hurricanes followed by fire.

nearby, seedlings become successfully established on their abandoned fields (*huamils*). Some farmers are reluctant to clear a fallow field where mahogany trees have regenerated. Currently, researchers are working with members of forest ejidos to establish experimental slash-and-burn fields where mahogany seeds are being sown along with corn, beans, and squash, to evaluate the costs and success of this agro-silvicultural system. Experimental patch clear-cuts and mechanical clearings imitating logyards are also being established to permit a comparison of the relative costs and results of creating mahogany regeneration conditions using these three intensive methods. It is expected that these systems will result in the establishment of even-aged, mixed-species stands with 50 to 100 mahogany trees/ha at harvest time, approximately a 50-fold increase over today's densities.

Sustainability: Beyond Mahogany

Maintaining future yields of mahogany is only one rather simple criterion for determining the sustainability of forestry practices in the forests of Quintana Roo. For economic and ecological reasons many other species should be taken into account in designing silvicultural management plans for these forests. For example, chicle latex provides a significant portion of many families' annual incomes, so a healthy population of productive chicle trees must be maintained. Many species that do not reach commercial diameters are used for construction of houses and fencing. A number of animal species are also important to the subsistence of local people. In the process of refining the forest management system of the PPF, it should not be forgotten that the fruits of the sapodilla and ramón (*Brosimum alicastrum*) trees are major food sources for pacas and deer, two of the most important game species in the forest (Jorgenson 1993).

Even beyond their utilitarian values, in a tropical forest where little is known about pollination and dispersal, the maintenance of species diversity should be considered a safeguard for the future of many species. It is not known, for example, which species pollinate mahogany flowers, and which other species these creatures may require to survive. Both food supplies and habitat needs for fauna should be considered. Intensive silviculture for the production of mahogany timber need not reduce the diversity of tree species, because patchy catastrophic disturbance events have sustained the existing mixture of species for centuries. Nonetheless, if more species are harvested, more knowledge is required to ensure that they are not depleted. As part of the effort to sustain biodiversity, attention should also be paid to sustaining a mixture of ages and sizes of trees, including some ancient individuals. If the current diameter-limit harvesting plan is followed, by the end of the first cutting cycle the age/size structure of the forest will have been permanently altered. Once all the huge, old, rotten mahogany trees are harvested, the supply of nesting cavities for parrots and toucans, important seed dispersers and beautiful inhabitants of the forest, will have been severely depleted. A crisis in the availability of nesting cavities has already become apparent (pers. obs.).

Conclusions

The biological diversity of tropical forests like the Maya Forest represents a challenge to silvicultural management. However, the Maya communities that own, utilize, and benefit from this forest also provide a context within which forest management can be practiced in a more holistic fashion than that defined by the limited demands of the timber industry. Maya communities practice shifting agriculture, which mimics natural disturbance patterns, and utilize a wide range of resources, from building poles and thatch to chicle latex and game. Silviculture in the Maya Forest could integrate ecological understanding with local patterns of resource use, focusing on intensive management of small areas for multiple products in a mosaic of time and space. Mahogany could be sustained as part of the shifting milpa system and wildlife by ensuring mixed species and age structures, which also help maintain supplies of chicle and building poles. A diversified peasant economy may provide the best framework for a kind of silviculture that works with the complexity of these species-diverse tropical forests.

References

Anon. 1992. Area de Manejo 1992–1996. Ejido Noh-Bec. Informaciones técnicos, 10 pp.

Argüelles S., L. A. 1991. Plan de manejo forestal para el bosque tropical de la empresa ejidal Noh-Bec, Tesis, UACh, Dept de Bosques, Texcoco, México, 125 pp.

———. 1993. Conservacion y manejo de selvas en el estado de Quintana Roo, México in *Conservación y Manejo de Selva en el Estado de Quintana Roo, México*. Ponencia presentada en el I Congreso Forestal Centroamericano, III Congreso Forestal de Guatemala, Petén, Guatemala, 29 August–4 September 1993.

Argüelles, A., S. Gutiérrez, E. Ramírez, and F. Sánchez Román. 1993. Un modelo de inventario forestal adecuado para apoyar las operaciones de extraccion, de silvicultura e industriales de las empresas forestales ejidales de Quintana Roo, 9 pp. in Conservación y Manejo de Selva en el Estado de Quintana Roo, México. Ponencia presentada en el I Congreso Forestal Centroamericano, III Congreso Forestal de Guatemala, Petén, Guatemala, 29 August–4 September 1993.

Barrera de Jorgenson, A. 1993. Chicle extraction and forest conservation in Quintana Roo, Mexico. M. Sc. thesis, University of Florida, Gainesville, 122 pp.

Bauer, G. P. 1991. Line planting with mahogany (*Swietenia* spp): Experiences in the Luquillo Experimental Forest, Puerto Rico and opportunities in tropical America, 23 pp. Paper presented at the Humid Tropical Lowlands Conference: Development Strategies and Natural Resource Management, DESFIl Project/USAID, Panama City, Panama, June 17–21, 1991.

de Landa, Fr. Diego. 1566/1937/1978. *Yucatán Before and After the Conquest*. Dover Publications Inc., New York. 162 pp.

Edwards, C. R. 1986. The Human impact on the forest in Quintana Roo, Mexico. *Journal of Forest History* (July): 120–127.

Escobar, N. A. 1981. *Geografía General del Estado de Quintana Roo*. Fondo de Fomento Editorial del Gobierno del Estado de Quintana Roo, Chetumal. 140 pp.

Flachsenberg, H. 1993a. Aspectos socioculturales, técnicos, económicos y financieros en el manejo del bosque tropical. Pages 1–27 in *Conservación y Manejo de Selva en el Estado de Quintana Roo, México*. Ponencia presentada en el I Congreso Forestal Centroamericano, III Congreso Forestal de Guatemala, Petén, Guatemala, 29 August–4 September 1993.

———. 1993b. Descripción general. Unpublished presentation, 16 pp.

Galletti, H. A. 1994. Las actividades forestales y su desarrollo historico. Pages 109–171 in *Estudio Integral de la Frontera México–Belize*, CIQRO, Chetumal, Tomo I.

García C., X., B. Rodriguez S., and J. Chavelas P. 1992. Regeneración natural en sitios afectados por el huracán Gilberto e indencios forestales en Quintana Roo. *Revista Ciencia Forestal en México* 17 (72): 75–99.

Gates, 1937/1978. Introduction, pp. i–xv in Fr. Diego de Landa, *Yucatán Before and After the Conquest*. Dover Publications, New York.

Gerhardt, K. 1996. Germination and development of sown mahogany (*Swietenia macrophylla* King) in secondary tropical dry forest habitats in Costa Rica. *Journal of Tropical Ecology* 12: 275–289.

Hammond, N. 1982. *Ancient Maya Civilization*. Rutgers University Press, New Brunswick.

Holdridge, L. R., W. C. Grenke, W. H. Hatheway, T. Liang, and J. A. Tosi Jr. 1971. *Forest Environments in Tropical Life Zones: A Pilot Study*. Pergamon Press, Oxford, 747 pp.

Jauregui, E., J. Vidal, and F. Cruz. 1980. Los ciclones y tormentas tropicales en Quintana Roo durante el periodo 1871–1978. Pages 47–64 in *Quintana Roo: Problematica y Perspectiva*. Memorias del Simposio, Instituto de Geografía, UNAM & Centro de Investigaciones de Quintana Roo, Cancun, Quintana Roo, October 1980, 384 pp.

Johnson, M. S., and D. R. Chaffey. 1973. An inventory of Chiquibul Forest Reserve, Belize. Land Resource Study No. 14, Land Resources Division, Overseas Development Administration, England, 87 pp.

Jorgenson, J. P. 1993. Gardens, wildlife densities and subsistence hunting by Maya Indians in Quintana Roo, Mexico. Ph.D. dissertation, University of Florida, 336 pp.

Juarez B., C. J. (1988). Analisis del incremento periódico de caoba (*Swietenia macrophylla* King) y cedro (*Cedrela odorata*) en un relicto de selva en el estado de Campeche. Tesis, Ing. Agronomo Esp.en Bosques, Division de Ciencias Forestales, Universidad Autonoma de Chapingo, Chapingo, México, 87 pp.

Konrad, H. W. 1988. De la subsistencia forestal tropical a la producción para exportación: La industria chiclera y la transformación de la economia maya de Quintana Roo de 1890 a 1935. Pages 161–182 in *Etnohistoria e Historia de las Americas*. Memorias, 45 Congreso Internacional de Americanistas. Ediciones Uniandes, Bogotá, Colombia.

Lamb, F. B. 1966. *Mahogany of Tropical America: Its Ecology and Management*. University of Michigan Press, Ann Arbor, 220 pp.

Lloyds' Committee of Registry. 1850. *The Mahogany Tree*. Rockliff and Son, Liverpool, England, 120 pp.

López-Portillo, J., M. R. Keyes, A. González, E. Cabrera C., and O. Sánchez. 1990. Los incendios de Quintana Roo: Catástrofe ecológica o evento periódico? *Ciencia y Desarrollo* 16 (91): 13–57.

Lundell, C. L. 1938. The 1938 Botanical expedition to Yucatán and Quintana Roo, Mexico. Carnegie Institute of Washington Yearbook 37, pp. 143–147.

Medina R., B. 1948. La Explotación forestal en el territorio de Quintana Roo. Tesis, Ing. Agr. en Bosques. Escuela Nacional de Agricultura, Chapingo, 67 pp.

Medina R., B., A. Cuevas L., and M. de los Santos V. 1968. Ajuste al proyecto de ordenación forestal, UIEF MIQRO. Chetumal, México, 200 pp.

Mell, C. D. 1917. True Mahogany. *USDA Forest Service Bulletin* 474: 24 pp.

Miranda, F. 1958. Estudios acerca de la vegetación. Pages 213–272 in Beltran, E., ed., *Los Recursos Naturales del Sureste y su Aprovechamiento*. IMRNR, Mexico City, 326 pp.

Murphy, J. 1990. Indigenous forest use and development in the "Maya Zone" of Quintana Roo, Mexico. Master's paper, Graduate Program in Environmental Studies, York University, Ontario, Canada, 181 pp.

Murphy, P. G., and A. E. Lugo. 1986. Ecology of a tropical dry forest. *Annual Review of Ecology and Systematics* 17: 67–88.

Napier, I. A. 1973. A brief history of the development of the hardwood industry in Belize. *Coedwigwr* 26: 36–43.

Negreros C., P. 1991. Ecology and management of mahogany (*Swietenia macrophylla* King) regeneration in Quintana Roo, Mexico. Ph.D. dissertation, Iowa State University, Ames, 132 pp.

———. 1994. Evaluation of direct planting and post-harvesting natural regeneration in Quintana Roo, Mexico. Unpublished study supported by the Tropical Ecosystems Directorate of the U.S. Man and the Biosphere Program.

———. 1995. Enrichment planting as a silvicultural technique for sustaining Honduras mahogany (*Swietenia macrophylla*) and Spanish cedar (*Cedrela odorata*) production: An evaluation of experiences in Quintana Roo, Mexico. Paper presented at the conference Conservation and Community Development in the Selva Maya of Belize, Guatemala, and Mexico, Chetumal, Quintana Roo, November 8–11.

Negreros C., P., and C. Mize. 1994. El efecto de la abertura del dosel y eliminación del sotobosque sobre la regeneración natural de una selva de Quintana Roo. Pages 107–126 in Snook, L., and A. Barrera de Jorgenson, eds., *Madera, Chicle, Caza y Milpa: Contribuciones al Manejo Integral de las Selvas de Quintana Roo*. INIFAP/PROAFT/AID/WWF-US, Merida, México, 145 pp.

Parraguirre L., C. 1994. Germinación de las semillas de trece especies forestales comerciales de Quintana Roo. Pages 67–80 in Snook, L., and A. Barrera de Jorgenson, eds., *Madera, Chicle, Caza y Milpa: Contribuciones al Manejo Integral de las Selvas de Quintana Roo*. INIFAP/PROAFT/AID/WWF-US, Merida, México, 145 pp.

Pennington, T. D., and J. Sarukhan 1968. *Arboles Tropicales de México*. INIF/FAO, México, 413 pp.

Record, S. J. 1924. *Timbers of Tropical America*. Yale University Press, New Haven, pp. 348–356.

Rey, O. 1983. La Ruta del Rio Hondo. Fonde de Fomento Editorial del Estado de Quintana Roo, Serie Dzicbal, Chetumal, 48 pp.

Rodríguez C., R. 1944. La explotación de los montes de caoba en el territorio de Quintana Roo. Tesis, Ing. Agr. en Bosques. Escuela Nacional de Agricultura, Chapingo, 120 pp.

Rodríguez y Pacheco, A. A., and J. M. Barrio Chavira. 1979. Desarrollo de caoba (*Swietenia macrophylla* King) en diferentes tipos de suelos. *Ciencia Forestal* 4 (22): 45–64.

Rodríguez S., B. J. Chavelas P., and X. García Cuevas. 1994. Dispersión de semillas y establecimiento de caoba después de un tratamiento mecánico del sitio. Pages 81–90 in Snook, L., and A. Barrera de Jorgenson, eds., *Madera, Chicle, Caza y Milpa: Contribuciones al Manejo Integral de las Selvas de Quintana Roo*. INIFAP/PROAFT/AID/WWF-US, Merida, México, 145 pp.

Snook, L. 1991. Opportunities and constraints for sustainable tropical forestry: Lessons from the Plan Piloto Forestal, Mexico. Paper presented at the Humid Tropical Lowlands Conference: Development Strategies and Natural Resource Management, DESFIL Project, TR&D and the U.S. Forest Service, Panama City, Panama, June 17–21. DESFIL 5: 65–83.

———. 1993a. Stand dynamics of mahogany (*Swietenia macrophylla* King) and associated species after fire and hurricane in the tropical forests of the Yucatán Peninsula, Mexico. Ph.D. dissertation, Yale School of Forestry and Environmental Studies. University Microfilms International #9317535, Ann Arbor, Mich.

———. 1996. Catastrophic disturbance, logging and the ecology of mahogany (*Swietenia macrophylla* King): Grounds for listing a major tropical timber species on CITES. *Botanical Journal of the Linnean Society* 122: 35–46.

Stevenson, N. S. 1927. Silvicultural treatment of mahogany forests in British Honduras. *Empire Forestry Journal* 6: 219–227.

Synnott, T. J. 1995. Practices for sustainable silviculture at the Plan Piloto Forestal in Quintana Roo, Mexico. Unpublished Final Report to the Biodiversity Support Program, 10 pp.

Turner, B. L. II. 1976. Population density in the Classic Maya lowlands: New evidence for old approaches. *Geographical Review* 66: 73–82.

Verissimo, A., P. Barreto, R. Tarifa, and C. Uhl. 1995. Extraction of a high-value natural resource in Amazonia: The case of mahogany. *Forest Ecology and Management* 72 (1): 39–60.

Villaseñor A., R. 1958. Los Bosques y su explotacíon. Pages 273–326 in Beltran, E., ed., *Los Recursos Naturales del Sureste y su Aprovechamiento*. IMRNR, Ciudad de México, 326 pp.

Weaver, P. L. 1987. Enrichment planting in tropical America. Pages 259–277 in Figueroa, J., F. Wadsworth, and S. Branham, eds., *Management of the Forests of Tropical America: Prospects and Technologies*. International Institute of Tropical Forestry, U.S.D.A Forest Service, Rio Piedras, Puerto Rico, 469 pp.

Whigham, D. F., I. Olmsted, E. C. Cano, and M. E. Harmon. 1991. The impact of hurricane Gilbert on trees, litterfall and woody debris in a dry tropical forest in the northeastern Yucatan Peninsula. *Biotropica* 23 (4a): 434–441.

Whigham, D. F., J. F. Lynch, and M. B. Dickinson, in press. Ten years of studying dry tropical forests in the Yucatán Peninsula: What have we learned? Paper presented at the Conference Conservation and Development in the Maya Forest of Mexico, Guatemala, and Belize, Chetumal, Mexico, November, 1995.

Wilson, E. M. 1980. Physical geography of the Yucatán Peninsula. Pages 5–40 in Mosley, E. H. and E. D. Terry, eds. *Yucatán: A World Apart*. University of Alabama Press.

Wolffsohn, A. L. A. 1961. An experiment concerning mahogany germination. *Empire Forestry Review* 40 (1): 71–72.

———. 1967. Post hurricane forest fires in British Honduras. *Commonwealth Forestry Review* 46: 233–238.

Chapter 6

The Maya Forest in Campeche, Mexico: Experiences in Forest Management at Calakmul

Deocundo Acopa and Eckart Boege

Deforestation and forest degradation are common in the tropical forests of Mexico. Forests in Oaxaca, Chiapas, and the Yucatán Peninsula, as well as coastal forests of Michoacan, Jalisco, Nayarit, and Sinaloa are among those threatened, although the most badly degraded forests are found in Veracruz, Tabasco, and Chiapas. For geographic and social reasons, some forests in Campeche and Quintana Roo have experienced a slower rate of destruction. These forests in southeastern Mexico represent Mexico's best opportunity for preservation of existing forests and for restoration of degraded tracts because they are part of the largest unbroken forest mass in the northern hemisphere of Latin America. But this forest, along with adjoining areas of Guatemala and Belize, is not a "virgin" forest; it was historically the seat of ancient Maya civilization, and the remains of Maya cities are found throughout the forest. It is from this civilization that the Maya Forest, or Selva Maya, draws both its name and its status as a cultural and biological patrimony of humanity. The great challenge now before us is to preserve this forest and to plan regional development so that the forest is maintained as a permanent resource. However, causes of deforestation and forest degradation in Mexico are multiple, and it is necessary to understand their dynamics in order to plan suitable policies for preservation of these forests.

Forest Policy in Mexico

It is no small irony that "forest policy" in Mexico has historically encouraged removal of forests. The principal causes of deforestation and forest degradation include development of extensive cattle raising and commercial agriculture. These activities are supported by the state bank, the government, the World Bank, and the Inter-American Development Bank, and promoted by governmental agencies. Also, explicit colonization and land-clearing policies, led by the Programa Nacional de Desmontes (National Land-Clearing Program) in the 1970s, contributed to forest destruction by equating "improved"—that is, cleared—land with a claim to ownership of the newly converted tract. These colonization projects have been carried out in various regions of southeastern Mexico; they mostly focused on resettling displaced populations from elsewhere in Mexico, through both planned and spontaneous colonization, and lacked long-term assessments of the projects' impact on the environment.

Mexico's forest policy also favors private industries over local populations who directly depend on the resources. Historically, owners of forested land have been paid only a symbolic stumpage fee that does not represent the real value of the forest resource. Government forest agencies have been principally aligned with industry, and political structures at all levels—regional, state, and national—encourage the exploitation of common resources. Even where policies might favor sustainable use, lack of coordination among different levels of government reduce the policies' effectiveness. In some cases, policies are drawn up that are appropriate for temperate forests, not tropical ones.

Beginning in the 1980s, two alternative policies have been implemented to slow the process of destruction in Quintana Roo and Campeche: the creation of biosphere reserves (Map 1 in Introduction to this volume) and the management of natural resources by organized peasants. These two policies did not develop in tandem, but rather emerged as two parallel practices. In this chapter, we will focus on the interplay between these two alternatives as they have developed around the Calakmul Biosphere Reserve in southwestern Campeche.

Establishment of Biosphere Reserves in Southeastern Mexico

The biosphere reserve concept, which includes zoned and managed core and buffer areas, calls for the participation of local populations in reserve management. However, this principle has been difficult to implement. In the case of the Calakmul reserve, for example, local populations were not consulted before the reserve was declared by the Mexican government in 1989, nor did the decree take into account that there were already peasant communities existing in the presumably ecologically pristine core area. Furthermore, the creation of the reserve has done nothing to control activities such as the cultivation of narcotics, trade and sport hunting of rare and endangered species, and looting of archaeological sites. Nevertheless, the creation of the Calakmul Biosphere Reserve has initiated the challenge of turning the reserve into a focus for a regional development strategy that must extend the concept of sustainability even beyond the reserve proper if it is to successfully protect the forests of Calakmul.

One important instrument in such a strategy is land-use mapping and zoning. This activity can be implemented from above or develop from spontaneous land-use decisions of local producers, but the most effective way of implementing it is to approach it not as a theoretical mapping scheme but as an agreement among stakeholders to establish specific rules of conduct and resource use. Another instrument involves planning a biological corridor between Calakmul and the Sian Ka'an Biosphere Reserve in central Quintana Roo. This corridor includes permanent forest areas managed by communities.

The participation of local populations and resource users in all management decisions must be the basis of a regional development strategy organized around the biosphere reserve concept. Such participation is obviously taken for granted on their own ejido lands, but they should also take part in decisions affecting adjoining reserve land. This strategy gives them economic incentives for sustainable use of resources and generates self-organization, incomes, basic necessities, and stability for the forest. The local populations also tend to view the forests as a multiple-use resource, extracting not just high-value timber species, but also a multitude of nontimber forest products that can lend themselves to sustainable uses.

History of Natural Resource Use in Calakmul

Resource extraction in the forests of Campeche began with the exploitation of *tinta*, or logwood (*Haematoxylum campechianum*), a forest tree with a deep purple heartwood that was prized for the red and purple dyes that could be made from it. Although logwood had been exported since the seventeenth century, it became the principal export in the last decades of the nineteenth century. However, its use dropped dramatically after the invention of synthetic dyes in the early twentieth century. With the decline of the logwood market, two alternative products gained prominence: chicle latex, used in chewing gum, and timber.

Growth and Change in the Chicle Industry

In the late nineteenth century, latex from chicle (or *chicozapote*) trees (*Manilkara zapota*) emerged as a global commodity. At the industry's peak in 1940, 80% of the world's chicle came from Mexico, with over half of that coming from Campeche. In 1936, the powerful Chenes cooperative was created in Dzibalchén; this cooperative was granted a concession of 150,000 ha of national lands located in the core of the current Calakmul Reserve, which were to be used for chicle extraction. A few years later, all the forests of Campeche were divided into 50 concessions, which were later declared ejidal lands. From 1935 to 1940, 69 ejidos were established, 9 of which were given extensive forest lands. In the largest of these, each ejidatario was given 400 ha of land so that they could be assured of having sufficient trees available to make a reasonable living collecting chicle. Most of these chicle gathering areas remained uninhabited, and at least one community was given forest lands located two days' walk from their homes. Colonists from throughout Mexico flocked into the forests to gather chicle, despite the horrible working conditions prevalent at the time.

The extraction of chicle saw several periods of rise and decline, coinciding with World Wars I and II, due to the U.S. Army's custom of providing its soldiers with a daily ration of chewing gum. This important market went into decline, like the logwood market before it, when artificial bubble gum was introduced during the Korean War. Since the 1950s, chicle production has decreased continuously, although enough demand exists that chicle tapping continues to be an important secondary economic activity for many peasants. The process of chicle extraction in the area has slowly evolved from large concessions operated by contractors working for foreign companies toward production by independent ejidos. This change has reduced extraction pressures on some of the more distant forest areas.

Timber Extraction

At about the same time that chicle was developing as a prominent resource, enormous logging concessions were granted to eight North American companies, which had access to 1.3 million ha in Campeche by 1910. Large-scale timber exploitation in the modern-day Calakmul Reserve began with the construction of a railroad in the early 20th century, and followed in later years by the Escárcega-Chetumal highway. Previously, timber extraction was limited to areas accessible to the few rivers that traverse the southern Yucatán Peninsula, which were used to transport the logs to Chetumal Bay, where they could be loaded onto ships for export. Even after alternative routes became available for transporting timber, a factor which theoretically increased the value of the concessions, companies exploited hundreds of thousands of hectares of forested land while paying only a very modest stumpage fee.

The first ejidos organized around forest exploitation rather than chicle extraction were created by the Mexican government during the 1960s. By the early 1970s, the Ejido Forestry Association included nearly one hundred communities. In 1974, it was converted into the Forest Ejido Union (UEF) and became a provider of the technical assistance necessary to receive logging permits. However, the process of issuing logging permits became very corrupt, with the permits being bought and sold rather than issued on merit. This period in Mexico's timber industry was characterized by tremendous waste of the forest resources. Ejidos in the Escárcega region of Campeche were given logging permits even though they had no forested land; most of the permits were used to harvest timber from land that today is part of the reserve area. However, the ejidos received few benefits from this activity; the timber, primarily mahogany and cedar, was sold below its actual value to sawmills ostensibly owned by cooperatives, but which permitted the ejidos no participation in profits or decisionmaking. Uncontrolled logging produced impoverished forests and reduced benefits to the populations who lived closest to the forests; one particularly wasteful practice was the use of valuable tropical hardwoods for railroad ties despite the ready availability of more common species. Although a 1986 forestry law made management plans obligatory, few ejidos could afford the cost of putting the plans into effect, so they were seldom carried out.

The exclusion of peasant producers from an alliance established among government forest authorities, corrupt cooperatives, and influential businessmen triggered the beginning of a movement of independence of these producers from official organizations. This movement lasted ten years and sought control, management, and industrialization of natural resources. Peasants from the Alvaro Obregon ejido allied with other ejidos and fought government objections to gain the power to saw and market their own timber. After a long struggle, they were finally able to obtain their own sawmill. Although the government continued to deny them a logging permit, they began to mill the tips and branches left in the forest as waste by the logging industry. With this waste timber, they began making beehives, giving rise to beekeeping as a new economic activity in the region and creating a nontimber forest alternative. This period marked the beginning of the end of an exploitation regime that "mined" the forest, which coincided with the end of unorganized colonization.

Strategies for Comprehensive, Community-Based Forest Management

The Calakmul Biosphere Reserve was created in 1989 and was registered in the UNESCO Man and the Biosphere Program in 1993. Of the 723,185 ha that compose the reserve, 227,860 ha have been set aside as two core areas, with the remainder classified as buffer zones. Calakmul also adjoins the Maya Biosphere Reserve in the southern Petén in Guatemala and serves as the southern anchor for a vast 1.2 million ha corridor of permanent forest reserves managed by ejidos, with the Sian Ka'an Biosphere Reserve holding down the northern end (Figure 6.1). The reserve and its adjoining areas are populated by some 15,000 residents, including mestizo colonists from 23 states, as well as indigenous Yucatec, Chol, and Tzeltal Maya.

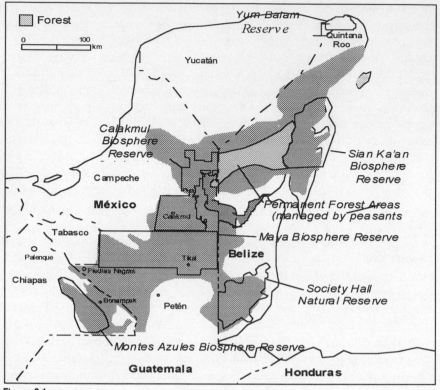

Figure 6.1

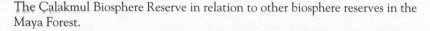

The Calakmul Biosphere Reserve in relation to other biosphere reserves in the
Maya Forest.

The organization of the ejido populations around and in Calakmul to manage their own forests was heavily influenced by the successful Plan Piloto
Forestal (PPF) methodology that had been applied in southern and central
Quintana Roo since the mid-1980s (Galletti, this volume; Flachsenberg and
Galletti, this volume). This methodology consisted of systematically training
local people to carry out sustainable silvicultural practices, to reforest, and to
manage their own forest industries. It is based on the assumption that natural
resources must benefit the local populations because they have the most direct impact on the resources and have a long-term interest in developing a
multiple-use strategy that includes both timber and nontimber forest products.

The fundamental strategy of this approach calls for a diversified management plan that includes timber and nontimber forest products (such as wildlife, chicle, honey, palms, and ecotourism), as well as sustainable agriculture.

The strategy also advocates the creation of inter-ejido organizations that support sustainable development. These organizations are composed of members from various production sectors, including timber workers, beekeepers, jalapeño farmers, and chicle workers. These organizations establish ecological zoning for the management of common goods, and introduce important elements of democratic decisionmaking in regions traditionally marked by authoritarian structures.

In addition, the strategy calls for the creation of technical capacity among the peasants to allow them to carry out the majority of the technical management of their forest. Ideally, this would include management structures to allow the peasants to supervise the work of forestry professionals they hire. Furthermore, the approach requires that industrial capacity developed for the ejidos be adjusted to the sustainable production potential of the forest, not the forest production to the size of the industry.

If the strategy is to work effectively, however, it requires an element of political planning as well as technical know-how. Political "cover" must be provided by seeking support from sympathetic government officials and foundations and by challenging destructive sectors when necessary. The project must negotiate differences between ejidos within the organizations, which may be of different ethnic groups and have very different resource endowments. The local organizations must also contend with contradictory policy directives emanating from state and federal authorities; they may frequently find themselves alone in promoting the most sustainable option. Since the natural tendency of both the state and the federal government in Mexico is to resist the actions and ideas of organizations they do not control, successful implementation of this strategy requires a high level of organization on the part of the peasants, but they have generally been able to meet this challenge. In Quintana Roo, peasant organizations established a precedent by refusing to be used as political springboards for the official party, and the Calakmul organizations have been able to achieve the same autonomy. They have developed enough organizational, economic, and political strength to negotiate with the state and federal governments.

The management plan the ejidos have developed has five principal elements, each of which can add value to the forest. The first and most crucial element is the creation by each ejido of areas of permanent forest (*áreas forestales permanentes* or AFPs), as well as wildlife habitats, foraging areas for apiculture, and management regimes for nontimber forest products. AFPs voluntarily established by 30 ejidos encompass some 125,000 ha. This element has halted the conversion of forest to agricultural fields and pasture over wide areas. Second, agroforestry regimes and timber plantations are being developed outside of the permanent areas. These areas can include sequenced harvesting cycles from 1 to 20 years that create open spaces needed for establishment of sun-loving species such as mahogany. The diverse vegetation of these

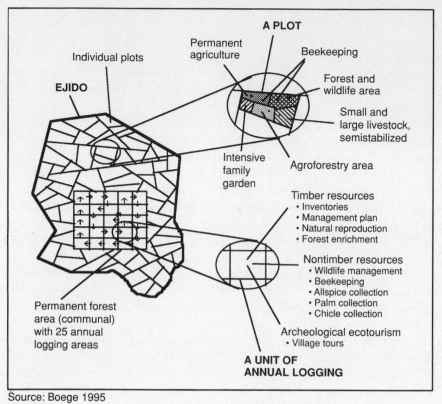

Source: Boege 1995

Figure 6.2

Proposed territorial and ecological zoning for ejidos with permanent forest areas in the areas of influence and buffer zones.

gaps also creates enriched habitats for wildlife populations. Third, the traditional milpa fields created using slash-and-burn cultivation techniques must become intensively farmed, fixed plots rather than migrating extensively across the landscape. The use of legumes as green fertilizer and control of soil humidity are key in managing the fragile soils of the tropics. Fourth, more intensive methods of stock raising that require less land are being developed. Fifth, the intensive use of family vegetable gardens must be encouraged. The ejidal proposal for territorial zoning is shown in Figure 6.2.

Timber Industry in Calakmul: Problems and Prospects

In the near future, it is likely that logging will be the most important economic activity for the region. The first major problem with this activity is that the intensity of logging in earlier periods in the Calakmul area has seriously

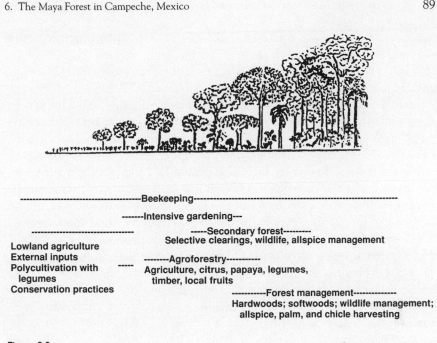

--Beekeeping--

--------Intensive gardening---

---   -----Secondary forest---------
Lowland agriculture   Selective clearings, wildlife, allspice management
External inputs   --------Agroforestry-----------
Polycultivation with   -----   Agriculture, citrus, papaya, legumes,
  legumes   timber, local fruits
Conservation practices   -----------Forest management--------------
                                                        Hardwoods; softwoods; wildlife management;
                                                        allspice, palm, and chicle harvesting

Figure 6.3

Schematic representation of different stages of forest succession showing activities
that can be supported by each stage.

compromised the future productivity of its forests. For commonly used tropical timbers, Calakmul has a production potential of 75 to 80 m³/ha, while nearby Quintana Roo and Chiapas have a production potential of 100 m³/ha and 120 to 180 m³/ha, respectively. Furthermore, only 10 m³/ha of this timber from Calakmul is currently commercial timber, such as mahogany, due to heavy logging during earlier periods. Thus, sustainable logging plans and the economic needs of the local populations must be carefully calibrated so that expectations about income from logging are realistic and sustainable. Although the PPF model emphasizes management of cedar and mahogany, Calakmul is trying to emphasize the importance of the lesser-known tropical species.

Important steps have been made in sustainable forest management. In addition to the establishment of the AFPs, the first complete forest inventories have been carried out on 35,000 ha in ten ejidos, a new generation of ejido paraprofessional foresters has been created, management plans have been formulated, and 75-year logging cycles for mahogany, consistent with the PPF methodology, have been established. This cycle is still regarded as an estimate since the exact growth rate of mahogany and other precious species is still under debate. Furthermore, ejidos have established permanent sampling plots to measure forest growth and ejido nurseries to enrich plantings on family plots and in secondary growth areas.

A major planning problem is the variation of forest resources held by each ejido. In fact, only 5 of the 30 ejidos that established AFPs have the potential to reach an economically important and sustainable annual yield. Differences in size and available species require that the organization, the territorial zoning plans, and the strategies of milling and marketing be adapted to the conditions in each ejido. For example, ejidos with small AFPs may permit logging only every three to five years, instead of annually; alternatively, wood could be extracted annually only from small exploitation areas. Under these difficult conditions, it is particularly important to find technical solutions to increase the value of production and obtain the highest profit with a small volume. Mobile sawmills shared among several smaller ejidos are one such technical solution that is being attempted. Enhanced income-generation on smaller ejidos is also obtained through the local processing of raw material using small carpentry workshops that experiment with different products for local use. This effort is interesting because it provides young people with jobs and generates products, such as beehives, that are bought locally, keeping money in the local economy.

In addition to mobile sawmills and carpentry workshops, more industrial milling operations also have their place. Efforts by the regional inter-ejidal organizations to operate their own sawmills have not proved profitable or efficient, but more recent efforts to associate established industry with the ejido organizations may prove to be more successful. This effort still requires external subsidies if the organizations are to move toward sustainable management. Requirements include a dependable supply of natural and secondary forests, in a framework of sustainable management; organization of production inside the ejidos; creation of a basic infrastructure by purchasing extraction equipment; construction of roads that can be used during the rainy season; the use of every extracted tree; an efficient system of transportation to reduce costs; and a system of reforestation. As mentioned before, enterprise size must be designed with the real sustainable production of the forest clearly in mind.

Finally, sustainability in the marketplace will also depend on getting the best possible prices at the regional, national, and international levels. Particularly important at the international level is the potential subsidy available from green labeling. If international consumers are willing to pay a somewhat higher price for timber sustainably harvested by these communities, the additional income could help support some of the expenses of sustainable harvesting, costs that sales of timber at regular market prices will not cover. Efforts to increase market demand for the lesser-known tropical hardwood species would also bring new value to the forest. With accurate inventories, which also will have to be subsidized, genuinely sustainable rates of harvest could be calculated in the AFPs. On the basis of these figures, a more finely calibrated agroforestry program could be developed that would make up for the deficiencies in production of a given species from the natural forest.

Exploitation of Nontimber Forest Resources

There are a number of experiments taking place in nontimber forest product industries, including chicle harvesting, allspice plantations, beekeeping, and agroforestry. Many of these have met with success, as described below.

Chicle

As remarked earlier, the chicle boom ended several decades ago. However, a consistent international market, principally sales to Japan and Italy, has remained. It is important to develop this market because the chicozapote tree is the single most abundant species in the forest, and its logging is still prohibited by law. Further, chicle gathering is now restricted to ejido lands and is prohibited in the core area of Calakmul, giving the communities an even greater incentive to preserve their forests, assuming their chicle can be sold for a reasonable price.

Chicle extraction is extremely laborious, requiring the movement of entire families into the forest during rainy months. A 1994 survey of ejido members revealed that 160 families were involved in chicle gathering. The average figures are probably higher because 1994 was a depressed year for chicle production, a result of poor rainfall. The price of chicle is affected by a monopoly imposed by the Bank of Foreign Trade (BANCOMEX), its concession (IMPEXNAL), and corrupt official peasant organizations, aggravated by a tax of questionable constitutionality. If producers can organize themselves to administer their own marketing and export, as is now being done with the Chicle Plan Piloto in Quintana Roo, they can increase their incomes from this source. Recently, Campeche's *chicleros* had some initial success in marketing their own chicle, exporting 50 tons directly to Japan. The existence of a working capital fund was key to this achievement.

Allspice

Stands of allspice are available in the entire area, including AFPs and peasants' plots, and the spice is widely harvested, but it has not been subject to any management plan. Prices have also been quite unstable, and competition with traditional producer areas is strong. In order to increase the production of allspice, nurseries of two ejidos are carrying out a program of plant propagation for agroforestry plantations. Because the harvesting process is relatively simple, it is another activity, like chicle gathering, that can generate income for the entire family. Further, a more intensive agroforestry management regime could create a more predictable income source. Markets could also be developed in organically grown allspice, achieving the kind of direct exporting that is now being developed for chicle.

Beekeeping

Honey production helps give added value to both secondary vegetation and primary forests. Beekeeping requires a low initial investment that can be recovered during a single cycle of production under normal weather conditions. However, as in other cases, its marketing has been hindered by corrupt official organizations. Beekeeping is a very useful economic activity that can be pursued during periods when there are few other options. Beekeeping can also produce a variety of other profitable products, like wax, pollen, and royal jelly.

Thus far, only the Yucatec and Chol indigenous ejidos in the area have practiced beekeeping. Production has been inhibited by traditional harvesting methods that had little technical assistance. The invasion of Africanized "killer" bees, which can hybridize with local varieties and lower honey production, forced changes in these methods, requiring the introduction of European bees in the hives. In these cases, subsidies from the Mexican government have had a significant multiplier effect, with beekeepers investing in new colonies and equipment. It has also stimulated the incorporation of 60 new families into beekeeping, with women being included in the activity for the first time. Further, as mentioned before, the construction of hives is done locally, using waste woods and supporting community carpentry shops. Beekeeping has also created a new interest in conservation, with one ejido putting a new area of primary forest into production as a "pasture" for the bees.

Beekeeping has been one of the most positive experiences thus far in the development of nontimber forest products, but further steps can be taken. First, greater local technical capacity needs to be developed. Second, product quality could be improved using local knowledge of the forest to locate apiaries where the most intensive flowering of particular species occurs, which could result in the introduction of different flavors in the market, giving new value to plant biodiversity. Export quality could be reached by establishing local packing centers with the adequate technology. Finally, marketing could be improved through locating national and international markets for certified organic and rainforest honey that could have a "Calakmul Biosphere Reserve" trademark.

Agroforestry and Intensive Agriculture

The last four years of work have revealed a great potential for agroforestry in the region. In ecological and economic terms, agroforestry has an important role to play in giving added value and biodiversity to degraded areas and to enrichment of natural forests. In Calakmul, the following sequence has been developed: in the first year, slash-and-burn agriculture for the production of corn is followed by the planting of fruit trees with medium-term maturation period and timber trees for longer-term cycles. Corn, other basic grains, and subsistence crops can continue to be planted on the same plot until the fifth year. In the third and fourth years, the fruit trees will start producing. As the timber trees mature, the terrain begins to look more like a forest. Under this kind of regimen, growth rates are greater than those of natural regeneration, so the logging of some trees is possible after 25 years. Under these plantation conditions, it is also possible to cut cedar and mahogany trees with smaller diameters than is allowable in natural forests.

The concept is very attractive, and in Calakmul the initial experimental plots seem to be working according to the concept. The first agroforestry plots established around Calakmul are beginning to produce citrus fruits, which are being sold in local markets. Ejido nurseries are also being established that encourage the cultivation of indigenous fruit-bearing trees. These include zapote mamey (*Pouteria sapota*), black zapote (*Diospyros digyna*), chicozapote (*Manilkara zapota*), and huaya (*Talisia olivaeformis*). Improving their genetic quality and management is this program's current challenge. New planting areas must also be sought, since the fruit trees will cease to flourish once the forest canopy begins to close.

The experience in Calakmul has raised difficult questions about the nature of agriculture in and around tropical forests. Can the milpa, the traditional corn field, be grown on permanent sites with shallow tropical soils? Can sustained production be achieved without rotation or clearing new areas? How can farmers achieve soil fertilization without burning?

These questions must also be answered by looking at agriculture as part of an integrated system of production that includes secondary forests as reforestation areas, nonmigrating multiple-use plots with some agroforestry elements to improve soils, and a diversified system of corn cultivation. Fertilization is based mainly on the management of animal fertilizers, compost, and green fertilizers, as well as a method of minimal tillage. An objective for the future is to gradually improve soil conditions and stabilize corn production using native seeds. In addition, a system of annual rotation is being tested in the cultivation of chili peppers, as well as the use of a variety of squash to provide additional cover to the vegetation.

However, the most important improvement has been achieved during the last few years with the introduction of native legume species as green fertilizer. The simultaneous use of these nitrogen-fixing legumes, including jícama (*Pachyrhizus erosus*), ib (*Phaseolus lunatus*), cocuite or xabyaab (*Gliricidia sepium*), and uaxim (*Leucaenia glauca*), along with other cultivars, allows the maintenance of a permanent layer of soil. Some cover crops, such as velvet bean (*Mucuna pruriens*), introduced by the peasants themselves, may generate up to 5 tons per year per hectare of dry organic matter and also control weeds and maintain soil humidity. As a consequence, land can be used continuously, avoiding long years of fallow and the need to clear fresh plots.

The use of legumes provides many alternatives for combining crops that could make production a continuous process: annual and biannual agriculture, fruit plantations with short- (3 years) and intermediate- (7 years) term yields, and with long- term (25 years) plantations of precious woods. This productive strategy would cushion the negative effects of price fluctuations under monocropping conditions and create a continuous gradient from forests to plantations, without severe interruptions in the flora and fauna. All these techniques are being used jointly for the first time in the Yucatán Peninsula, and hold the promise of a new kind of tropical forest agriculture for the region.

Ecotourism As an Alternative Industry

Development of archaeological ecotourism also has great potential in the Calakmul region. There are several important Maya sites located two to six hours from the airport in Chetumal, Quintana Roo. What might be called "archaeo-ecotourism" presents another opportunity to bring new value to the forest's natural and cultural resources. The current plan attempts to base tourism in the local communities and discourages more destructive forms of tourist development. It will target those segments of the local, national, and international markets interested in the educational and recreational aspects of the forest and the Maya ruins it conceals. To avoid the concentration of tourists in a single place, two tourism circuits have been planned. One of these two regional circuits includes visits to several Maya sites located around the Calakmul town of X'pujil, including the well-known sites of Becán, Chicanná, Río Bec, and Hormiguero. The second circuit involves the archaeological sites of Calakmul and Balamku.

The biosphere reserve designation gives added tourist value to the region, and two ejidos have established wildlife reserves close to the ruins of Hormiguero and Río Bec to capitalize on this value. Ejidos have also established new regulations that forbid hunting close to the ruins, further increasing their value to tourists. An infrastructure of cabins and restaurants and a luxury hotel in Chicanná have been built in the town of X'pujil, providing various services for different market segments. Other programs related to ecotourism include artisan production, the framing of rainforest insects for marketing, and a workshop for ecotourism guides. This last program has stimulated the interest of young people in learning English and becoming guides.

Institutional Design

The most important element in community forest management in Calakmul has been the emergence of a consolidated regional peasant organization.

Calakmul benefited from the precedent of organizations in Quintana Roo, such as the Sociedad de Productores Ejidales Forestales de Quintana Roo in Chetumal, that had formed a common front for forest management and timber marketing. These organizations had no links with the forestry organizations of the government's ruling party, the Institutional Revolutionary Party (PRI), which had played a significant part in creating the policies that encouraged the destruction of Mexican forests. Inspired by this history, the Consejo Regional Agrosilvopastoril y de Servicios de X'pujil, S.C. (Regional Council for Agriculture, Silviculture, Farmland, and Services of X'pujil) was formed in Calakmul in 1991, and eventually included more than 40 ejidos.

As with ecological sustainability and economic sustainability, the sustainability of local organizations managing their own resources is crucial. The Consejo emerged as a strong representative organization capable of managing its affairs and its region. But the organizational process has not been free of conflicts. In the last two years, two additional organizations have split from the original Consejo, each having stronger affiliations with political parties; one organization has strong ties to the ruling PRI, and the other is affiliated with a rival political party, the Party of the Democratic Revolution (PRD). The challenge for biosphere reserve management now is to find a common ground for the three organizations to meet and form common strategies for regional development.

All three organizations operate on the same basic principles. Ejidos aligned with the organizations are asked to organize themselves internally and to nominate two representatives to participate in the Regional Councils or Rural Committees. Both development programs and sources of funding from the government, national nongovernmental organizations (NGOs), and international assistance are analyzed by these bodies. From this gradual process the following structure has arisen: inter-ejidal peasant organizations have been created, based on a concept of sustainable regional development and respect for each other's autonomy. Each organization independently seeks governmental and nongovernmental support for their development programs, and sends representatives to sessions of the Council, assuring that information is fed back to the communities. Monthly meetings include community representatives, peasant organizations by sector (forestry, apiculture, women's enterprises, etc.), and technicians. The foresters who work for the organization and who have the forest technical services concession from the government are included in the Council, and they and the peasants together design forest strategies, disseminate information, and train rural technicians.

In general these organizations serve to transmit information, provide technical assistance through contracted staff, create a united front during negotiations over forest policy, supply the organizational vehicle for funding by governments and NGOs, promote all of the activities mentioned above, and provide a forum where peasants can learn parliamentary techniques and build their negotiating skills—even if negotiations do sometimes end up in fights!

A basic challenge has been finding technicians who can work with the communities in providing some of the planning and technical tools for sustainability, and who can explain it in terms acceptable to them. The basic technique here has been to use "farmer-to-farmer" training techniques, in which a technician, frequently of a peasant background himself, provides training to a group of peasants who, in turn, provide training to their fellow farmers. This has been particularly successful in the agroecology programs, which hire farmers part-time as promoters over a several-year period. The empowerment of peasants and their organizations with knowledge of alternative paths has proved to be a powerful tool, and one that has met with considerable resistance from powerful interests in the region.

Conclusion

The last four years in Calakmul have constituted a sustained effort to incorporate peasant organizations and give them a major role in conservation and development decisionmaking in the region where they live. This constitutes a new element in biosphere reserve management, one that goes beyond mere "involvement" of local people. The creation of economic incentives is a long-term process, and some of the resources may not be abundant enough to permit intensive exploitation. However, unlike the Plan Piloto Forestal experience, multiple use of the forest was promoted from the very beginning in Calakmul, giving rise to the system of territorial and ecological zoning that has been discussed, and holding out the promise of a diversified economic base that depends on a diverse ecosystem. The Calakmul experience has been distinguished by a positive organizational experience, a new approach to biosphere reserve management, the agroforestry and agroecological experiences, and the incorporation of beekeeping as a major new source of NTFP economic activity. From the Plan Piloto experience in Quintana Roo, community members have learned about forest and wildlife management and new methods for chicle extraction. The last four years have shown that, as long as the political space is allowed by the state and federal governments, peasants can become leaders in the management of lowland tropical forests in general and biosphere reserves in particular.

References

Boege, E., and R. Murguía. 1989. Diagnóstico de las actividades humanas que se realizan en la Reserva de la Biósfera de Calakmul, Estado de Campeche. Pronatura-Península de Yucatán, Mérida, Mexico.

Bunch, R. 1986. Dos mazorcas de maíz: Una guía para el mejoramiento agrícola orientado hacia la gente. World Neighbors, Oklahoma City, Okla.

Consejo Regional Agrosilvo Pastoril y de Servicios Xpujil, S.C. 1994. Bosque modelo para Calakmul. Ecología productiva. Propuesta (CRASX), Zoh-laguna, Campeche, Mexico.

García, G. 1993. Cartografía temática para el manejo de la Reserva de la Biósfera de Calakmul, Campeche. Pronatura-Península de Yucatán, Mérida, México.

García, G., and I. J. March. 1990. Cartografía temática básica y base geográfica de datos para la zona de Calakmul, Campeche. Pronatura-Península de Yucatán, Mérida, México.

Garrett, W. E. 1989. La ruta Maya. *National Geographic* 176: 424–479.

Janka, H. 1981. La alternativa forestal comunal: Una alternativa para el trópico húmedo? Acuerdo México–Alemania: Alternativas para el uso del suelo en áreas forestales del trópico húmedo. SARH-INIF, Ciudad de México, D.F., México.

Konrad, H. 1984. Plantation labor systems in tropical forests: The case of chicle tappers. Unpublished manuscript.

López, G. 1994. Memoria del taller de capacitación e intercambio de experiencias campesinas efectuado en Zoh-laguna, Campeche, 3–5 de febrero de 1994.

SEDESOL. 1993. Areas naturales protegidas. Secretaría de Desarrollo Social (SEDESOL), Ciudad de Mexico, D.F., Mexico.

Snook, L. 1991. Opportunities and constraints for sustainable tropical forestry: Lessons from the Plan Piloto Forestal, Quintana Roo. In *Developmental Strategies for Fragile Lands Project*, Tropical Research and Development, Inc., U.S. Forest Service.

Chapter 7

Forestry Policy and Protected Areas in the Petén, Guatemala

Ismael Ponciano

Public policy in Guatemala traditionally has been developed through a process of negotiation and agreement between the controlling elements of the government and pressure groups, both national and international. Forest policy is no exception to this tradition. In the recent history of Guatemala, five successive forestry laws have served as guidelines for policy. The first law, enacted in 1924 by the civil government of Carlos Herrera, remained in effect until 1945, at which point a radical change in the management of public affairs took place. This change came about because a modernizing government, which held office from 1944 through 1954, was attempting to push the economy toward a capitalist model. This "revolutionary government," as it called itself, passed new legislation on October 6, 1945. This second law, Decree 170, formed a new forestry bureaucracy inspired by the North American model, consisting of two divisions: the Department of Forestry and the Department of Fish and Wildlife.

The third law, Decree 58-79, developed financial incentives and administrative independence. This legislation was an important step forward; it established an autonomous forestry institute and granted it maximum independence, although this autonomy was later diminished. The law was amended in 1984, fundamentally strengthening, broadening, and deepening the concepts of fiscal incentives, subsidies, and debt-forgiveness for reforestation. In 1989, the forestry law was modified again in all aspects, but it was supplanted by yet another new forestry law enacted by the Guatemalan Congress in October 1996. The most important change in the new law is the return to an autonomous forestry agency that gives increased prominence to the idea of sustainable development.

Protected areas policy had its first modern expression in 1944 with the signing of a regional protocol for the protection of national parks, flora, fauna, and other scenic attractions. This protocol is still on the books today, although it is not enforced. In 1955, the national government of Guatemala signed agreements for the creation of ten national parks, selected for their aesthetic, scenic, touristic, and cultural values. The most important of the new protected areas were Tikal National Park, Río Dulce National Park, Riscos de Momostenango National Park, El Baúl National Park, United Nations National Park, and Mira Mundo National Park. But these were all "paper parks," with the notable exception of Tikal National Park. The rest of the areas, because of failures to provide both administrative structures and funds, were either lost entirely or were transformed into recreational areas.

Forest Policy and Protected Areas in the Recent History of El Petén

In 1969, a forestry inventory for the department of El Petén was concluded. This inventory was done under the auspices of a project of the Petén Promotion and Development Association (FYDEP), and the United Nations Food and Agriculture Organization (FAO). The results showed that 96% of the territory of the Petén was covered with primary forests. This inventory, at a cost of $2 million, was carried out as part of the development policies of the Guatemalan government. FYDEP had been created in 1962 with the goal of incorporating the department into the rest of the country in a more effective and rational manner. The forest policy of FYDEP had as a principal objective the logging of wood, especially mahogany and Spanish cedar. After the inventory, concessions of approximately 50,000 ha blocks were granted to several logging companies. The key variable was the volume of harvestable wood and not the means by which it was harvested. The traditional logging practices required sites with the best conditions for harvest; sites with either very old or very young trees, where logging would not be profitable, were discarded.

This policy dominated from 1962 through 1990, the date by which FYDEP was eliminated and the Maya Biosphere Reserve was created, which will be further discussed below. During the FYDEP period, there was basically no protected areas policy operative. However, the Institute of Anthropology and History (IDAEH) did establish a policy of protection of archaeological sites that coincided with the core of what would later become protected areas. However, as a result of this policy several archaeological parks were created that currently can be considered true protected areas. These were Ceibal National Park, Petexbatun Archaeological Park, and Dos Pilas Archaeological Park.

In 1989, the National Protected Areas Council (CONAP) was founded as a coordinating institution for policy and management for protected areas in the country. The first effect of the creation of CONAP was the establishment of protected areas in the north of Guatemala. Most importantly, the Maya Biosphere Reserve (MBR) was founded; the reserve incorporated the pre-existing Tikal National Park, Laguna del Tigre Biotope, El Zotz Biotope, and the Dos Lagunas Biotope into a more comprehensive conservation program. Additionally, the Laguna del Tigre and Sierra del Lacandón National Parks were created. In 1993, CONAP supported the technical studies for the creation of three more protected areas in the Petén, which added an additional 400,000 ha of healthy forest to the conservation area, the creation of which, at the time of this writing, had obtained the approval of the Congress.

Political and Social Process in the Creation of the Maya Biosphere Reserve

The creation of the MBR in 1990 was more a product of a unique opportunity—the proposal of the "Ruta Maya" tourism project and paving of 200 km of highway between Cadenas and Flores, with financing from the German government—than part of a clear-cut environmental policy of then President Marco Vinicio Cerezo Arevalo (1986–1990). Opposition to the highway project quickly arose and began to focus attention on the state of the forests in the Petén. Another contributing factor in the policy momentum for this important reserve was the collective image among Guatemalans of the Petén as a forested area. This image was rooted in the fact that, since 1969, the people of the Petén as well as Guatemalans in general had considered the territory north of the 17°10' parallel as a forest preserve. This forest preserve was never really delineated nor managed as such, and for many years it was exploited and "high-graded" (selective cutting of the highest-value trees) throughout virtually its entire area. When the MBR was declared, only the most inaccessible areas, particularly along the borders, were still pristine.

At the time of the proclamation of the MBR there were a number of important conditions that led to Congress's decree. First, there existed in Guatemala the first democratically elected government in many years, one strong enough to exercise its dominance in matters of public policy. Second, CONAP had been created as a coordinating body for conservation policy in the country and had political support, allowing it to play a lead role in forest and protected areas policies, particularly with reference to the other relevant agency, the General Forestry Directorate (DIGEBOS). DIGEBOS was created in 1988, replacing the National Forestry Institute (INAFOR), an organization that had been weak and lacking in prestige. Unfortunately, DIGEBOS would prove to be no stronger than its predecessor, and protected areas and wildlife responsibilities were not contained within its mandate. However, the

National Commission on the Environment existed as a politically strong and effective entity, which served as a pivot for all conservation activities at this time. Third, there were no existing plans or projects for petroleum exploration or exploitation in the region, except for one small 2,000 ha concession. The Guatemalan government considered both conservation and tourism as priority activities to increase its prestige, and the project had the personal support of the Office of the President. In addition, studies and evaluations already existed for the creation of the MBR.

However, it was the aforementioned highway project that really awakened concern over the consequences that the road might have on the Petén's forests. The Law for the Protection and Improvement of the Environment required a study of environmental impacts for projects like the Petén highway. A team of German experts brought in to carry out the study helped to create the environmental impact assessment; conservation groups found an opportunity to advise the German government of the serious consequences that could result from the highway project unless protected areas were first declared. As a result of this process, the government of Guatemala did decide to suspend the highway project until new protected areas were created. Further, funds originally intended to be a loan for highway construction were transformed into a grant to aid in the implementation of the Integral Development Plan of the Petén, including the creation of the three additional protected areas already mentioned.

The interest awakened by a special edition of *National Geographic* (vol. 176 no. 4, October 1989) was highly influential. This issue called for an integrated road and tourist attraction network that would highlight the cultures, ecosystems, and archaeological sites of the region. Dubbed the Ruta Maya (Maya Route), it would include five countries: Mexico, Belize, Guatemala, Honduras, and El Salvador (Garrett 1989). The Ruta Maya was proposed as a project that would make a significant contribution to conservation and development in the region.

Forest Policies That Affect the Petén

It is not easy to discern the impact of forest policy on the Petén in the last decade because of the frequent changes in agencies and policies. An examination of the most relevant policies during this period shows a primary focus on continued logging of natural forests. This trend is shown in the granting of annual concessions for the selective logging of mahogany, cedar, and several other species, and the absence of management plans and long-term concessions. Additionally, clandestine logging has recently been more locally destructive because conservation measures have given greater degrees of protection to some areas, which together with general deforestation, reduces the forest area susceptible to logging.

Clandestine logging has always been present to a degree, but beginning in the 1980s, with a loss of control by government agencies and the increasing intensity of armed conflicts in the region, the cutting of trees with chainsaws and subsequent transportation and illegal sale grew slowly. The illegal loggers focus on trees close to rivers and highways to facilitate their removal. They cut them, convert them into boards, then transport them any way they can— using tractors, pickup trucks, animals, or even hauling them on their shoulders. This wood is bought by local carpenters and sawmills. In 1992, 6 million bf were cut illegally in the MBR near the Belizean border. The authorities confiscated the logs, then promoted the private or public sale of the wood. The issue of the public sale of confiscated logs has been a controversial one, with sales delayed at one point due to Decree 72-92 in November 1992. But the decision was finally made two years later to allow the municipalities to sell the logs to the Petén timber-processing industry to generate income.

The exploitation of the forests of the Petén continues for two primary reasons: first, public and private industries and individuals seek ways to create capital for themselves in a region where development is incipient. In a subsistence agricultural economy, timber is an important vehicle for capitalization or income. Second, the Guatemalan government continues to promote agriculture in the Petén as it has since 1944, when the first agricultural colony was founded in Poptun, bringing as a consequence daily elimination of primary forest. Despite acknowledgment of the importance of tropical forests by governments the world over, there is still a tendency to view cleared land as "productive" and therefore more valuable than "unproductive" forested land.

In the Petén, timber is virtually a short-term currency that is spent quickly, rather than—as would be the ideal situation—a long-term income-generating resource. In countless cases, settlements of poor farmers have traded the timber of their forests to loggers in exchange for the construction of roads in the belief that roads would enable them to market their produce more easily. Unfortunately, the roads serve primarily as a means to extract timber from the forest, and they quickly become impassable due to lack of maintenance. The consequence has been that the communities, rather than strengthening themselves, contribute to their own deterioration, and their ability to participate economically continues to decline. They are poorer than when they had no road but still had their timber. These communities have only rudimentary levels of organization, do not realize the true value of the timber, and do not have the training or capital to produce value-added timber products. Most community members are subsistence farmers, living from the planting of corn and beans, who aspire to own a herd of cattle someday.

Forest Conservation Legislation and the Petén

Guatemala's prolific Congress has enacted approximately 20 current laws related to the forestry sector, including the municipal code and the hydrocarbon law, among others. This legislation has rarely been applied due to weaknesses in the agencies responsible for its implementation. No agency can force compliance with a forestry law if it lacks human resources, equipment, and financing—much less political support. Moreover, several of the provisions of these laws are flatly contradictory. Article 126 of the law refers to reforestation, conservation, and the rational use of the forests, in order to stimulate industrialization. This article is the basis for the current forestry law and of any future laws. In Article 125, referring to the use of nonrenewable natural resources, the exploitation of hydrocarbons is declared a matter of public benefit and need, thus sustaining all of the petroleum legislation and contributing to the predominance of the development lobby over that of conservation of natural resources. Article 15, a temporary measure referring to the integration of the Petén, declares economic development of the department a matter of national urgency, even though poorly conceived economic development could well destroy the resources that sustain the Petén's residents.

Forest Management and Protected Areas Laws

Decree 89-26 is the law administered by INAFOR that regulates forest management in Guatemala. It is relatively well balanced on behalf of forest conservation and the ratification of incentives for restoration. But application of the law is very weak, since INAFOR has had constant cutbacks in both budget and staff.

Decree 4-89 provides specifically for the protection and management of biodiversity in the country. This law determines the process by which a protected area can be declared, the standards by which a protected area must be managed, and the regulation of the production and marketing of wild flora and fauna. This legal instrument was approved by the Guatemalan Congress with last-minute modifications that called for technical studies for declaration of protected areas and the formation of the CONAP Council with participation from 14 governmental agencies, nongovernmental organizations (NGOs), and the private sector. However, only four members of the board are representatives of conservation NGOs, while most of the government agencies are development-oriented and the private sector is represented by logging interests. With this composition, decisions made do not necessarily lean toward the environment. For example, it was the Council that authorized the sale of the 6 million bf of timber clandestinely cut from the MBR in 1992, and that allowed the settlement of refugees in the core zone of the Lacandón Forest in March of 1995. The most difficult aspect of compliance with this new law has been the formation of new protected areas. At the time of this writing, there are five protected areas awaiting approval by the CONAP Board of Directors, with only one receiving endorsement in June of 1995—four years after completing the technical requirements specified by the law. By late

1996, technical studies had been approved for two of the protected areas, Bocas del Polochic and Cerro San Gil.

Agencies, Private Groups, and Local and International NGOs

Here we refer to both public and private agencies with a role in forest conservation and protected areas in northern Guatemala. As already discussed, the Petén, although the largest department in the country, has been slighted when it comes to development throughout its history. It is still the department that receives the least public and private investment; for example, the Petén's 1995 public investment fund was only 150 million quetzales, representing 0.6% of the total national budget. As a consequence, the presence of government agencies has been weak, with little capacity for monitoring or follow-through.

There are ten government agencies directly related to conservation, natural resources, or related mandates. These are the Urban and Rural Development Council of the Petén (CUDEP), the National Commission on the Environment, the Vice-Ministry of Agriculture, the Protected Areas National Council (CONAP), the National Institute of Agrarian Transformation (INTA), the General Directorate for Forests and Wildlife (DIGEBOS), the Anthropology and History Institute (IDEAH), the General Directorate for Mining and Hydrocarbons, the Guatemalan Tourism Institute (INGUAT), and the Guatemalan Army. The programs of each of these agencies are independent, and the levels of coordination between them vary according to circumstances.

NGOs began to play an important role in 1990. Before then there existed only two or three NGOs in the Petén: the Development Association of the Petén and the Cultural Centers of Flores and Poptún, respectively. Currently there are more than 20 NGOs, the majority of them focused on the environment. These NGOs arose under the shelter of large amounts of governmental and international foreign assistance and NGO projects, and they still depend on them for financial support. This fact suggests that their program goals are constrained by the agendas and vision of these national or international organizations. Their financial dependence means that if the parental programs stop funding them, they will have to close up shop.

Private sector organizations are the strongest in the department. The principal ones are the Chamber of Commerce of the Petén, the Hotel Owners Association, and the Timber Industry Association of the Petén, which together represent the largest businesses of the department. Most of the businesses, except for timber extraction, are in the service sector. The two groups with the strongest ties to the forests are the hotel owners and the timber industrialists, but the two have conflicting interests. Both groups depend on the forest and the natural environment, but the hotel owners need a conserved forest environment, depending as they do on ecotourism, while the timber industrialists want to consume that very environment. Considering the weak presence of government agencies in the department, it is the struggle between these two private sector actors that will determine whether logging or conservation will win out.

As has been noted, beginning in 1990 the international government-to-government foreign assistance and international NGOs began to play an increasingly important role in the department. These entities were focused principally on the conservation of the natural resources, and developed the two largest conservation programs ever seen in the Petén. The Maya Biosphere Project (MAYAREMA), with an investment of $20 million over three years coming principally from the U.S. Agency for International Development (USAID), was dedicated exclusively to the management and conservation of the Maya Biosphere Reserve. From the German government came the project for integral development of the Petén, with a budget of 23 million German marks. This project was an effort to develop a master plan for the Petén, and within it a program for the conservation of the southern buffer zone of the MBR. These two programs have supported five international NGOs in the Petén, each of which supports individual conservation programs. These NGOs have the best and most professional staffs and have sufficient funds to complete the tasks contracted with CONAP and sufficient flexibility to adapt to new situations as they arise. The achievements of these two programs are positive, if narrow in scope. They have advanced in some specific areas, but have not been able to reverse the process of deterioration of the forest and biodiversity in the Petén. They have been a new and active force in the social and economic dynamic of the department, but have also been forced to become more modest in their goals.

Responses to the Forest and Protected Areas Policy

Responses to the implementation of forest and protected areas policy in the Petén have been diverse as *Peténeros* absorb the government's attempts to control logging, reduce threats of displacement of the local population, and supervise petroleum operations. The 1989 Law of Protected Areas created systems of administration and control that had not previously existed in the Petén. For the people of the Petén it was most extraordinary, something they had never experienced before. Efforts to reduce clandestine logging, wildlife trafficking, and the plunder of archaeological objects caused violent reactions against CONAP, the organization in charge of the protected areas.

The two sites where the most violent reactions occurred were in El Naranjo (Río San Pedro) and El Cruce de Dos Aguadas, settlements established in the 1970s around petroleum and logging activities, respectively. The inhabitants of both communities reacted violently against the forest guards of CONAP, going so far as to expel them from their communities in 1990 and 1991, respectively. CONAP has not been able to return to either of the two sites, and the buildings occupied by the forest guards were burned. Government authorities could not regain control of the region immediately after the incident, and those responsible were not captured. This situation allowed clandestine logging to continue, especially in the zone of Laguna del Tigre. However, in July of 1995 a new guardpost was installed in El Cruce de Dos Aguadas, with the protection of the Guatemalan Army, in an effort to once again halt the destruction of this protected region.

The primary reason for this violent reaction by Petén residents has been the perceived threat of displacement from the land that is their livelihood, especially in circumstances where communities occupy MBR lands. Although government policy did not call for or contemplate any such measure, government agencies have had to reassure the local populations that resettlement is not an option. Yet fear of displacement is a tremendous source of anxiety for local people, many of whom were originally displaced from lands in highland Guatemala. At the root of the expulsion of the forest guards in El Naranjo is the fact that this location has been the principal point of entry for new settlers in the MBR.

Although not a response to public policy, Guatemalan refugees currently living in Mexico have seen the possibility of settling themselves in the MBR as a quick and cheap option. The validity of this perception was demonstrated when 240 families settled in the Finca El Quetzal, with 80% of the settled area falling in the core zone of the Sierra del Lacandón National Park; the settlement became permanently occupied by the refugees despite the opposition of CONAP. If not a response to the conservation policy of the government, this attitude is a response to the weakness of CONAP and governmental agencies in general.

Responses to petroleum policy came principally from conservation NGOs, universities, and the urban population. Responses to these policies focus on the slender profits these operations ostensibly report and attempts to paint the companies as instigators of the destruction of the natural patrimony and as a possible source of contamination by spilled oil. Responses of conservation NGOs were channeled through major media in Guatemala, but are sporadic and have minimal impact.

Community Forestry Concessions

As an option for achieving more positive relations between local communities and the administration of the MBR, the concept of community forestry concessions was created by both the international NGOs and the Forestry

Consulting Committee of the MAYAREMA Project (see Gretzinger, this volume). It is hoped that this concept will contribute to more sustainable logging, improvement in community income, and better control by the government over forest activities. After a difficult bureaucratic process, four initial experimental concessions have been approved by CONAP: San Miguel, La Palotada, La Pasadita, and Bethel. The community concessions are valid, but their impact is relatively small, especially because the communities suffer from organizational deficiencies and the natural conditions of the forests in the concessions do not allow the immediate achievement of high levels of productivity. All the projects are strongly subsidized.

Petroleum Concessions

Forty percent of the territory of the MBR overlaps with the area defined as having petroleum production potential. The Ministry of Energy and Mines has offered these zones for exploitation in public international auction. International corporations obtained the respective concessions between 1985 and 1993. The simultaneous existence of two policies with profoundly different purposes has caused challenges for the conservation and petroleum interests. Neither conservation policy nor the policy of petroleum concessions has attempted to reconcile the opposing interests, and no government agency has had sufficient power to seek a compromise solution. In 1994 the Ministry of Energy and Mines expressed an interest in reaching some agreements on the matter. But unfortunately this initiative failed because it required that the mining interests play the dominant role. Nonetheless, there were several meetings that produced a draft agreement requiring the signature of the president of the Republic, which attempted to resolve this threat to the biodiversity of the Petén. However, the agreement was never finalized or signed.

The threat of petroleum extraction is grave because of the high levels of investment required by drilling, which would immediately attract strong migratory flows to work in the region. Additionally, drilling would presumably require more roads and urban infrastructure, which would also attract settlers. Additionally, petroleum companies represent large global economic interests, providing Guatemala with development opportunities. Their power would give them a major influence over national politics, not to mention local politics in the Petén. Transnational oil companies make large investments without considering the protection of the environment as a part of the investment. Environmental impact studies and efforts at mitigation and environmental monitoring are considered unnecessary expenses. Petroleum companies typically confine themselves to the completion of the required environmental impact study because once the project is approved by the governing bodies, there is little monitoring for compliance. When a company complies with one or another part of the study, it is only due to pressure brought by conservation NGOs. Because of the large percentage of the MBR with petroleum production potential, petroleum extraction must be considered the principal threat of destruction for the forests of the Petén, one that could become reality over the next decade.

Returned Refugee Settlements

The return of refugees from Guatemala as part of the peace process has created an aggressive and rapid program of human settlements in the Petén, as mentioned earlier. The great support that United Nations agencies are giving to the refugees, without taking into account environmental considerations, is resulting in the establishment of settlements in and around the protected areas. Clear examples are the previously mentioned settlement in the Finca El Quetzal in the Lacandón National Park and the settlement of Los Limones.

There are also other high biodiversity areas of Guatemala, such as northeastern Huehuetenango, that have not been studied or considered by the conservation NGOs. This region was one of the hardest hit by the war, but many refugee settlements are being placed here; these settlers are resorting to traditional agricultural patterns that depend on cutting the forest to plant basic grains. This resettlement process also brings investments by international organizations in infrastructure, creating the possibility for further destruction of natural resources, including rare and endangered species. In a recent study conducted by the Center for Conservation Studies at San Carlos University (CECON), a new species of butterfly and two endemic species of fish were identified in the region, all of which are potentially threatened by development. Sustained support in conservation and development activities is crucial for the relocated communities, who could quickly return to levels of poverty that could generate new social conflicts. The Guatemalan government also faces serious logistical and economic difficulties, now and in the foreseeable future, in providing services to these dispersed and remote communities.

Conclusion

It is imperative that forest and protected areas policies, and the policies regarding resettlement of populations and petroleum concessions in virgin forests with high concentrations of biodiversity, become the focus of wide public debate in Guatemala. A continuation of the present policies—such as they are—will result in the disappearance of rainforest resources, denying Guatemala a potential base for development forever. It is crucial for these issues to be discussed publicly and openly, and with the objective information necessary for making rational decisions on behalf of sustainable development.

References

Basic Resources International, Bahamas and Ltd. 1996. *Estudio del Impacto Ambiental Significativo de la Expansión del Campo Petrolero Xan*. Contrato 2-85. Guatemala City, Guatemala. n.d.

Cabrera Gaillard, C., and J. Morales Dardón. 1996. Diagnóstico Forestal de Guatemala. IUCN Mesoamerican Regional Office.

Congreso de la República de Guatemala. 1924. Ley Forestal (Decreto 1364, 24 de marzo de 1924).

————. 1945. Ley Forestal (Decreto 170, 17 de octubre de 1945).

————. 1963. Ley de Fomento y Desarrollo de El Petén. Creación de FYDEP (Decreto 72-63).

————. 1986. Ley de Mejoramiento del Medio Ambiente (Decreto 68-86, 5 de deciembre de 1986).

————. 1988. Ley de Mejoramiento del Medio Ambiente (Decreto 24-88, 21 de junio de 1988).

————. 1989. Ley de Areas Protegidas y Vida Silvestre (Decreto 4-89, 14 de febrero de 1989).

————. 1995. Declaratorio de la Reserva de la Biosfera Río Chiquibul, Santa Amelia y San Román (Decreto 63-95, 11 de septiembre de 1995).

————. 1996. *Proyecto de Ley Forestal*. Guatemala City, Guatemala. n.d.

DIGEBOS (Directorado General de Bosques, Guatemala). 1993. *Dirección General de Bosques y Vida Silvestre*. Guatemala City, Guatemala. n.d.

Garrett, W. E. 1989. La Ruta Maya. *National Geographic* 176: 424–479.

Gobierno de Guatemala. 1993. *Agenda del Gobierno para el Periodo 1994–1995*. Guatemala City, Guatemala. n.d.

Payeras, M. 1993. *Latitud de la flor y el granizo*. Instituto Chiapaneco de Cultura, Chiapas, México.

Chapter 8

Community Forest Concessions: An Economic Alternative for the Maya Biosphere Reserve in the Petén, Guatemala

Steven P. Gretzinger

One of the great challenges in the Maya Forest is discovering ways in which forests can be protected while simultaneously providing sustainable livelihoods to the local people. The Man and the Biosphere Program's approach is one possible method of encouraging people to live in a harmonious balance with the natural world. The Maya Biosphere Reserve (MBR) was established in 1990 to become Guatemala's first unit of the International Network of Biosphere Reserves (Aguilar and Aguilar 1992). The 2.1 million ha MBR includes 747,800 ha under strict protection, 864,300 ha destined for multiple use, and 487,900 ha of private holdings in the buffer zone (Figure 8.1; MAGA 1996). Although most of the MBR is state land that may not be bought or sold as private property, several villages have existed since the 1930s in the area now designated as reserve lands; roads, homes, schools, churches, stores, and clinics all lie within the borders of the MBR. Population figures are speculative, but there are probably more than 30,000 inhabitants in the reserve (ProPetén 1993). Kekchi Maya and mixed-blood "Ladino" settlers contribute to an annual immigration rate for the Petén of 5.5% (Southgate and Basterrechea 1992). Since the early 1960s, at least 50% of the department's population growth has been due to immigration (Schwartz 1990). Incorporating the needs of these people with the conservation of forest resources represents an important aspect of the MBR's conservation strategy; this chapter offers suggestions for how such a goal might be accomplished.

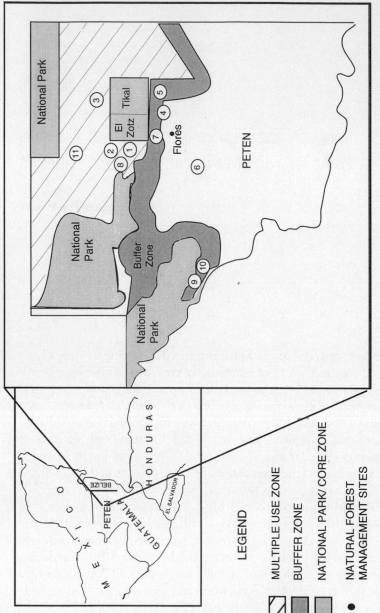

Figure 8.1

The Maya Biosphere Reserve, El Petén, Guatemala, includes national parks, biotopes, and archaeological sites. Numbers indicate the location of proposed and actual natural forest management sites in the Maya Biosphere Reserve.

Resource Use in the Maya Biosphere Reserve

In past decades before the influx of new immigrants, traditional Petén residents spent 60% to 70% of their time extracting forest products for income generation, and the remainder growing crops for family consumption (Reining et al. 1992; Soza-Manzanero 1996). Agriculture was not intensive, and most dwellers intermixed crops with forest patches to provide seeds, fruits, and other products (Nations and Nigh 1980; Remmers and Koeijer 1992). The use of long fallow periods and two- to three-year rotations among cultivated plots helped maintain soil fertility (Cowgill 1961; Urrutia 1967). This agroforestry system minimized the need to cut primary forest and remains appropriate for the Petén, where only 20% to 30% of the soils are suitable for agriculture (FAO/FYDEP 1970; Schwartz 1990; MAGA 1996). Current resource use, however, is dominated by landless immigrants who rely upon imported agricultural practices to sustain themselves in an unfamiliar ecosystem (Soza-Manzanero 1996). They typically follow a pattern of forest felling, burning, cultivation, cattle ranching, and abandonment of degraded soils in search of new forest (Purata 1986; Gómez-Pompa 1987). This approach requires great effort, provides low earnings, and exacerbates a precarious environmental situation (Schwartz 1990). Colonists have few alternatives and little luxury to consider the opportunity costs of their actions—actions that are, in fact, logical responses to policies that grant property rights based on "improvements," which are defined under Guatemalan law as removal of natural vegetation (Southgate and Basterrechea 1992).

Other land-use practices affect the MBR's forests to varying degrees. Although logging is prohibited in the MBR (except under terms to be discussed later), illegal selective harvesting of high-value species such as *Swietenia macrophylla* (mahogany) and *Cedrela odorata* (Spanish cedar) continues to be an attractive economic option. Such "high-grading" involves no management, depletes the forest's economic value, and provides little financial incentive for long-term conservation efforts (Bojorquez et al. 1988; Gretzinger 1994).

Nontimber forest products industries (chicle, allspice, xate), which generate roughly $5 million in exports and 378,200 person-days of employment per year (Reining et al. 1992), can also create problems. Newcomers to the Petén either are unfamiliar with proper harvesting techniques or overharvest the resource out of short-term economic necessity. For instance, xate harvesters are paid for quantity rather than quality, prompting overcutting as workers strive to fill quotas. The chicle industry is threatened as fewer trees in a diminishing forest area are tapped by more harvesters with increasing frequency (Dugelby 1995). Traditional workers cut only branches to collect allspice seeds, but new harvesters fell entire trees for the same purpose.

While Petén residents depend heavily on products derived from the MBR, they have no legal resource rights and thus have little ability to protect the forest from agriculture, cattle ranching, or illegal logging. Conflicting and misguided land-use policies have led to general confusion, land speculation, and increasingly intense resource use (Gretzinger 1995).

Justification for Community Forest Concessions

The aforementioned situation is not conducive to traditional protected area management based on control of access. The role of human demographics in Guatemalan conservation, as discussed by Nations and Komer (1984), has changed little in the past decade, and the relocation of residents to areas outside the reserve is generally implausible. The government is plagued by problems that hinder its ability to control resource use. Despite assistance by the Guatemalan military, law enforcement is minimal.

The government recognizes that resource use in the multiple-use zone cannot only strengthen the economy but also aid the greater conservation agenda. In Guatemala's National Council of Protected Areas (CONAP), with legal jurisdiction over the MBR, response to this possibility has established a community forest concession policy (Synnott 1994). Community organizations potentially can be more effective at maintaining forest cover than traditional governmental protection (Morell 1992; Bray et al. 1993; MacFarland et al. 1994; Chapela and Lara 1995). Active forest management by communities can inhibit the invasion of unmanaged, common lands by individuals with nonforest-based economic interests.

The private sector in the Petén, which includes community groups as well as timber and NTFP industries, has the experience and resources necessary to conduct forest management activities, and should be viewed as an ally in the conservation movement (Synnott 1994). Several of the five major villages located within the MBR (Carmelita, Cruce a Dos Aguadas, La Pasadita, San Miguel la Palotada, and Uaxactún) all existed prior to the reserve's establishment and had developed a traditional forest society based on the extraction of chicle, allspice, xate, and, to a lesser degree, timber (Schwartz 1990). This reliance upon the forest has yielded conservation benefits: for example, despite being the oldest settlements in the MBR, Carmelita and Uaxactún have the lowest deforestation rates (Sader et al. 1994). Industry has been less successful; timber and nontimber forest industries provided high returns in the past, but limited access to the MBR, consistent overharvesting, and changing markets have reduced their profitability. Substitute activities have yet to satisfy the needs of local residents.

One strategy that might alleviate the strain on the MBR's resources and improve the long-term economic conditions of the people who rely on those resources is to grant concessions for use rights. Concessions in the multiple-use zone help ensure a constant supply of natural resources for the local populace, thus reducing exploitation in core areas. Multiple-resource management helps keep the natural diversity, structure, and functions of the forest ecosystem relatively intact, and extends the range of wildlife habitat around core areas (Stanley and Gretzinger 1996). Given the wide range of conflicting economic interests in the MBR (cattle, crops, timber, nontimber products, tourism), traditional concessions that grant large areas to only one particular user group are not feasible. Multi-resource concessions maintain a mix of raw materials for different industries, provide varied opportunities for employment, and increase the local tax base. Contractual, payment, and conflict resolution mechanisms must allow for multiple users to obtain benefits from the same forested area (Colom 1996). Legally enforceable, long-term access rights and responsibilities must also be clearly stipulated to ensure that investments are protected, approved management regimes are respected, and forest cover is maintained (Gretzinger 1995).

How Community Forest Concessions Work

Community-based forestry concessions are a priority for the MBR. CONAP policy, as defined in the concession procedures (1994) and the MBR Master Plan (1996), recognizes the legitimacy of traditional forest use by established communities within their sphere of influence. This policy accords certain communities the a priori right to receive a concession without going through the competitive licensing process required for industrial concerns.

CONAP has approved forest concession procedures for the multiple-use zone with the intent of distributing responsibilities, benefits, and rights among the different players (CONAP 1994; Synnott 1994). CONAP establishes the rules, oversees concession granting, and supervises compliance. Community members and contractors implement management activities in the field. Monitoring and technical assistance are provided by independent organizations, which should ultimately be funded by income generated from concessions. This delegation of roles minimizes dependence upon the government and reduces opportunities for corruption.

CONAP has initiated a public consultation process to define concession units for communities with traditional forest uses (Gretzinger and Carrera 1996). The interested community must create a map of the area within its sphere of influence and justify its request based upon traditional use, an approach similar to that taken in other parts of Central America (Denniston 1994). A unique aspect of the Guatemalan community concessions is that agricultural lands are included in the grant area as long as the permanent forest estate is not reduced and is managed according to CONAP guidelines.

Upon receiving approval from local authorities, the concession proposal is presented to CONAP. Although CONAP has an approved zoning plan and procedures, community concession boundaries often are heavily disputed, and consistent decision making rationale is not always evident. To date, only San

Miguel la Palotada, La Pasadita, and Carmelita have approved boundaries; boundaries for Barrio Suchitan and Uaxactún are pending. The planning process is not yet complete, as concession areas for nontimber and timber industries (to be granted by competitive award) must be defined after the community areas are resolved.

Once a community's concession area is approved, a forest inventory must be conducted, followed by a management plan and environmental impact assessment (EIA) developed with standardized methodologies. The plan proposes three uses for different parts of the concession: timber production, strict preservation, and agriculture. It also defines the timber cutting schedule and cycle, the annual allowable cut, commercial species of interest, minimum cutting limits, silvicultural treatments, and protection strategies (CONAP 1994).

Upon acceptance of the management plan and EIA, a 25-year contract is written to define rights and responsibilities. While a concession does not grant land title, communities do gain rights to all resources within the area, and they must protect the forest. Failure to do so can result in cancellation of the concession. Prior to expiration of the allotted period, CONAP must renew the concessionaire's request for an additional contract unless the community has repeatedly committed infractions (CONAP 1994).

The community concessionaire must pay a one-time fee (less than $1 per acre for agricultural and forest lands) over a ten-year period, a performance bond for 1% of the total bid, and standard production-based taxes for timber and nontimber products. Concession agreements may be revoked if the community does not follow the management plan, lacks operating capacity, stops operations without just cause, or declares bankruptcy (Johnston and Lorraine 1994).

Forest management in the MBR is based upon the type of polycyclic felling system viewed by Buschbacher (1990) as the norm for the tropics. For unevenly aged forests, future harvests of the same cutting block are planned to occur when advanced regeneration from lower diameter classes reaches marketable size (Davis and Johnson 1987). The standard interval between harvests (i.e., the cutting cycle) in the Petén is 25 years. The minimum cutting limit for mahogany and cedar is 60 cm dbh, and for lesser-known species is usually 45 cm dbh. Forest dynamics are being monitored to determine specific cutting limits for different species (Stanley and Gretzinger 1996).

Silvicultural treatments are being developed to address the ecological requirements of threatened, high-value species (such as mahogany and cedar) that regenerate most effectively in the high light conditions prompted by disturbance (Putz 1993; Snook 1993). Diagnostic sampling, a tool originally developed in Malaysia, has been modified for use in the Petén to help define appropriate silvicultural prescriptions (Stanley and Gretzinger 1996).

The silvicultural use of liberation thinning to favor desired timber species is proving successful on an experimental basis. Liberation thinning involves allowing future harvestable timber trees to achieve maximum growth by removing neighboring trees that compete for light and other limited resources. The average annual diameter and basal area increases for commercial species on treated sites has been up to double that of untreated, control sites monitored over a three-year period (Pinelo-Morales 1997). Liberation thinning also reduces natural mortality rates and increases recruitment. On an operational basis, the combination of these benefits will allow the cutting cycle to be shortened.

Achievements in Community-Based Natural Forest Management

CONAP's promotion of community-based natural forest management in the MBR is producing economic and social benefits for reserve inhabitants while also serving to protect the natural functions of the Petén's forest ecosystem. Consider the following example: in 1994, the 33 families of San Miguel la Palotada became the first community to receive a concession of 7,039 ha (5,115 ha for forest production). The management plan stipulated an annual allowable cut of 795 m^3 for mahogany, Spanish cedar, and 11 other secondary species (CATIE 1993). Due to the degraded populations of mahogany and cedar, the proposed cutting cycle for these species is 40 years; the minimum cutting limit is 60 cm dbh; and 20% of the harvestable individuals were recommended to be left uncut as seed trees. Lesser-known species have a lower minimum cutting limit (40 cm dbh) and shorter cutting cycle (25 years) due largely to their growth characteristics and abundance (CATIE 1993).

For the 1994 harvest, an independent contractor was hired to extract via tractor an average of 1.45 trees/ha (Galvez-Ruano 1996) yielding 4.03 m^3/ha (Ammour et al. 1995) from the 40 ha cutting area. The community received U.S. $0.35/bf for mahogany and cedar, and U.S. $0.17/bf for lesser-known species sold as roundwood. Undried mahogany and cedar cut to variable-width rough-planks earned U.S. $0.63/bf. Wood sales of 47.06 m^3 yielded gross earnings of U.S. $8,758 ($186/m^3 or $218/ha), and provided 661 person-days of employment for community members (Ammour et al. 1995).

In 1995, the community used oxen to extract 1.54 m^3/ha from a larger 180 ha block, and sold chainsawed, dimensional lumber for $1.00/bf (mahogany and cedar) and $0.46/bf for secondary species (Ammour et al. 1995). Compared to the 1994 operations, total costs incurred by the community in 1995 increased 35% due to greater labor and processing, but gross earnings from a total volume sold of 57.35 m^3 increased to $21,845 ($380/m^3 or $121/ha), and provided 879 person-days of employment. By processing the wood rather than just selling roundwood, San Miguel generated more profits and wages from a forest that had less commercial timber than the stand harvested in 1994. Despite earning less on an area basis in 1995, the community increased its earnings by over 100% on a volume basis. The community reinvested some of its profits in a Guatemalan-designed portable sawmill (which is not yet functioning to capacity) and processing equipment.

As a result of San Miguel's incipient success, other communities in the multiple-use zone are applying for concessions. CONAP recently approved the forest inventory, management plan, and environmental impact assessment for an 18,000 ha concession in La Pasadita; harvesting should commence in 1997. As a variation on the timber-oriented model, the Center for Tropical Agricultural Research and Higher Learning (CATIE) has helped Uaxactún document its historic forest use to justify the community's request for a 70,000 ha concession to be used primarily for the extraction of nontimber resources. A consortium of three communities called Los Impulsores Suchitecos is soliciting a 13,000 ha timber concession on the Guatemala–Belize border. Finally, the village of Carmelita has recently initiated management of a 50,000 ha concession that incorporates both timber and nontimber products.

CONAP has also approved regulations governing private forest lands in the buffer zone. The first contract was signed in 1994 with the 50 families of the Bethel Cooperative located along the Usumacinta River bordering Mexico. Although most of the cooperative lies within the MBR's buffer zone, Bethel holds title to 4,149 ha of private land, of which 2,876 ha (69%) is selectively logged and unlogged old-growth tropical forest (Gretzinger et al. 1993). Bethel initiated forest management activities in 1994 following an approved management plan that recommended the selective cutting of mahogany and cedar (minimum cutting limit 60 cm dbh) and six other lesser-known species (minimum cutting limit 50 cm dbh) from a 100 ha block of primary swamp forest (Gretzinger et al. 1993). The 1994 operation was financed by a private wood buyer who paid an independent contractor to fell, skid, and transport the roundwood to a local sawmill. Bethel dwellers offered "unskilled" labor, a community committee supervised the operation, and a local nongovernmental organization called Centro Maya offered technical assistance (Salazar and Ruano 1995).

The 1994 cut yielded 5.63 m³/ha, or 57% of pre-harvest estimates. The 2.14 m³/ha of mahogany and cedar extracted was 90% of the estimate, while only 47% of the secondary species were cut (Gretzinger 1996). This discrepancy reflects the large price difference between primary and secondary species. Given the same extraction costs, a mediocre market for secondary species, and a short harvest period, the contractors made a logical economic decision to focus on high-value species. Adjusting volume estimates from the management plan by the actual efficiency of the first year's operations revealed that 14,163 m³ of the 2,278 ha available are actually suitable for forest production. Taking into account the 1994 harvest, and following a 20-year cutting cycle, the average annual allowable cut in subsequent years should be approximately 745 m³ (Gretzinger 1996).

Bethel sold its standing timber for $0.36/bf for mahogany and cedar, and $0.09/bf for secondary species. The 1994 operating costs for felling, skidding, loading, log transport to mill, road maintenance, taxes, and paperwork totalled $0.21/bf. The total processing cost (not including management or wood purchase costs) for conversion of standing timber to sawn timber ready for export at Puerto Barrios, Guatemala, was $0.48/bf (Gretzinger 1996). Gross earnings for all participants in the operation based on the sale of 491 m³ were $36,200 ($362/ha or $74/m³). The community received gross earnings of $19,068 ($190/ha or $39/m³), and less than 200 person-days of employment. The wood buyer covered 90% of the variable costs and received 74% of gross earnings ($15,519), while Bethel paid less than 2% of the variable costs and received 20% of gross earnings. Bethel's attractive earnings on a per hectare basis are due mainly to having a rich forest with large quantities of mahogany. Following the San Miguel example, however, Bethel could dramatically increase its earnings on a per cubic meter basis by selling processed timber.

Utilizing 1994 volume, logging, processing, and management cost data, three scenarios differing by degree of community involvement and investment were analyzed for Bethel. Financial projections calculated over the 20-year cutting cycle with an effective interest rate of 20% indicated that the most profitable route for Bethel is to actively process its timber (Gretzinger 1996). In fact, sustainable timber production (as opposed to mining of the timber resource) will prove unprofitable if Bethel continues to sell standing timber; value must be added to the final product for good forestry to "pay its way." In 1995, the Bethel cooperative took steps to improve its earnings: it purchased a tractor, chainsaws, and portable sawmill, and carried out logging activities without independent contractors. Although earnings from the 1995 and 1996 operations have yet to be analyzed, they appear to be quite attractive. Profits have been distributed to cooperative members and used to purchase additional equipment (Salazar and Ruano 1995).

Neighboring cooperatives to Bethel have also expressed interest in forest management as an alternative to slash-and-burn agriculture and cattle ranching. The La Tecnica cooperative, for example, completed an inventory of its privately owned 5,000 ha forest and submitted a management plan to CONAP in 1995. In 1996, the first harvest was implemented with financial backing from a local sawmill and assistance from Centro Maya. Guatemalan refugees returning to their lands in other parts of the Usumacinta region are interested in following suit. Another community in the buffer zone, the village of San José, established the 3,600 ha Bio-Itzá Forest Reserve in 1991 on communal land (Stanley and Gretzinger 1996; see also Chayax Huex et al., this volume). The reserve's goals are to maintain forest cover and support traditional Maya Itzá culture. CATIE technicians assisted the community in implementing a forest inventory in 1992 and finished a management plan in 1995. The plan incorporates timber and nontimber products into one management strategy and is the first contemporary indigenous effort at integrating different resource uses in the Petén. Unfortunately, internal political struggles in the community of San José have prevented active management from occurring.

Where to from Here?

An ironic situation exists: as the Petén forest shrinks, various communities are beginning to manage forests for profit; nongovernmental organizations (NGOs) appear to have the will to assist local efforts; and the Guatemalan government's forest policies are becoming clearer. Despite good intentions, numerous legal and technical obstacles still inhibit the implementation of community concessions on a large scale. To resolve some of these obstacles, Petén foresters are trying to learn from other projects in the Maya Forest region. The Plan Forestal Estatal (PFE) actively assisted communities in the management of similar forest types in Quintana Roo, Mexico, since 1983, and offers several useful lessons for the relatively recent initiative in the Petén (Putz 1993; Gretzinger 1995).

A large part of the PFE's success is attributed to the fact that it received strong political commitment and substantial financial backing from the beginning (Bray et al. 1993). One of the biggest problems facing community-based forestry in the MBR is the lack of stability in both governmental (CONAP) and donor support. The stronger tenure structure in Mexico promotes long-term investment in forestry, whereas the concession concept in Guatemala is still doubted by some who expect the government to change its policies in the near future, annulling previously established concessions. Despite providing critical assistance for some villages, NGOs and their donors have been notoriously fickle in their support of community forestry in the MBR. Several villages have been abandoned midstream, and it is not uncommon to find community members who feel betrayed by the NGOs.

Mexico's tradition of social progress, activism, and community involvement is another reason for the PFE's success. Guatemala's very different history, shadowed by military dictatorships and repression, makes public participation a novel issue; consequently, community groups are not effectively organized. Administration of funds and personnel, negotiating with government officials, and resolving internal conflicts are new skills that Guatemalan farmers must learn if they are to make their concessions work.

Forest management in both the Petén and Quintana Roo is based upon a polycyclic system that relies on seed trees, minimum cutting limits, and a 25-year cutting cycle to sustain timber production. Petén foresters use liberation thinning to produce higher growth rates for existing individuals, but have yet to experiment with the group (or "patch") cut methods advocated in Quintana Roo. Such methods seem particularly appropriate for encouraging new regeneration of high-value species such as mahogany (Putz 1993). Petén foresters have made great strides in pre-harvest planning, low-impact logging, and long-term forest monitoring; advances in these areas have been shared with Mexican colleagues.

Most Petén and PFE foresters understand that timber and nontimber products must be managed together (Snook and Barrera de Jorgenson 1992; Johnson and Cabarle 1993). In communities such as Carmelita and Uaxactún, the extractive reserve concept developed in the Brazilian Amazon (Pendzich et al. 1994) may prove to be a particularly appropriate model. Despite the Petén's long history of nontimber forest product exploitation, little active management of these resources has occurred to date (Dugelby 1995). Integrated forest management is more advanced in Quintana Roo (Snook and Barrera de Jorgenson 1992), and forest producers there receive higher profits from nontimber industries than in the Petén. One key obstacle is that CONAP is legally obligated to establish prices and control the exportation of chicle, thus limiting the market's ability to dictate higher prices for Guatemalan producers.

Few people in the region doubt that markets for lesser-known timber species must be developed or that wood must be processed to achieve sufficient earnings given the generally degraded conditions of forests in both countries. Several ejidos (community organizations analogous to cooperatives) in Quintana Roo have received independent "green" certification of their wood by the Rainforest Alliance's "SmartWood" Program, thus granting them access to new markets with more favorable prices. Despite some interest in this area in the Petén, no concessions have been certified. Further, while prices paid for wood purchased from concessionaires have been rising (Ammour et al. 1995), new markets outside of Guatemala have yet to be entered. Some of the larger Mexican ejidos have advanced production capacities (sawmills, trucks, skidders, etc.) that have been purchased with profits earned over the last 15 years. While both Bethel and San Miguel have invested some of their profits in equipment, the operations are too economically incipient to allow for greater purchases. The communities' production capacity remains limited due to the shortage of capital, and they must rely on intermediaries to help finance operations.

Similarities and differences clearly exist between the community-based forestry systems being implemented in Mexico and Guatemala. To date, a healthy interchange of ideas has characterized the relationship between the founders of the PFE and those involved in community concessions in the MBR. Such collaboration is crucial to ensure that the first tentative steps toward community-based forest management in the Maya Biosphere Reserve become firmly implanted as a critical component of a regional conservation strategy for the Maya Forest.

References

Ammour, T., J. Kent, R. Reyes, and H. Monroy. 1995. *Evaluación financiera de dos aprovechamientos forestales de la concesión comunitaria de San Miguel, Petén, Guatemala.* CATIE, Turrialba, Costa Rica.

Aguilar, J. M., and M. A. Aguilar. 1992. *Arboles de la Biosfera Maya, Petén: Guía para las especies del Parque Nacional Tikal.* CECON, Guatemala City, Guatemala.

Bojorquez, S. N., R. A. Cabrera, W. R. Chavez, L. D. Enriquez, H. N. Lopez, and R. A. Sagastume. 1988. *Diagnostico del recurso forestal del departmento de Petén.* IN-AFOR, Guatemala City, Guatemala.

Bray, D. B., M. Carreón, L. Merino, and V. Santos. 1993. On the road to sustainable forestry. *Cultural Survival Quarterly* 17: 38–41.

Buschbacher, R. J. 1990. Natural forest management in the humid tropics: Ecological, social, and economic considerations. *Ambio* 19: 253–258.

CATIE, 1993. *Plan de Manejo Forestal: Unidad de Manejo San Miguel, San Andrés, Petén, Guatemala.* Flores, Guatemala.

Chapela, F. M., and L. P. Lara. 1995. *El Papel de las Comunidades Campesinas en la Conservación de los Bosques.* Consejo Civil Mexicano para la Silvicultura Sostenible. México, D.F.

Colom, E. 1996. *Definición y análisis del marco legal para concesiones de productos forestales no maderables en la Reserva de la Biosfera Maya, Petén, Guatemala.* CATIE, Turrialba, Costa Rica.

Consejo Nacional de Areas Protegidas (CONAP). 1994. *Normas de adjudicación de concesiones.* Guatemala City, Guatemala.

CONAP. 1996. *Plan Maestro: Reserva de la Biosfera Maya.* CATIE, Turrialba, Costa Rica.

Cowgill, U. M. 1961. Soil fertility and the early Maya. *Transactions of the Connecticut Academy of Arts and Sciences.* New Haven, Conn. Vol. 42.

Davis, L. S., and K. N. Johnson. 1987. *Forest Management*, 3rd edition. McGraw-Hill, New York.

Denniston, D. 1994. Defending the land with maps. *World Watch* (January/February): 27–31.

Dugelby, B. L. 1995. *Chicle Latex Extraction in the Maya Biosphere Reserve: Behavioral, Institutional, and Ecological Factors Affecting Sustainability.* Ph.D. dissertation, Duke University, Durham, N.C.

FAO/FYDEP. 1970. *Estudio de preinversion sobre desarrollo forestal: Guatemala.* United Nations Organization for Food and Agriculture, Rome and Guatemala (seven volumes).

Galvez-Ruano, J. J. 1996. *Elementos técnicos para el manejo forestal diversificado de bosques naturales tropicales en San Miguel, Petén, Guatemala.* M.S. thesis, CATIE, Turrialba, Costa Rica.

Gómez-Pompa, A. 1987. Tropical deforestation and Maya silviculture: An ecological paradox. *Tulane Studies in Zoology and Botany* 1: 19–37.

Gretzinger, S. P. 1994. *Response to Disturbance, Community Associations and Successional Processes on Upland Forest in the Maya Biosphere Reserve, Petén, Guatemala.* M.S. thesis, North Carolina State University, Raleigh.

———. 1995. *El manejo forestal comunitario en la selva Maya: La perspectiva campesina.* CATIE, Turrialba, Costa Rica.

———. 1996. *Analisis financiero del manejo forestal comunitario en la Reserva de la Biosfera Maya: Caso de la cooperativa Bethel.* CATIE, Turrialba, Costa Rica.

Gretzinger, S. P., and J. R. Carrera. 1996. *Procedimientos simplificados para el otorgamiento de concesiones forestales en la Reserva de la Biosfera Maya, Guatemala.* CATIE, Turrialba, Costa Rica.

Gretzinger, S. P., M. E. Salazar, M. A. Manzanero, J. R. Carrera, R. A. Morales, and G. I. Pinelo. 1993. *Plan de Manejo Forestal Cooperativa Bethel, La Libertad.* Conservation International, Flores, Guatemala.

Johnston, G., and H. Lorraine. 1994. Analysis of forest management policies in Central America. In *The Green Book*, volume 3: *Applications.* RENARM/USAID. Guatemala City, Guatemala.

MacFarland, C., J. C. Godoy, S. Heckadon, R. Popper, and J. Posadas. 1994. *Evaluation of the Maya Biosphere Project.* Management Systems International, Washington, D.C.

Ministerio de Agricultura, Ganadería y Alimentación (MAGA). 1996. *Política sectorial agrícola de Petén: 1996–2000.* Petén, Guatemala.

Morell, M. 1992. Iniciativas forestales a nivel de campo en America Central y México: El papel de las organizaciones campesinas. *Unasylva* 171: 43.

Nations, J. D., and R. B. Nigh. 1980. The evolutionary potential of Lacandon Maya sustained-yield tropical forest agriculture. *Journal of Anthropological Research* 36: 1–30.

Nations, J. D., and D. I. Komer. 1984. *Conservation in Guatemala.* Center for Human Ecology. Final Report (presented to WWF/US). Austin, Tex.

Pendzich, C., G. Thomas, and T. Wohlgenant. 1994. *The Role of Alternative Conflict Management in Community Forestry.* FAO, Rome.

Pinelo-Morales, G. I. 1997. *Dinamica del bosque Peténero: Avances de investigación en Petén, Guatemala.* Projecto CATIE/CONAP, Petén, Guatemala.

ProPetén. 1993. *Información sobre el sistema de áreas protegidas de la Reserva de la Biosfera Maya, Petén.* Conservation International. Flores, Guatemala.

Purata, S. E. 1986. Floristic and structural changes during old-field succession in the Mexican tropics in relation to site history and species availability. *Journal of Tropical Ecology* 2: 257–280.

Putz, F. E. 1993. *Considerations of the Ecological Foundation of Natural Forest Management in the American Tropics.* Center for Tropical Conservation, Duke University, Durham, N.C.

Reining, C., R. M. Heinzman, M. Cabrera Madrid, S. Lopez, and A. L. Solórzano. 1992. *Productos no maderables de la Reserva de la Biosfera Maya, Petén, Guatemala.* Conservation International, Washington, D.C.

Remmers, G. G. A., and H. de Koeijer. 1992. The T'olché, a Maya system of communally-managed forest belts: The causes and consequences of its disappearance. *Agroforestry Systems* 18: 149–177.

Sader, S. A., T. Sever, J. C. Smoot, and M. Richards. 1994. Forest change estimates for northern Petén region of Guatemala—1986–1990. *Human Ecology* 22: 317–332.

Salazar, M. E., and S. Ruano. 1995. *Desarrollo de un modelo de manejo forestal comunitario en las cooperativas de la region del Usumacinta, estudio de caso: Cooperativa Bethel.* Centro Maya, Santa Elena, Guatemala.

Schwartz, N. B. 1990. *Forest Society: A Social History of Petén, Guatemala.* University of Pennsylvania Press, Philadelphia.

Snook, L. K. 1993. *Stand dynamics of mahogany* (Swietenia macrophylla King) *and associated species after fire and hurricane in the tropical forests of the Yucatán Peninsula, México.* Ph.D. dissertation, Yale University, New Haven, Conn.

Snook, L. K., and A. B. de Jorgenson, eds. 1994. *Madera, chicle, caza y milpa: Contribuciones al manejo integral de las selvas de Quintana Roo, México.* Chetumal, México.

Southgate, D., and M. Basterrechea. 1992. Population growth, public policy and resource degradation: The case of Guatemala. *Ambio* 21: 460–464.

Soza-Manzanero, C. A. 1996. *Factores que Inciden en la Conciencia Ecológica de los Habitantes de la Reserva de la Biosfera Maya en el Departamento de El Petén.* San Carlos University, Guatemala City, Guatemala.

Stanley, S. A., and S. P. Gretzinger. 1996. Timber management of forest patches in Guatemala. Pages 343–365 in *Forest Patches in Tropical Landscapes*, J. Schelhas and R. Greenberg, eds. Island Press, Washington, D.C.

Synnott, T. 1994. *Concesiones de manejo forestal para la Reserva de la Biosfera Maya, Petén, Guatemala.* Technical Report, Tropical Forest Management Trust. Gainesville, Fla.

Urrutia, V. M. 1967. *Corn production and soil fertility changes under shifting cultivation in Uaxactun, Guatemala.* M.S. thesis, University of Florida, Gainesville, Fla.

Chapter 9

Forest Management and Conservation in Belize: A Brief Background

Elizabeth Platt

As part of the Maya Forest, Belize shares many species and communities with its neighbors, Mexico and Guatemala. However, Belize has a unique perspective on the ways in which these species should be managed and conserved—an outgrowth of its special history, which is unlike that of any other nation in Central America. As a result of this history, particularly the establishment of policies that favored utilization of a small, select range of timber resources rather than promoting agriculture, the country has been left with extensive, relatively diverse forests that include healthy populations of species that are threatened or extinct elsewhere in the region. A commonwealth country with a parliamentary government modeled on the British system, Belize also has been spared many of the internal conflicts that have adversely affected both the citizens and the natural resources of neighboring Mexico and Guatemala (see Ponciano, this volume; Galletti, this volume). However, though the land under forest is still fairly extensive, external and internal pressures to convert it to other uses are growing. Moreover, the forests have been high-graded—that is, stripped of all marketable individuals of preferred species, leaving behind the less-valuable species—to the point that valuable species, such as mahogany and cedar, are fairly rare. Like its northern and western neighbors, Belize has reached a point at which direct intervention is necessary if these species are to recover and if remaining forests are to remain productive.

Historical Background

The area of Belize was originally claimed by the Spanish as part of the territory comprising Guatemala. Like the Petén, Belize was not formally settled by the Spanish in the seventeenth and eighteenth centuries. The Spanish concentrated most of the military and economic activities of colonization in centers such as Merida and Antigua, none of which were sufficiently close to the Belizean coast by standard means of transportation of the time to allow expansion into this region. The Spanish ignored the lowland areas, primarily because this land was considered marginal at best for agriculture, but perhaps also because military dominance over the indigenous Maya residents of the lowland forests remained tenuous until the end of the seventeenth century. Although the Spanish logged significant quantities of mahogany during the sixteenth century, most of it was extracted from Cuba, the West Indies, and Mexico (Lamb 1966).

In the late seventeenth and eighteenth centuries, small British logging settlements were established along the Belize River (Finamore 1994). The British loggers, some of whom were former buccaneers, originally extracted logwood (*Haematoxylum campechianum*), a tree with a dark purple heartwood valued for making red dye (Craig 1969; Hartshorn et al. 1984). Because this species grows in low-lying swamps (*bajos*) and logging technology of the day relied upon the presence of rivers to transport the logs, the first British settlements were concentrated along the watersheds and stayed relatively small and ephemeral (Finamore 1994). However, as demand for logwood declined, British efforts shifted to logging mahogany (*Swietenia macrophylla*), a wood highly prized in shipbuilding for both its durability and the ease with which it could be worked (Lamb 1966). British logging settlements encountered some opposition by the Spanish colonial government, but treaties between Britain and Spain forbade permanent agricultural settlements, and conflicts were limited to occasional raids and skirmishes (Hartshorn et al. 1984). As Spanish influence in the Caribbean waned during the eighteenth century, permanent logging operations, owned by British-born timber barons and manned primarily by slaves imported from Africa and the Caribbean, became common. Mahogany resources eventually became the justification for formal annexation of Belize in 1862 (Lamb 1966; Hartshorn et al. 1984), at which point a de facto British colony had been in existence for some time. Although the Spanish disputed the British claim—a dispute that continued in spirit until formal recognition of Belize by Guatemala in 1991—the area eventually became British Honduras, a legal colony of Great Britain, which it remained until independence was granted in 1981.

Evolution of Colonial Forest Policy

During the initial, informal stage of the colony, mahogany extraction was somewhat arbitrary. Cutting rights for specific areas called "works" were often allocated on the basis of wealth and political influence (Nicolait and Franklin 1995). Many of the strongest logging barons were also merchants who controlled the importation of goods on which the colony depended. Most of the reasonably accessible tracts of land containing mahogany stands were bought or claimed by such individuals early in the colony's history; by the time a formal governing forest department was created in 1922, nearly all of northern Belize and the richest mahogany stands of southern Belize were in private hands. As a result, most of the government-owned forests found in Belize today are located in the south, and much of that is restricted to the less accessible lowland areas, the highland regions where mahogany is less common, and parts of the southern coast and swamplands (Arnold et al. 1989).

Formalization of the British claim to Belize led to a more structured forest management policy. Much of this policy was based on experience that had been gained by colonial administrations in other tropical colonies, particularly India, during the eighteenth and nineteenth centuries (Primack 1993). Timber exploitation had been the preeminent resource in these colonies, leading the British colonial governments to develop strong forestry departments and encourage scientific investigation of forest and ecosystem dynamics. Belize ultimately benefited greatly from the experience and scientific knowledge obtained in other tropical colonies. These experiences taught the Belizean colonial government the value of practices such as leaving stands of forest intact to maintain rainfall levels and prevent erosion (Hartshorn et al. 1984; Primack 1993).

Some of these practices were codified in colonial law well in advance of independence. The Forest Department was founded in 1922, shortly before a permanent forest estate was formally established to protect remaining public lands (Johnson and Chaffey 1973; Nicolait and Franklin 1995). Control of timber extraction was instituted by the Forest Department almost from its inception; department records from as early as 1925 indicate the establishment of a formal concession system to regulate and collect royalties from timber operations (Johnson and Chaffey 1973). As the timber industry grew, other methods of forest management were explored. For instance, natural forest silviculture was investigated in the 1920s (Stevenson 1927; Johnson and Chaffey 1973), while a few plantations of pine (*Pinus caribaea*), cedar (*Cedrela odorata*), and other valuable timber species were established in the 1940s and 1950s to prevent overexploitation of commercial species in natural forests (Johnson and Chaffey 1973; Arnold et al. 1989). Various pieces of legislation were specifically aimed at promoting sustainable timber harvest: the 1954 Forest Policy of British Honduras included recommendations that land be set aside to conserve forest both for "sustained yield management" and for protection of watersheds and climate (Arnold et al. 1989). Other laws were explicitly conservation-oriented, emphasizing ecological concerns rather than economic ones. The Forest Ordinance of 1927, for example, established a legal basis for the creation of protected areas, legitimizing the Silkgrass Forest

Reserve established five years earlier, and furthermore called for conservation to coincide with development of the forestry industry (Nicolait and Franklin 1995)—although it is important to note that "conservation" probably was used in the sense of maintaining viable habitat for timber species, rather than in the currently popular sense of preserving communities or maintaining biological diversity. Timber development and conservation were simultaneous objectives; one goal mentioned in the 1954 Forest Policy decree was to "bring about an increased appreciation of the need for and aims of forest conservation amongst the general public . . . and [in] the schools" (Arnold et al. 1989).

Despite policies aimed at protecting timber resources, the main species of interest to loggers, mahogany (characteristically located in subtropical moist forests of northern and western Belize) and pine (primarily found in the western portion of Mountain Pine Ridge and in an extensive pine savanna north of the Western Highway), declined in the 1950s (Hartshorn et al. 1984); 300 years of continuous logging had virtually exhausted these species. In the face of this decline, in the late 1950s the colonial government made a decision that would strongly affect the way in which forests contributed to the national economy: it cut back dramatically on its investment in forestry, reducing the overall importance of the Forestry Department in the colonial budget, despite recommendations for continued management (Hartshorn et al. 1984; Arnold et al. 1989). This action had repercussions that modern Belize still feels: programs aimed at replenishing depleted stocks of timber species were ended, scientific studies were continued only on a sporadic basis, fire prevention programs were halted, and efforts to oversee use of public lands decreased. In these circumstances, replenishment of the depleted forests became difficult, if not impossible, under the colonial administration. More importantly, however, the gutted Forestry Department was too small to perform many of the management and conservation functions for which it was originally created. As a result, many activities and restrictions mandated by law, such as enforcement of cutting limits, could not be pursued for lack of manpower—a problem that continues today (Hartshorn et al. 1984; Nicolait and Franklin 1995).

Culture and Economy in Modern Belize: Where Do Forests Fit In?

In the brief overview of Belizean colonial history above, several factors stand out: first, throughout all stages of the colony's development, no policy of agricultural expansion and large-scale settlement of the countryside was ever promoted by colonial administrators. This factor stands in sharp contrast to both Guatemala and Mexico, where agrarian policies were aggressively pursued, first by the Spanish, and later by the independent governments. Second, although a certain amount of uncontrolled forest exploitation occurred before the formal British claim to Belize was established, the colonial government recognized the value of intact forests and began a concerted effort to manage forest resources fairly early in the country's history—well in advance of such efforts elsewhere in Central America. Finally, Belize has not encountered the same scale of forest conversion seen in Mexico and highland Guatemala for the simple reason that Belize's colonial and modern population has never been as dense as its neighbors', although recent decades have seen a rapid growth of population, primarily a result of immigration from other areas of Central America (Hartshorn et al. 1984). Lower population means that subsistence farming using milpa techniques does little damage to forests (Whitacre, this volume), and that large-scale agricultural holdings are less likely to be at maximum production, as has indeed been the case in Belize throughout much of its history (Hartshorn et al. 1984).

These factors meant that by 1981 a newly independent Belize had largely escaped the deforestation seen in Mexico and in highland Guatemala. Though certain species had suffered from overexploitation, the Belizean forests were still basically intact. The one significant government action that adversely affected the condition of Belize's forests—namely, the decision to drastically cut back funding for the Forest Department, leaving only a skeleton staff insufficient to fulfill the department's intended functions of regulatory enforcement and scientific study—occurred relatively recently, a response to declines in productivity of the primary timber species. In spirit, the policies of the colonial government were conscientious efforts to manage forest resources in a sustainable manner; in practice, however, implementation of these policies suffered from insufficient staffing and funding for enforcement.

Unfortunately, the decline of the timber industry in the 1950s meant that the economy and culture of modern Belize has become increasingly oriented toward industries that are not conducive to forest management. As timber extraction declined in productivity, it was replaced primarily by agriculture. The most serious trend was the establishment of large-scale, permanent fields of cash crops such as sugarcane in the north and citrus and bananas in the south. A significant number of Belizean men and teenage boys earn at least part of their yearly income working either as cane cutters or as truck drivers transporting loads of cane to the Belize Sugar Industry's single processing plant near Orange Walk. Both jobs are seasonal, and income levels may vary depending on the year-to-year changes in planting and harvesting, so cane harvesting and hauling may not provide a secure or steady source of income for many workers. Moreover, Mennonite communities that traditionally farm permanent fields of vegetables for their own use and for market have expanded into cash crops such as sorghum, and other local inhabitants have plantations of citrus and cacao. Some of these agricultural developments are of questionable sustainability; for example, citrus groves planted on poor-quality soils in southern Belize are unlikely to thrive there (Arnold et al. 1989). More recently, efforts to promote tourism based upon ecological and archaeological attractions have developed (see Matola and Platt, this volume; Horwich and Lyon, this volume). These efforts hold promise, as sites such as Lamanai, Caracol, and Lubaantun are both attractive and reasonably accessible, but at present the most advanced tourist outfits focus upon the coastal cays, which has helped raise popular consciousness regarding the fragility of the reef but does not advance forest conservation.

Transition to Independence: Changes in Forestry in Modern Belize

The last important piece of colonial forestry legislation was the Forests Act (Chapter 176, Laws of Belize, 1980), which conferred authority upon government ministries to regulate the use of forests on both public and private lands and to create forest reserves by decree upon "Crown Lands" (now called "National Lands") (Nicolait and Franklin 1995). Following its independence in 1981, Belize built upon this legacy of the colonial government by creating the National Park System Act of 1981 to provide the legal basis for establishing national parks, natural monuments, wildlife sanctuaries, and nature reserves. A series of acts protecting threatened wildlife and specialized ecosystems such as mangroves followed during the 1980s, as the new Belizean government took stock of its resources and sought to protect them (Hartshorn et al. 1984; Arnold et al. 1989).

Yet the major problem, enforcement of forestry policies, was never addressed. Though timber extraction on public land is only done under concession licenses administered by the Forest Department, it is common knowledge that government officials are spread too thin to effectively monitor logging operations. The Forest Department makes as efficient use of its limited personnel as possible; the number of trees to be felled in a given concession is determined by Forest Department officials prior to the actual cutting, and only trees that meet the minimum diameter requirements can be extracted. Diameter limits are designed to make certain that loggers leave some reproductive individuals as seed sources for regeneration, and concessionaires are permitted to extract only those trees marked by the Forest Department during the site assessment (Hartshorn et al. 1984). Despite these precautions, there are too few foresters to ensure that loggers adhere to the cutting limits for particular species; where valuable species such as mahogany and cedar are concerned, loggers may take a short-term, profit-oriented perspective, knowing that chances are good that they will not get caught—and, as Forest Department officers cannot be on site for all logging operations, the loggers may be correct. At best, the officers can spot-check the timber during transport; if the loggers have exceeded cutting limits, any harm done is a fait accompli, and there is little the Forest Department officials can do about it. Forest Department reg-

ulations alone cannot prevent poor logging practices without adequate enforcement, and unscrupulous timber companies may attempt fraud and
bribery on the occasions that they are inspected (Nicolait and Franklin 1995).

The enforcement problem is complicated by lack of a clear-cut division of
responsibilities among ministries and departments designated to oversee natural resources. Assignment of departments to individual ministries occurs at
the discretion of the prime minister, which in theory means that oversight of
natural resources can vary among ministries from one administration to the
next. Currently, creation and oversight of protected areas is divided among
three departments—Forestry, Fisheries, and Archaeology—while responsibility for protection and "rational use" of natural resources lies with the Department of the Environment (Nicolait and Franklin 1995). Compounding matters, these four departments report to different ministries: the Forestry
Department works within the Ministry of Natural Resources, while Fisheries,
Archaeology, and Environment all report to the Ministry of Tourism and the
Environment. Such division of labor must at least occasionally create situations where two departments either are working at cross-purposes or are du-
plicating each others' efforts. There is also a certain amount of inherent conflict in these divisions: for example, mangrove forests often act as hatching
grounds for many species of fish; so should they be administered by Forestry or
by Fisheries? And if a government-owned tract of forest contains valuable
timber, but logging would damage a unique archaeological site, which department—Forestry or Archaeology—has the authority to make a decision on
whether or not to cut timber? Such questions are made more urgent by the
fact that the "minister in charge" of National Lands (a definition that changes
according to the wishes of the current administration) has the power to reverse the protected status of reserve lands.

Tropical Forestry Action Plan

In 1989 Belize commissioned a Tropical Forestry Action Plan (TFAP) to be
carried out by a team composed of experts from Britain, Canada, the United
States, and the United Nations Food and Agriculture Organization (Arnold
et al. 1989). This report observed that a sound legal structure for conservation
and sustainable forestry had existed in Belize for decades, but that the poorly
funded and understaffed Forest Department was incapable of implementing
the existing laws. One notable problem cited by the TFAP was the de-reser-
vation of protected lands. Ministers in charge of national protected lands
have the ability to remove the restrictions for resource exploitation when
"overriding public interest" dictated that such action was appropriate—but
only after Forest Department personnel had collected adequate data on the
current condition of the land, assessed the potential impacts of new land uses
upon species there, and determined whether proposed uses of that land were

appropriate for the region. In practice, these precautions were virtually ignored; protected lands often were released for private use in a haphazard, arbitrary fashion irrespective of their ecological value, in large part because there were too few Forest Department officials to keep track of, much less slow down, the pace of development (Arnold et al. 1989). In short, forest management became a matter of policy but not practice, leading to ill-considered land conversion and waste of potentially valuable timber.

The TFAP recommended a number of changes to halt the trend toward forest degradation. First, the "high-grading" method by which most logging was done does not encourage regeneration of the preferred species. Because mahogany and other valuable species depend on high light levels, they do not regenerate well in the small gaps created by this system of timber extraction (Flachsenberg and Galletti, this volume; Snook, this volume). A more viable practice proposed by the TFAP would be to exploit a wider range of species so that forest gaps from logging are larger, allowing greater regeneration of high-quality timber. Monocyclic logging, rather than the polycyclic management system that had been in place, was deemed more appropriate to maintaining stocks of commercial species. In support of this point, the TFAP investigators observed that Belize's forests were adapted to catastrophic disturbance caused by occasional hurricanes and therefore regenerated best under conditions of high disturbance (Arnold et al. 1989). In conjunction with such intensive logging activity, however, the TFAP proposed increasing silvicultural research to determine the best methods of restocking the valuable species, as the available information was anecdotal at best (Brokaw et al., this volume).

A second proposal was to create the industrial capacity to process timber into high-value end products. It has been pointed out in other chapters (Galletti, this volume; Ponciano, this volume; Chayax Huex et al., this volume) that sale of raw timber brings the least revenue to the owners of forested land and therefore is not an effective or efficient way to transform timber resources into capital. Unfortunately, creation of processing plants requires capital, which most Belizeans—like the Peteneros and Mexican *ejidatarios*—simply do not have in sufficient quantity to support the cost of a brand new mill. The TFAP solution to this problem was to make gradual improvements by investing in small changes, purchasing used equipment from North American or European mills, and most importantly, investing in education and training for mill operators (Arnold et al. 1989). As mills gradually upgrade to the ability to produce high-value end products, they will require less timber to produce higher profits.

A final priority for the TFAP was increased efforts at data collection and scientific analyses. Of the three countries that comprise the Maya Forest, Belize is perhaps the best studied as a result of efforts by the colonial government (e.g., Lamb 1946; Wright et al. 1959), yet there is still too little information for effective resource management. Information on forest composition, growth rates and seedling requirements of important timber species, and the effects on regeneration of different land-use regimes are all topics of vital importance to the future sustainability of Belize's forests that require further investigation. In recognizing this fact, the TFAP sounded a precautionary note against the all-too-common practice of simply granting permission for resource extraction without taking into account its potential effects on the environment.

Beyond TFAP: Priorities for Belize in the Twenty-First Century

The Tropical Forestry Action Plan is now nearly a decade old. In the intervening years, a number of significant changes have taken place. Most important of these is the fact that the country has gradually gained a reputation as a superior tourist destination, a process accelerated by the publicity surrounding the Ruta Maya concept (Garrett 1989), which became widely known shortly after the TFAP was completed. Much of the tourism generated by this publicity focuses upon so-called archaeo-ecotourism or adventure tourism based upon Maya ruins and tropical forest species. This industry holds a strong potential to generate income—*if* the forests themselves remain intact to draw the tourists. This potential, however, can only be realized if TFAP's proposals to maximize production of timber by making more intensive use of forest species are carried out with an eye to maintaining a good environment for tourism. Moreover, timber production, no matter how carefully managed, has additional environmental repercussions that may be problematic. Even when programs to reseed or reforest logged areas are present and functional, there is still a possibility of topsoil erosion, which can lead to siltation of rivers and coastal waters (Primack 1993)—a potentially serious situation in light of the fact that Belize's coastal waters contain a major portion of the second-largest coral reef ecosystem in the world. Aside from its role as a major tourist attraction, the reef is home to many species of fish and coral, some of which are endangered or even extinct in other parts of the Caribbean (Primack 1993). Thus, logging that is not undertaken with considerable care could have far-reaching implications for both the economic and ecological future of Belize.

The TFAP's assertion that information collection is a priority is still valid; even if the Belizean government had the resources to embark on large-scale ecological and managerial research projects, it would still take decades to acquire comprehensive and detailed information given the sheer number of species that exist in these forests. Some of the missing information has been filled in through the efforts of nongovernmental organizations such as the Belize Audubon Society and the Programme for Belize. To its credit, the Belizean government has actively encouraged such efforts. For this reason, in spite of its budgetary constraints, Belize has never suffered from a lack of personnel conducting research; a small army of forest researchers, botanists, ornithologists, archaeologists, and other specialists descend upon Belize each year, drawn by the wealth of information still hidden in the forests, funded by universities, private foundations, and government scientific and cultural organizations such as the U.S. National Science Foundation. This situation benefits Belize because the data generated from such foreign-funded projects are automatically made available to Belize's government agencies—interim and final reports are mandated in government-issued research permits, although most data are offered to appropriate departments as a professional courtesy anyway. However, the hidden drawback to this setup is that data analysis generally takes place in the researchers' institute of origin; although the information is returned to Belize, one valuable aspect—the learning process that occurs when the data are analyzed—departs the country when the researchers leave. This problem may be addressed through sponsorship of promising young Belizean students to university programs abroad, and through advanced degree programs for experienced departmental personnel, both of which have been undertaken to a limited extent as opportunities and funds present themselves. However, the urgent need for trained local researchers, both for Belize and for the Maya Forest as a whole, cannot be overstated.

The TFAP focuses on increasing the productivity of its forests in terms of timber extraction. However, several additional economic uses of the forest should be considered, as mentioned in the TFAP. While it is unrealistic to imagine that timber production will be excised from the Belizean economy, it is perfectly reasonable to suggest that perhaps timber, historically large in this small country's livelihood, should become in the modern era one piece of the total economic pie. Forests do have a role to play in the Belizean economy, but the challenge is to create a system involving national parks, watershed management, nature reserves, ecotourism, and nontimber forest products in which the presence of healthy, well-managed forests is the source of local income.

Acknowledgments

Thanks are due to three anonymous reviewers whose thoughtful, detailed criticisms greatly improved the chapter. Richard Primack and David Bray provided invaluable advice, and Nick Brokaw kindly assisted in obtaining sources. Finally, Dan Finamore unintentionally taught me more than he may realize about Belizean colonial history, for which I am grateful.

References

Arnold, J. E. M., F. B. Armitage, W. L. Bender, N. V. L. Brokaw, H. Hilmi, J. R. Palmer, and S. L. Pringle. 1989. *Belize Tropical Forestry Action Plan*. Overseas Development Administration, London, U.K.

Craig, A. K. 1969. Logwood as a factor in the settlement of British Honduras. *Carib Studies* 9: 53–62.

Finamore, D. 1994. *Sailors and Slaves on the Wood-Cutting Frontier: Archaeology of the British Bay Settlement, Belize*. Ph.D. dissertation, Boston University, Boston, Mass.

Garrett, W. E. 1989. La Ruta Maya. *National Geographic* 176: 424–479.

Hartshorn, G., L. Nicolait, L. Hartshorn, G. Bevier, R. Brightman, J. Cal, A. Cawich, W. Davidson, R. DuBois, C. Dyer, J. Gibson, W. Hawley, J. Leonard, R. Nicolait, D. Weyer, H. White, and C. Wright. 1984. *Belize Country Environmental Profile: A Field Study*. Robert Nicolait and Associates Ltd., Belize City, Belize.

Johnson, M. S., and D. R. Chaffey. 1973. An Inventory of the Chiquibul Forest Reserve, Belize. Land Resource Study No. 14, ODA, Surbiton, U.K.

Lamb, A. F. A. 1946. Notes on forty-two secondary hardwood timbers of British Honduras. Forest Department Bulletin No. 1. Belmopan, Belize.

Lamb, F. B. 1966. Mahogany of Tropical America: Its Ecology and Management. University of Michigan Press, Ann Arbor, Mich.

Nicolait, L., and S. Franklin. 1995. Forestry and Protected Areas Policies of Belize. Report prepared for the U.S. Man and the Biosphere Program, U.S. Department of State, Washington, D.C.

Primack, R. B. 1993. *Essentials of Conservation Biology*. Sinauer Press, Sunderland, Mass.

Stevenson, N. S. 1927. Silvicultural treatment of mahogany forests in British Honduras. *Empire Forestry Journal* 6: 219–227.

Wright, A. C. S., D. H. Romney, R. H. Arbuckle, and V. E. Vial. 1959. Land in British Honduras. Colonial Research Publication No. 24. Her Majesty's Stationery Office, London.

Part III

Nontimber Forest Products in Conservation Strategies

The preceding section addressed a topic of paramount importance in conservation and management of the Maya Forest: the ways in which the three nations of the region seek to alter their timber extraction strategies in order to prevent destruction of the forest. Yet we must not lose sight of the fact that there is far more to the Maya Forest, or indeed any tropical forest, than mere timber. In the most literal sense, we must not become blind to the forest by seeing only the trees. Within any tropical forest exist countless species of plants, animals, insects—even microbes—that also are vital components of the forest ecosystem. For this reason, studies of these species are equally important as studies of the valuable timber species; if we ignore them, we run the risk of inadvertently damaging a vital link in the ecological chain.

Of equal importance is the fact that some of these nontimber species are extracted by local people for various products that are important both for sale in the marketplace and for household use. Some conservationists have seen in this fact an opportunity to promote nontimber forest products (NTFPs) as a less destructive source of income for local people than timber harvesting. This strategy rests on the assumption that NTFP extraction is inherently sustainable—and on the surface, why shouldn't that assumption seem valid? After all, haven't local people been extracting these products for centuries, or even (as is demonstrably the case in the Maya Forest) millennia?

On closer inspection, however, the assumption clearly has several flaws: first, markets for these products may not be well developed, especially if the species or product is newly identified as a marketable commodity, a problem identified by Belsky and Siebert in their analysis of tie-tie crafts in Belize. Second, the scale of extraction for market may be vastly greater than extraction for household use; O'Hara's discussion of *huano* (*Sabal mauritiiformis*) monitoring, for example, suggests that the growing use of this resource for commercial construction may place pressure on the species far beyond that of household use. Yet previous analyses of NTFPs (Godoy and Bawa 1993; Ganesan 1993) indicate that even household use of forest species might not be sustainable in all cases. As pointed out by Bawa and Godoy (1993: 216),

> Scholars assume that because rural people have harvested a product for a long time, harvesting must be sustainable. Sustainability can only be determined by directly measuring the rate of extraction and comparing it to the rate of natural replacement, however. Few natural scientists have measured sustainability directly, whether with plants or with animals.

The chapter by Jorgenson seeks to partially address this problem for the Maya Forest by examining how hunting by local people in Quintana Roo affects the populations of game species in the area.

Finally, as NTFPs become more widely used and extracted, there is a potential for extraction methods to become more intensive and harmful to the species involved. Dugelby's discussion of chicle harvesting demonstrates the problems that can occur even when a product has a well-established market and is demonstrably sustainable under the right conditions. Competition for limited resources, poor regulation of resource extraction, and lack of understanding of the species' biology and ecology can contribute to direct harm to the species involved. An especially pertinent point is the fact that successful chicle harvesting must be done with care and consideration for the future well-being of both the harvesters' colleagues and the trees themselves.

Despite these obstacles, nontimber forest products still have a promising role to play in conservation of the Maya Forest. There is no question that any factor that demonstrates that standing forests can provide equal or greater economic rewards to local people than clearing the forests will assist local people, government officials, and conservation organizations in conserving these forests; indeed, though government policies have been slow to recognize that anything but cleared land has value, local people are unlikely to need many incentives to leave the forests intact beyond the hope of a secure, steady income. The key to successful use of NTFPs in conservation is integrating them with other industries to increase the forest's economic value. Though it is unreasonable to see NTFPs as the "savior" of the forest, when considered in conjunction with industries such as ecotourism and selective logging that also rely upon intact forests, these extractive industries represent a significant argument in favor of maintaining forests. To this end, Barborak discusses the ways in which buffer zones in the Maya Forest permit a balance between "locking up" forests for conservation and permitting controlled, diversified economic activities—a strategy that allows people to benefit from forest resources while preventing wholesale destruction of the forest.

References

Ganesan, B. 1993. Extraction of nontimber forest products, including fodder and fuelwood, in Mudumalai, India. *Economic Botany* 47: 268–274.

Godoy, R. A., and K. S. Bawa. 1993. The economic value and sustainable harvest of plants and animals from the tropical forest: Assumptions, hypotheses, and methods. *Economic Botany* 47: 215–219.

Chapter 10

Nontimber Forest Products in Community Development and Conservation: The Palm *Desmoncus schippii* in Gales Point, Belize

Jill M. Belsky and Stephen F. Siebert

Nontimber forest products (NTFPs) have been advocated as a means to promote forest conservation and community development because of their widespread use and value, as well as their purported potential for sustainable harvesting with few adverse effects on other flora and fauna (Nepsted and Schwartzman 1992). Enthusiasm for NTFPs in community development and conservation stems in large part from reports extolling their high economic value. For example, Peters, Gentry, and Mendelsohn (1989) reported that the net value of fruit and latex extraction in the upper Amazon was $6,330/ha, while Balick and Mendelsohn (1992) noted that the current value of medicinal plant harvesting in western Belize was $726/ha. In contrast, LaFrankie (1994) found that sustained production of wild cinnamon (*Cinnomomum mollissimum*) and incense (*Aquilaria malaccensis*) in Malaysia was worth only about $0.10/ha/year, while sustained-yield harvesting of rattan (*Calamus exilis*) in Sumatra is estimated to generate only about $1.50/ha/year (Siebert 1995).

In theory, when extraction of a species that exhibits high population densities, year-round product availability, and strong demand has little adverse effect on other flora and fauna, this species could be expected to have high extractive development potential (Salafsky, Dugelby, and Terborgh 1993). However, in many studies the potential value of NTFPs is exaggerated by the assumption of unrealistically high discount rates, unlimited market demands, no transportation difficulties, and an assumed absence of product substitution potential (Phillips 1993; Tremaine 1993). NTFPs also are rarely the mainstay of the rural household or community economy, serving primarily to supplement other resource and income flows during particular seasons in the year (Arnold 1995). Collectors and NTFP artisans frequently are farmers with high labor demands tied to agricultural calendars, or landless workers who take wage work whenever it is available (Siebert and Belsky 1985; Richards 1993; Belsky and Siebert 1995).

The unwillingness of states to recognize and legalize customary resource tenure and community management institutions has led to the breakdown of local access and management rules, especially when harvesting of NTFPs occurs in protected areas or areas subjected to commercial logging pressures (McCay and Acheson 1987; Berkes 1989; Poffenberger 1990; Peluso 1992). Case studies from around the world have shown that villages with strong community management institutions and secure property rights have sustained access to and use of forests for generations (Poffenberger 1990). However, political, economic, and social changes within and beyond communities have led to the loss of traditional methods of access control, usufruct allocation, and conflict resolution. Overuse and degradation frequently accompany the progressive transfer of resource management decisions to central states, and many previously common-managed resources now operate essentially as unregulated "open access" resources, despite laws and policies that constrain their use (i.e., "paper parks") (Poffenberger 1990). In other cases, possibly due to low population densities, limited product demand, extensive resource frontiers, and/or particular cultural traditions and development histories, no common-managed resources or common management institutions have developed. Whatever their etiology, the lack of management efficacy—whether state- or community-based—seriously threatens the viability of implementing sustained-yield harvest guidelines for NTFPs, even if they are ecologically possible.

Analysis of an NTFP currently at a low level of use in a community in Belize demonstrates that creation of an economically viable industry is not simply a matter of identifying an underutilized, easily renewed resource. We examined current NTFP extraction of tie-tie (*Desmoncus schippii*) a common liana species, used in basketry by the Belizean community of Gales Point. By combining ecological research into the reproductive and growth habits of the plant with sociological data gathered from individuals who utilize the resource, we assessed the viability of tie-tie extraction for a potentially expanded NTFP industry.

Species Characteristics

Desmoncus is a diverse genus of climbing palms found throughout the Neotropics from Mexico southward to Brazil and Bolivia. The group is poorly known botanically, but it may include as many as 61 species (Uhl and Dransfield 1987). *Desmoncus* spp. are reported to be most common in lowland forests, particularly open areas and along river banks, and are rarer in the undergrowth of closed canopy forests (Uhl and Dransfield 1987). Henderson and Chavez (1993) reported that *Desmoncus* spp. appear to prefer light gaps and other open areas in western Amazonia. Similarly, Quero (1992) found that *D. quasillarius* and *D. chinantlensis* are widespread in disturbed areas and secondary forests throughout southern Mexico.

Canes from *Desmoncus* have been used for centuries by forest-dwelling and rural people. Over a century ago, Alfred Russell Wallace (1853) noted that *D. macroacanthus* was used by Amazonian Indians in the construction of manioc pressing grates. The anthropologist Claude Levi-Strauss (1952) observed *Desmoncus* spp. use in basketry among South American Indians. More recently, Balick (1979) reported widespread *Desmoncus* spp. use by Guahibo Indians in the Amazon Basin, Williams (1981) noted the use of *Desmoncus* spp. throughout Central America for weaving and basketry, and, in a comprehensive review, Phillips (1993) reported that *Desmoncus* spp. provide fiber for weaving and cottage industries as well as edible fruit. In Belize, *Desmoncus* cane is used in whole or split form for weaving baskets and handicrafts.

Despite the widespread distribution of *Desmoncus* spp. and its economic importance, the group remains poorly known ecologically (Henderson and Chavez 1993) and economically. In this chapter, we assess the ecology and use of *Desmoncus schippii* Burret (known locally as "tie-tie") and its potential integration with forest conservation and community development efforts in Belize.

Research Site and Study Methods

We selected Gales Point, Central Belize, a rural Creole village located on a narrow peninsula on the Southern Lagoon about 30 km south of Belize City (three hours by small boat) (see Map 1 in Introduction to this volume), to conduct research on *D. schippii* because of recent activities by the Belizean government and foreign consultants to promote community-based ecotourism and wildlife conservation in the area (GPPC 1992; Horwich et al. 1993; Horwich and Boardman 1993). The natural attractions of Gales Point are many. Of utmost conservation importance are one of the largest Central American populations of the West Indian manatee (*Trichecus manatus*), a hawksbill turtle (*Enetmochelys imbricata*) nesting beach, and waterfowl rookeries (GPPC 1992). In 1992, Gales Point Village and the surrounding estuaries, karst hills, lowland savanna, and broadleaf forests were designated by the government of Belize a special conservation and development zone (known as the Manatee Conservation and Development Area). Volunteers from nongovernmental organizations (NGOs) such as Community Conservation Consultants and governmental officials are planning the Manatee Community Reserve (MCR), 170,000 acres of public and private land and three large lagoons (Horwich et al. 1993). The specific tourism and local development objectives of the MCR are to develop a locally supported reserve that integrates the use of private and government-owned lands and ensures sustainable use of resources; to maintain and strengthen the local rural culture; and to develop supplementary sources of income through tourism. Integrating tourism with economic development that builds on local culture is a major objective of the MCR, as stated by Horwich et al. (1993): "The sanctuary will concentrate on developing tourism around the community lifestyle, giving tourists an authentic experience of village life, something like the exposure to Creole culture at the Community Baboon Sanctuary."

Since 1992, the planners have worked with interested residents of Gales Point to develop community management institutions built around the model of legal cooperatives to organize and equitably distribute access to and benefits from local ecotourism activities including bed-and-breakfast accommodations, boat operation and tour guiding, farming, and handicrafts based largely on *Desmoncus* basket weaving.

In 1993, 1994, and 1996 the authors and ten Belizean and American students lived in Gales Point and collected data on household assets, livelihood strategies, decision making underlying participation in tourist activities, concerns related to community-managed tourist institutions, and conservation attitudes. The field research methodologies included participant observation, key informant interviews, oral histories, and, in 1994, in-depth household interviews using standard random sampling techniques and a questionnaire developed by one of the authors. Thirty-four households comprise the survey sample (or 56% of 61 permanent-resident households) and included all members of the bed and breakfast and craft associations; the rest were chosen randomly from the remaining village household population.

Ecological research on *D. schippii* was conducted in Gales Point as well as in four other forest types in Belize to estimate the abundance, distribution, and growth patterns of *D. schippii* plants and canes (individual plants produce multiple canes). Twenty-five 10 x 10 m sample plots were established at random intervals off line transects in each site, providing a total of 0.25 ha of forest sampled. Within each plot, *D. schippii* plants and canes were counted and cane lengths were measured.

Ecological Potential for Sustained Yield Management of *Desmoncus* spp.

Desmoncus schippii plants are abundant and widely distributed in a variety of forest types in Belize (Table 10.1). In a cane collection area near Gales Point, we observed an average of 228 *D. schippii* plants, 92 harvestable canes, and a

Table 10.1. *Desmoncus schippii*. Plant and cane populations in Belizean forests. Numbers indicate the mean number/ha (N = 25 sample plots/site).

	Plants	Harvestable Canes	Meters of Cane
Río Bravo broadleaf forest	172	104	952
Río Bravo secondary broadleaf forest	84	532	4816
Mountain Pine Ridge montane forest on limestone	160	216	2264
Manatee broadleaf forest on karst hills	228	92	844
Cockscomb secondary broadleaf forest	40	72	720

total of 844 m of cane per ha. Plant populations varied by forest type from 40 to 228 individuals per hectare; the number of harvestable canes varies from 72 to 532 per hectare, and the amount of cane ranges from 720 to 4,816 m per hectare in forests from southern to northern Belize. The number and amount of harvestable canes (i.e., those greater than 5 m in length) was highest in disturbed sites (compare the well-developed broadleaf forest in Río Bravo with the young secondary forest in the same location, Table 10.1). In fact, significantly greater numbers of plants and harvestable canes were observed in disturbed environments with high light intensity (e.g., canopy gaps) than in undisturbed, low-light environments ($P < 0.05$). These data confirm observations that *D. schippii* appears to prefer disturbed and early successional sites. This preference may bode well for the future availability of cane supplies, as the area of disturbed forest is increasing in Belize.

Use and Value of *Desmoncus schippii*

Desmoncus schippii canes were collected or used by approximately 35% of the households interviewed in Gales Point (N = 34). Respondents reported that at least one member of the household either collected or wove *D. schippii* during the previous year. Women are the primary weavers, producing baskets, hats, and handicrafts predominantly intended for sale to tourists. A few of the older residents (including one man) also weave baskets for home use.

Most weavers rely on one of five young village men to collect canes from nearby forests, although male family members collect canes while hunting or farming in some instances. A common order is one to two dozen vines (approximately 3 to 4 m each) worth about U.S. $4 to $5 in total (U.S. $1 = BZ

$2). The whole cane is cut lengthwise into strips; one to two dozen vines are sufficient to make about four small baskets worth $2.50 to $7.50, or one large basket worth $7.50 to $25. Cane length, basket size, and quality vary enormously, making it difficult to specify size, price, and cane requirements precisely.

Of the approximately one-third of village households involved in the trade, approximately 46% reported collecting or weaving *D. schippii* crafts "often" (i.e., at least once each month during the previous year); 54% said they did so "rarely" or only a few times during the previous year. Whether a household collects or weaves cane (at either level) was not significantly related to class differences, defined in terms of the households' self-identified level of food security. Some older residents noted that they wove baskets for household use before plastic items were available, but now no longer do so.

The sale of *D. schippii* crafts is not a major source of income in the village. Wage labor (30%), selling "bush meat" (27%), and remittances from family members working elsewhere (16%) are the primary household income sources; income from newly initiated ecotourist activities was the major source of household income for only 14% of survey respondents (see Table 10.2). The latter reflects mostly boat operators/tour guides and bed-and-breakfast operators. These respondents reported per capita income higher than that reported for members of the craft and farming associations (see

Table 10.2. Primary source of household income in Gales Point.

	Frequency	Percentage
Wages[a]	11	29.7
Sell bush meat[b]	10	27.0
Remittances/pension[c]	6	16.2
Tourism-related[d]	5	13.9
Sell fish	3	8.1
Sell farm goods[e]	1	2.7
Rent	1	2.7
TOTAL[f]	37	100

[a] From working at nearby Whiteridge citrus plantation and Manatee Fishing Lodge, and providing services within Gales Point Village (teacher, postal worker, carpenter).

[b] Predominantly gibnut or agouti, but also deer, peccary, and, to a lesser extent, armadillo.

[c] From relatives in the United States and Belize City.

[d] Mostly as boat operators/tour guides and from providing bed-and-breakfast services.

[e] This applies largely to root crops, bananas, and vegetables, as well as roasting cashew nuts (in season) and collecting coconuts for sale.

[f] Percentages do not add to exactly 100 due to rounding.

Table 10.3). That income from crafts remains very low is substantiated by the fact that only one household reported that income derived from selling or weaving *D. schippii* was "very" important to their household's economy; over half of the households in the trade (55%) characterized it as a supplementary income source, while 36% utilized it only for emergency or sporadic income.

The low economic value of *D. schippii* to Gales Point residents is not related to its access or supply. As noted above, *D. schippii* is abundant in the Manatee forest, where it is an "open access" resource—that is, cane harvesting is not restricted. Similarly, there are no efforts by the community, currently or historically, to manage cane or plant populations. Villagers report that wild plants are simply cut and new canes coppice from basal clusters (Figure 10.1), which are harvested again after several years. There are no reports of anyone ever cultivating *D. schippii*. Most survey respondents and key informants characterize the plant as plentiful in the nearby forest, although some noted that it is now unusual to find vines longer than 16 m (reportedly common decades ago), and that it is increasingly difficult to locate even short

Table 10.3. Average per capita income by membership in community management associations.[a]

Category	N	%[b]	Average per capita income ($BZ)[c]	Standard deviation
All	29	14	872 (US 436)	597
B & B members	10	16	1,020 (US 510)[d]	747
Boat operators and tour guides	7	12	1114 (US 557)[e]	773
Farm association	10	16	852 (US 426)[f]	680
Crafts association	7	12	885 (US 442)[g]	535

[a]Survey respondents were asked to tell us their average household monthly income over the previous year. Twenty-nine households responded (8 households did not respond). To calculate average per capita income, the mean for each group was divided by 5 (the average size of the household) and multiplied by 12 (total months in a year). N refers to the number of households with at least one member participating in the association.

[b]Percent of households in the village as a whole.

[c]BZ $2 – US $1

The following values refer to statistical comparisons of the income of particular group members with nonmembers. F is the statistical value of the test, and P refers to its significance.

[d]F = 4.281; P = .048 (mean scores B & B members and nonmembers)
[e]F = 3.02; P = .094 (mean scores BO/TG members and nonmembers)
[f]F = .008; P = .931 (mean scores FA members and nonmembers)
[g]F = .402; P = .531 (mean scores CA members and nonmembers)

Figure 10.1
....

Tie-tie (*Desmoncus schippii*) plant, showing spiny
stem, inflorescence, and compound leaf.

canes (e.g., 4 m long) in the closest collecting areas on the west side of the lagoon. These observations are confirmed in the Manatee sample site, where
cane lengths averaged 9.2 m (± 2.0 m) and no canes longer than 12 m were
observed.

The Potential of *D. schippii* in Community Development and Conservation in Gales Point

Desmoncus schippii possesses a number of characteristics favorable to sustained
extraction and use in forest conservation efforts. These characteristics include: (1) high population densities in a variety of forest types and soil conditions, (2) preference for disturbed habitats and secondary forests, which are
becoming increasingly common, and (3) use by rural Belizeans as cash income
through the production and sale of baskets and other woven products. These

traits, in conjunction with the plant's clustering growth habit and ability to resprout following cutting, suggest potential for sustained extraction.

Despite favorable ecological attributes, there are a number of potential constraints to sustainable *D. schippii* extraction. First, the rate of cane growth and effects of repeated harvesting are unknown. Collectors reported that canes can be repeatedly harvested at three- to four-year intervals; several plants sampled in this study showed evidence of previous harvesting, particularly in the Manatee site.

Secondly, the effect of cane harvesting on other flora and fauna is unknown. Harvesting does not appear to have any direct adverse effects on trees or epiphytes that grow in association with these lianas. However, *Desmoncus* spp. fruits are consumed by frugivorous birds (Hess 1994), and they and other palm species could be a significant, even "keystone," food resource for birds and mammals (Terborgh 1992). If protected area managers in Belize wish to pursue sustained-yield harvesting of NTFPs, the viability and ecological effects of product harvesting must be carefully investigated. Peters (1994) recommends a series of basic procedures before and during any extractive operation, including forest inventory, regeneration studies, and harvest assessments and adjustments. If product extraction is to be compatible with conservation objective, the effects of extraction on plant pollinators, seed consumers, and dispersers, as well as other mutualistic relationships with vertebrate and invertebrate populations, must be assessed. In addition, it will be necessary to monitor the health and vigor of plant populations over time. For example, cane collectors in Gales Point reported that *D. schippii* growth and resprout rates have recently been adversely affected by insects consuming the apical meristems. Such factors could greatly affect the viability of the populations used for NTFP extraction.

Prospects for *D. schippii* harvesting and handicrafts to contribute to community development and forest conservation efforts are constrained by its low market value, uncertain future market demand, and the difficulties inherent at both the community and state levels in establishing and enforcing harvesting guidelines under open-access resource conditions. The latter is exacerbated by the fact that there have never been traditional common management institutions in Gales Point or state policies that monitor or enforce sustainable levels of cane extraction, nor viable producer or community organizations that might assume monitoring and enforcing roles in the future. Contemporary efforts at developing a community craft association are centered primarily on teaching cane plaiting skills and facilitating marketing.

At present, *D. schippii*–based cottage industries in Gales Point do not provide sufficient income to contribute significantly to conservation efforts. Wage labor, farming, and sale of wild game are more important sources of household income than collecting and producing *D. schippii* handicrafts. The minor role of *D. schippii* in the rural economy—especially one characterized by limited access to land—is striking when compared to the role of rattan in the Philippines and Indonesia (Siebert and Belsky 1985; Belsky and Siebert 1995). In the latter areas, income derived from selling rattan canes and/or making rattan handicrafts are the primary livelihood for many households, particularly those who are landless or without access to producing their own rice supply. While the majority of Gales Point residents are also landless and must purchase basic food staples, *D. schippii* harvesting and handicraft manufacturing have not assumed a similarly important role in the household economy. The considerably higher market demand for Asiatic rattans and the centuries-long trade history and community-managed traditions are important differences between these two NTFPs.

We suggest that the relatively low socioeconomic importance of *D. schippii* in Gales Point can be attributed largely to the fact that cane harvesting and handicraft manufacturing have not been traditionally widespread in the village, and hence are not a significant part of the "community lifestyle." *Desmoncus* baskets have gained commercial value only recently with the burgeoning tourist trade, and even that is limited and sporadic. Marketing outlets and logistics remain poorly developed. A major impetus for rejuvenating and expanding cane handicrafts has come from an older part-time Gales Point resident who has been teaching local residents to weave handicrafts (Figure 10.2). Thus far, women with young families have expressed the most interest in learning how to weave. Women with small children find weaving attractive because it provides an opportunity to socialize while working and because it can be done in or around the home in conjunction with other domestic responsibilities. Outside of selling small home-cooked foods, women stressed the limited availability of necessary income-generating opportunities for them in the village.

Handicraft marketing is constrained by the small and unpredictable number of tourists traveling to Gales Point. This situation creates little demand and small incentive for people to manufacture handicrafts. Villagers expressed hope that ecotourism and efforts to establish a crafts center will increase tourist visitation and opportunities to sell handicrafts. Indeed, many survey respondents indicated that they are "watching" the trade and might take up weaving if demand increases and they can be assured a market outlet and reasonable returns for their labor.

Opportunities may exist to improve the *D. schippii* handicraft market. For example, in the village of Teakettle in western Belize, a small group of women weave handicrafts and baskets. One community member transports them to ecotourist lodges and craft centers throughout Belize City. When interviewed, the handicraft producers said that reliable market outlets and good prices underlie their involvement in the trade beyond producing handicrafts for home use. In Teakettle, a major limitation facing handicraft production is that cane supplies are located far from the village. The strength of the demand

Figure 10.2

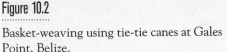

Basket-weaving using tie-tie canes at Gales
Point, Belize.

for *D. schippii* handicrafts in Belize remains to be determined. Personal observation of current quality and cost suggest that it is unlikely the trade could
compete in global markets. Additionally, there is some risk of villagers becoming dependent on a single, potentially volatile, tourist-based marketing
outlet.

If marketing constraints are overcome and the *D. schippii* trade increases in
Gales Point, problems with resource access and supply could arise due to the
open-access nature of the resource (McCay and Acheson 1987; Berkes 1989).
A reconsideration of property rights would become critical at the village and
state levels to determine which individuals in which communities would have
access and control over cane supplies, as would monitoring and enforcing
sustainable cane harvesting rates. Based on work elsewhere, user or producer
groups should play an important role in NTFP management, specifically to
ensure that more powerful groups within communities do not overshadow the

concerns of NTFP collectors and producers—typically the least wealthy stratum in rural communities (Belsky and Siebert 1995). Additionally, efforts at legalizing NTFP collection and promoting equitable community management could create additional competition or conflicts beyond communities, involving state agencies, merchant groups, and NTFP collectors and producers in other areas. Conflicts over NTFP policies and practices in Belize could be mediated, however, by the presence of community-oriented conservation consultants to assist with developing harvesting guidelines, monitoring impacts on both people and wildlife, and providing political support for the role of local property rights and community development in conservation.

Conclusion

Despite favorable ecological attributes, the potential of *D. schippii* to contribute to community development and forest conservation is constrained by low market values, uncertain future market demands, open-access resource management and control problems, and the absence of community traditions, local organizations, and state sanctions to develop and support sustainable cane harvesting. Efforts to promote community development and conservation in Gales Point should address primary livelihood activities—hunting, wage labor opportunities, and farming. Local economic viability and environmental conservation are more likely to result from the sustainable development of these activities than on supplementary activities such as NTFPs. These conclusions are likely to be relevant to the management of *Desmoncus* spp. and other NTFPs throughout the Maya Forest region of Belize, Guatemala, and Mexico.

Acknowledgments

We greatly appreciate the assistance provided by Pio Saqui, Jennifer Snorsky, the participants of the 1993, 1994, and 1996 University of Montana/University College of Belize study group, and Natalie Uhl of the Bailey Hortorium at Cornell University for identifying the specimens. Assistance for the project was provided by the U.S. Man and the Biosphere Program, the University of Montana, the Belize Forestry Department and Program for Belize. Voucher specimens of *Desmoncus schippii* are deposited in the Bailey Hortorium, Cornell University.

References

Arnold, J. E. M. 1995. *Tree Management in Farmer Strategies: Responses to Agricultural Intensification.* Oxford University Press, Oxford, U.K.

Balick, M. J. 1979. Economic botany of the Guahibo. I. Palmae. *Economic Botany* 33: 361–376.

Balick, M. J., and R. Mendelsohn. 1992. Assessing the economic value of traditional medicines from tropical rain forests. *Conservation Biology* 6: 128–130.

Belsky, J. M., and S. F. Siebert. 1995. Property rights, rattan and forest conservation in Kerinci-Seblat National Park. *Selbyana* 16: 58–64.

Berkes, F., editor. 1989. *Common Property Resources: Ecology and Community-Based Sustainable Development.* Belhaven, London.

Gales Point Progressive Cooperative (GPPC). 1992. *Gales Point Progressive Management Plan.* Gales Point, Belize.

Henderson, A., and F. Chavez. 1993. *Desmoncus* as a useful palm in the western Amazon basin. *Principes* 37: 184–186.

Hess, S. 1994. Patterns of plant reproductive phenology, food resource availability to vertebrates and implications for forest management in the Río Bravo Conservation and Management Area, Belize. M.S. thesis, University of Montana, Missoula.

Horwich, R. H., D. Murray, E. Saqui, J. Lyon, and D. Godfrey. 1993. Ecotourism and community development: A view from Belize. Pages 152–168 in *Ecotourism: A Guide for Planners and Managers.* K. Lindberg and D. E. Hawkins, editors. The Ecotourism Society, North Bennington.

LaFrankie, J. V. 1994. Population dynamics of some tropical trees that yield nontimber forest products. *Economic Botany* 48: 301–309.

Levi-Strauss, C. 1952. The use of wild plants in tropical South America. *Economic Botany* 6: 252–270.

McCay, B., and J. M. Acheson, editors. 1987. *The Question of the Commons: The Culture and Ecology of Communal Resources.* University of Arizona Press, Tucson.

Nepsted, D. C., and S. Schwartzman, editors. 1992. *Nontimber Products from Tropical Forests: Evaluation of a Conservation and Development Strategy.* Advances in Economic Botany 9. The New York Botanical Garden, New York.

Peluso, N. L. 1992. The ironwood problem: (Mis)management and development of an extractive rainforest product. *Conservation Biology* 6: 210–219.

Peters, C. M. 1994. *Sustainable Harvesting of NonTimber Plant Resources in Tropical Moist Forest: An Ecological Primer.* Biodiversity Support Program. Corporate Press, Landover, Md.

Peters, C. M., A. H. Gentry, and R. O. Mendelsohn. 1989. Valuation of an Amazonian rainforest. *Nature* 339: 655–656.

Phillips, O. 1993. Using and conserving the rainforest. *Conservation Biology* 7: 6–7.

Poffenberger, M., editor. 1990. *Keepers of the Forest: Land Management Alternatives in Southeast Asia.* Kumarian Press, New Haven, Conn.

Quero, H. J. 1992. Current status of Mexican palms. *Principes* 36: 203–216.

Richards, E. M. 1993. The potential of nontimber forest products in sustainable natural forest management in Amazonia. *Commonwealth Forestry Review* 72: 21–27.

Salafsky, N., B. L. Dugelby, J. W. Terborgh. 1993. Can extractive reserves save the rain forest? An ecological and socioeconomic analysis of nontimber forest product extraction systems in Petén, Guatemala and West Kalimantan, Indonesia. *Conservation Biology* 7: 39–52.

Siebert, S. F. 1995. Prospects for sustained-yield harvesting of rattan (*Calamus* sp.) in two Indonesian national parks. *Society and Natural Resources* 8: 209–218.

Siebert, S. F., and J. M. Belsky. 1985. Forest-product trade in a lowland Filipino village. *Economic Botany* 39: 522–533.

Terborgh, J. 1992. *Diversity and the Tropical Rain Forest.* Scientific American Library, New York.

Tremaine, R. 1993. Valuing tropical rainforests. *Conservation Biology* 7: 7–8.

Uhl, N. W., and J. Dransfield. 1987. *Genera Palmarum: A Classification of Palms Based on the Work of Harold E. Moore, Jr.* Allen Press, Lawrence, Kans.

Wallace, A. R. 1971. *Palm Trees of the Amazon and Their Uses.* Coronado Press, Lawrence, Kans. Reprint of a work first published by John Van Voorst, London, in 1853.

Williams, L. O. 1981. The useful plants of Central America. *Ceiba* 24: 1–297.

Chapter 11

Governmental and Customary Arrangements Guiding Chicle Latex Extraction in Petén, Guatemala

Barbara L. Dugelby

Scientists and resource managers increasingly are calling for conservation efforts to better accommodate the needs and expectations of local communities. A community-based approach, it is argued, can better combine development objectives with those of conservation and offers an alternative to traditional conservation strategies that impose heavy restrictions on resource exploitation (Western and Wright 1994). On a similar front, recent studies stress the important role of local knowledge and institutions in the strategies adopted by resource users (e.g., Agrawal 1993, 1995; Gadgil et al. 1993; Browder 1995). This chapter describes and analyzes institutional factors affecting the exploitation of chicle latex, a natural base for chewing gum extracted from the forest tree *Manilkara zapota*, in the Maya Biosphere Reserve in northern Guatemala (Figure 11.1). Specifically, it examines the role that both governmental regulations and customary arrangements play in guiding resource extraction, and ways in which these factors might contribute to sustainable management of the resource.

Study Region

In 1990, the Guatemalan government established the Maya Biosphere Reserve in the northern Petén (CONAP 1990). Of particular importance to rural populations living in and near the reserve are the nontimber products extracted from the forests. In 1991, chicle production was worth approximately U.S. $1.4 million and employed 2,000 seasonal workers (Santiso

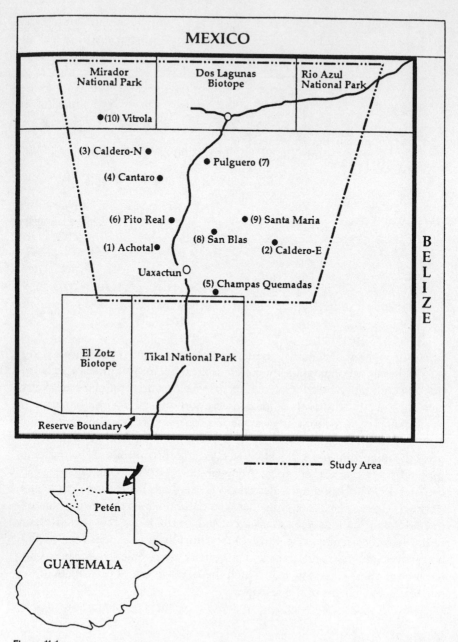

Figure 11.1

Study area in the Maya Biosphere Reserve.

1993; Dugelby 1995). Other nontimber products such as xate palm fronds (*Chamaedorea* sp.) and berries of the allspice tree (*Pimenta dioica*) contribute an additional U.S. $2 to $5 million to Guatemala's economy, employing some 7,000 people full or part time (Nations et al. 1988; Heinzman and Reining 1988). The study described below was undertaken to determine whether the chicle industry was operating in a sustainable fashion, and whether any changes were needed to improve its use of forest resources.

Study Methods

The analysis presented here is based on a 13-month interdisciplinary study of factors affecting the sustainability of chicle latex extraction in the Maya Biosphere Reserve (Dugelby 1995). The study region, located in the northeastern corner of the reserve, extends from the northern boundary of Tikal National Park to the border with Mexico and includes the multiple-use area surrounding the community of Uaxactún as well as the core areas of Dos Lagunas Biotope and the recently created Río Azul National Park. The area encompasses approximately 2,500 km^2 and is locally known as the Uaxactún and Dos Lagunas harvesting regions.

During the tapping season of 1992–93 (the tapping season coincides with the rainy season, which typically begins in late August and continues into early February), I monitored the movements of all chicle tapper groups (n = 34 groups) working in the study area and visited eight groups managed by seven out of the nine chicle contractors in the area. Of the eight tapper groups studied, three were composed of local tappers and five of migrants. Four out of five of the migrant groups were composed of workers from areas in highland Guatemala far south of the Petén—*Cobaneros* from the Cobán area of the Department of Alta Verapáz, located approximately 90 km north of Guatemala City, and *Salamatecos* from the Salamá area of the Department of Baja Verapáz, roughly 40 km southeast of Cobán. Group sizes ranged from 6 to 28 tappers (mean = 15).

For all trees tested and/or tapped, I recorded latex yields (in kg fresh weight), tree size (dbh), and approximate time since the most recent tapping event (years since tapping, YST). Tapping wounds take several years to heal and the age of recent wounds (up to ten years old) can be determined fairly easily by changes in color of the exposed bark and scar tissue formation in crevices of the cut. In each of the ten camps, data on M. *zapota* size and tapping history were collected along four 2 m wide, 2.5 km long transects radiating out from the camp base (n = 40, 0.5 ha plots). Along the transects, dbh and YST were recorded for all M. *zapota* ≥ 10 cm. We also noted signs indicating that a tree was suffering as a result of a previous tapping and recorded the size of any dead trees.

Ecology and Exploitation of *Manilkara zapota*

Manilkara zapota (L.) van Royen (Sapotaceae) is a dominant emergent tree native to the forests of the Yucatán Peninsula whose range extends south as far as Costa Rica. The tree grows best in upland broadleaf forests, although it is found in most other forest types throughout the region (Brokaw et al. 1990). A slow-growing tree, M. *zapota* may attain a height of 40 m (Lundell 1937) and a diameter of over 125 cm (Pennington 1991). The tree produces a sticky, milky-white sap that is at present its principal economic product, though its edible fruit and dense wood may once have been used by the ancient Maya.

Variations in latex yields per tree are common. It is widely held that genetic variability, along with differences in microclimatic conditions, may play an important role in the availability and quality of resin, although the question has not been studied formally. Such differences may be significant to the industry; for example, trees that produce very little latex (nicknamed by tappers *zapote mula*) are found in all size classes. Among M. *zapota* populations in the Petén, it is possible to distinguish three or four varieties (Leon 1987), possibly different species or subspecies. Chicle tappers distinguish the varieties by the color and depth of the inner bark, the appearance of the fruit, and color and consistency of the latex (Figure 11.2). Industry participants also distinguish between two types of latex based primarily on consistency, which affects its suitability for chewing gum production. First-quality latex (*chicle de primera clase*) is extracted almost exclusively from the northern portion of the Petén, coinciding in large part with the area of the reserve. Second-quality latex (*chicle de segunda clase* or *chiquibúl*) is extracted from trees in the southern Petén. Chiquibúl is not sold in Guatemala, but tappers occasionally smuggle it into Belize for sale to that country's chicle manufacturers.

Densities of M. *zapota* are quite high in the Petén, corresponding to the low overall species diversity of the region's subtropical forests (on the order of 50 to 100 species per ha) (Lundell 1937). In the study region, densities of live chicle trees ranged between 20 and 50 trees per ha, although densities of what tappers consider as latex-producing chicle trees ranged from 14 to 38 trees per ha.[1] Reining et al. (1992) found similar densities in the Uaxactún area and slightly higher and lower densities in the Carmelita and Yaxhá areas, respectively.

In a study of forest structure and composition in neighboring forests of northern Belize, Alcorn (1994) found that the Sapotaceae family was ecologically the most important. With only 4% of the total number of species, the Sapoteaceae family accounts for 20% of the individuals and 23% of the total basal area. Although little research has been done on M. *zapota* regeneration in Yucatán forests, Alcorn (1994) found a mean density for M. *zapota* of 64 trees > 10 cm dbh, but a lower density of smaller-size classes (10 to 20 cm dbh) in both old-growth (4 individuals/ha) and transition forests (13 individu-

Figure 11.2

Cooking latex in a chicle camp.

als/ha) compared to that of upland forest (24.7 individuals/ha). Chicle seedlings and saplings seem to maintain a low height and slow growth rates under the forest canopy (Alcorn 1994), a pattern typical of primary forest species (Hartshorn 1980). These data indicate that gaps in the forest canopy may be the most important component of this species' regeneration.

The Chicle Extraction Process

The latex of M. *zapota* is extracted by chicle tappers during the rainy season (late August to early February) by severing vessels in the tree's inner bark. Using a sharp machete, tappers cut grooves in the bole of the chicle tree in a herringbone design beginning at the bottom of the trunk and working their way up the trunk as far as possible (Figure 11.3), occasionally making incisions in large branches (*gajos*) as well. Experienced tappers take care not to damage the vascular cambium (just below the inner bark) when making inci-

Figure 11.3

Chicle tappers make herringbone-pattern cuts on
the trunk and main branches of the tree. As
these cuts heal, they can be used by the tapper to
determine when a tree is ready to be retapped.

sions. Tapping incisions, whether done with or without care, automatically
increases the risk of predation by insects and fungus through the removal of
the protective bark layer and by interrupting the natural flow of water and nutrients from the roots to the crown. Healing of incisions and restoration of
latex flow after tapping is a slow process. According to experienced tappers, a
chicle tree should be allowed to rest for at least three years, and preferably between four and six years, before being retapped.

In any given year there are 1,600 to 1,900 chicle tappers[2] and 60 to 90 contractors and subcontractors working in the Maya Biosphere Reserve. Based on
the records maintained by contractors and CONAP and on my own interviews, I estimate that 40% to 50% of the tappers working in the Maya Biosphere Reserve are seasonal migrant tappers from southern Guatemala. Com-

paring my data with that of Schwartz (1990 and pers. comm.), it appears that the proportion of migrants in the industry has grown significantly in recent years. Contractors claim that they prefer hiring migrants over local residents because they are more dependable and do not leave camp to visit their families (primarily because it is a one- to two-day journey to their homes). An analysis of differences in tapping behavior between migrant and local tappers revealed that migrants tap more trees per day on average than local residents, but they are less selective than local residents in determining whether a tree is rested or healthy enough to be tapped (Dugelby 1995).

The forests of the Maya Biosphere Reserve are latticed with roads built for logging operations and oil exploration. These roads, along with thousands of footpaths, serve as an infrastructure for transporting men and supplies in and out of forest camps. Hundreds of forest camps are scattered throughout the reserve, each located adjacent to a water supply, such as a small pond, lake, creek, or river. Few camps are located directly on major (i.e., all-weather) roads, but many are close to secondary roads. Most secondary roads are not passable by automobiles during the rainy season, when chicle is harvested, forcing contractors to rely heavily on mules for transportation of chicle, food supplies, and occasionally people.

In order to establish a camp, contractors must locate forest areas displaying the necessary characteristics for a successful harvesting season. Tappers need a camp with sufficient water and tappable trees. Many contractors hire scouts to investigate the availability of chicle trees and water in forest camps before the beginning of the season. Other contractors prefer to conduct the investigations themselves. The number of tappers in a camp ranges between 5 and 40. Tappers begin each season by tapping those trees closest to the camp base and day by day working their way out farther from the camp to find additional tappable trees. Once the nearest tappable trees lie beyond 1.5 to 2 hours' walking distance, tapper groups relocate to another camp. Tappers also will abandon a camp if the water supply is depleted, or if the density (individuals per hectare) of tappable trees is not economically viable.

History and Importance of Chicle Exploitation in the Petén

According to Schwartz (1990), from 1890 to around 1970 chicle extraction "dominated the political economy of Petén and the imagination of Peténeros" (Figure 11.4). During the first part of the century, when the Petén was still sparsely populated[3] and not economically marginalized, the chicle industry directly contributed economically to the lives of between 29% and 50% of the population of the Petén (Schwartz 1990). From the late 1800s until around 1945, chicle latex served as the primary base for chewing gum production, after which it was replaced in importing countries by petroleum-derived synthetics. Production declined briefly during the economic depression of

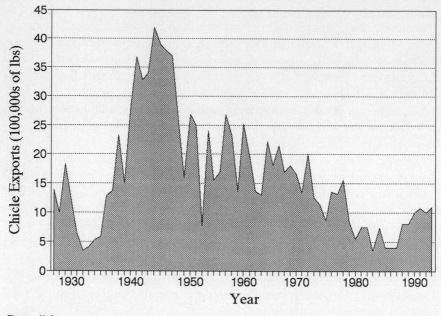

Figure 11.4
....

Chicle production in the Petén, 1927–1993.

1929–33 and then peaked between 1942 and 1948. A 1947 export level of 49,000 *quintales* (1 quintal or qq = 100 lb) is more than four times that of 1993.[4] The majority of exports in the early part of the century were purchased by U.S. companies. In the mid-1970s, the U.S. role in purchasing Guatemalan chicle began to decline. Shortly after, Japan absorbed the entire production. Presently, two Japanese companies, Mitsui and Sumitomo, buy all chicle produced in the Petén.

With the exception of a brief two-year period, since 1949 the national government of Guatemala has maintained control over chicle extraction in the Petén. In 1949, INFOP (National Institute for the Promotion of Production, Instituto Nacional de Fomento de Producción) was created to be the sole intermediary between chicle producers and foreign purchasers (Schwartz 1990). From 1959 to 1962, the government gave control over chicle management to the newly created cooperative of contractors (Consorcio de Empresarios de Chicle del Petén, today called Itzalandia). In 1962, the government again took control over chicle management through the creation of a new agency, FYDEP (the National Agency for Economic Development and Promotion of the Petén, Empresa Nacional de Fomento y Desarrollo Económico del Petén). FYDEP, along with the contractors' cooperative, Itzalandia, outlined new regulations for the exploitation of chicle. These regulations gave rise to the law

(Decree 79-79) that currently controls latex extraction and the distribution of the industry's economic benefits.

In 1990, with the creation of the Maya Biosphere Reserve, FYDEP was liquidated, and responsibility for chicle extraction was handed over to CONAP, the agency responsible for management of the reserve. The regional headquarters of CONAP in the Petén is authorized to manage the day to day operations of purchasing, processing, and quality control of chicle during the tapping season. Although this department of CONAP is most knowledgeable about the industry, the majority of key policy, regulatory, and managerial decisions regarding chicle are made or must be approved by personnel in CONAP's central office (CONAP-Central) in Guatemala City.

Various elements of the exploitation process have been strongly shaped by political, economic, and cultural factors in the Petén, including the organization of the industry, interactions among contractors, the recruitment of tappers, and tapper behavior in the forest. The most important formal regulations or factors that influence the industry are property and resource use rights, government regulations concerning chicle processing, and cooperation between the contractors' cooperative and CONAP on industry management.

Property Rights

Chicle extraction in the Petén operates under overlapping property regimes. Elements of state, open-access, and common property regimes all govern the industry's operations. The entire northern portion of the Petén is national land in which no private holdings are permitted. Restrictions on agriculture and colonization in the region are based on results from various studies indicating that the thin soils supporting the forests of the northern Petén are better adapted to managed extraction of forest products than to farming (Schwartz 1990). It is primarily for these reasons that forests north of latitude 17°10' have remained relatively intact (Nations et al. 1988). Currently, no legal concessions or other form of resource tenure are granted to any forest-based industry (including timber, as timber concessions have been halted until the approval of a biosphere-wide management plan), nor have legal user rights ever been granted to the chicle industry.

Although contractors and tappers currently are allowed to collect chicle latex from the forests, they have no guarantee of future access and collection rights. In addition, there are no legal restrictions on who can collect nontimber forest resources. There are, however, technical and financial barriers to entering the industry as a new participant, which will be discussed in greater detail below. Harvest of forest products, including timber, nontimber, and wildlife resources, is not permitted in core protected areas, such as national parks and biotopes (nature reserves set aside for the protection, enjoyment, and study of biological diversity). Restrictions on harvesting in Tikal National Park have been in place since the park's creation in 1953, but regulations governing biotopes and national parks in other areas of the Maya Biosphere Reserve were established in 1990 when the reserve was created. These regulations have yet to be fully enforced due to lack of manpower and some disagreement over how rigid the restrictions should be.[5]

From a technical point of view, therefore, nontimber forest products are harvested on state-owned land under an open-access property regime (cf. Schwartz 1990). However, in the absence of a governmentally imposed resource allocation system, contractors have developed their own internal system for partitioning the forest among themselves. These common-property-like arrangements have developed in part due to the nature of the resource, but are also conditioned by the lack of strong management on the part of government agencies (FYDEP and CONAP) into the affairs of the industry.

Regulations on Chicle Exploitation

The regulation of chicle extraction and marketing of the latex vary slightly from that of other nontimber forest products harvested in the Petén (e.g., xate fronds and allspice berries). These differences are due largely to the age of the chicle industry and its historical role in the political economy of the department. Most important, chicle is purchased from contractors and sold to overseas buyers by a government agency rather than private exporters.

There are few government regulations on chicle exploitation. Those that exist include the following:

(1) Contractors must obtain a license from the government to collect chicle in the Maya Biosphere Reserve. CONAP provides licenses and collects taxes and other fees (e.g., for transportation permits). Quotas based on amounts negotiated by CONAP with buyers are allocated to licensed contractors. A contractor's quota is determined by an evaluation of the contractor's chicle production in recent years and his or her record for repaying loans. Corruption historically has benefited particular contractors, however, by awarding larger quotas to a few influential individuals (Schwartz 1990; pers. obs.). In recent years contractors have been allowed to surpass quota limits without sanctions from CONAP.[6]

(2) Licenses themselves do not designate where contractors may and may not place their teams, but chicle extraction is prohibited in core protected areas of the Maya Biosphere Reserve, such as Tikal, other national parks, and all biotopes.

(3) CONAP accepts from contractors only the blocks of latex that are of export quality. To be of export quality, the cooked latex cannot have more than 30% moisture content (uncooked chicle contains approximately 80% water; Reining et al. 1992) and must be free from impurities.

(4) At the end of each season, CONAP receives an additional payment from the Japanese companies, representing the increase in the value of the U.S. dollar

to the Guatemalan quetzal between the time the year's contract was signed, typically in May or June, and the time the latex was delivered to Japan, in March or April of the following year. The profits are shared among all industry participants, including tappers, according to their production for that season. Contractors must keep track of individual tappers' production and turn in a list of names with production levels at the end of the season so that tappers may be awarded their share of the profits, which the contractors distribute. However, some contractors do not comply with this requirement and have been subjected to legal denunciations from chicle tappers who were never paid (pers. obs. 1993).

Important here is the fact that of the few government regulations that exist, none represents an effort to effect a more ecologically sound or sustainable extraction system. Moreover, government regulations and actions do not recognize or utilize customary arrangements that have developed over decades. For the most part, monitoring and control of chicle extraction has been left to the tappers and contractor themselves, without providing them with strong incentives for sustainable resource use.

Itzalandia's Contribution to Industry Management

CONAP is legally responsible for all management and regulatory matters involving the chicle industry, yet it is assisted in many managerial tasks by Itzalandia, the chicle contractors' cooperative. Itzalandia's role in management probably began in 1959 when the cooperative was placed in charge of the industry after INFOP was disbanded. Itzalandia provides assistance in maintaining up-to-date lists of contractors and tappers, distribution of licenses and quotas, distribution of payments for chicle, and advising CONAP on various matters. Despite Itzalandia's assistance to CONAP in managing the industry and resource, however, industry participants have no legal voice in important management and regulatory decisions made by CONAP, in particular those made by CONAP-Central in Guatemala City. As a result, participants have very little influence over such central issues as when contractor licenses are distributed, how prices are negotiated with importers, and how and when restrictions on harvesting in biotopes and other areas in the Maya Biosphere Reserve will be phased in. In rare cases, Itzalandia is brought in to help resolve a problem, but typically only at the last minute (M. Soza, pers. comm. 1993), and its invaluable assistance frequently goes unappreciated.

The tight control exercised by CONAP-Central over industry management decisions and finances has resulted in significant problems for industry participants. The fact that the majority of important managerial, administrative, and financial decisions must first pass through CONAP-Central creates a serious bottleneck in daily operations in the Petén. To make matters worse, at times there is no clear chain of command in CONAP-Petén. As a result, neither government workers in the Petén nor industry leaders are motivated to try to improve industry operations. Managers hesitate to dictate changes, knowing that any new policies, industry standards, or management strategies they establish may be meaningless as a result of decisions or inaction on the part of CONAP-Central.

Customary Institutional Arrangements Guiding Chicle Extraction

Customary institutions often are based on expectations of reciprocity among participants, rules regarding access and membership, standards of behavior, and the enforcement of sanctions against rule violators (Bromley et al. 1992). Expectations may vary over time due to the effect of environmental changes on the availability of the resource, sociopolitical factors, and market fluctuations (Gupta 1986). Several of the customary arrangements guiding chicle extraction are "nonbinding" (Taylor 1987) because there are no formal constraints currently enforced that "would keep men to their agreements." Other agreements, such as informal ones between contractors and tappers, are enforced through competition over labor and worker reputations (Schwartz 1990; pers. obs. 1993). The key finding of this study is that current customary arrangements strongly influence extraction activities and could play a more significant role in future resource management strategies.

Forest Partitioning among Contractors

Although the forests of the Maya Biosphere Reserve have never been parcelled into legal concessions for resource management, from the industry's point of view, the northern Petén forest is divided into several nontimber working regions to which groups of contractors consider they belong (Figure 11.5). These nontimber working regions are based primarily on the existing transportation infrastructure throughout the forest. Contractors who work in the same region historically have shared information with each other concerning the availability of camps and cooperated on various tasks such as transporting tappers, supplies, and chicle. Within each working region, economically powerful contractors often have control over key areas of the forest, creating a network of large contractors' "territories" around which smaller contractors establish their camps and territories. Thus, the financial strength of a few contractors and cooperation among relatives and friends play key roles in the division of forest areas among the larger population of contractors, creating a semi-predictable pattern of contractor distribution.

Ideally, these customary boundaries should facilitate a more efficient distribution of harvesting teams throughout the forest. However, they are not permanently fixed and occasionally overlap. In addition, information is rarely shared between contractors regarding the exact boundaries of their territories

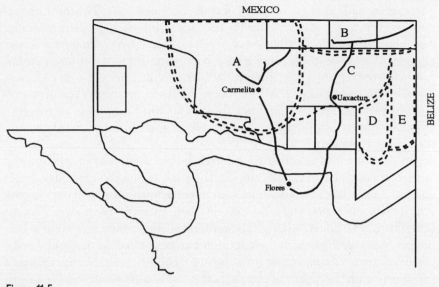

Figure 11.5

Chicle contractors' historical division of Petén forests based on access and stopover points. Names for the region used by chicleros and CONAP are: (A) Carmelita, (B) Dos Lagunas, (C) Uaxactún, (D) Yaxhá, and (E) Melchor.

for the upcoming season. The result is that tapper groups or contractors occasionally choose camps where the trees have been harvested recently or that intersect with another group's harvesting area. The nature of the camp selection process therefore increases the potential for inefficient and unsustainable harvesting, as well as for inter-group conflict.

Information Sharing and Uncertainty among Contractors

Resource users with poor information about the options and outcomes of their actions face high levels of uncertainty and typically have lower levels of efficiency in resource use. The greater an individual's uncertainty regarding the possible results of an action, the shorter is the time horizon upon which his decisions are based and the less attention he can give to long-term efficiency (Jochim 1981). A chicle contractor seeks to obtain information concerning the quality and tapping history of camps and the location of other groups in his area. The more information he has, the lower is his uncertainty regarding the outcomes of his decisions.

Uncertainty can be generated by factors external and internal to the chicle industry. External sources of uncertainty include the timing and quantity of rainfall, availability of chicle trees and water in camps, market prices, and government actions (e.g., awarding of timber concessions). The most important internal source of uncertainty is the lack of information sharing among contractors about the distribution of available chicle trees, water, and tapper groups. Information concerning recent harvesting activities in forest camps can help contractors predict the availability of chicle trees in a given camp. In addition, uncertainty is high concerning future access to resource-rich areas because of the possibility that these areas will be set aside by the government. As a result, information is closely guarded and shared only among the closest confidants.

An assessment of contractors' relative levels of certainty regarding the availability of chicle trees and camps in the study region indicated that larger and more experienced contractors were more knowledgeable about tapping activities in the region and more certain about plans to move tapper groups (Dugelby 1995). To test whether the ranking of contractors according to certainty levels correlated with their actions and success rate in the field, I compared contractor certainty, size (in numbers of chicle tappers contracted), and experience with the quality of camps chosen and the mean number of changes per tapper group, for each contractor monitored in the study. Camp quality

Table 11.1. Relationships between contractor size, experience, camp quality, and group changes.

Contractor	Uncertainty[a]	Size[b]	Experience[c]	Camp Quality[d]	Avg. # Changes[e]
1	96	L	H	4	1
2	60	S	L	3	3
3	60	S	L	2.5	2
4	72	S	M	3	0.5
5	74	M	H	4	1
6	96	M	H	5	0
7	90	M	M	4	0.5

[a]Uncertainty based on average of qualitative scores regarding knowledge of various characteristics in study region camps: quality of resource base, distribution of tapper groups, activities and plans of other contractors, certainty regarding options for relocating tapper groups.

[b]Size based on number of tappers employed in 1992–93 with consideration of average number of tappers in past years. L = large, M = medium, S = small.

[c]Experience based on number of years as contractor and chiclero. H = high, M = medium, L = low.

[d]Camp quality was assessed using averages of dbh, latex production, years since tapping, and density of M. zapota trees in each camp. High numbers indicate high quality.

[e]Number of camp changes per group, averaged across all groups managed by the contractor.

was quantified using averages of diameter at breast height (dbh), latex yield, and years since tapping for all sampled trees as well as the density of trees in each camp's territory. The analysis revealed that larger and more experienced contractors, whom I had ascertained were more informed about resource, water, and camp availability, chose camps of higher quality and their groups changed camps less often than the smaller, less experienced contractors (Table 11.1; Figure 11.6).

Both experience and the size of a contractor's operations confer different advantages and information to extraction operations. Higher levels of certainty among more experienced contractors could be rooted in the fact that they (1) have more extensive knowledge of forest camps, resource densities, and potential water availability due to many years of managing groups, (2) employ scouts with more experience and knowledge of the forest and camps, and (3) receive constant feedback from cooperating contractors and other contacts established over the years. Larger contractors have two important advantages: (1) they have more scouts and other informants in the forests and, related to this, (2) they receive information throughout the season as muleteers (men who manage the mules carrying supplies and chicle to and from camps) bring back information from tappers in the various camps through which they pass, as well as from people they encounter on the road. However,

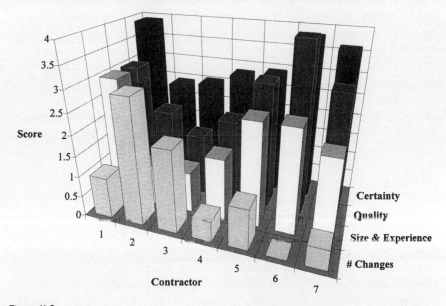

Figure 11.6

Correlation of contractor size, certainty, and experience with camp quality and number of changes.

being large does not always confer an advantage. For example, contractors operating in territory with which they are unfamiliar or in which they do not have many established contacts will not have access to complete and accurate information.

Tapper Interactions and Tapping Strategies

Voluntary cooperation and mutual trust are strong among tappers in both camp and forest activities. They speak proudly of their camaraderie and respect for territories of their fellow tappers while working in the forest. Tappers working in the same general forest area assist each other in finding good patches of trees. Once a tapper has located a good patch (a patch typically consists of between five and ten tappable trees), however, the patch is considered "his" and is not intruded upon by fellow tappers.

Local and migrant tappers show strikingly different natural resource management strategies, corresponding to their differing levels of compliance with customary management systems. Most tappers appear to be aware of the major ecophysiological factors driving chicle latex production; local tappers can discuss in detail how an open canopy or a windy day can reduce latex production of a tree by exposing the leaves to more wind, sun, and dry air, all of which draw moisture out of the leaves instead of allowing it to flow down through the vessels in the trunk. Local (as opposed to migrant) tappers claim that there is social pressure in camps to tap in a manner that does not fatally injure or overtax the tree, a claim that was confirmed in observations of tapper behavior (Dugelby 1995).

Most local tappers followed in this study often voiced concerns about making sure that a tree was not too small, had rested sufficiently, and was not suffering from a previous injury. On numerous occasions, a local tapper would realize that a latex-producing tree had been injured and that further tapping might kill the tree. In such cases the tapper almost always left the tree untapped. Similarly, local tappers who found trees that had been tapped within the past few years yet showed good latex producing potential would nonetheless refrain from retapping the tree to avoid harming it. We frequently heard comments such as, "I can get a bag out of this tree, but it may kill it and then nothing would be left for the next guy" (pers. comm. 1993).

Such attitudes were never expressed by migrant tappers followed in the study. Migrant tappers not only are unaffected by customary rules developed by local tappers regarding the selection of trees for tapping, but are more aggressive tappers in general. It is a common sentiment among local tappers that "los Cobaneros matan el bosque," or, "Cobaneros (i.e., migrants) kill the forest." Migrant tappers typically tap the majority of trees in the area that were sufficiently rested for another round of tapping, leaving fewer than average for the following year. A statistical test of the proportion of tappable trees remaining

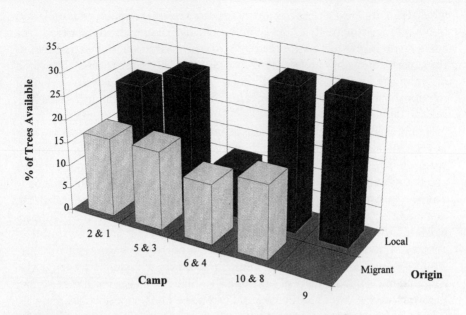

Figure 11.7

Percent of trees available for tapping in camps after occupation,
by origin of tappers.

in local versus migrant camps after the season supported this perception (Figure 11.7; one-tailed $t = 2.13$; $p > 0.04$; $n = 9$ camps) (Dugelby 1995).

General Industry Relations

In addition to those mentioned above, other standards and norms play an important role in how contractors and tappers interact. Three important aspects of industry relations affect chicle exploitation: the selection process by which contractors choose their tappers, and likewise tappers their contractors; the unspoken commitments inherent in the social contract between contractor and tapper; and the personal nature of the learning and traditions developed over years of interaction and cooperation among contractors, camp foremen, and tappers.

Selection of personnel plays a central role in the success of both contractors' and tappers' work. Contractors seek to hire tappers who have good reputations for tapping productivity, are faithful to the contractor, and do not generate social conflict in camps. Tappers may switch contractors in mid-season or simply abandon tapping activity altogether. In both cases, the tapper's actions leave the contractor with substantial debts. When considering whether to hire new tappers, a contractor often relies on the recommendation of other tappers he trusts, such as camp foremen or experienced tappers. Contractors rarely provide novice tappers with cash advances for the first two to three years, until they are sure that the tapper will be accountable, both in a discipline and a production sense. Some contractors try to develop personal relationships with their workers in large part to ensure their performance during the tapping season.

There is also competition among contractors for good tappers. Although not statistically tested, I observed that contractors who had many years of experience, who visited camps, and who in general expressed personal concern about the welfare of their tappers tended to have fewer tappers that abandoned the camp. Many of the tappers in these camps had worked with the same contractor for several years, in some cases more than a decade. Tappers who are badly treated by contractors have the option of switching to another contractor and recommending to comrades that they not work with the offending contractor. In a similar vein, contractors who suffer losses at the hands of misbehaving tappers will refuse to hire them again and may spread the word among other contractors and foremen. Thus, sanctions against violations of the unwritten contract between tappers and contractors are subtle, but nonetheless present a clear disincentive to potential infractors if they perceive that there is a high chance that sanctions will be carried out and will affect their chances of future success in the industry.

External Threats to Chicle Extraction

Several activities external to the chicle industry and for the most part illegal in the biosphere reserve present additional problems for the chicle industry in that they reduce the total area of forest to which tappers have safe or priority access, reducing the incentives for long-term sustainable resource management. These external threats include contraband activities, illegal and legal forest clearing, and the illegal entry of tappers from Mexico and Belize.

Contraband Activity

The northern regions of the Petén, bordering Mexico and Belize, have become increasingly unsafe for forest workers due to the risk of encountering *contrabandistas*, people involved in illegal smuggling activities. According to many sources in the Petén, contraband timber, drugs, weapons, and looted Maya artifacts frequently are transported through (or in the case of marijuana, cultivated in) these areas. According to several contractors, contrabandistas have been present in the northern border area for a long time, particularly those looting Maya ruins, but only recently have the risks become so great that tappers and muleteers may refuse to work in a particular area. Most threatening are the contrabandistas growing marijuana or looting ruins, as they often are armed with automatic weapons and have harassed and even murdered numerous people in recent years (A. Aldecoa, pers. comm. 1993).

Forest Clearing

The current rate of forest clearing in the Maya Biosphere Reserve is difficult to gauge; it varies with season and location in the reserve. Legal residents of the Maya Biosphere Reserve[7] are the only people allowed to clear forest, and then only for subsistence agriculture in specified areas near their villages. Any other type of forest clearing, unless otherwise approved by CONAP (e.g., for the construction of a new road), is illegal. Even legal clearing, however, can affect nontimber harvesters when it occurs near forest camps, as it destroys the natural habitat of the nontimber species, lowering short-term productivity by killing or injuring individual plants.

Foreign Tappers in Guatemalan Camps

The forest regions bordering Belize and Mexico are unguarded from the Guatemalan side, far from Guatemalan population centers, and, as a result, less heavily exploited by Guatemalans for nontimber products. Not surprisingly, people familiar with the area report that they often observe Mexicans and Belizeans from border communities working in Guatemalan camps, extracting chicle and other forest products such as allspice and wild animals; in some cases, these intruders loot Maya ceramic pieces from the ubiquitous ancient mounds. Although there is no reliable information on how many illegal tappers enter from Belize and Mexico, based on reports from contractors and tappers regarding the camps that had been occupied over a period of several years, I estimate that the number of foreign tappers working in the El Mirador/Dos Lagunas/Ixcan Río area is between 75 and 200 men. It is possible, however, that in areas where the forest extends across both sides of the border, some tappers may not even realize they have crossed the border. Needless to say, the presence of foreign tappers creates additional uncertainty for Guatemalan contractors and reduces the forest area available to Guatemalan tappers.

Conclusions

Neither government regulations nor customary institutions, alone or operating together, provide the conditions and incentives necessary for the development of a sustainable resource management regime. A central conclusion of this study is that a combination of the government's failure to recognize and support local resource use arrangements and the lack of necessary incentives for harvesters and contractors to manage the resource wisely has led to the weak management regime found today. Three factors in particular have impeded the development of a sustainable resource management regime: the lack of secure resource use rights or resource tenure; a failure to formalize the participation of industry participants in resource management; and the presence of external threats. To resolve these problems, two significant steps should be taken. First, the government of Guatemala should grant formal user rights to the chicle industry. Formal user rights, for example in the form of concessions awarded to groups of contractors, could provide industry participants with both the incentive and opportunity to strengthen and comply with customary rules regarding extraction activities and become part of a monitoring and enforcement network. Second, cooperation between CONAP and Itzalandia should be formalized, strengthened, and expanded. CONAP, established in 1989, is an agency with little experience in chicle management and therefore can benefit enormously from the combined years of experience and knowledge of the most experienced contractors. CONAP also has a very small budget and inadequate personnel to handle its many tasks; passing key management tasks over to Itzalandia simplifies and reduces the workload of CONAP.[8] This process of inter-institutional collaboration may be setting the foundation for a future comanagement regime, perhaps the best way to manage the chicle resource (Dugelby 1995), as keeping the government at least partially in control protects the industry from possible buyouts or other monopolistic moves by powerful private companies (M. Soza, pers. comm. 1993).

It is crucial that both industry participants and CONAP perceive incentives to cooperate in designing and implementing a management regime that ensures resource sustainability and long-term viability of the industry. The recommended changes and improvements represent only a beginning, but should generate the appropriate incentives and a forum for industry participants and CONAP to collaborate in developing a sustainable chicle management regime.

Notes

1. Nonlatex-producing chicle trees include all trees occurring in seasonally flooded forests (*bajo* forest), dying trees, and trees that chicle tappers considered of a nonproducing variety (locally called *mulas*, or trash).

2. My estimate of the total number of tappers working in the Petén in 1992–93 is based on two calculations. One method used the average production of latex per tapper per season and the total latex produced during 1992–93. The other method used data from interviews with contractors in which they stated the number of tappers they managed each year (Dugelby 1995).

3. The population of the Petén in the late 1800s was no more than 9,000 people and by 1964 it had grown to a mere 25,000. Current estimates place the population of the rapidly growing department at over 400,000.

4. Early peaks in chicle export levels may be explained by several factors. First, during the 1930s, importing companies operated directly out of the Petén and probably exported chicle harvested not only from Guatemalan forests, but as well from forests of southern Mexico and western Belize. Second, up until the late 1960s, the Petén was heavily forested. Since the 1960s, however, much of the region's forest has been converted to farm and pasture land. Thus, during the early decades of the chicle industry, the quantity of latex harvested was much greater possibly due to the larger expanse of forest being tapped, which included forest areas in Mexico and Belize. In earlier times, both first- and second-class chicle were purchased, occasionally indiscriminately. At present, Guatemala sells only first-class chicle. Thus, in addition to a larger expanse of forest, a significantly larger pool of trees (first- and second-class chicle-producing trees) was available to provide latex for the export market in the 1940s.

5. There is strong animosity among industry participants toward the proposed restrictions on tapping in new biotopes and national parks (particularly those along the northern border with Mexico) because, according to many knowledgeable forest workers, these areas include some of the richest chicle-producing forests in the Petén. Contractors and tappers also are convinced that the forests in these protected areas will not go unexploited, but rather that Mexican and Belizean tappers will enter to harvest latex. In addition, there are few guards posted in these parks, none of them are allowed to carry guns, and many have been restricted from patrolling the entire park area due to the risk of violence.

6. This lack of compliance actually originated with Itzalandia, as it was a negotiating point they used to get particularly powerful contractors to rejoin the cooperative. The contractors had left the cooperative because they objected to the policy that forbade them to surpass pre-established quotas (pers. obs. 1993).

7. I define legal residents as those who were living within the boundaries of the multiple-use area of the Maya Biosphere Reserve when it was established in 1990. According to the law establishing the Maya Biosphere Reserve, no immigration is permitted into this area. However, there are people living in villages just south of the Maya Biosphere Reserve who have small ranches and milpas in the Maya Biosphere Reserve that were established prior to the reserve.

8. It is interesting that officers of Itzalandia claim that they want CONAP to remain essentially the legal owner of chicle use rights. On the surface at least, this appears to be an attempt to prevent the cooperative and other contractors from selling out (i.e., to prevent self-destruction). It is puzzling why contractors do not trust each other or the group as a whole to manage the industry successfully on their own, controlling licensing, pricing, and design of restrictions, and this is worth further investigation.

References

Agrawal, A. 1993. Mobility and cooperation among nomadic shepherds: The case of the Raikas. *Human Ecology* 21: 261–279.

———. 1995. Dismantling the divide between indigenous and scientific knowledge. *Development and Change* 26: 413.

Alcorn, P. 1994. The chicle tree (*Manilkara zapota*) in Northwest Belize: Natural history, forest floristics, and management. Master's thesis, University of Florida, Gainesville.

Barrera de Jorgenson, A. 1993. Chicle extraction and forest conservation in Quintana Roo, Mexico. M.A. thesis, University of Florida, Gainesville.

Brandon, K. E., and M. Wells. 1992. Planning for people and parks: Design dilemmas. *World Development* 20: 557–570.

Brokaw, N., B. Brokaw, and P. Alcorn. 1990. *Trees of the Rio Bravo Conservation Area.* Report to the Manomet Bird Observatory, Manomet, Mass.

Bromley, D. W., D. Feeny, M. A. McKean, P. Peters, J. L. Gilles, R. J. Oakerson, C. F. Runge, and J. T. Thomson, eds. 1992. *Making the Commons Work: Theory, Practice, and Policy.* California Institute for Contemporary Studies, San Francisco.

Browder, J. O. 1995. Redemptive communities: Indigenous knowledge, colonist farming systems, and conservation of tropical forests. *Agriculture and Human Values* 12: 17.

Consejo Nacional de Areas Protegidas (CONAP). 1990. *Reserva de la Biosfera Maya.* Guatemala City, Guatemala.

Dugelby, B. L. 1995. Chicle latex extraction in the Maya Biosphere Reserve: Behavioral, institutional, and ecological factors affecting sustainability. Ph.D. dissertation, Duke University, Durham, N.C.

Gadgil, M., F. Berkes, and C. Folke. 1993. Indigenous knowledge for biodiversity conservation. *Ambio* 22: 151.

Gupta, A. 1986. Socioecology of stress: Why do common property resource management projects fail? In *Proceedings of the Conference on Common Property Management.* National Academy Press, Washington, D.C.

Hartshorn, G. S. 1980. Tree falls and tropical forest dynamics. In *Tropical Ecological Systems: Trends in Terrestrial and Aquatic Research,* F. B. Golley and E. Medina, eds. Springer-Verlag, New York.

Heinzman, R., and C. Reining. 1988. *Sustainable Forest Management in the Northern Petén, Guatemala.* Report to USAID/Guatemala.

Jochim, M. A. 1981. *Strategies for Survival: Cultural Behavior in an Ecological Context.* Academic Press, New York.

Leon, J. 1987. *Botánica de los Cultivos Tropicales,* M. S. Snarkis, ed. Instituto Interamericano de Cooperación para la Agricultura, Costa Rica.

Lundell, C. L. 1933. Chicle exploitation in the sapodilla forest of the Yucatán Peninsula. *Field and Laboratory* 2: 15–21.

―――. 1937. *The Vegetation of Petén.* Carnegie Institute of Washington, Washington, D.C.

McKean, M. A. 1992. Success on the commons: A comparative examination of institutions for common property resource management. *Journal of Theoretical Politics* 4: 247–281.

McKean, M., and E. Ostrom. 1995. Common property regimes in the forest: Just a relic from the past? *Unasylva* 180: 3–15.

Nations, J. D., B. Houseal, I. Ponciano, S. Billy, J. C. Godoy, F. Castro, G. Miller, D. Rose, M. R. Rosa, C. Azurdia. 1988. *Biodiversity in Guatemala: Biological Diversity and Tropical Forests Assessment.* World Resources Institute, Washington, D.C.

Peluso, N. L. 1992. The ironwood problem: (Mis)management and development of an extractive rainforest product. *Conservation Biology* 6: 210–219.

Pennington, T. D. 1991. Sapotaceae. *Flora Neotropica,* Monograph 52. The New York Botanical Garden, New York.

Puleston, D. E. 1982. The role of ramón in Maya subsistence. In *Maya Subsistence*, K. Flannery, ed. Academic Press, New York.

Reining, C. C. S., R. M. Heinzman, M. Cabrera Madrid, S. López, and A. Solórzano. 1992. The non-timber forest products of the Maya Biosphere Reserve, Guatemala: Results of ecological and socioeconomic surveys. Unpublished draft report to Conservation International, Washington, D.C.

Santiso, C. 1993. The Maya Biosphere Reserve in Guatemala. *Man and Natural Resources*. UNESCO quarterly journal.

Schwartz, N. B. 1990. *Forest Society: A Social History of Petén, Guatemala*. University of Pennsylvania Press, Philadelphia.

Standley, P., and M. Steyermark. 1958. *The Flora of Guatemala*. Fieldiana: Vol. 24. Field Museum of Natural History, Chicago.

Taylor, M. 1987. *The Possibility of Cooperation*. Cambridge University Press, Cambridge, U.K.

Western, D., and R. M. Wright, with Shirley C. Strum, eds. 1994. *Natural Connections: Perspectives in Community-Based Conservation*. Island Press, Washington, D.C.

Chapter 12

The Impact of Hunting on Wildlife in the Maya Forest of Mexico

Jeffrey P. Jorgenson

Subsistence hunting has a long history in the Maya Forest of Mexico, Belize, and Guatemala. Archaeological studies have confirmed that the Maya have consumed many species of fish, mollusks, birds, mammals, reptiles, and amphibians for at least 1,500 years (Pohl 1976, 1985; Hamblin 1984), and perhaps for as long as 4,000 years. Contemporary studies have documented hunting for domestic consumption (Leopold 1972; Chávez-León 1983; Greenberg 1992; Jorgenson 1995a), the use of live animals as pets, and the use of wild animal products in homes and for religious ceremonies (Redfield and Villa Rojas 1962; Villa Rojas 1987). Wildlife also plays an important role in the oral histories of the Maya (Burns 1983).

Despite its significance in the lives of local people, there are indications that the abundance of wildlife in the Maya Forest is diminishing. Reasons for this decline may include overexploitation through subsistence hunting, although this possibility has not yet been explored. The objective of this chapter is to discuss the impact of hunting on wildlife in the context of the current socioeconomic situation of the region and the management of the Maya Forest. Specifically, I will present a case study of Maya hunters at Ejido X-Hazil y Anexos, State of Quintana Roo, Mexico, and discuss subsistence hunting in terms of the following topics: patterns and intensity of hunting in the Maya Forest, sustainability of hunting, impact of hunting on biological communities in the region, and local management of subsistence hunting. These topics are important individually as well as collectively. The patterns and intensity of hunting are important in order to identify those species that are hunted and to analyze differences by species in terms of the number of animals killed and the amount of meat obtained by the hunters.

Maya hunters do not take all species at the same frequency. This fact, as well as biological differences between game species, means that some game species may be unable to sustain viable populations at the current level of hunting. To ensure the continued survival of game species as well as the continuation of this important Maya cultural activity, it is important to determine the level of hunting that is sustainable.

The impact of hunting on biological communities in the region is important because many of the species of birds and mammals are seed dispersers or seedling predators. Thus, hunting has potential positive and negative impacts on the flora. Such impacts on biological communities can vary according to the abundance of the associated wildlife. Based on the above information, and taking into consideration how difficult it is to manage many game species, it seems clear that local management of wildlife ought to occur within a framework of bilateral cooperation between officials of Maya communities and national entities responsible for the management of natural resources. By means of this chapter, I hope to show on the one hand the complexity of Maya hunting practices, and on the other the tremendous opportunity that exists for fruitful cooperative efforts between local and national officials to manage this activity.

Study Area

The study took place at Ejido X-Hazil y Anexos, primarily in the vicinity of the village of X-Hazil Sur, Quintana Roo, Mexico, during 1989–1990 (17 months; additional data obtained during a 1-month trip in 1992: Figure 12.1). The ejido area, where the residents have the legal right to exploit and manage natural resources found in the area to benefit the community, measures approximately 20 km x 30 km and has a surface area of 55,295 ha. There are three villages in the ejido: X-Hazil Sur, Uh-May, and Chancah Veracruz. In 1989, the population of X-Hazil Sur, the largest village, was 950 residents (479 males and 471 females) in approximately 200 family units. In addition to maintaining many of their cultural traditions, ejido residents participate in a wide range of socioeconomic activities outside of the ejido.

The study area typically has a dry season between December and May, and a wet season between June and November, with an annual precipitation of 1,300 mm (Jorgenson 1993). Temperatures fluctuate daily between 22° and 32° C. The principal vegetation type of the ejido is medium-height, semi-evergreen forest (Téllez Valdés and Sousa Sánchez 1982). Approximately 100 species of trees with dbh > 15 cm have been recorded for the area, with chacá (*Bursera simaruba* Burseraceae) and chicozapote (*Manilkara zapote* Sapota-

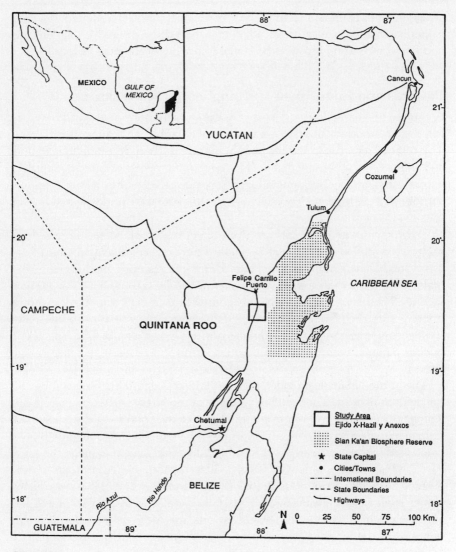

Figure 12.1

Study area: Ejido X-Hazil y Anexos, Quintana Roo, Mexico.

ceae) the most abundant (Barrera de Jorgenson 1993). On the ejido, the area in permanent forest measures 25,000 ha, while the area used for agriculture and livestock grazing is 30,295 ha (Guatemala Biempica, pers. comm.).

Patterns and Intensity of Hunting in the Maya Forest

A total of 584 animals were reported as taken by hunters at X-Hazil Sur during the 17 months (June 1989–October 1990, Table 12.1; Jorgenson 1993). The total of reported animals was 66% mammals (N = 385 individuals) and 34% birds (N = 199 individuals). There were no reports of hunting reptiles, amphibians, or insects. Some villagers practiced fishing, but it was a limited activity (few outings and few fish caught); thus data were not collected on the species or quantities.

Eight species of mammals and four species of birds were harvested by hunters for subsistence purposes at X-Hazil Sur. The coati (*Nasua narica* Procyonidae; N = 167 individuals) occupied first place among the hunted mammals, while the pocket gopher (*Orthogeomys hispidus* Geomyidae; N = 53) was second and the paca (*Agouti paca* Agoutidae; N = 47) was third. Among hunted birds, the plain chachalaca (*Ortalis vetula* Cracidae; N = 167 individuals) occupied first place. According to hunters, however, the other species of hunted mammals and birds were also important for cultural and nutritional reasons.

The hunted animals provided the residents of X-Hazil Sur with a substantial amount of meat. The total body weight of the 584 animals was 2,700 kilograms (kg) (Table 12.1). Of this total, 95% of the total weight was derived from mammals, and only 5% came from birds. Three species of mammals provided 68% of the total weight: white-tailed deer (*Odocoileus virginianus* Cervidae; 709 kg, average weight = 30kg), collared peccary (*Pecari tajacu*, previously identified as *Tayassu tajacu* [see Wilson and Reeder 1993], Tayassuidae; 618 kg total weight, average weight = 16 kg) and coati (505 kg total weight, average weight = 3 kg). With few exceptions, this meat was consumed by the hunters and their immediate families or sold in small quantities (ca. 1 to 2 kg) to neighbors in the village. Hunters did not have to leave the ejido to sell meat.

The group of acknowledged hunters at X-Hazil Sur was relatively small (Jorgenson 1995b,), including 84 men (older than 15 years of age) from 70 family units and two women from two family units, for a total of 86 persons. Other individuals either did not hunt or denied hunting. It is estimated that these 86 hunters harvested approximately 67% (two-thirds) of the game kills. With respect to those persons who did not report kills, the majority only harvested one to two animals per year.

The number of kills per hunter varied greatly (Jorgenson 1995b). The average was 6.8 kills per hunter over 17 months (equivalent to 4.8 kills annually

Table 12.1. Total number of individuals and total weight of game species harvested by Maya Indians in X-Hazil Sur, Quintana Roo, Mexico (6/89–10/90).[a]

Game species Spanish / English Scientific name	Total number of individuals[b]	Total weight (kg)[c]	Mean weight (kg)[c]
Mammals			
Tuza / Pocket gopher *Orthogeomys hispidus*	53 (51)	22.3	0.4
Sereke / Agouti *Dasyprocta punctata*	47	278.4	2.8
Tepescuintle / Paca *Agouti paca*	35	96.8	5.8
Tejón / Coati *Nasua narica*	167	504.9	3.0
Puerco de monte / White-lipped peccary *Tayassu pecari*	3	94.3	31.4
Jabalí / Collared peccary *Pecari tajacu*	40 (36)	618.5	17.2
Temazate / Brocket deer *Mazama americana*	16	250.0	15.6
Venado cola blanca / White-tailed deer *Odocoileus virginianus*	24 (22)	709.0	32.2
SUBTOTAL	385 (377)	2,570.6	
%	66	95	
Birds			
Perdíz / Thicket tinamou *Crypturellus cinnamomeus*	13	4.9	0.4
Faisán / Great curassow *Crax rubra*	13	40.9	3.1
Chachalaca / Plain chachalaca *Ortalis vetula*	67	64.9	0.4
Pavo de monte / Ocellated turkey *Agriocharis ocellata*	6	19.7	3.3
SUBTOTAL	199	130.4	
%	34	5	
COMBINED TOTAL (MAMMALS & BIRDS)	584 (576)	2,700.1	

[a]Source: Jorgenson (1993)

[b]The weight in parentheses indicates the total number of individuals summed to calculate the total weight if the weight was not available for all individuals.

[c]Total weight or mean weight for each species. The precision of the weight varies according to the scale used.

per hunter; Figure 12.2). However, the average is not indicative of the extent of variability; for instance, one individual took 85 animals, while 35 hunters took one animal each. Seven hunters harvested 27 or more animals each and were responsible for 54% of the kills. For the purpose of this study, these hunters were categorized as "dedicated hunters," a category representing approximately 2% of the male population in X-Hazil Sur. The 79 individuals who harvested one to 26 kills each were categorized as "occasional hunters" (approximately 26% of the male population in the village). A total of 216 men did not hunt (72% of the male population).

Sustainability of Hunting

Maya hunters have practiced subsistence hunting in the Maya Forest for as much as 4,000 years. It is interesting to note that the same species of wildlife almost always appear in the harvest lists compiled by scientists. Archaeological studies in Mexico (Hamblin 1984), Belize, and Guatemala (Pohl 1976, 1985), for example, have documented the abundance and diversity of wildlife species in the diet of the ancient Maya. Recent studies have also documented

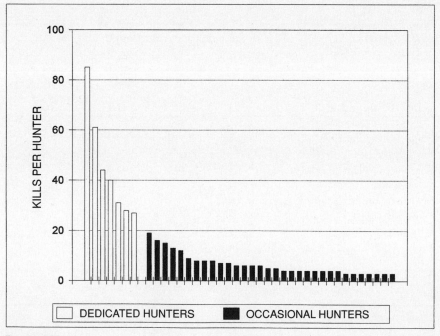

Figure 12.2

Number of kills per hunter. A total of 47 hunters had one or two kills each and are not shown here.

the importance of bush meat to modern residents (Nations and Nigh 1980; Murphy 1990). The fact that current hunters are harvesting roughly the same species that have been taken for 4,000 years suggests a hypothesis that hunting, as practiced by the Maya, may be sustainable. However, this hypothesis needs to be critically examined in light of increasing human populations and socioeconomic changes that are now occurring in the region (Edwards 1986, Sullivan 1989; Bray et al. 1993; Barrera de Jorgenson and Jorgenson 1995).

According to local hunters at X-Hazil Sur, certain species are no longer as abundant as they were previously. According to elderly hunters, there are three species of mammals and three species of birds that are in danger of being extirpated due to hunting: white-lipped peccary (*Tayassu pecari* Tayassuidae; 3 animals killed during 1989–1990), spider monkey (*Ateles geoffroyi* Cebidae; 0), howler monkey (*Alouatta pigra* Cebidae; 0), great curassow (*Crax rubra* Cracidae; 13), ocellated turkey (*Agriocharis ocellata* Meleagrididae; 6), and guan (*Penelope purpurascens* Cracidae; 0). The local reduction in abundance of these species, however, does not mean that it would not be possible to have a sustainable harvest of these taxa. Other factors besides hunting may be involved in the decline in abundance of these species, such as changing land-use patterns, animal diseases, and exotic species introductions. The population decreases and their causes need to be evaluated.

Impact of Hunting on Biological Communities in the Region

Hunting has a direct potential impact on wildlife populations, especially birds and mammals. The removal of large animals, however, is not the only impact of this activity. Hunting also has an impact on ecosystems by reducing the populations of animals engaged in herbivory and seed predation, seed dispersal, and predation of other animals (Redford 1992). From Mexico (Dirzo and Miranda 1990) to Brazil (da Fonseca and Robinson 1990), there is evidence that hunting can result in negative changes in the structure and composition of biological communities, thus affecting plants as well as animals. The impact of these changes is poorly understood, but there is evidence that herbivory and seed predation by mammals can reduce tree recruitment. In Panama, for example, mammals are predators on seeds and seedlings of two species of trees (*Dipteryx panamensis* Leguminosae, De Steven and Putz 1984; *Faramea occidentalis* Rubiaceae, Scupp 1988). Additional examples of seed and seedling predation by mammals are expected. These examples will provide additional information about the relationship between wildlife consumption and structure and composition of the forest. Given that large mammals in other areas of the Neotropics have an important role in regulating the structure and function of biological communities (Terborgh 1988), their absence or low numbers in the Maya Forest also might modify biological communities there.

It has been documented through an analysis of stomach contents that the game species at Ejido X-Hazil y Anexos eat a wide variety of plant species (Table 12.2). In the study of the diet composition of white-tailed and brocket deer (*Mazama americana* Cervidae; Jorgenson 1995c) with respect to the plant parts consumed, it was possible to determine that the diet of the white-tailed deer was composed of 42% leaves (percent volume), 32% fruits and seeds, and 26% other, while the diet of the brocket deer was composed of 58% leaves, 24% other, and 19% fruits and seeds. The diet of these species also varied in terms of the species composition of the consumed plants. The white-tailed deer used a greater diversity of plants than did the brocket deer (43 taxa vs. 32). For the brocket deer (N = 8 stomachs analyzed), the principal stomach contents were shrubs of the genus *Psychotria* (Rubiaceae; rank order = 1; occurrence = 88% of the individual samples and volume = 58% of the total combined samples) and the ramón tree (*Brosimum alicastrum* Moraceae; rank order = 2; occurrence = 62% and volume = 1.6%). For the white-tailed deer (N = 11), the principal stomach contents were *Psychotria* spp. (rank order = 1; occurrence = 73% and volume = 43%) and unidentified plants (rank order = 2; occurrence = 54% and volume = 0.7%; Table 12.2).

Suggestions for Local Management of Subsistence Hunting

Despite the experience, contacts, good intentions, and economic resources of national and international entities, these organizations cannot undertake by themselves the task of wildlife management in the Maya Forest. Based on the results and experiences obtained during this study, it is clear that the national and state governments must develop wildlife management plans with the active participation of the Maya communities. Government biologists and wildlife experts can provide technical information and a wide geographical perspective (external advice), while local Maya communities can provide extensive knowledge of the area and wildlife species contained therein (internal advice). In this manner, it would be possible to take advantage of the different levels or kinds of experience and information that each party possesses, with the local communities ultimately taking responsibility for the management of resources in their areas. To a certain extent, the community of Tres Garantías in the southern part of Quintana Roo has been able to organize a program for sport hunting and ecotourism to attract visitors to their ejido (F. Quinto, pers. comm.). Supported by field data about wildlife habitat use and relative abundance, local officials at Tres Garantías have obtained the necessary permits from state officials to continue their program. It is important to emphasize that the residents of Tres Garantías also design and benefit from their program through their employment as guides, cooks, and field assistants for the visitors. In this way, these people have an economic alternative to extensive timber harvest on their lands. This program can serve as an example of cooperation between local and state officials.

Table 12.2.

Principal stomach contents organized by family for brocket deer (*Mazama*; N = 8 stomachs analyzed) and white-tailed deer (*Odocoileus*: N = 11) at Ejido X-Hazil y Anexos, Quintana Roo, Mexico, 1989–1990.

Species	Family	Mazama			Odocoileus		
		% Occ.[a]	% Vol.[b]	Rank order[c]	% Occ.[a]	% Vol.[b]	Rank order[c]
Ipomea triloba	Convulvulaceae				36.4	0.7	6
Galactia stricta	Leguminosae				36.4	5.6	5
Brosimum alicastrum	Moraceae	62.5	1.6	2	45.5	1.0	4
Trophis racemosa	Moraceae	37.5	1.1	5	45.5	7.7	3
Eugenia spp.	Myrtaceae	50.0	0.4	3	36.4	0.6	7
Psychotria spp.	Rubiaceae	87.5	58.3	1	72.7	42.7	1
Manilkara zapota	Sapotaceae	37.5	0.7	6			
Unidentified plants		50.0	0.3	4	54.5	0.7	2
Animal material	Class Mammalia	37.5	<0.1	7	36.4	<0.1	8

Source: Jorgerson (1995c)

[a] % Occ. = % occurrence

[b] % Vol. = % volume

[c] Rank order based on percent occurrence and volume

In order to develop a local plan to manage subsistence hunting, it is necessary to gather information to answer several basic questions about short-term and long-term matters. The short-term questions include the following: Which species are being hunted? How much is being hunted? Who hunts? Where do people hunt? When do people hunt?

The purpose of obtaining this information is to be able to develop a basis to identify patterns and characterize the intensity of hunting. With this information, obtained through studies at the community or ejido level, it will be possible to determine which species and how many species are subject to hunting. It also will be possible to determine the quantity of animals harvested (the number of animals as well as their weight). With regard to the hunters, it is necessary to know who is using the wildlife resources in order to evaluate the cultural and nutritional importance of the game. It is also necessary to know what proportion of the community benefits from hunting. If wildlife is considered to be a community resource, but benefits only a few people, there will be problems in convincing the majority of the local people to abide by management rules. In order to avoid these problems, a way must be developed so that those who do not hunt still receive benefits from this activity. This is necessary to ensure that nonhunters understand that they must take wildlife into consideration when undertaking other economic activities such as timber harvest or the extraction of nontimber forest products. Finally, it is important to know where and when game is harvested in order to develop our knowledge of the biological characteristics of the species (for example, diet, preferred habitat, and reproductive period). If this information is gathered in a systematic manner, it can be used to develop long-term management plans.

There are two critical aspects regarding local management of wildlife on ejidos in the Maya Forest of Mexico. First, there must be common agreement among ejido members, by hunters as well as nonhunters, to develop and implement the wildlife management plan. It is important that hunters recognize that wildlife is a resource that belongs to all the members of the community, and not just to the hunters. Thus everyone must participate in the decision-making process regarding this resource. Hunters must look for ways to compensate the community for the game harvested. Nonhunters must accept that wildlife is an important resource for the community and that management of forest species implies limits to activities that could be detrimental to animals (for example, timber harvest and the extraction of nontimber forest products). Second, there must be agreement between the communities and the government officials to share management responsibilities for the wildlife. As their contribution, government officials should give up a certain degree of autonomy to the communities in the establishment of hunting regulations such as harvest dates and the legal bag limit. As their contribution, community authorities should assume responsibility for the implementation and enforcement of these regulations. Local authorities, as members of these communities, are in a better position than outside enforcers to assure compliance with these rules.

Examples of Cooperative Projects in Other Regions

Local participation in the management of wildlife and other natural resources has been a critical element in several projects in Latin America (Vega 1994). The following are two such projects:

In Colombia, national legislation recognizes the right of indigenous and black communities to manage their lands collectively, as well as to use forest resources. Fishing and hunting along the west coast, where agricultural production is low (Jimeno et al. 1995) are important activities for local people's subsistence. There is evidence, however, that some species of wildlife in the Choco region cannot sustain current harvest levels. During a cooperative study with Emberá Indians at Utría National Park, Rubio Torgler (1995) was able to confirm the extirpation of two major game species: white-lipped peccary and tapir (*Tapirus bairdii* Tapiridae). Now, based on a joint evaluation of the situation, researchers and local residents have created wildlife refuges and are establishing no-hunting periods for selected species. The results of these local management actions will be obtained through established methods and criteria made jointly by researchers and local residents (Ráez Luna and Rubio Torgler 1994).

Local management of wild flora and fauna in combination with external consultancies is the basis for a community development project in Peru. Established in 1991, Tamshiyacu-Tahuayo Community Reserve aspires to develop a program for the sustainable use by local residents of animals (Bodmer 1995a) and plants (Penn 1995) in order to eliminate some of the causes that promote the overexploitation of wildlife. In order to develop this program and propose a sustainable system, Bodmer (1995b) had to analyze historical aspects of community management of wildlife, evaluate the sustainability of current harvest levels, and undertake a socioeconomic analysis of the current overharvest. Bodmer (1995b) concluded that it was possible to exploit these resources in a sustainable manner. However, he was able to foresee that a short-term consequence of implementing the program (0 to 5 years) would be severe economic costs for the residents, while local people would obtain important benefits over the long term (6 to 30 years). Due to the severe poverty of the region, it would be difficult to expect major sacrifices from these people. By not adopting this program, however, their poverty would only increase as they used up the available natural resources.

In order to respond to this critical situation, the program for the Tamshiyacu-Tahuayo Community Reserve adopted two strategies (Bodmer 1995b). First, the program sought to develop short-term economic support to help the people in the reserve. Second, it proposed a long-term project for the local management of plants and wildlife to be implemented in steps or phases so that incremental changes will be instituted to modify hunting practices, the extraction of wood, and the use of nontimber forest products. In order to assure the success of the project, according to Bodmer and his colleagues, the support and participation by local residents in the development of management plans is indispensable.

Conclusions

The socioeconomic situation of the Maya in Mexico, Belize, and Guatemala is changing rapidly; it appears that hunting can no longer continue without effective controls on legal harvest dates and bag limits. Many hunters at X-Hazil Sur indicated their concerns about the increasing scarcity of wildlife on the ejido. They were not interested in changing their personal hunting practices, however, thereby limiting dates or quantities, because there was no way to assure that other hunters would adopt the same changes.

The problem of hunting in the Mexican portion of the Maya Forest represents an excellent opportunity to join the themes of wildlife conservation and management with the needs of rural communities to develop socioeconomic alternatives without exhausting the natural resources of the ejido. The organizational structure of the ejido, with legally recognized boundaries and officials sanctioned by the State, favors the development and implementation of management plans that include not only agriculture, chicle exploitation, and timber harvest as economic resources, but also the incorporation of wildlife products from hunting. The critical element for the development and implementation of these plans is local participation. Thus far, the State has not been able to manage natural resources at the local level, and it will not be able to do so because of a shortage of time and money. The solution is to promote a joint effort combining local knowledge with national and international experience. At Ejido Tres Garantías, local officials have developed a program for ecotourism. In other countries, such as Colombia and Peru, local officials are cooperating with state and international entities to design long-term plans for the sustainable exploitation of local natural resources. To date, these successes have been quite modest, but the opportunities are great. To assure the cultural and biological conservation of the Maya and their surroundings in the Maya Forest, it is imperative to identify solutions that respond to the socioeconomic needs of people as well as to the biological needs of the wild flora and fauna in the region. For perhaps as long as 4,000 years the Maya have shared these lands with the surrounding plants and animals. With careful management, perhaps they can continue to share them for another 4,000 years.

Acknowledgments

This study was undertaken with the financial support of World Wildlife Fund–US, World Nature Association, Roger and Benita Jorgenson, Organization of American States, Centro de Investigaciones de Quintana Roo, and Program for Studies in Tropical Conservation/Tropical Conservation and Development Program (University of Florida). The Secretaría de Desarrollo Urbano y Ecología (SEDUE) kindly granted a research permit for Quintana Roo, Mexico. Marcelo Carreón Mundo and Victoria Santos Jiménez (Plan Estatal Forestal) provided maps and information about the forest in the study area. Kent H. Redford and John G. Robinson assisted in the design of the study. Amanda Barrera de Jorgenson, Armando Balam Xiu, and Rufino Ucan Chan (X-Hazil Sur) collaborated in the field work. I thank Richard Primack, David Bray, Hugo Galletti, and the anonymous reviewers for their comments on an earlier version of the manuscript. Finally, I would like to thank the residents of Ejido X-Hazil y Anexos for their friendship and cooperation without which this study would not have been possible.

References

Barrera de Jorgenson, A. 1993. Chicle extraction and forest conservation in Quintana Roo, Mexico. M.A.thesis, University of Florida, Gainesville.

Barrera de Jorgenson, A., and J. P. Jorgenson. 1995. Use of forest resources and conservation in Quintana Roo, Mexico. In *Integrating People and Wildlife for a Sustainable Future*. J. A. Bissonette and P. R. Krausman, eds. The Wildlife Society, Bethesda, Md.

Bodmer, R. E. 1995a. Manejo de fauna silvestre con las comunidades locales en la Reserva Comunal Tamshiyacu-Tahuayo. II Congreso Internacional sobre Manejo de Fauna Silvestre en la Amazonia 7–12 de mayo de 1995, Iquitos, Perú (Summary).

———. 1995b. *Linking Conservation and Local People through Sustainable Use of Natural Resources: Community-Based Management in the Peruvian Amazon*. Case study requested by the WWF Wild Species Use Study, C. H. Freese, ed. World Wildlife Fund, Washington, D.C.

Bray, D. B., M. Carreón, L. Merino, and V. Santos. 1993. On the road to sustainable forestry. *Cultural Survival Quarterly* 17: 38–41.

Burns, A. F. 1983. *An Epoch of Miracles: Oral History of the Yucatec Maya*. University of Texas Press, Austin.

Chávez-León, G. 1983. Determinación de las relaciones hombre-fauna silvestre en una zona rural de Quintana Roo. *Boletín Técnico del Instituto Nacional de Investigaciones Forestales (México, D.F., México)* No. 94.

da Fonseca, G. A. B., and J. G. Robinson. 1990. Forest size and structure: Competitive and predatory effects on small mammal communities. *Biological Conservation* 53: 265–294.

De Steven, D., and F. E. Putz. 1984. Impact of mammals on early recruitment of a tropical canopy tree, *Dipteryx panamensis*, in Panama. *Oikos* 43: 207–216.

Dirzo, R., and A. Miranda. 1990. Contemporary Neotropical defaunation and forest structure, function, and diversity: A sequel to John Terborgh. *Conservation Biology* 4: 444–447.

Edwards, C. R. 1986. The human impact on the forest in Quintana Roo, Mexico. *Journal of Forestry* 30:120–127.

Greenberg, L. S. Z. 1992. Garden hunting among the Yucatec Maya: A coevolutionary history of wildlife and culture. *Etnoecológia* 1(1):23–33.

Hamblin, N. L. 1984. *Animal Use by Cozumel Maya*. University of Arizona Press, Tucson.

Jorgenson, J. P. 1993. Gardens, wildlife densities, and subsistence hunting by Maya Indians in Quintana Roo, Mexico. Ph.D. dissertation, University of Florida, Gainesville.

———. 1995a. Maya subsistence hunters in Quintana Roo, Mexico. *Oryx* 29:49–57.

———. 1995b. Cambios en los patrones de la cacería de subsistencia a través de mejoramientos socio-económicos: El ejemplo de los cazadores mayas en México. II Congreso Internacional sobre Manejo de Fauna Silvestre en la Amazonia 7–12 de mayo de 1995, Iquitos, Perú (Summary).

———. 1995c. Aproximación a la dieta de dos especies de venado en el suroriente de México, III Congreso Latinoamericano de Ecología, 22–28 de octubre de 1995, Mérida, Venezuela.

Leopold, A. S. 1972. *Wildlife of Mexico: The Game Birds and Mammals*. University of California Press, Berkeley.

Murphy, J. 1990. Indigenous forest use and development in the "Maya Zone" of Quintana Roo, Mexico. M.E.S. thesis, York University, Ontario, Canada.

Nations, J. D. and R. B. Nigh. 1980. The evolutionary potential of Lacandon Maya sustained yield tropical forest agriculture. *Journal of Anthropological Research* 36(1): 1–30.

Penn, J. 1995. El proyecto de palmeras (*Mauritia flexosa*) en la Reserva Comunal Tamshiyacu-Tahuayo, Loreto, Peru. II Congreso Internacional sobre Manejo de Fauna Silvestre en la Amazonia 7–12 de mayo de 1995, Iquitos, Perú (Summary).

Pohl, M.E.D. 1976. Ethnozoology of the Maya: An analysis of fauna from five sites in Petén, Gautemala. Ph.D. dissertation, Harvard University, Cambridge, Mass.

———, ed. 1985. *Prehistoric Lowland Maya Environment and Subsistence Economy*. Papers of the Peabody Museum of Archeology and Ethnology, Vol. 77. Harvard University Press, Cambridge, Mass.

Ráez Luna, E. F., and H. Rubio Torgler. 1994. Manual básico para el estudio de la cacería de animales silvestres y su impacto ecológico, con especial referencia a la cacería de subsistencia en el Chocó Biogeográfico Colombiano. Proyecto BioPacífico, Santa Fe de Bogotá.

Redfield, R., and A. Villa Rojas. 1962. *Chan Kom, a Maya Village*. Carnegie Institution of Washington, Publication No. 448.

Redford, K. H. 1992. The empty forest. *BioScience* 42: 412–422.

Rubio Torgler, H. 1995. Demanda de fauna por parte de comunidades indígenas Emberá y estratégias para el manjo de especies de caza en el área de influencia del Parque Nacional Utría (Chocó, Colombia). II Congreso Internacional sobre Manejo de Fauna Silvestre en la Amazonia 7–12 de mayo de 1995, Iquitos, Perú (Summary).

Sullivan, P. 1989. *Unfinished Conversations: Maya and Foreigners between Two Wars*. Alfred A. Knopf, New York.

Téllez Valdés, O., and M. Sousa Sánchez. 1982. *Imagenes de la flora quintanarroense*. Centro de Investigaciones de Quintana Roo (CIQRO), A.C., Puerto Morales, Q.R., México.

Terborgh, J. 1988. The big things that run the world: A sequel to E. O. Wilson. *Conservation Biology* 2: 402–403.

Vega, A., ed. 1994. *Corredores conservacionistas en la Región Centroamericana: Memorias de una conferencia regional auspiciada por el Proyecto Paseo Pantera*. Tropical Research and Development, Gainesville, Fla.

Villa Rojas, A. 1987. Los Elegidos del Dios: Enografia de los Mayas de Quintana Roo. Instituto Nacional Indigenista, México, 574 pp.

Wilson, D. E., and D. M. Reeder, eds. 1993. *Mammal Species of the World: A Taxonomic and Geographic Reference*. 2nd edition. Smithsonian Institution Press, Washington, D.C.

Chapter 13

Monitoring Nontimber Forest Product Harvest for Ecological Sustainability: A Case Study of Huano (*Sabal mauritiiformis*) in the Río Bravo Conservation and Management Area, Belize

Jennifer L. O'Hara

During the past decade, management of protected areas has undergone a significant shift in strategies—from merely "locking up" resources to actively integrating economic development and conservation objectives (Goodland 1987; Shaffer and Saterson 1987; McNeeley 1992). Conservation organizations and funding agencies alike have recognized that protected areas cannot be sustained over the long term without the approval and support of local inhabitants (McNeeley 1992); these organizations thus have turned to the implementation of integrated conservation and development programs (ICDPs) as a solution. A primary goal of ICDPs has been to promote conservation of biodiversity while improving human living standards (Kremen et al. 1994). Development ventures have included ecotourism projects and the harvest of renewable resources such as timber and nontimber forest products (NTFPs). Nontimber forest products (also known as "minor" or "natural" forest products) have included animals, fruits, nuts, latexes, oils, and all plant parts other than wood.

Funding agencies have recognized only recently the need for monitoring and evaluating ICDPs (Brown and Wykoff-Baird 1992; Wells et al. 1992); as a result, very few programs have undertaken monitoring activities (Kremen et al. 1994). Is there cause for concern? A review of 36 ICDPs found that only five projects exhibited successful conservation of biological diversity (Kremen et al. 1994) This finding suggests that there is a critical need for incorporating monitoring and assessment procedures into NTFP programs in order to ensure that larger conservation goals are achieved.

Background

The Brazilian government first accepted the idea of extractive reserves as a legitimate form of land tenure in 1988. Since then, harvesting of nontimber forest products has been proposed as an effective strategy that integrates the dual objectives of biodiversity conservation and economic development. Many scholars subsequently have assumed that NTFP extraction is occurring or can occur on a sustainable basis (Prance 1989; Allegretti 1990; Soemarwoto 1992; Godoy and Bawa 1993; Dore and Nogueira 1994) despite the absence of systematic studies that support this assumption (Godoy and Bawa 1993; Kremen et al. 1994). Basic information such as distribution, abundance, productivity, and regeneration of nontimber forest product species typically is lacking, yet it is urgently needed in order to determine optimal productivity and capacity for harvest in natural habitats (Gunatilleke et al. 1993). In response to this absence of information, NTFP research has focused on determining the distribution, abundance, and effects of harvesting on population structure and dynamics of the NTFP species. Notably missing from these studies are efforts to address the effects of harvesting on ecosystem processes and functions. If the harvest of NTFPs is to serve as a positive strategy in biosphere reserves and other protected areas, it is necessary to assess whether current rates of extraction threaten harvested species and whether extraction deteriorates ecosystem processes and functions. A decision-making framework is needed to help determine where and when this land-use technique is or is not appropriate. For example, there may be particular habitats or specific products that are more conducive to ecologically sustainable harvest.

Current State of the Art of NTFP Monitoring

Since the beginning of this century, the concept of maximum sustainable yield has been used by foresters and fisheries biologists to manage single utilitarian resources (Steen 1984). It has also been applied to the management of soils, game populations, livestock forage, and even recreational use (Salwasser 1990). More recently, sustained yield principles have been utilized as part of NTFP management.

Maximum sustainable yield is a scientific doctrine that emphasizes the management of a single resource for maximum and continuing production, consistent with the maintenance of a constantly renewable stock (Tivy and O'Hare 1982). Although maximum sustainable yield has been practiced in the United States for over 80 years in the fields of forestry and fisheries, many problems remain. In fact, this paradigm has more recently been deemed inadequate for today's ecological concerns. For example, forestry managers are increasingly turning toward an ecosystem approach, an evolving management paradigm that more effectively addresses not only uses and outputs but also the effects of management on ecosystem interactions and processes (Gordon 1994). Is the sustained yield paradigm, by itself, adequate for the management of NTFPs?

NTFP management is in many ways far less evolved than that of the aforementioned fields, primarily because little basic biological information is available for many tropical NTFP species. In this regard, NTFP managers are playing a "catch-up" game. In instances where monitoring of NTFP harvesting is occurring, studies have focused on the abundance, distribution, and population structure and dynamics of the species of interest. This research is characteristic of the maximum sustained yield approach to management. Abundance and distribution data can be used to delineate suitable harvesting areas and to construct age/size class distributions (Hall and Bawa 1993). Studies of population dynamics appear to be following a trend toward using matrix models, sensitivity analyses, and elasticity analyses to identify the potential consequences of varying management schemes (e.g., Olmsted and Alvarez-Buyalla 1995; Peters 1989; Ratsirarson et al. 1996). Despite the multitude of articles that address economic concerns and NTFP harvest processes and use, very little literature specifically discusses methods for monitoring the harvest of NTFPs.

More recently, researchers have emphasized that NTFP managers must consider not only the long-term sustainability of harvested populations but also the effect of harvesting on ecosystem structure and function (Nepsted et al. 1992; Hall and Bawa 1993) and on other species in the community (Hall and Bawa 1993). For example, harvesting seeds and fruits may lead to decreases in forage for frugivore populations, which in turn may lower the diversity of frugivores in a community (Hall and Bawa 1993). Harvesting products such as leaf litter over long periods of time (e.g., 40 years) can lead to decreases in nutrient cycling rates (Brown et al. 1995) and organic matter pools (Mo et al. 1995), both of which affect soil mineralization rates and soil nutrient availabilities (Brown et al. 1995). Extractive activities that remove critical nutrients faster than they can be replenished may cause nutrient depletions in ecosystems (Salafsky et al. 1991), which may lead to decreases in productivity (Stone 1979).

Scientists recently have begun to understand that a plant species' unique characteristics or functions can mean that individual species have a significant effect on the local environment. For example, a plant may modify or control decomposition and nutrient cycling rates by accumulating particular secondary defensive compounds in its tissues (Vogt et al. 1995), by accumulating beneficial elements (e.g., magnesium, nitrogen, calcium, or phosphorus), thereby enriching its living space with these elements (Bloomfield et al. 1993), or by accumulating aluminum, which can inhibit growth of other plant species (Vogt et al. 1995). Other plant species, such as the cohune palm (*Orbignya cohune*), affect soil development through the addition of large amounts of organic litter (Furley 1975). Some tree species may even lower soil pH through a variety of processes, including increasing the quantity of anions in soil solution (Binkley and Richter 1987).

As demonstrated by the above examples, an individual plant species may play a key role in an ecosystem. Loss or significant alteration of the population dynamics of a species may have significant effects on the sustainability of ecosystem processes. Therefore, it is crucial to examine not only the effects of harvesting on plant populations, but also potential effects on ecosystem processes and interactions.

Huano Harvest in the Río Bravo Conservation and Management Area: A Case Study

In the greater Petén area, as in many tropical regions, palm species supply necessary products ranging from medicines and foods to construction materials. *Sabal mauritiiformis* (formerly known in Belize as *Sabal morrisiana*) is harvested widely for the production of thatched roofs (Figure 13.1). Within the Maya Forest this species is known by several names. For example, *huano* refers specifically to *Sabal mauritiiformis* and the leaf products it supplies. In Belize the terms *bayleaf* and *botan* also refer to *Sabal mauritiiformis*. The fan-shaped leaves of this species are prized above all others for their pliability and durability (Lundell 1937; Horwich and Lyon 1990). Recently, habitat destruction and overharvesting have caused huano supplies to become increasingly scarce. It is therefore critical that information be gathered on this utilitarian species in order to ensure not only its ecological viability but its availability as a nontimber forest product.

Located in the northwestern corner of Belize, the Río Bravo Conservation and Management Area is managed by a nonprofit conservation organization called Programme for Belize for the dual purposes of conservation and sustainable economic development (see Map 1 in Introduction to this volume). This protected area consists of over 92,000 ha of subtropical moist forest and is home to a rich variety of flora and fauna. Programme for Belize has identified several projects that support the organization's dual objectives, one of which is the harvest of huano. Given the management philosophy of this protected area, it is of paramount importance that harvesting be carried out in an ecologically sensitive manner.

Figure 13.1

Sabal mauritiiformis growing in the Río Bravo Conservation and Management area.

Resource Use

The leaves of *S. mauritiiformis* are harvested for both subsistence and market purposes in the construction of thatched roofs for work shelters, homes, and resort cabanas. Leaves are either cut by local people for their own homes or by individuals hired as contractors to construct thatched roofs for lodges or other tourist facilities (Figure 13.2).

According to the 1991 Belizean population census, 13.5% of all Belizean residences (5,073 residences) had thatched roofs, second only to sheet metal, which is by far the most common roofing material (78.1%; Table 13.1). Thatch is used primarily in rural areas. Of the 5,073 thatched roof residences it is estimated (based on geographic location and the likelihood of using *S. mauritiiformis*) that approximately 52% of the domiciles had roofs constructed with *S. mauritiiformis* fronds. With the recent increase in ecotourism projects, a substantial commercial market has developed for thatched roofs. Although the extent of the true demand for huano has yet to be determined, one has only to look through *Destination Belize*, an annual publication of the Belize Tourist Industry Association, to get a sense of the extensive use of this product. Typically, 3,500 to 4,500 leaves are used to create a roof for an average-size home (approximately 18' x 15') while over 20,000 leaves are used to con-

Figure 13.2

Examples of thatch roofing on Ambergris Caye, Belize. The huts shown here are part of a tourist resort.

Table 13.1. Roofing material for domestic residences in Belize, Central America.

Type of Roofing Material	Total	%	Urban	%	Rural	%
Total	37,658	100.0	19,036	100.0	18,622	100.0
Sheet metal (zinc aluminum)	29,414	78.1	17,613	92.5	11,801	63.4
Shingle	152	0.4	91	0.5	61	0.3
Tile	28	0.1	19	0.1	9	0.0
Concrete	1,651	4.4	976	5.1	673	3.6
Thatched	5,073	13.5	108	0.6	4,967	26.7
Other	1,340	3.6	229	3.6	1,111	6.0

Source: 1991 Population Census of Belize

struct roofs for the main lodges of tourist resorts. Given the large demand for this resource, the potential for overharvesting is substantial.

Resource Management and Harvest

In Belize, *S. mauritiiformis* is not yet managed in any official capacity and has not been grown in home gardens or plantations. Leaves are simply harvested from natural forest stands (Figure 13.3). Harvesting practices, however, do vary. For example, some harvesters cut unusable leaves in order to improve access to usable ones, while others just cut usable leaves. Careless cutting, whether of usable or unusable leaves, can damage the apical meristem, the growing tissue of the plant, thereby inhibiting future growth. Not only do the harvesting practices differ but the concept of "sustainable" harvest also varies from person to person. Some harvesters claim that *Sabal* harvest is sustainable

Figure 13.3

Harvest of *Sabal mauritiiformis* in Maskal, Belize.

as long as two leaves are left on the plant; others assert that all of the leaves can be cut except for the new shoot. In some cases, however, sustainability is not considered at all; some harvesters fell tall trees to harvest leaves that are out of reach by other means. This practice not only kills the tree but also removes reproducing individuals from the population.

Harvesting can occur throughout the year, but resource users believe that it must be timed with the correct lunar phase. The exact period varies among extractors, although it typically falls between the full moon up until the new moon. Leaves harvested outside the correct lunar phase are reported to deteriorate much more rapidly.

The Monitoring Program

In June of 1993 Programme for Belize initiated a monitoring program to evaluate the feasibility of sustainable huano harvest. The first objective was to determine population densities and distributions (Table 13.2). Studies revealed that *S. mauritiiformis* occurred in many of the forest types within the reserve. Densities were greatest in transitional forest (Figure 13.4), an area characterized as a gradation from upland mesic to swamp forest (Brokaw and Mallory 1993).

In order to gain information on potential yields, effects on the population dynamics, and effects on harvested plants, a pilot harvesting project was conducted in an area of prime habitat (transitional forest). The pilot harvest revealed that harvesters typically extract leaves that are at least 1.5 m in diameter. Given this size requirement, resource users are most likely to extract

Table 13.2. Outline of huano monitoring program in the Río Bravo Conservation and Management Area.

- Determination of abundance and distribution
  - densities
  - height class distributions
- Implementation of harvesting pilot project
  (1) Estimation of yields
  - average number of harvestable individuals by forest type per unit area
  - average number of harvestable product per individual plant
  (2) Assessment of the effect of NTFP extraction on species leaf productivity
- Assessment of the effect of NTFP harvesting on the population dynamics of the species of interest
- Estimation of countrywide demand for the product
- Examination of potential ecosystem level effects of harvesting

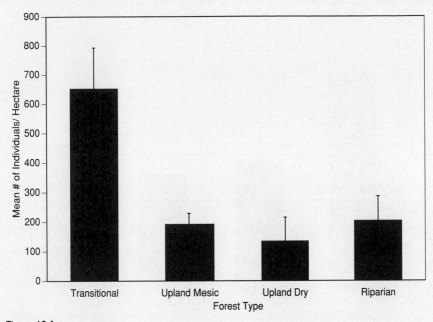

Figure 13.4

Density per hectare for *Sabal mauritiiformis* in the Río Bravo Conservation and Management Area, Belize.

leaves from plants 2 to 5 m in height. The mean number of harvestable plants per hectare was then estimated by determining the average number of individuals in these height classes. Based on this approach, transitional forest contained the greatest number of harvestable huano plants (Figure 13.5).

The harvest pilot project was also used to assess the effects of extraction on leaf productivity. Leaf productivity measurements were taken on a monthly basis for two years to provide an estimation of annual leaf growth for plants harvested under varying intensities. This study revealed that S. *mauritiiformis* grows relatively slowly and that plants of harvestable size classes produce an average of three leaves per year. However, the added stress of a drought in 1994 has caused the trees observed in the study to grow more slowly; the harvested plants have yet to fully recover their original amount of leaf tissue. Such factors will have repercussions on the frequency of extraction. The next course of action will be to examine the effects of harvesting on the population dynamics of S. *mauritiiformis* and ecosystem processes such as nutrient cycling.

Palm leaf litter often plays an important role in the ecology of tropical forests. For example, in Brazilian swamp forests arborescent palms are a sig-

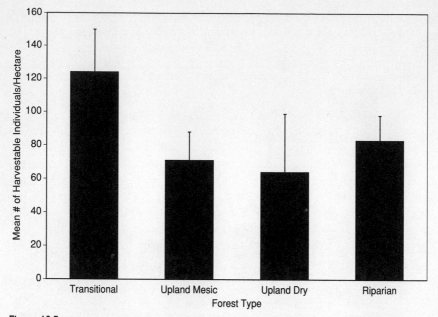

Figure 13.5

Mean harvestable *Sabal mauritiiformis* plants per hectare for four forest types in the Río Bravo Conservation and Management Area, Belize.

nificant source of leaf litter; approximately 14 tons of leaf litter are added annually by palms alone (Kahn and de Granville 1992). The above-ground biomass production and recycling of *Orbignya phalerata* leaf litter is found to contribute significantly to soil fertility (Anderson 1985). In Belize, *Orbignya cohune* is used as an indicator of fertile soils. Other palms, such as *Asterogyne martiana* and *Eugeissona minor* trap nutrients from litter and rainfall in their funnel shaped crowns, enriching their growing space (Raich 1983; Holbrook et al. 1985). The crown of *S. mauritiiformis* is also funnel shaped and enables the plant to effectively channel rainwater to the base of its stem. This water is enriched with nutrients, most notably with potassium (Castellanos 1995). Preliminary studies reveal that *S. mauritiiformis* accumulates significant amounts of potassium in its leaf tissues (O'Hara unpublished). It may be that its crown shape and its ability to effectively capture soluble potassium from rainwater allows *S. mauritiiformis* to act as a potassium accumulator.

After nitrogen and phosphorus, soils are most commonly limited in potassium. Potassium is essential for plant photosynthesis, respiration, and activating enzymes that are necessary for starch and protein formation. Potassium is also a highly soluble nutrient and therefore easily lost from tropical ecosystems. Based on these conditions, it is possible that long-term harvest of huano could lead to a significant loss of potassium from extraction areas.

Conclusions

Currently NTFP management focuses upon the principles of maximum sustained yield, a management paradigm that has demonstrated its utility in many fields, including those of forestry and fisheries. However, as in the aforementioned fields, the principles of maximum sustained yield have proven inadequate in addressing today's complex management concerns, since management objectives are no longer single-resource oriented. Instead, when managing NTFPs, the concept of maximum sustained yield must be combined with other approaches that are capable of addressing the effects of harvesting on ecological processes and interactions.

To date, far too many NTFP projects lack monitoring and assessment components. It is crucial that these measures be incorporated into NTFP programs especially for those located in protected areas such as biosphere and extractive reserves. The original purpose for creating these protected areas was to enhance rural incomes, incorporate local participation in conservation efforts, and conserve biological biodiversity. Monitoring and assessment will facilitate successful achievement of these goals by identifying potential obstacles and successes.

There is a need to develop NTFP monitoring protocols that address both population and ecosystem-level concerns and that are appropriate regardless of the product harvested. Biosphere reserves are ideal places to develop these protocols because of their management goals (conservation of biodiversity and economic development), and also due to the fact that many NTFP projects are occurring in the buffer zones of these reserves. With the creation of NTFP monitoring protocols, which, for example, outline particular techniques for determining abundances, distributions, population dynamics, and structures as well as potential ecosystem-level effects, managers will be able to compare data, results, and management issues with other managers in the region. Coordinating monitoring protocols will not only benefit the management at the local level but will also help to determine when and where the harvest of NTFPs can serve as an effective conservation strategy.

Acknowledgments

The author wishes to acknowledge Kristiina Vogt, Dan Vogt, Nick Brokaw, and Joel Tilley for their assistance with the design and implementation of the huano project, and Joy Grant and Roger Wilson of Program for Belize for their support of this project from its beginning. Thanks to Bruce Larson and Peter Palmiotto for their comments on drafts of this chapter. Special thanks go to Río Bravo field assistants: Claudia Groutche, Darryl Novelo, and Alfredo Leal. Financial support for this study came from the Perkin Elmer Corporation, the Charles A. and Anne Morrow Lindbergh Foundation, a Hutchinson Research Fellowship, and the Tropical Resource Institute at Yale University.

References

Allegretti, M. H. 1990. Extractive reserves: An alternative for reconciling development and environmental conservation in Amazonia. Pages 255–264 in *Alternatives to Deforestation: Steps Towards Sustainable Use of the Amazon Rain Forest*. Columbia University Press, New York.

Anderson, A. B. 1985. Productivity of a forest-dominant palm (*Orbignya phalerata* Mart) in Brazil. Abstracts of the Association for Tropical Biology Meetings, 1985: 38.

Binkley, D., and D. Richter. 1987. Nutrient cycles and H^+ budgets of forest ecosystems. *Advances in Ecological Research* 16: 1–51.

Bloomfield, J., K. A. Vogt, and D. J. Vogt. 1993. Decay rate and substrate quality of fine roots and foliage of two tropical tree species in the Luquillo Experimental Forest, Puerto Rico. *Plant and Soil* 150: 233–245.

Brokaw, N. V. L., and E. P. Mallory. 1993. *Vegetation of the Río Bravo Conservation and Management Area, Belize*. Manomet Observatory and Program for Belize.

Brown, M., and B. Wykoff-Baird. 1992. Designing integrated conservation and development projects. The Biodiversity Support Program, U.S. Agency for International Development/World Wildlife Fund, Baltimore, Md.

Brown, S., M. Lenart, and J. Mo. 1995. Structure and organic matter dynamics of a human-impacted pine forest in a MAB reserve of subtropical China. *Biotropica* 27: 276–289.

Castellanos, J. J. G. 1995. El ciclo del P y K en una selva alta perennifolia del sur de Quintana Roo, México. Tesis, Universidad Autonoma de Yucatán, Yucatán, México.

Dore, M. H. I., and J. M. Nogueira. 1994. The Amazon rain forest, sustainable development and the Biodiversity Convention: A political economy perspective. *Ambio* 23: 491–496.

Furley, P. A. 1975. The significance of the cohune palm, *Orbignya cohune* (Mart.) Dahlgren, on the nature and in the development of the soil profile. *Biotropica* 7: 32–36.

Godoy, R. A., and K. S. Bawa. 1993. The economic value and sustainable harvest of plants and animals from the tropical forest: Assumptions, hypotheses, and methods. *Economic Botany* 47: 215–219.

Goodland, R. J. A. 1987. The World Bank's wildlands policy: A major new means of financing conservation. *Conservation Biology* 1: 210–213.

Gordon, J. 1994. From vision to policy: A role for foresters. *Journal of Forestry* 92: 17–19.

Government of Belize. 1991. Belize population census. Central Statistical Office, Ministry of Finance, Belmopan, Belize.

Gunatilleke, I. A. U. N., C. V. S. Gunatilleke, and P. Abeygunawardena. 1993. Interdisciplinary research towards management of nontimber forest resources in lowland rain forests of Sri Lanka. *Economic Botany* 47: 282–290.

Hall, P., and K. Bawa. 1993. Methods to assess the impact of extraction of nontimber tropical forest products on plant populations. *Economic Botany* 47: 234–247.

Horwich, R., and J. Lyon. 1990. *A Belizean Rainforest: The Community Baboon Sanctuary*. Orangutan Press, Gays Mills, Wis.

Kahn, F., and J. J. de Granville. 1992. *Palms in Forest Ecosystems of Amazonia*. Springer-Verlag, New York.

Kremen, C., A. M. Merenlender, and D. D. Murphy. 1994. Ecological monitoring: A vital need for integrated conservation and development programs in the tropics. *Conservation Biology* 8: 388–397.

Lundell, C. L. 1937. *The Vegetation of Petén*. Carnegie Institute, Washington, D.C.

McNeeley, J. A. 1992. The biodiversity crisis: Challenges for research and management. Pages 15–26 in *Conservation of Biodiversity for Sustainable Development*, D. T. Sandlund, K. Hindar, and A. H. D. Brown, eds. Oxford University Press, New York.

Mo, J., S. Brown, and M. Lenart. 1995. Nutrient dynamics of a human-impacted pine forest in a MAB reserve of subtropical China. *Biotropica* 27: 290–304.

Nepstad, D. C., I. F. Brown, L. Luz, A. Alechandre, and V. Viana. 1992. Biotic impoverishment of Amazonian forest by rubber tappers, loggers, and cattle ranchers. *Advances in Economic Botany* 9: 1–14.

Olmsted, I., and E. R. Alvarez-Buyalla. 1995. Sustainable harvesting of tropical trees: Demography and matrix models of two palm species in Mexico. *Ecological Applications* 5: 484–500.

Peters, C. M. 1989. Reproduction, growth and the population dynamics of *Brosimum alicastrum* in a moist tropical forest of central Veracruz, Mexico. Ph.D. dissertation, Yale University, New Haven, Conn.

Prance, G. T. 1989. Economic perspectives from tropical rainforest ethnobotany. Pages 61–74 in *Fragile Lands of Latin America: Strategies for Sustainable Development*, J. O. Browder, ed. Westview Press, Boulder, Colo.

Raich, J. W. 1983. Understory palms as nutrient traps: A hypothesis. *Brenesia* 21: 119–129.

Ratsirarson, J., J. A. Silander, and A. F. Richard. 1996. Conservation and management of a threatened Madagascar palm species: *Neodypsis decaryi*, Jumelle. *Conservation Biology* 10: 40–52.

Salafsky, N., B. Dugelby, and J. Terborgh. 1991. Can extractive reserves save the rain forest? An ecological comparison of nontimber forest product extraction systems in el Petén, Guatemala, and West Kalimantan, Indonesia. *Conservation Biology* 5: 39–52.

Salwasser, H. 1990. Sustainability as a conservation paradigm. *Conservation Biology* 4: 213–216.

Shaffer, M. L., and K. A. Saterson. 1987. The biological diversity program of the U.S. Agency for International Development. *Conservation Biology* 1: 280–286.

Soemarwoto, O. 1992. Forestry and nonwood products: A developing country's perspective. Pages 64–69 in *The Rainforest Harvest: Sustainable Strategies for Saving the Tropical Forests?* S. Counsell and T. Rice, eds. Friends of the Earth, London.

Steen, H. K. 1984. *History of Sustained Yield Forestry*. The Society for the International Union of Forestry Researchers, Santa Cruz, Calif.

Stone, E. L. 1979. Nutrient removals by intensive harvest—some research gaps and opportunities. Pages 366–386 in *Impact of Intensive Harvesting on Forest Nutrient Cycling*. State University of New York, Syracuse, NY.

Tivy, J., and G. O'Hare. 1982. *Human Impact on the Ecosystem*. Oliver and Boyd, Edinburgh, Scotland.

Vogt, K. A., D. J. Vogt, H. Asbjornsen, and R. A. Dahlgren. 1995. Roots, nutrients and their relationship to spatial patterns. *Plant and Soil* 168–169: 113–123.

Wells, M., K. Brandon, and L. Hannah. 1992. *People and Parks: Linking Protected Area Management with Local Communities*. World Bank, Washington, D.C.

Chapter 14

Buffer Zone Management: Lessons for the Maya Forest

James R. Barborak

The Maya Forest, which straddles the joint borders of Mexico, Belize, and Guatemala, contains one of the largest remaining blocks of contiguous forests in Mesoamerica. In this region, human population growth, poverty, and inappropriate land use pose a triple threat to remaining wildlands and wildlife (see Petén case study in IUCN 1992). For this reason, much of the current investment in conservation programs in the Maya Forest region is "people-centered" and attempts to integrate conservation and development programs in buffer zones that border protected areas. Such projects, according to Wells et al. (1992), " . . . attempt to ensure the conservation of biological diversity by reconciling the management of protected areas with the social and economic needs of local people."

Can such projects really reduce pressure on core conservation areas? Can they maintain and enhance the ecological values of adjoining buffer zones as well? If so, what types of projects will work best? In what settings? At what spatial and temporal scale? Done by whom, for whom? Within what regulatory and legal framework? For what time frame, and with what guarantees of financial and institutional sustainability?

These questions are of particular concern to the Wildlife Conservation Society (WCS), which has been working worldwide to save wildlife and habitats for over a century (Carr 1988). WCS's Mesoamerican and Caribbean Program supports several conservation projects in the Maya Forest, ranging from research on endangered vertebrates to environmental education, park management, and corridor mapping (Carr et al. 1994). The Society's regional flagship project since 1991, Paseo Pantera, has focused on efforts to consolidate the region's protected areas through creation of a linked network of parks and reserves that spans the Mesoamerican land bridge from Mexico to Colombia. The crown jewels of this Mesoamerican Biological Corridor are the great parks of the region, such as the core zones of the Calakmul and Sian Ka'an Biosphere Reserves in Mexico, Tikal National Park in Guatemala, and the Chiquibul National Park in Belize's Maya Mountains.

Such core conservation areas need to be linked by extractive reserves and buffer zone corridors to permit the continued ebb and flow of genes, species, and communities—the factors that have made Mesoamerica a center of biological diversity for several million years (Vega 1994). Also, the Maya Forest has had a long history of human occupation and impact (Denevan 1992; Gomez-Pampa and Kaus 1992) and is endowed with greater potential for production of agricultural and forest products than wetter and steeper tropical forests to the south in Central America. "Locking up" sizable additional areas in strict reserves therefore is not a viable social or political alternative in the Maya Forest region.

Since 1990, the U.N. University for Peace and the Wildlife Conservation Society have cosponsored an annual international buffer zone management workshop for conservation professionals from throughout the Neotropics. Although the workshop is held in Costa Rica, more of the nearly 150 participants have come from the countries that share the Maya Forest than from any other geographic region.

The mobile workshop focuses on site visits to a number of buffer zone projects. Discussions with project staff and local residents focus both on site-specific problems and on principles that apply to many successful buffer zone management efforts regardless of the country or the sociocultural and biophysical setting.

The conceptual framework and guidelines that follow are based in large part on the fruitful debate and discussions that have taken place during those workshops, and reflect the input of the participants, instructors, and staff of the projects visited during the workshop. Readers are forewarned that the conclusions and recommendations presented are based on empirical results from field practitioners of conservation, and these results are not necessarily politically correct or ideologically in vogue.

Conceptual Framework

Few question the logic behind the concept of buffer zone management, defined by Sayer (1991) as follows: "A zone, peripheral to a national park or equivalent reserve, where restrictions are placed upon resource use or special development measures are undertaken to enhance the conservation value of the area." Protected areas are social constructs, the limits of which seldom coincide with ecosystem boundaries. Most are open systems, both socioeconomically and ecologically. Like many institutions, protected areas use both buffering and bridging strategies to protect themselves from outside threats and avail themselves of outside resources.

It is hard to argue with the proposal that providing alternative sources of employment and income for local residents and promoting productive and stable land-use systems around protected areas will reduce external pressures on parks and reserves and thereby increase their ecological viability. However, even after major investments for over a decade around the globe one can point to few widely replicable examples of successful buffer zone management on a sufficiently large scale to improve human welfare and save wild species and spaces (Oviedo and Sylva 1994; Western et al. 1994; West and Brechin 1990). Most reviews of buffer zone projects, such as the recent one by Beavers (1995) for community ecotourism initiatives in the Maya Forest, stress that most such projects are still in their infancy and acknowledge the scarcity of successful examples of community-based ecotourism ventures. Wells et al. (1992), after examining case studies throughout the tropics, concluded that "while the [buffer zone] concept has strong intuitive appeal, there are many difficulties in trying to put it into practice, and actual working examples of buffer zones among the case study projects were virtually nonexistent."

Objectives of Buffer Zone Management

There are three interrelated justifications often cited for buffer zone management projects and interventions. The first of these, clear in Sayer's definition of the concept, is ecological: to increase the effective size of conservation units through the promotion of land uses that are as similar as possible to natural ecosystems in adjoining parks and reserves—in effect, to buffer the protected area from negative influences of surrounding human activity. This justification is especially important as reserve size and ecological diversity decline and as individual reserves become more isolated from other natural areas. Where natural areas are surrounded by intensively used landscapes, and where competing uses for nearby lands or political and economic concerns preclude direct land acquisition, buffer zone management may be the only option available to land managers to improve the ecological viability of their protected areas and reduce rates of species loss. In the Maya Forest, a good example of problems faced by small reserves that lack effectively functioning buffer zones is the Cerro Cahui Biotope along Lake Petén Itzá in northern Guatemala. In this small (under 1,000 ha) reserve, now surrounded by pastures and subsistence agricultural plots, ecological isolation and poaching have already led to extirpation of the ocellated turkey, the conservation of which was a main reason for establishing the reserve.

A second common objective of buffer zones, not explicitly stated in Sayer's definition but generally accepted, is sociological: to promote equitable and sustainable human development in communities around core reserves. Since many parks and reserves in developing countries tend to be located in remote areas with standards of living far below already dismal national levels, social investments in such regions usually make sense regardless of the presence of a protected area nearby. But for a rural development project in a region next to a park to really qualify as a buffer zone initiative, it must do more than improve the standard of living: it must also reduce pressure on the adjoining core conservation area and improve or stabilize land-use patterns in the buffer. Such goals do not always harmonize; for example, introducing nonnative tilapia fish to improve protein-deficient diets in buffer zone communities might make good sense to a nutritionist, but could endanger native fish populations in nearby lakes and streams.

The final common justification for buffer zones is to reduce conflicts and pressure on core conservation areas from incompatible uses and activities, either outside or within park limits (Ghimire 1991), by providing direct, targeted opportunities for obtaining food and raw materials, employment, and income to the very individuals who are the source of pressure on parks. Many park managers spend most of their time and devote much of their personnel and budgets to skirmishes with individuals and communities living near or within protected area boundaries. These persons carry out proscribed activities such as poaching, extraction of forest products, or squatting and grazing livestock on protected lands. Combatting these major threats diverts scarce resources that are needed to promote activities such as research, education, or recreation programs. Obviously adversarial situations also do little to improve the already strained relationships between conservation authorities and rural communities.

Guidelines for Improving Chances of Buffer Zone Success

In spite of the diversity of socioeconomic and ecological settings in which buffer zone management is undertaken, a relatively limited set of principles is repeatedly claimed to be associated with successful efforts. Listed below are 12 such principles that are most often cited in the literature concerning buffer zone management, and that have also been repeatedly endorsed by University for Peace workshop participants with a wealth of real-world experience with such projects. All are directly applicable to the Maya Forest:

(1) *Establish appropriate limits, management categories, and legal frameworks for protected areas.* Most protected areas in the Maya Forest share a problem common to many Neotropical parks and reserves: their limits, management category, and legal frameworks often are vague or seriously flawed. Many such areas were created by taking advantage of ephemeral political opportunities, but lacked adequate field investigation. Such reserves and their limits are often defined without sufficient ecological inventories or land tenure and

census information. As a result, most reserves contain at least some legal in-holdings and squatter populations at the time of their establishment. A recent study showed that 86% of all South American national parks and equivalent reserves have permanent human occupation inside their limits (Amend and Amend, 1994). Many Maya Forest protected areas (such as Tikal National Park and other core zones of the Maya Biosphere Reserve in Guatemala) have straight-line limits that cut across watersheds and wildlife corridors and ex-clude localized but unique ecosystems. Other reserves have mineral or timber concessions outstanding, contain indigenous communities, or include good cropland. In some cases areas very well suited for sustainable timber harvest or wildlife utilization have been declared as strictly protected national parks or biological reserves. Other extremely fragile and uncommon ecosystems have been designated as extractive forest reserves or wildlife refuges when a strict protection policy would be more appropriate.

A number of mechanisms are available for resolving land-use conflicts within protected areas. These include land swaps, direct purchase from land owners, changing protected area laws and limits to exclude human settle-ments, and changing management categories to less or more restrictive op-tions. "Special use" zoning within parks and reserves may be applied to permit problematic uses and occupancy, at least temporarily, while other options are explored. Where possible, the selection and definition of limits for protected areas and strategies for buffer zones can be best accomplished as part of re-gional land-use planning initiatives, such as that being undertaken for special development regions in Belize.

Although it is not a politically popular solution, relocation of individuals or even communities from within strict reserve limits is an option that must be considered. This consideration is particularly valid when small numbers of individuals live in isolated regions with extremely limited potential for agri-culture and animal husbandry but with great ecological or watershed values. Maintaining such communities is a very costly proposition in the long run, often condemning the involved individuals to "sustainable misery." Regard-less of these problems, resolving land-use, occupancy, and tenure conflicts within park boundaries is almost always more important, although not neces-sarily easier, than embarking on social development projects beyond core pre-serve limits.

(2) *Involve local communities in wildland and buffer zone planning from the outset.* Quoting World Bank vice president Moeen A. Qureshi, "Participation and empowerment are questions of efficiency. Communities are more likely to have a stake in, contribute to, and maintain projects which respond to their needs, knowledge and initiatives" (Anon. 1991). In general, the relative suc-cess of rural development is greater when local stakeholders are directly in-volved in project planning, decision making, and implementation (Western et al. 1994). Rural inhabitants in general are always looking for improved

ways to farm, fish, harvest forest products, and meet their usual daily needs. They look for ideas that are inexpensive, reduce risks, save manpower, generate income, and are compatible with their customs and normal practices.

Unfortunately, parks and reserves established in the Maya Forest region are usually created with little or no prior consultation with affected populations and interest groups. Too many conservationists believe they know what is best for park neighbors. Too few are willing to truly listen to the knowledge, opinions, needs, wants, and priorities of local residents. From the ejidos of Quintana Roo, to the leading edge of the colonization front in the northern Petén, to the indigenous communities on the edge of the Maya Mountains in Belize, long-term success of conservation efforts will depend as much on dialogue as it will on direct development investments.

(3) *Work with governments and national participants to address large-scale problems.* After several decades of intensive research and field testing in Mexico and Central America, fast growing, multiple-use trees have been identified, agroforestry systems and improved crop and livestock varieties have been developed, soil conservation techniques have been tested, community ecotourism projects are underway, natural forest management trials have moved ahead, and integrated pest management approaches have been applied and refined (Beavers 1995; Gretzinger 1995; Palma 1995). But most efforts to successfully and widely disseminate such techniques, as well as wildlife management initiatives, have floundered, and almost none of these have been proven to work in "real world" situations in the Maya Forest.

Some such failures are a result of the fact that technically "adequate" systems are too expensive or difficult to maintain to be useful. Often, however, such failures are caused by grassroots myopia: microlevel project implementation and a focus on technical solutions without attention to regional and national root causes of symptoms seen in buffer zones. Inappropriate agricultural policies, such as price controls and subsidies for land clearing, can make marketing the increased corn yields from successful agricultural intensification projects difficult or impossible. Likewise, counterproductive or conflicting legislation and poorly functioning government institutions can foil plans to implement long-term logging concession systems in extractive reserves. Obstacles to land titling, agricultural loan policies that discriminate against small landholders, and extremely high interest rates hamper agricultural diversification and intensification. Fiercely independent buffer zone inhabitants might be reluctant to organize cooperatives for improving marketing clout and reducing costs of agricultural inputs through volume purchasing. While opening of new roads and even logging trails in frontier areas often leads to forest destruction, at the same time lack of investments in improving existing road infrastructure makes getting crops to market (when there is a market) a high-risk venture.

A discussion by participants in a recent trinational mobile seminar for peasant and community leaders of the Maya Forest illustrated that the failure of efforts to improve buffer zone land use is often caused by market, pricing, tenure, and institutional failures rather than by technical inadequacies. The participants in the workshop listed nine major priority problems for community forest management: poor community organization; lack of governmental support; lack of land use rights; inadequate funding; marketing problems; no industrialization (e.g., value added) to products; inadequate technical assistance and extension; lack of the will to change; and lack of planning and diversification (Gretzinger 1995; Palma 1995). Yet grassroots conservation and development practitioners and their organizations are often powerless to combat such problems, as these issues and policies are often decided at the state or national level or by bilateral and multilateral development agencies. Conservationists need to form strategic partnerships with groups and individuals working in the macroeconomic and national political arenas to resolve "big-picture problems" that often explain the field failures of projects.

(4) *Address issues of land tenure and population growth.* Two situations, almost always found in concert, frequently are associated with failure of efforts to manage buffer zones: runaway population increase deriving from both natural increase and in-migration, and weak, conflictive, or absent land tenure rights. Guillen (pers. comm., 1995) describes in detail, for example, how the combined impact of colonization and land tenure inconsistency has contributed both to forest destruction and to poverty in the Selva Lacandona of Chiapas, Mexico. On the other hand, some of the best examples in the Maya Forest of innovative approaches to timber and nontimber forest management are found in the long-established ejidos of Quintana Roo, where secure land tenure, economies of scale, and a focus on value-added enterprises have guaranteed benefits to all members of the communities (Palma 1995). Lynch and Alcorn (1995) argue convincingly that it may be more effective to promote long-term efforts to title land individually or communally in buffer zones, to promote family planning initiatives, and to improve the lot of women, than to focus exclusively on improving land use productivity. The hundreds of thousands of landless peasants that inhabit the Maya Forest cannot be expected to invest in long-term improvement of the productive capability of land they occupy but do not own. Without clear individual or communal title, they lack access to credit and are shut out of most extension programs. Even with credit and technical assistance, most individuals are unwilling to invest significant amounts of effort in improving property that could be confiscated at any time.

(5) *Understand how relative resource scarcity and degradation affects buffer zone management strategies and success.* Areas that already are quite degraded and have stable or declining human populations and those that have suffered

recent environmental disasters (major floods, droughts, or landslides) are good targets for successful buffer zone projects. In such areas, both the causes and consequences of resource degradation are often better understood by local communities than in new frontier settings. Conversely, in buffer zones where natural forests or wildlife are still relatively abundant but are rapidly being depleted, such as in the Petén of Guatemala, it is often difficult to convince recent immigrants from other, more degraded regions that there is anything to worry about in their new home.

(6) *Beware of perverse incentives and unintended results.* Short-term success at improving human standards of living in buffer zones can actually breed long-term failure in both buffers and core conservation areas. This seemingly contradictory notion stems from the fact that highly successful rural development efforts in buffer zones can act as magnets for impoverished people from many kilometers away. Unless buffer zone success stories can be rapidly replicated in a larger region, or very clear mechanisms exist to limit population growth in buffers (e.g., clear and enforced land tenure systems and community edicts barring new settlers), initial success can lead to major population influxes. These can quickly surpass the ability of buffer zone projects to meet the additional demands for assistance of the newcomers, causing spillover effects within park and reserve limits and greater degradation of buffer zones. The best social investments one can make in such cases are often far from the frontier in the distant, environmentally degraded regions from which new colonists are coming.

(7) *Stick to institutional mandates and competencies.* Some argue that buffer zone management should take priority over core zone management in efforts to stem threats to parks. Those who espouse this view feel that conservation agencies should reduce effort and resources spent on protection, visitor services, and investigation, and devote most of their energies to working with park neighbors.

However, most agencies that manage protected area are young and weak. Most have suffered through years of budget cuts, staff reduction, and worsening morale. Management staff often lack the mandate, experience, staff, and budget to work effectively in rural development. In addition, by expanding the breadth and scope of their activities to include development projects in buffer zones, these managers are often indirectly encouraging lapses by other government agencies and private voluntary organizations, some of which may be falling woefully short of fulfilling their mandates.

Only with strong research and monitoring programs can we monitor the status of biotic resources within protected areas and assess the impacts of surrounding land use on those resources. If baseline data are limited, what yardstick does one have to judge against? Without a certain level of visitor services and facilities, parks cannot serve as magnets for ecotourists, who provide employment and income opportunities for local residents. Finally, if the core areas of parks are underprotected, their important role as "water factories" and as nursery grounds for wildlife and fisheries stocks will be reduced.

What, then, are the appropriate roles for managers of protected areas in buffer zones? Their greatest contribution to improving the long-term development prospects for nearby communities is by maximizing the generation of local employment and income through proper stewardship of core zones—in other words, focusing on their core competencies and legal mandates. Few core conservation areas in Mesoamerica are being used at anywhere near their "carrying capacity" for research, recreation, education, and national and international tourism. Such development usually creates an even greater surge in indirect employment in tourism services, construction, and new markets for artisanry and foodstuffs outside preserve limits. At the same time, protected area management agencies should be active promoters and catalytic agents for change in buffer zones—lobbying, cajoling, and challenging other public and private agencies with mandates and competencies in rural development to do a better job. Such activities should be coupled with strengthening existing national and local government social development agencies, and empowering NGOs and community organizations working in the buffer zone arena (Barborak 1995).

A simple rule of thumb is that efficient and effective management of a national park is much less complex than proper stewardship of a government-owned extractive reserve. Extractive reserves are in turn much easier to administer than efforts to improve land use on private lands, particularly in regions undergoing population explosions that lack clear land tenure. Turning a highly specialized land management agency into an all-powerful regional government is not the answer to buffer zone dilemmas.

(8) *Recognize the vital role of law enforcement.* Conservation practitioners in the Maya Forest uniformly prefer nonconfrontational approaches to dealing with conservation law violators whenever possible. They have good reason: a strong emphasis on law enforcement in the years after the creation of the Maya Biosphere Reserve in Guatemala earlier in this decade led to torching of ranger posts, physical violence against reserve staff, and deep-seated resentment between government rangers and local residents. However, weakening or eliminating protection programs usually does lead to increases in prohibited activities. Some inhabitants of all societies are prone to break the law at least occasionally. In any country, if conservation law-breakers are never caught in the act, taken before a magistrate, and punished in a meaningful way, it becomes more likely that more citizens will break the law. It is crucial that investments in buffer zone activities not be seen as an excuse for reducing law enforcement within parks and reserves. In fact, expanded and more rigorous protection efforts are also needed in most Maya Forest parks and reserves within the region. As McNeely (1993) points out, park regulations need to be applied strictly and in an equitable fashion. He also stresses the im-

portance of reaching consensus with local communities on restrictions and involving local residents in enforcement efforts.

(9) *Buffer preserves with reserves.* It is increasingly common to find complexes of protected areas, including a national park or similar strictly protected "core area," surrounded at least in part by extractive reserves and
forested portions of tribal lands. The largest and most ecologically representative of such reserve complexes forms part of the UNESCO MAB Biosphere
Reserve Network, such as the Maya and Sian Ka'an Biosphere Reserves.

The biosphere reserve model reflects the fact that the best buffer zones for
strictly protected parks and preserves are often extractive reserves without
permanent human settlements that have clear limits and effective management in their own right, such as forest reserves and wildlife management
areas. From a social and political standpoint, it is also usually easier to obtain
support for creation of such extractive reserves than for strict preserves (Mc-
Neely and Ness 1995). The next best thing are private lands devoted primarily to conservation (natural forest management, ecotourism, etc.). The network of private and NGO nature reserves in Latin America is growing quickly
(Alderman 1994); many are found adjoining government-owned and -man-
aged parks and preserves. Conversely, the worst buffer zones from a conflict
and managerial standpoint are densely populated by impoverished, landless
peasants, where women have low standing, family size is large, and land
tenure systems are poor or absent.

(10) *Adopt flexible definitions of the outer limits of buffer zones.* The ideal
buffer zone from a conservation standpoint would contain progressively more
intensive land uses as one moves outward from a core reserve, with corridors
of more natural habitat linking nearby core reserves. Few examples of such
landscapes exist in the real world. Instead, land use around protected cores is
often a mosaic of cropland, pastures, urban landscapes, and parcels devoted to
forestry and agroforestry.

Except in the case of extractive reserves adjoining core conservation areas,
however, it is usually best to think of buffer zone management as a concept
not necessarily bounded by firm outer limits. On privately held lands in buffer
zones, different problems occur at different intensities at different times of the
year. Rather than focusing on a physical outer boundary, attention should go
to defining targets for intervention—high-priority human communities and
problem hotspots. Limited resources can be best used through regulations, incentives, and programs that promote improved land use, clear tenure, and reductions in human pressure toward core zones in these areas.

One point brought up many times in the University for Peace buffer zone
workshop by participants from reserves with important aquatic resources has
been that very often, the worst threats to a protected area might originate
some distance from its limits. For example, though sewage and pollutants
from urban centers or agricultural areas may originate tens of kilometers from

a park border, these pollutants may constitute the major threats to streams, lakes, and estuaries in that protected area. In such situations, buffer zone management focusing on lands immediately adjacent to a park or reserve would do little to mitigate the most critical threats to the protected area.

(11) *Encourage formation of a strong network of stakeholders and prepare for the long haul.* Conflict is inevitable when resources and land are scarce. Buffer zone problems will change, but they will never entirely disappear. Perseverance, along with the strengthening of a network of local public, NGO, and for-profit institutions, is needed to survive reductions or collapses in outside funding and local political crises. Investments in strengthening local institutions, developing human resources, and designing and promoting improved production systems can enhance chances for sustainable improvements in buffer zone land use and human welfare, long after the umbilical cord to outside financial aid and technical assistance is cut.

Great effort should be expended on developing the proper institutional framework for management of protected areas. There is a general trend in Latin America toward decentralization of decision making within national agencies, downsizing of central governments, devolution of power to local and regional authorities, and increasingly, privatization of former government functions. These trends pose great opportunities for saving wildlands. Those protected areas that instill a sense of responsibility and ownership in large and diverse constituencies that include local communities, NGOs, and the private sector in general, have a brighter long-term future than those managed in a monolithic and unparticipatory fashion by distant bureaucracies. What is very much needed is to find appropriate institutional frameworks that combine the positive features of governments, the for-profit sector, communities, NGOs, and individual citizens to enhance stewardship of protected areas.

(12) *Work with all buffer zone interest groups.* Not all protected area neighbors, even in the poorest of developing countries, are impoverished peasants or tribal peoples. Many areas next to core protected areas are owned by prosperous farmers or ranchers, timber interests, or even multinational corporations. Some would argue that such protected area neighbors are the "enemy" and should at best be ignored in conservation programs. The reality is that prosperous neighbors with long-range economic interests in a region can be stable allies in the cause of conservation, particularly if they depend to some extent on ecotourism or the harvest of timber or wildlife for their income. Conversely, such individuals or groups can also be powerful obstructionists and adversaries if good relations with them are not cultivated. Thus, protected area managers should work with all sectors of surrounding societies, from peasants and indigenous peoples to wealthy ranchers and local business people, and with both small landholders and owners of large blocks of land.

One mechanism for working with a broad array of buffer zone actors is through the formation of protected area advisory councils that meet regularly to discuss protected area and buffer zone management. Such a regular forum, while difficult to sustain, is a much more effective means for working with buffer zone constituencies than one-time meetings or crisis-driven management.

Conclusions

International experience with buffer zone management and integrated conservation and development projects is still in its infancy. Most such efforts in the Maya Forest have begun within the past decade. However, mounting evidence points to common obstacles to success in project implementation and to a number of basic principles that are often associated with more successful efforts. The guidelines presented in this paper, gleaned from the literature and the collective wisdom of Maya Forest practitioners, should provide useful food for thought for individuals and institutions muddling through the murky world of buffer zone management.

Acknowledgments

Thanks are due to all participants and instructors in the University for Peace International Buffer Zone Management Workshops for sharing their experience and ideas, and to the donors that have made the annual workshop possible, particularly U.S. AID, the Peace Corps, the World Heritage Fund, the European Community, the World Wildlife Fund, and the Wildlife Conservation Society. I would also like to thank the U.S. Man and the Biosphere Program for supporting my participation at the Chetumal conference, Kathleen Jepson of WCS for her editorial assistance, and the anonymous reviewers.

References

Alderman, C. 1994. The economics and the role of privately owned lands used for nature tourism, education, and conservation. Pages 273–318 in *Protected Area Economics and Policy: Linking Conservation and Sustainable Development*. M. Munasinghe and J. McNeely, eds. World Bank, Washington, D.C.

Amend, S., and T. Amend, eds. 1994. *Espacios sin Habitantes? Parques Nacionales de America del Sur*. IUCN, Gland, Switzerland.

Anon. 1991. World Bank Approaches NGOs. *ISTF News* 12: 2.

Barborak, J. 1995. Institutional options for managing protected areas. Pages 30–38 in *Expanding Partnerships for Conservation*. J. McNeely, ed. Island Press, Washington, D.C.

Beavers, J. 1995. *Community-Based Ecotourism in the Maya Forest: Six Case Studies from Communities in Mexico, Guatemala and Belize*. The Nature Conservancy, Flores, Petén, Guatemala.

Carr, A. C. III. 1988. Beyond parks. *Animal Kingdom* 91: 12–24.

Denevan, W. M. 1992. The pristine myth: The landscape of the Americas in 1992. *Annals of the Association of American Geographers* 82: 369–385.

Ghimire, K. B. 1991. Parks and people: Livelihood issues in national parks management in Thailand and Madagascar. Discussion Paper 29. U.N. Research Institute for Social Development, Geneva, Switzerland.

Gomez-Pampa, A., and A. Kaus. 1992. Taming the wilderness myth. *BioScience* 42: 271–279.

Gretzinger, S. 1995. *El Manejo Forestal Comunitario en la Selva Maya*. Serie tecnica, Informe tecnico 256. CATIE, Turrialba, Costa Rica.

IUCN. 1992. *Protected Areas and Demographic Change: Planning for the Future*. IUCN, Gland, Switzerland.

Jukofsky, D. 1992. Path of the panther. *Wildlife Conservation* September/October: 18–24.

Lynch, O. J., and J. B. Alcorn. 1995. Tenurial rights and community-based conservation. Pages 373–392 in *Natural Connections: Perspectives in Community-Based Conservation*. D. Western, R. M. Wright, and S. C. Strum, eds. Island Press, Washington, D.C.

McNeely, J. 1993. People and protected areas: partners in prosperity. Pages 249–257 in *The Law of the Mother: Protecting Indigenous Peoples in Protected Areas*. E. Kemf, ed. Sierra Club Books, San Francisco.

McNeely, J., and G. Ness. 1995. People, parks, and biodiversity: Issues in population-environment dynamics. Paper presented at the AAAS Conference on Human Population, Biodiversity, and Protected Areas: Science and Policy Issues. IUCN, Gland, Switzerland.

Oviedo C., G. Sylva C., and P. Sylva C. 1994. *Areas Silvestres Protegidas y Comunidades Locales en America Latina*. Oficina Regional de la FAO para America Latina y el Caribe, Santiago, Chile.

Palma, E. 1995. *El Manejo Forestal Comunitario en la Selva Maya: Version Campesina*. CATIE, Turrialba, Costa Rica.

Sayer, J. 1991. *Rainforest Buffer Zones: Guidelines for Protected Area Managers*. IUCN, Gland, Switzerland.

Vega, A., ed. 1994. *Conservation Corridors in the Central American Region: Proceedings of a Regional Conference Sponsored by the Paseo Pantera Project*. Tropical Research and Development, Inc., Gainesville, Fla.

Wells, M., and K. Brandon, with L. Hannah. 1992. *People and Parks: Linking Protected Area Management with Local Communities*. The World Bank, Washington, D.C.

West, P. C., and S. R. Brechin, eds. 1990. *Resident Peoples and National Parks: Social Dilemmas and Strategies in International Conservation*. University of Arizona Press, Tucson.

Western, D., R. M. Wright, and S. C. Strum, eds. 1994. *Natural Connections: Perspectives in Community-Based Conservation*. Island Press, Washington, D.C.

Part IV

Biodiversity Research for Conservation

In the earlier discussion on nontimber forest products, it was apparent that one factor limiting effective management of resource extraction in the Maya Forest is the lack of baseline data on the biology and ecology of the majority of forest species. The problem is partly one of manpower; the staggering number of species in these forests presents a sharp contrast to the relatively few trained biologists available to record their characteristics. This difficulty is even more acute in the face of the rapid expansion of the agricultural frontier—the shortage of scientific personnel would hardly matter if the forests could remain untouched in perpetuity, but the reality is that species are disappearing faster than they can be recorded. This reality presents a dilemma for managers and conservationists: should management plans be instituted for threatened species despite the minimal information available, risking the possibility that the plan will overlook some vital aspect of the species' biology and thus prove inadequate, or worse still, do more harm than good? Or should the plan wait on the collection of adequate data, despite the fact that any delay in the creation of conservation strategies might lead to irreversible decline in the species of interest? The ideal compromise is for managers to create a plan based on the limited knowledge made available by baseline studies of rare and endangered species—including data on population size, habitat, diet or nutrient needs, and reproductive biology—reevaluating and adjusting their methods as more data become available.

However, it has also become clear that research projects must use integrated approaches to address their topics. Time works against the goals of conservation biologists; each day that passes represents more destroyed or degraded forests, and no amount of "pure" biological research collecting baseline data will slow down the factors that harm the Maya Forest. The best way to combat the threats is to combine basic biological research on forest species with examination of current land-use practices and consideration of social questions. Such studies typically begin with baseline research in forests with minimal human impact to determine what healthy natural populations *should* look like, before turning to areas that have been degraded or deforested by logging, agriculture, and other land uses. The projects described by Brokaw et al. and Whigham et al., for instance, progressed naturally from baseline studies of undisturbed forests to an examination of the effects that various natural disturbances, human activities, and silvicultural regimes have on populations of trees, birds, and butterflies. Such comparisons allow researchers to determine the extent to which natural disturbances, such as hurricanes, and different land uses affect these species, which in turn permits fine-tuning of management plans.

Yet the contribution of baseline studies to conservation efforts, as demonstrated in the chapter by Whitacre, can be even greater than data collection. The act of studying forest species is an opportunity to involve local people in conservation efforts. In the case of The Peregrine Fund's Maya Project, the researchers' efforts caused the project to expand in several directions; not only did they take up studies of effects of land use on forest species, as occurred with the projects described by Brokaw and Whigham, but they also created a number of initiatives designed to encourage participation of local people. The efforts of The Peregrine Fund to train local people as field scientists highlights a theme that is beginning to take center stage in conservation: successful management of forest resources can occur only where conservation and management plans have the support and active participation of local people. Sometimes gaining this support is simply a question of making people more knowledgeable about conservation issues, but more often the most effective means of garnering support is to encourage local people to become economically, intellectually, and emotionally invested in threatened species and ecosystems.

In all three projects, the researchers realized that simple data collection, valuable though it may be, is not the most efficient way to protect the Maya Forest from degradation and destruction. Because time is not on the side of conservation, researchers must make their studies proactive—that is, data collection must integrate other strategies to promote conservation. By learning the differences between natural forests and degraded ecosystems, scientists have the opportunity to understand the human factors that lead to degradation. Such understanding can then help researchers to propose less harmful techniques of farming, forestry, or resource extraction and work with local people to institute changes in unsustainable practices.

Chapter 15

Toward Sustainable Forestry in Belize

Nicholas V. L. Brokaw, Andrew A. Whitman, Roger Wilson,
John M. Hagan, Neil Bird, Elizabeth P. Mallory, Laura K. Snook,
Paul J. Martins, Darrell Novelo, Dominic White, and Elizabeth Losos

The best hope for conserving the biodiversity of tropical forests is to develop economically viable land uses that require large areas of relatively natural forest cover. Strict reserves are essential for conservation, but they usually are too few or too small to contain all the necessary elements of a tropical forest ecosystem, and their integrity may depend on being surrounded by zones of compatible economic land uses. One such land use is sustainable forestry (Frumhoff 1995), defined here as forestry in which present harvests do not irreversibly reduce future harvests, viable populations of all native species are maintained at the landscape level, and harvesting practices are economically viable in both the short and long term. In this paper we describe projects aimed at developing sustainable forestry in Belize, Central America.

Belize is a favorable setting for this effort. First, about 55% (1,262,800 ha) of Belize is still covered with forest (estimated from Programme for Belize 1995; cf. 22.8% forest in Costa Rica [Sader and Joyce 1988]). Second, Belize has a low population (c. 200,000 in 1991) and consequently has less pressure for forest conversion than other Central American countries (Costa Rica's population is 15 times greater, with land area only 2.2 times larger). Third, some 44% (551,000 ha) of Belize's forest is currently under government or private management for conservation and sustainable forestry (Programme for Belize 1995). In contrast to other parts of Central America, Belize has relatively more time and opportunity to develop sustainable forestry, supported by both public and private commitment to conserving forest resources.

Belize has great biological diversity. Its total angiosperm flora is about

4,000 species (Hartshorn et al. 1984); by comparison, Ecuador, a country almost 20 times larger, on the equator, and with a greater range of habitats, has 13,000 species (Gentry 1993). Belize also has large populations of animals threatened elsewhere in the region, such as jaguars, ocelots, and other big cats, Baird's tapir, white-lipped peccary, and great curassow. Supporting this biodiversity are ecological and evolutionary processes that operate unimpeded in the country's broad areas of relatively undisturbed habitat.

Although the present situation of forests in Belize is good, it is nevertheless at risk. Forest land in Belize is threatened with conversion to agriculture, because the main economic use of forest land, logging, is declining as valuable timber becomes depleted from forests. Since 1977, 34,131 ha of Belize's national forest reserves have been de-reserved for conversion to agriculture (Smith 1991). In addition, the 540,810 ha of national lands in Belize, much of which is forested, eventually will be assigned to some economic use—perhaps forestry if it proves viable, otherwise agriculture (Smith 1991). Population pressures on the land are increasing due to immigration and a high annual birth rate of 36.1 per 1,000 women (SPEAR 1990). And the number of Belizeans will soon multiply greatly: in 1989, 45% of the population was under 14 years old (SPEAR 1990).

Our projects aim to increase and maintain the economic value of forest in Belize, as an incentive to conserve forest cover and biodiversity, i.e., the species and biological communities of the area. Conversely, economic uses of the forest depend on biodiversity, because of the interspecific relationships on which exploited species rely (Putz 1993). The forestry research we outline below includes (1) studies on the impact of traditional selective logging on regeneration of timber species (mahogany and species of secondary value) and on birds, (2) timber stock surveys and monitoring of forest dynamics in permanent sample plots, (3) three different silvicultural experiments designed to improve growth and regeneration of timber species, (4) monitoring of silvicultural impacts on forest structure, birds, butterflies, and the plant community, and (5) economic evaluation of the silvicultural treatments and development of markets for secondary species. We preface discussion of current research with background on the forest industry in Belize and our research on traditional selective logging.

The Forest Industry and Forest Management in Belize

Until 1950, logging was the largest sector of the Belize economy; since then it has declined, both as a percentage of Gross Domestic Product (2% in 1993 [Embassy of Belize, pers. comm.]) and in absolute terms (ODA 1989). Between 1952 and 1977 log harvest fell from 161,500 to 28,300 m³. Much of the decline has been in the "primary," i.e., the highest value, timber species. Recovery of forest-based industries is a priority in the government's current economic plan (Embassy of Belize, pers. comm.).

Until recently Belizean loggers focused on one primary (high value) species, mahogany (*Swietenia macrophylla*), while harvesting a low volume of secondary (low value) species (Lamb 1946), which are, nonetheless, "fully commercial and commonly used for joinery and construction" (Alder 1993). Whereas a typical mahogany tree is worth about U.S. $324 in log form and $1,500 on import as sawn wood to the United States (Rodan et al. 1992), a similar-sized tree of a typical secondary species is worth half as much and is rarely exported (ODA 1989). From 1985 through 1988, primary species made up about 94% of exported lumber, secondary species 6% (ODA 1989).

This emphasis on mahogany sharply reduced its availability, imperiling the timber industry. Yet overharvesting of mahogany continues. Using estimates of current stock, growth, and mortality, and assuming constant regeneration, Alder (1993) calculated an "annual allowable cut" of primary species in Belize of 6,041 m^3, the amount that might be sustained indefinitely. He compared this figure with the "actual annual cut" of 20,000 m^3, the amount harvested in 1992. The supply and its capacity to regenerate is dwindling. By contrast, he estimated an annual allowable cut of 85,000 m^3 of secondary species against an actual annual cut of 40,000 m^3. These imbalances suggest two needs that must be met to establish a long-term, economically viable timber industry in Belize: first, forests must be managed to promote growth and regeneration of mahogany and secondary species, and second, uses and markets for secondary species must be developed.

The only significant management prescription for timber species in the broadleaf forests of Belize has been a prohibition against harvesting trees under a certain diameter. This policy leads to traditional selective logging, in which the forest is combed for trees of legal size. It is assumed that there is ample recruitment of timber species through seed, seedling, and larger stages, continually replenishing the supply of trees of legal size. Unfortunately, these assumptions about population structure and dynamics do not hold for mahogany (see below), and little is known about populations of secondary species. Thus traditional selective logging has been termed "inappropriate and unsustainable" in Belize (ODA 1989).

Study Areas

Our forestry research takes place in two locations: the 97,166 ha Río Bravo Conservation and Management Area (RBCMA) in northwest Belize and the 76,554 ha Chiquibul Forest Reserve (CFR) in southwest Belize. The RBCMA is owned and managed by the Programme for Belize, a Belizean nongovernmental organization. Programme for Belize's goal is to conserve the biodiversity of the RBCMA and to support management of the area with economic activities that are compatible with conservation, such as sustainable forestry. Programme for Belize has zoned 17,900 ha of the RBCMA as a Timber Extraction Zone, designated for silvicultural research and income from logging.

The CFR is owned by the government of Belize and managed by the Belize Forest Department for sustainable production of forest products and conservation of the forest ecosystem.

The Extraction Zone in the RBCMA supports subtropical moist forest, while the CFR study area is near the transition between subtropical moist and subtropical lower montane moist forests (Holdridge system, Hartshorn et al. 1984). Rainfall in both areas is about 1,500 mm per year, with a dry season from January or February to May. The Extraction Zone is about 20 m above sea level, with level topography. The CFR study area is about 600 m above sea level, in a setting of low hills. Soils in both areas are calcareous clays (Wright et al. 1959). Both areas probably were cleared by the ancient Maya, then abandoned some 1,000 years ago. They are now entirely covered by forest, although the Extraction Zone was selectively logged from the mid-1800s through the early 1990s and the CFR from the 1920s into the present. Hurricanes have affected both forests, the RBCMA less than the CFR (Friesner 1997).

Traditional Selective Logging: Impacts and Lessons for Silviculture

We studied the effects of traditional selective logging (removal of ~1 tree/2 ha every five to ten years [Whitman, Brokaw, and Hagan 1997]) on regeneration of timber species and on the bird community in the RBCMA Extraction Zone. Sites were logged by previous owners.

At a site logged two to five years earlier, we found about one mahogany above the diameter limit (60 cm) in every 9 ha (Figure 15.1). Some of these were hollow or malformed trees of no value to loggers. The number of harvestable mahogany was insufficient to support a forestry enterprise. Nor did the numbers in smaller size classes promise much future yield: there were about two mahogany >10 cm diameter in every hectare of forest. Seedlings and saplings <2.5 cm diameter were more common (Figure 15.1), but, considering the high mortality of small stems, the study population was reproducing poorly (Verissimo et al. 1994). Mahogany regeneration was most abundant, grew fastest, and survived best along major roads or in similar open areas (Figure 15.2). The gaps left after removal of single trees contained a few seedlings, but these survived and grew poorly.

Nearby we noted higher densities of large mahogany, probably reflecting patchy, intermittent regeneration following major canopy opening by disturbances such as hurricanes (Snook 1993; Gullison et al. 1996). Such disturbance produces even-aged stands in which all individuals reach harvestable size at about the same time. In this situation logging can remove the whole population, leaving no small stems to replace those logged, nor large stems to provide seed (Gullison et al. 1996; Snook 1996). Foresters therefore recommend harvesting patches of trees rather than single trees, using all cut trees,

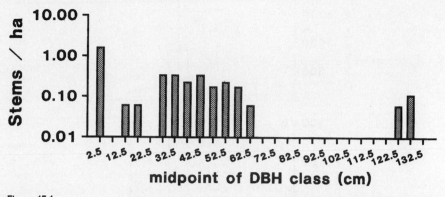

Figure 15.1
....

Diameter-class distribution of mahogany (*Swietenia macrophylla*) in the Timber Extraction Zone (Río Bravo Conservation and Management Area), Belize. Most diameter classes occur at low densities (<1/ha). Densities of large individuals are low and those of the smallest classes seem too low to replace harvested trees. The diameter-class distribution is discontinuous, indicating periodic recruitment. Data are from censuses in ten 500 × 10 m transects. (A. Whitman, unpublished data.)

and creating better conditions for regeneration of mahogany and timber species with similar ecology (ODA 1989; Snook 1993).

Studies of secondary species in the selectively logged area revealed various diameter-class distributions (Figure 15.3). Some had abundant regeneration, indicating seedling tolerance of shade and an easily sustainable supply of timber, while others had little regeneration, because, like mahogany, recent canopy openings have not been large enough to promote establishment and growth (Figure 15.4).

Traditional selective logging had little effect on the bird community, based on mist net and census data from forest logged within the past two years and intact canopy forest not logged for at least ten years (Whitman, Hagan, and Brokaw 1997). The number of bird species was similar in logged and intact canopy forests. Of 26 ecological guilds tested, 4 (canopy species, edge-using species, Neotropical-Nearctic migrants, and live foliage–using species) had significantly more species in logged forest. No guilds had significantly more species in intact canopy forest. Of the 66 species analyzed, only 1 species, the tawny-crowned greenlet, was significantly less frequent in recently logged than intact canopy forest, but it was still present in logged forest. Five species were more frequent in recently logged forest.

The low impact of logging on birds in this forest (cf. Johns 1991; Thiollay 1992) is partly due to the comparatively low impact of traditional selective logging on forest structure in the Extraction Zone (Whitman, Brokaw, and

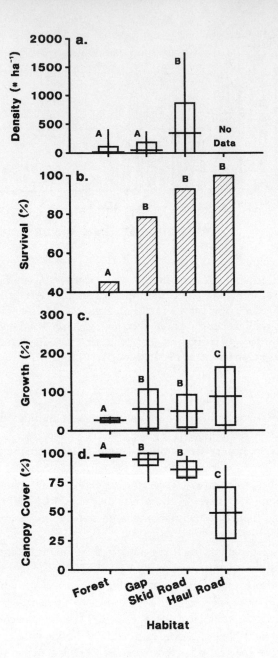

Figure 15.2

Mahogany performance in intact forest, in logging gaps, on skid roads, and along major roads at a site in the Timber Extraction Zone (Río Bravo Conservation and Management Area), Belize. (a) seedling density, (b) seedling survival, (c) seedling growth, and (d) canopy cover. Seedling density, survival, and growth were lowest in intact forest and greatest in logging gaps and along roads (a, b, and c). The disturbance created by logging gaps and roads decreases canopy cover (d) and allows more light into the understory, leading to greater mahogany regeneration, survival, and growth at these sites. (A. Whitman, unpublished data.)

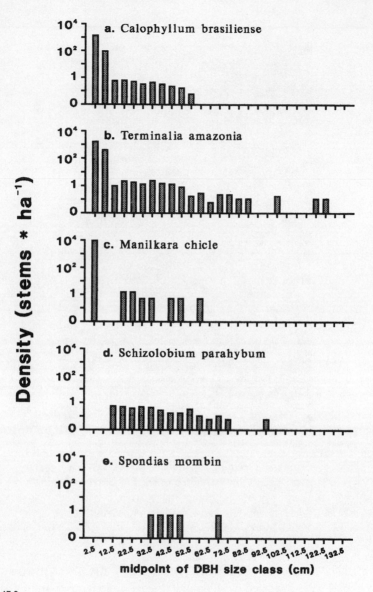

Figure 15.3
....

Diameter-class distributions of tree species of secondary commercial value at a site in the Timber Extraction Zone (Río Bravo Conservation and Management Area), Belize. *Calophyllum brasiliense* and *Terminalia amazonia* have high densities of small diameter classes, indicating frequent regeneration, and a continuous distribution, indicating continuous recruitment. *Manilkara zapota* has high levels of recruitment into small diameter classes but low recruitment into larger classes. *Schizolobium parahybum* and *Spondias mombin* have few recruits in small diameter classes and a discontinuous diameter class distribution, indicating periodic and low recruitment. Data are from censuses in ten 500 m × 10 m transects. (A. Whitman, unpublished data.)

Figure 15.4
....

Mahogany seedling (*Swietenia macrophylla*) in a
gap where a tree was felled in the Río Bravo
Conservation and Management Area, Belize.
Mahogany persists for a while but does not
thrive in logged tree gaps.

Hagan 1997), as elsewhere in Belize (pers. obs.). Only 4.8% of trees (stems
≥10 cm dbh) were damaged by traditional selective logging in the Extraction
Zone, compared with a mean of 37.0 % in three other studies. Canopy loss
was 2.0%, compared to a mean of 43.7% in three other studies. Damage was
low because few trees were harvested per hectare (0.5 compared to a mean of
3.0 in eight other studies). In any case, it is unlikely that many bird species
strongly sensitive to logging would be found in this region, with its historically
high levels of disturbance from Maya agriculture and hurricanes.

Forest Management Research

Details of forest management in the Extraction Zone will be based on results
of a stock survey to gain information on the overall amount of harvestable

timber in the area, the population characteristics of timber species, and the distribution and abundance of nontimber products such as chicle (*Manilkara zapota*) and thatch palm (*Sabal mauritiiformis*). In addition, we are installing 16 one-hectare permanent sample plots in the Extraction Zone, with all trees tagged, mapped, and repeatedly measured to accumulate information on long-term community and population dynamics. Twenty-four of these one-hectare plots have been established in seven forest types by the Forest Department in the CFR and other forest reserves.

Traditional selective logging must be replaced with new silivicultural methods. We are experimenting with three different silivicultural treatments in the Extraction Zone and two in the CFR. These treatments are designed to promote growth of standing stock, i.e., trees to be harvested within about 40 years, as well as establishment and growth of regeneration, i.e., trees that would be harvested in about 80 years. The first of these treatments, "selection felling," was undertaken by the Forest Planning and Management Project of the Forest Department. This treatment is defined as "selection, marking and directional felling of trees under strict silvicultural rules in a harvesting system which is ecologically and environmentally compatible and is in strict accordance with the traditional rules of good forest management and the principles of sustainability" (Bruenig 1996). Particular goals of this method in Belize are to use more species, enhance growth of remaining trees, promote regeneration, and reduce damage associated with traditional selective logging (Bird 1994). In practice, more trees of more species are removed per unit area than in traditional selective logging.

To carry out the selection felling treatment, the Forest Department established two 18-ha plots in the Extraction Zone, and four 18-ha plots in the CFR, in which all trees ≥30 cm dbh were tagged, mapped, measured, and identified, while smaller trees were likewise inventoried in subplots. With maps of the trees, the Forest Department planned a harvest route in the forest that minimized the distance traveled and damage inflicted by log skidders. Using directional felling to reduce damage to the residual stand, six trees per hectare were removed from a 9-ha half of each plot; 46 different species were harvested overall (Bird 1995). Trees ≥100 cm dbh were not cut to maintain a heterogeneous habitat structure beneficial to wildlife. Post-treatment studies will extend 40 years and focus on growth of remaining trees ≥10 cm dbh and on regeneration.

The second treatment, "liberation thinning" (Hutchinson 1987), is part of the Production from Natural Forests Project undertaken by CATIE (Centro Agronómico Tropical de Investigaciones y Enseñanza, based in Costa Rica) in the Extraction Zone and the CFR. This treatment (girdling) kills trees in the vicinity of selected individuals to improve the productivity, quality, and number of selected species. The goal of the project is to examine the effects of liberation thinning on the structure and dynamics of the treated forest stand.

Liberation thinning has been carried out for several timber species in 12

thinning plots at each of three sites in the Extraction Zone and at several locations in the CFR. Liberated trees are species of commercial value that meet
standards of form and condition that promise good timber yield. Generally
the treatment only kills trees of noncommercial species that overtop future
crop trees. When two trees of commercial species stand closer than 2 m to
each other, the one of inferior condition is killed.

The third treatment is a system of "patch cuts," from which all trees are removed, created in 1996 by the Programme for Belize in the Extraction Zone.
The goals of this treatment are to create sites favorable for regeneration of mahogany and other timber species with similar ecology, to reduce skidder travel
costs and damage associated with extensive, traditional selective logging, and
to promote use of more tree species (cf. Hartshorn 1989; ODA 1989; Snook
1993).

We cut patches in a range of sizes to determine a size that achieves the
combined goals of promoting regeneration, especially of mahogany, and efficiency of harvest. We used a randomized block design consisting of eight 7.5-
ha blocks, each with a random array of four patches (one each of 500, 1,000,
2,500, and 5,000 m^2) with an additional patch of 500 m^2 in two blocks and
closed-canopy control sites in all blocks. The patches were hand-felled and
cleared with a skidder, except for the 5,000 m^2 patches, which were mostly
cleared with a bulldozer. We used a bulldozer because it is the cheapest way to
clear large areas and maximally eliminate competition with mahogany.

We planted mahogany seedlings in each patch and control site, in patterns
designed to test the impact of patch size and edge effects, and, in the largest
sites, to test the effect of bulldozing versus hand-clearing. Our experiment
with patch cuts is complemented by studies in Quintana Roo, Mexico, on
timber regeneration in patch cuts of 200 and 500 m^2 (D. Whigham and M.
Dickinson, pers. comm.) and on timber regeneration after milpa agriculture
(Snook, this volume).

Ecological Sustainability

The silvicultural treatments involve greater and different kinds of disturbance
to the forest than did the relatively benign traditional selective logging. Logging can have various negative impacts, including structural damage to the
forest with associated changes in plants and animals; soil compaction, with effects on soil organisms and processes and on seed germination; erosion and
consequent deposition of sediment in streams and rivers, which changes
stream ecology; direct reduction of populations and altered gene pools of harvested species, with possible indirect effects on dependent species; and increased access, leading to hunting and forest clearing. Some of these effects
are negligible for the study areas. For instance, erosion is not a problem in the
study areas, as they are level or have little surface drainage. Access to the Ex-

traction Zone is well controlled by Programme for Belize, and the CFR is remote from human settlements. The other three problems listed above, however, could be significant.

We are studying impacts of selection felling and patch cuts on forest structure and selected animal groups as indicators of ecological sustainability. As one method of evaluating changes in forest structure due to selection felling in the CFR, we measured canopy openness (percentage of open sky) above grid points in the 18-ha study plots before and after treatment. Logging caused dramatic but localized changes in openness (Figure 15.5), reflecting changes in canopy structure. Tropical forest birds are sensitive to changes in forest structure (Johns 1991; Thiollay 1992), while butterflies are sensitive to plant species composition as well as structure (Sparrow et al. 1994). We monitored birds (mist net and census methods) before and after the selection felling in the Extraction Zone and the CFR, and we began monitoring birds and butterflies (trap and census) before the patch cuts in the Extraction Zone. It is too early to tell if selection felling will have had significant effects on birds in the 18-ha plots.

Patch cutting on a landscape scale would represent an extreme incident of disturbance that could alter the plant community. Size and frequency of the cuts as well as compacted soil may enable colonization by enough individuals of weedy species over the landscape to jeopardize plant species characteristic of older growth and their dependent animals. To evaluate this possible problem we are measuring soil compaction and comparing the regenerating plant communities in the different patch sizes with communities in control areas.

Economic Evaluation and Marketing

We can develop ecologically sustainable methods for promoting regeneration and growth of timber species in natural forest, but will those methods be economically sustainable? Would those methods be adopted by a logger needing to make a profit? To answer these questions we are analyzing the costs and benefits of management alternatives. Costs are being determined for all silvicultural treatments, to include all operations and fixed costs, e.g., field labor, transport, milling, road building, and administrative expenses. Income from management under the three treatments will be calculated. We can then compare treatments for economic as well as ecological costs and benefits. Logging can likewise be compared to alternative land uses. Preliminary analysis of selection felling in the CFR showed that this treatment is economically profitable, despite, or perhaps because of, added planning effort (N. Bird, unpublished data).

An important part of the economic equation will be profits from secondary species. Efforts to promote these species in Belize date at least from Lamb's (1946) monograph on their uses, published about the time mahogany harvest

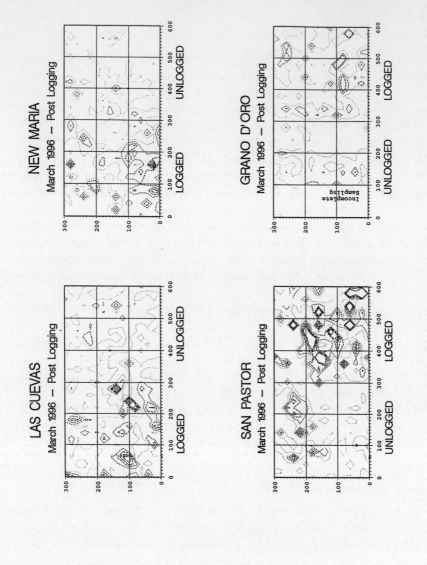

Figure 15.5

Canopy openness (percent open sky) on logged and unlogged plot halves in four 18 ha experimental logging plots in the Chiquibul Forest Reserve, Belize. Measurements on logged halves were made in 1996, ten months after logging; measurements on unlogged halves were made in 1995. Concentric contour lines are drawn around adjacent points that have the same value. Canopy openness was measured with a spherical densiometer (Lemmon 1957). (E. Mallory and N. Brokaw, unpublished data.)

began to decline. Since then, information on qualities and uses of Belize's secondary species has increased (Echenique-Manrique and Plumptre 1990), but this information is not widespread among potential users and these species have little name recognition in the international market. We are promoting the secondary species harvested in the Extraction Zone through product development and "value added" at a local wood products mill, and through sales to buyers and consumers concerned with the environment, known as the "green market." Access to the green market is achieved through certification of the sustainability of Programme for Belize's timber operations.

Conclusion: Can Forestry Be Sustainable in Belize?

"Sustainable" has become the watchword for all development projects in tropical forest areas. However, Rice et al. (1997) have pointed out some serious obstacles to sustainable forestry in tropical forests, based partly on their experience in Bolivia. We face many of these obstacles in Belize, yet the situation in Belize is significantly different and more encouraging than in countries such as Bolivia. Belize has the following conditions, some illustrated in this chapter, that facilitate sustainable forestry: (1) there is substantial political and social support for sustainable forestry; (2) many forest organisms in Belize are already adapted to a pattern of disturbance, caused by hurricanes; (3) markets for less valuable timber species can be developed; (4) timber companies are interested in sustainability, because they cannot simply cut and move on as in larger tropical countries; (5) some logging is currently subsidized with research and monitoring aimed at sustainability; and (6) many timber concessions are surrounded by large, protected forest areas. Perhaps more important than the particular situation in Belize, we think that some of the favorable conditions that exist there may increasingly prevail elsewhere in the tropics. If we are right, working toward sustainable forestry in Belize may ultimately help achieve sustainable tropical forestry more generally.

Acknowledgments

We thank the Natural History Museum (London) for use of facilities at the Las Cuevas Research Station (jointly operated with Belize Forest Department) in the Chiquibul, and particularly John Howell and Chapal and Celia Bol for many kinds of assistance at Las Cuevas. Alan Herrera has been a big help at the Hill Bank Field Station, operated by the Programme for Belize. We greatly appreciate the volunteer help of Vanessa Hill, Mic Murphy, Jennifer DeLucia, Matt Myer, Denise Bohon, Lynda Cobb, Paul Champlin, Paul Rodewald, Lisa Zweede, Bill Thevenin, Sherry Hudson, Patricia O'Neill, and Amanda Dumin. Juan Laeva and Julie Arnold, both of the Forest Department, did excellent work on logging impacts in the Chiquibul. Dennis Whigham and anonymous reviewers helped improve the manuscript. Funds for this research have come from the Commission of the European Community, the Overseas Development Administration, the United States Agency for International Development, the W. Alton Jones Foundation, the National Fish and Wildlife Foundation, the U.S. Man and the Biosphere Program, and the Prospect Hill Foundation.

References

Alder, D. 1993. *An Assessment of Broadleaf Forest Resources and Sustainable Yield in Belize*. Consultancy Report No. 11. Forest Planning and Management Project, Forest Department, Ministry of Natural Resources, Belmopan, Belize.

Bird, N. 1994. *Experimental Design and Background Information*. Silvicultural Research Paper No. 1. Forest Planning and Management Project, Forest Department, Ministry of Natural Resources, Belmopan, Belize.

————. 1995. *The Logging Treatment*. Silvicultural Research Paper No. 2. Forestry Planning and Management Project, Ministry of Natural Resources, Belmopan, Belize.

Bruenig, E. F. 1996. *Conservation and Management of Tropical Rainforests: An Integrated Approach to Sustainability*. CAB International, Wallingford, U.K.

Echenique-Manrique, R., and R. A. Plumptre. 1990. *A Guide to the Use of Mexican and Belizean Timbers*. Oxford Forestry Institute, Oxford, U.K.

Friesner, J. 1993. *Hurricanes and the Forests of Belize*. Occasional Series No. 1. Forest Planning and Management Project, Forest Department, Ministry of Natural Resources, Belmopan, Belize.

Frumhoff, P. C. 1995. Conserving wildlife in tropical forests managed for timber. *BioScience* 45: 456–464.

Gentry, A. H. 1993. *A Field Guide to the Families and Genera of Woody Plants of Northwest South America (Colombia, Ecuador, Peru), with Supplementary Notes on Herbaceous Taxa*. Conservation International, Washington, D.C.

Gullison, R. E, S. N. Panfil, J. J. Strouse, and S. P. Hubbell. 1996. Ecology and management of mahogany (*Swietenia macrophylla* King) in the Chimanes Forest, Beni, Bolivia. *Botanical Journal of the Linnean Society* 122: 9–34.

Hartshorn, G. S. 1989. Application of gap theory to tropical forest management: Natural regeneration on strip clear-cuts in the Peruvian Amazon. *Ecology* 70: 567–569.

Hartshorn, G. S., L. Nicolait, L. Hartshorn, G. Bevier, R. Brightman, J. Cal, A. Cawich, W. Davidson, R. Dubois, C. Dyer, J. Gibson, W. Hawley, J. Leonard, R. Nicolait, D. Weyer, H. White, and C. Wright. 1984. *Belize: Country Environmental Profile: A Field Study*. Robert Nicolait and Associates, Ltd., Belize City, Belize.

Hutchinson, I. D. 1987. Improvement thinning in natural tropical forests: Aspects and institutionalization. Pages 113–133 in *Natural Management of Tropical Moist Forests: Silvicultural and Management Prospects of Sustained Utilization*, F. Mergen and J. R. Vincent, eds. Yale University School of Forestry and Environmental Studies, New Haven, Conn.

Johns, A. D. 1991. Responses of Amazonian rain forest birds to habitat modification. *Journal of Tropical Ecology* 7: 417–437.

Lamb, A. F. A. 1946. *Notes on Forty-two Secondary Hardwood Timbers of British Honduras*. Forest Department Bulletin No. 1. Belize City, Belize.

Lemmon, P. E. 1957. A new instrument for measuring forest overstory density. *Journal of Forestry* 55: 667–669.

ODA (Overseas Development Administration). 1989. The Belize Tropical Forestry Action Plan. Overseas Development Administration, London.

Programme for Belize. 1995. *Towards a National Protected Area Systems Plan for Belize.* Programme for Belize, Belize City, Belize.

Putz, F. E. 1993. *Considerations of the Ecological Foundation of Natural Forest Management in the American Tropics.* Center for Tropical Conservation, Duke University, Durham, N.C.

Rice, R. E., R. E. Gullison, and J. W. Reid. 1997. Can sustainable management save tropical forests? *Scientific American* 276: 44–49.

Rodan, B. D., A. C. Newton, and A. Verissimo. 1992. Mahogany conservation: Status and policy initiatives. *Environmental Conservation* 19: 331–342.

Sader, S. A., and A. T. Joyce. 1988. Deforestation rates and trends in Costa Rica, 1940 to 1983. *Biotropica* 20: 11–19.

Smith, C. F. 1991. *Economic Aspects of Forestry Management in Belize.* Consultancy report for the Forest Department, Ministry of Natural Resources, Belmopan, Belize.

Snook, L. K. 1993. Stand dynamics of mahogany (*Swietenia macrophylla* King) and associated species after fire and hurricane in the tropical forests of the Yucatán Peninsula, Mexico. Ph.D. dissertation, Yale University School of Forestry and Environmental Studies, New Haven, Conn.

————. 1996. Catastrophic disturbance, logging and the ecology of mahogany (*Swietenia macrophylla* King): Grounds for listing a major tropical timber species in CITES. *Botanical Journal of the Linnean Society* 122: 35–46.

Sparrow, H. R., T. D. Sisk, P. R. Ehrlich, and D. D. Murphy. 1994. Techniques and guidelines for monitoring Neotropical butterflies. *Conservation Biology* 8: 800–809.

SPEAR (Society for the Promotion of Education and Research). 1990. *Profile of Belize 1989.* SPEAReports 3, Cubola Productions, Benque Viejo, Belize.

Thiollay, J.-M. 1992. Influence of selective logging on bird species diversity in a Guianan rain forest. *Conservation Biology* 6: 47–63.

Verissimo, A., P. Barreto, R. Tarifa, and C. Uhl. 1994. Extraction of a high-value resource in Amazonia: The case of mahogany. *Forest Ecology and Management* 72: 39–60.

Whitman, A. A., N. V. L. Brokaw, and J. M. Hagan III. 1997. Forest damage caused by selection logging of mahogany (*Swietenia macrophylla*) in northern Belize. *Forest Ecology and Management* 92: 87–96.

Whitman, A. A., J. M. Hagan III, and N. V. L. Brokaw. 1997. Effects of selection logging on tropical forest birds in northern Belize. *Biotropica* (in press).

Wright, A. C. S., D. H. Romney, R. H. Arbuckle, and V. E. Vial. 1959. *Land in British Honduras.* Colonial Research Publication No. 24. Her Majesty's Stationery Office, London.

Chapter 16

The Peregrine Fund's Maya Project: Ecological Research, Habitat Conservation, and Development of Human Resources in the Maya Forest

David F. Whitacre

To conduct field research in neotropical forests today is to be confronted by myriad and complex factors leading to the rapid shrinkage of these forests, and often, to the marginalization of segments of society. No ecologist can long indulge in basic research here without attempting to understand and combat these forces. When research can respond to the needs of land managers and others involved in conservation efforts and also contribute to the development of human resources and sustainable development objectives, the best of all worlds is achieved. The Peregrine Fund's Maya Project is an example of a program that has endeavored to respond to local conservation and development needs while conducting original research in basic ecology and conservation biology. Originally purely a research effort seeking to describe the region's poorly known forest raptors, the Maya Project has broadened to embrace a significant component of community outreach, including the education and training of local people in ecology and field research, as well as efforts to alter farming practices in ways that will help spare forest and enhance farmers' standards of living.

The Maya Forest, one of the few remaining blocks of intact forest in Central America, provides the dynamic setting of the project, which is centered mainly in Guatemala's Tikal National Park and Maya Biosphere Reserve (MBR). Originally taking advantage of the protected status of these areas, the project has increasingly been directed toward helping reserve managers confront a multitude of threats—from the encroachment of agricultural and pasture lands on reserve boundaries, to the aggressive extraction of resources such as timber and petroleum, to the increasing pressure brought on by a growing population. Initiated in 1988, the Maya Project began as a conservation research and training program intended "to aid in the preservation of tropical raptors, forests, and associated wildlife communities by using birds of prey as key indicators of environmental quality and indices for determining size and design of reserves" (Burnham et al. 1988). As many Neotropical forest raptors are poorly known, the first priority was to gather baseline data on the natural histories of these species. In addition, the project investigated the habitat and spatial needs of raptor species, requiring researchers to develop methods for censusing raptors in tropical forest.

While the project has maintained its initial focus on raptor ecology—some results of our studies are presented in brief below—it has broadened to include studies of forest vegetation and nonraptorial birds. In its current configuration, the project focuses on birds and forest vegetation to provide basic information on the biota within reserves, to reveal how different land uses affect birds and vegetation (and by extension, the forest biota in general), to aid in monitoring the ecological integrity of reserves, and to facilitate the training of local natural resource personnel. In the discussion that follows, we trace the evolution of the project, describing its achievements and lessons learned in the eight years since its inception. As the Maya Project has developed over the years, the project's philosophy and approach have been shaped by the input of local participants. Community outreach has become a significant component of the program—a component with important and positive implications for long-term involvement of community members in the conservation of the region's biota. As we learn more about the complex factors contributing to forest conversion, our project examines new, diverse methods of promoting conservation. Some of these methods may seem far removed from raptor studies, but all of them ultimately contribute to the conservation of these majestic birds and their forest home.

Biology of a Tropical Forest Raptor Community

The adequacy of conservation efforts may be judged in part by the intactness of predator communities, as predators often are among the first species to disappear when pristine habitat is altered by humans (Noss and Cooperrider 1994). Despite the difficulty of retaining full predator complements, doing so is vital to conserving an intact biota because predators help to maintain community integrity and diversity (Terborgh 1992). Thus, information that helps to retain viable predator populations is important for conservation.

Initial descriptions of raptor faunas of certain Neotropical forest areas have been published (Thiollay 1984, 1985, 1991; Robinson 1994), but the Maya

Project is the first to attempt to gather detailed data on the breeding biology, diet, and habitat requirements of an entire tropical forest raptor fauna. This community-level investigation is the Maya Project's central scientific goal. About 21 forest-dwelling raptors are common enough to study at Tikal National Park, Guatemala, the project's main study site. We now have gathered basic natural history data on 19 of these species.

As we began our investigations, we found that methods for censusing raptors in tropical forests are poorly developed. Hence, we first had to devise methods for documenting their abundance in areas of unbroken forest. We experimented with seven census methods and published our recommendations (Burnham et al. 1988; Turley 1989; Whitacre and Turley 1990; Whitacre et al. 1992). In brief, we recommend determining relative abundance by taking visual "point counts" conducted over the forest canopy from emergent tree tops, tall buildings, towers, hills, or other vantage points, in combination with pre-dawn auditory point counts. These techniques can be supplemented by acoustical luring, i.e., playback of taped vocalizations of raptors and distressed prey. Our methods have been incorporated into research programs in Costa Rica, Colombia, Honduras, Brazil, and Madagascar; moreover, these methods are effective not only for raptors, but also for several other bird species and monkeys—70 species in all, described more fully in a later section of this chapter.

To ensure the validity of comparisons across time and space, we studied seasonality of detection rates over a 12-month period. Several species showed marked seasonal differences, with conspicuousness often enhanced by heightened display activity early in the breeding season. These results led us to recommend that censusing for this suite of species take place during the early breeding season, which occurs from February through May for many bird species in the Maya Forest.

Spatial Needs of Forest Raptors

For most raptors at Tikal, we have gathered data on habitat and spatial requirements such as nesting density and/or home-range size. These data allow us to estimate, for example, that the 576 km^2 of Tikal National Park may harbor as many as 400 or more pairs of barred forest falcons (Micrastur ruficollis) (Thorstrom 1993), but only about 65 pairs of the larger ornate hawk-eagle (Spizaetus ornatus) (Figure 16.1), while the number of pairs of orange-breasted falcons (Falco deiroleucus) within the park is quite low—it varies between zero and two—because of the species' specialized cliff-nesting habits. Such information can be useful in planning and managing protected areas by helping to provide a rationale for reserve size, and it can contribute to analysis of population viability.

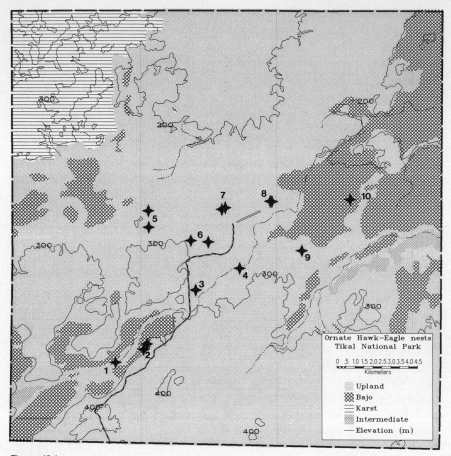

Figure 16.1

Map of Tikal National Park, El Péten, Guatemala, showing nest locations of ten pairs of ornate hawk-eagles studied in Tikal. Paired nests are alternate sites within a given territory. Areas without nests indicated were not searched for nests. (Map by R. Bjork.)

Monitoring the Population Status of Vulnerable Species

The bird species most in danger of extirpation from the Maya Forest are probably the harpy eagle (*Harpia harpyja*), scarlet macaw (*Ara macao*), and orange-breasted falcon. One of the world's least-known and possibly rarest falcons, the orange-breasted falcon attracted the attention of The Peregrine Fund in the late 1970s, when initial studies were made in the Petén, Guatemala (Jenny and Cade 1986). Since 1991, we have worked annually to document this species' ecology, distribution, and population size in the Maya Forest (Baker et al. 1995). We annually monitor occupancy and breeding success at 19 nest sites—6 in Petén and 13 in Belize—making this the best-studied population of this species. This falcon's population in northern Central America appears to be disjunct from the main bulk of the species' range in South America, so it is unlikely to be "rescued" by immigration from the south. Accordingly, it is important to secure the future of this northernmost population. We hope to continue research and monitoring until we feel confident of the current population size and trend, and to spur a local commitment to continue monitoring thereafter.

Habitat Affinities of Forest Birds: Conservation Potential in Milpa Farming Landscapes

As pressures on tropical forests increase, effects of human activities are demonstrable even in those areas set aside for protection of forest biodiversity. We believe that goals of conserving tropical forest biota cannot be met solely within protected areas. Rather, we must also conserve as much forest biota as possible in human-dominated landscapes. With this in mind, we have sought to help answer the question of how much avian conservation can be achieved in landscapes devoted largely to slash-and-burn, or milpa cultivation.

Recently, we completed field work documenting the types of forest utilized by some 90 bird species at Tikal. We sampled birds over the entire spectrum of mature forest types and on abandoned cornfields after 2 to 30 years of succession. Our goal was to determine what fraction of the bird community requires mature forest, and what fraction can make use of the abundant young secondary growth produced by milpa cultivation. Through multivariate ordination procedures, we identified eight tentative habitat "response types" among these 90 bird species (Whitacre et al. 1995b). Figure 16.2 shows patterns representative of four response types: a "bajo (swamp forest) specialist," a "second growth species," a "mature upland forest obligate," and a "forest generalist."

Forty to 50 percent of Tikal's forest bird species appeared strongly linked to mature forest (Whitacre et al. 1995b). These species can be expected to decline or disappear in deforested landscapes. Of the remaining half of the forest avifauna, the majority can probably persist in moderately deforested landscapes, but most would disappear from landscapes entirely converted to cattle pasture. Those species that thrive in young successional vegetation generally are not threatened by current land-use patterns. Thus, conservation efforts must be focused on that portion of the avifauna and other biota reliant on mature forest.

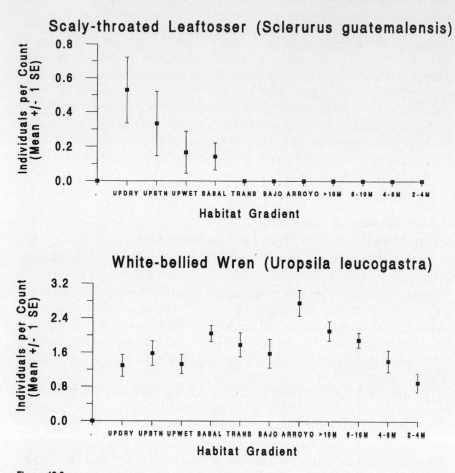

Figure 16.2

Habitat affinities of four bird species as determined by point counts. Habitat types from left to right are seven pristine forest types (upland dry, upland standard, upland wet, hillbase, transitional, bajo, and arroyo (true swamp), followed by four age/height classes of second growth (>10 m, 6–10 m, 4–6 m, and 2–4 m tall). Based on 428 point counts—two at each of 214 sites. On average 20 point count sites were censused per habitat.

Conservation Research on Migrant Songbirds

Millions of migrant songbirds that breed in the eastern U.S. and Canada spend six months or more each winter in the Maya Forest (Terborgh 1989). Of some 344 bird species occurring regularly in the Petén, Guatemala, one quarter of the species are Nearctic-Neotropical migrants (Beavers 1992). Several migrant species that winter partly in the Maya Forest are believed by

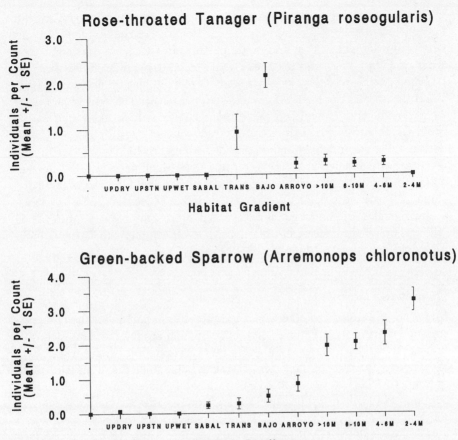

Rose-throated Tanager (Piranga roseogularis)

Individuals per Count (Mean +/- 1 SE)

Habitat Gradient

UPDRY UPSTN UPWET SABAL TRANS BAJO ARROYO >10M 6-10M 4-6M 2-4M

Green-backed Sparrow (Arremonops chloronotus)

Individuals per Count (Mean +/- 1 SE)

Habitat Gradient

UPDRY UPSTN UPWET SABAL TRANS BAJO ARROYO >10M 6-10M 4-6M 2-4M

many researchers to have experienced population declines during the past few decades (Askins et al. 1990). Factors causing these apparent declines are poorly understood, but probably include environmental changes on both breeding and wintering grounds.

We have pursued two lines of research related to conservation of migrant songbirds. First, we have studied the relative abundance of nine migrant species (those reliably mist-netted) in mature forest and in fallow vegetation on abandoned milpas. We found that many migrant species can utilize the ample supply of young second growth resulting from shifting cultivation. Examples are the indigo bunting (*Passerina cyanea*), gray catbird (*Dumetella carolinensis*), magnolia warbler (*Dendroica magnolia*), and ovenbird (*Seiurus aurocapillus*) (Lynch 1989, 1992; Whitacre et al. 1993). Other species, such as the wood thrush (*Hylocichla mustelina*) and to a lesser extent the Kentucky warbler (*Oporonis formosus*), showed markedly greater use of old-growth forest (Lynch 1989, 1992; Whitacre et al. 1993, 1995a). For these species, expansion of shifting cultivation and cattle pastures in the Selva Maya and elsewhere in Central America may have contributed to population declines.

Based on this result, we began a study of the population dynamics of the wood thrush and the Kentucky warbler in a 25-ha plot in mature forest at Tikal. We recently completed our third season of field work, documenting densities, year-to-year return rates, and over-winter survival of these species; data analyses are underway. Individuals of both species held winter territories, often showing fidelity to the same territories between years. Our results will add to the limited existing knowledge of the population dynamics of these disturbance-sensitive species (Winker et al. 1990; Mabey and Morton 1992; Conway et al. 1995) and serve as reference points for future monitoring. They will also help reveal the extent of geographic variation in the winter demography of these species (Madrid et al. 1995).

Quantitative Description of Forest Vegetation

Managers of forested protected areas require information about the composition and dynamics of the tree community, which are fundamental determinants of the characteristics of the overall biotic community. Little research on the woody vegetation of the Petén has taken place since the pioneering work of Lundell (1937) 60 years ago. We conducted a gradient analysis of the tree community of Tikal (Schulze 1992). The forest varies dramatically along a subtle topographic gradient from well-drained hilltops to low-lying ("bajo") areas that are alternately flooded during the rainy season (June through November) and drought-stressed during the dry season (February through May). We characterized the forest floristically and structurally along this topographic/edaphic gradient, describing several forest "types" (Schulze 1992). Our classification should assist workers over much of the north-central Petén to accurately match and describe vegetation. Figure 16.3 illustrates the individualistic response of four tree species along this environmental gradient, as well as close correlations among topographic position, soil clay content, and forest structure.

This high degree of vegetation differentiation along topographic gradients has implications for conservation. Biological corridors linking core areas ideally should include the full topographic range throughout their length, so that plant and animal species that use only a portion of the topographic gradient can satisfy their habitat requirements over the full length of the corridor. Failing this, a corridor may not provide the degree of connectivity hoped for by planners. For example, among the birds, bajo specialists may be unlikely to disperse freely along corridors composed solely of upland forest; examples are the rose-throated tanager (*Piranga roseogularis*), gray-throated chat (*Granatellus sallaei*), Yucatán flycatcher (*Myiarchus yucatanensis*), and man-

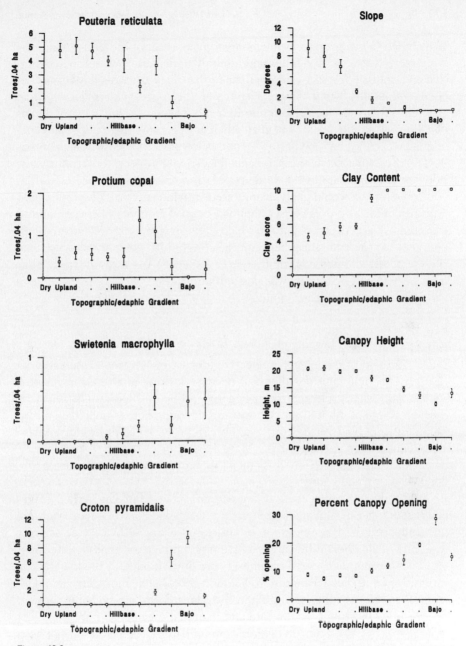

Figure 16.3

Some correlations between tree species distributions, vegetation structure, and edaphic factors along a topographic continuum at Tikal National Park. Mean ± one SE are given for 10 topographic positions, from driest hilltops at left to low-lying, seasonally flooded bajos at right; extreme right is "mesic bajo," with permanently saturated soil. Clay score is by manual method, and was highly correlated with % clay in lab analyses ($R^2 = 0.71$); clay scores of 1 averaged 30% clay, while scores of 10 averaged 76% clay. Canopy opening is by spherical densiometer; trees reported were those > 10 cm dbh. (Adapted from Schulze and Whitacre [in prep.].)

grove vireo (*Vireo pallens*). A much larger proportion of the bird community is characteristic of upland forest and unlikely to disperse well through extensive areas of bajo forest. Examples include the black-throated shrike-tanager (*Lanio aurantius*), scaly-throated leaftosser (*Sclerurus guatemalensis*), great tinamou (*Tinamus major*), plain antvireo (*Dysithamnus mentalis*), and dozens of additional species (Whitacre et al. 1995b). Regarding the trees, Figure 16.3 allows prediction that populations of trees such as *Croton pyramidalis* and mahogany (*Swietenia macrophylla*), for example, should disperse well through corridors containing bajo forest, while population expansion of species such as *Pouteria reticulata* would likely be inhibited by wide expanses of such habitat. Another implication concerns sampling design. Differences between bird or tree communities of an upland and a bajo site only a few hundred meters apart often exceed the differences between the communities of two upland or bajo sites scores of kilometers apart (Seavy et al. 1995). As a result, study plots must be matched by topographic position and forest type in order to serve as valid replicates or comparison units.

Effects of Selective Logging on Forest Birds

Little is known of the effects of selective logging of Neotropical forest biota (Mason 1996 and citations therein). Because logging in the Maya Forest is traditionally highly selective for mahogany and Spanish cedar (*Cedrela mexicana*), it results in limited canopy opening. Hence, there is hope that meaningful levels of biodiversity conservation can be achieved in logging concessions. Since large portions of the Maya Forest are destined to be managed partly for timber production, it is crucial to explore the compatibility of timber production and conservation goals.

We conducted a pilot study of logging impacts on birds at Bethel, Petén, and recently began similar research in and near Tikal National Park. Here we are comparing bird communities of unlogged areas with areas selectively logged 12 years prior. While analyses are not complete, it appears that direct effects of logging on the bird community are quite modest at the low logging intensities we studied (Schulze and Whitacre 1996). The most detrimental effects of traditional styles of logging in the Maya Forest are probably those of uncontrolled hunting (of a few bird and mammal species) and, for the forest at large, uncontrolled human colonization and attendant deforestation; both hunting and colonization are facilitated by construction of logging roads into previously inaccessible wilderness. There is an urgent need to restrict access and especially colonization along logging and oil field roads.

Also needed is additional research on the ecological impacts of alternative forestry practices. There has been much promotion in the Maya Forest of the idea of intensifying timber harvest by taking a dozen or more species in addition to mahogany and cedro. The rationale is that such diversification would give the forest greater economic value, which would aid in its conservation. No information exists, however, on the effects of such intensified timber harvest on the forest biota. This question should be investigated before such a strategy is promotcd. The main factor impeding such research in the Petén is the lack of appropriate, controlled logging trials to which biological research may be coupled.

Biotic Inventory and Monitoring

The importance of biotic inventory and monitoring of protected areas is increasingly recognized among conservation biologists and resource managers. Without such efforts, we do not know what species are present nor whether they are being conserved effectively. Ecological monitoring in tropical forest regions is in its infancy; the joint efforts of several institutions in the Maya Forest region are at the forefront of such efforts globally.

Development of Methods and an Initial Inventory and Monitoring Network

One goal of the Maya Project has been to gather baseline data that would allow detection of ecological changes over time. To facilitate these efforts, we have established a network of permanent 1 km^2 census plots within the Maya/Calakmul reserve complex—10 plots at each of three sites (Biotopo El Zotz, Biotopo Dos Lagunas, and the Calakmul Biosphere Reserve), 16 plots in Tikal National Park, and 8 in the farming landscape south of Tikal.

On each plot, we have censused birds repeatedly during at least two years, using methods described above (canopy emergent and pre-dawn point counts). More than 70 bird species and two primate species were censused via these methods: 35 species of raptors, 4 tinamous, 5 cracids and allies, 9 doves, 4 nightjars, 7 parrots, and 8 other bird species, as well as the howler monkey (*Alouatta pigra*) and spider monkey (*Ateles geoffroyi*). These groups include species with a great diversity of biological traits, so that collectively their population tendencies should reveal ecological changes occurring in the forest. In addition, a slightly overlapping set of 90 bird species is censused in some cases via ten-minute aural/visual point counts from the forest floor. This group is even more ecologically diverse, constituting a powerful "indicator complex."

Before organisms can be used as environmental indicators, one must know (at least in part) how they respond to the changes one hopes to detect. To facilitate such use of the two species suites described above, initial data have been analyzed in a way that elucidates habitat affinities of each bird species, revealing the "indicator" properties of individual species and the bird community as a whole. In practice, we do not focus on individual species, but rather we use the entire species suites sampled by each census method as an "ecological indicator complex." These census programs provide a systematic and repeatable measure of deviation from pristine conditions—an index of ecological integrity (Angermeier and Karr 1994) as revealed by the bird community.

Differences in bird communities of the four main monitoring sites have been detected, reflecting both habitat differences and biogeographic patterns. Calakmul differs notably from the three more southern sites, reflecting the shorter, drier forest that prevails as one moves northward in the Yucatán Peninsula. In addition, some year-to-year changes have been observed; for example, a proliferation of black vultures (*Coragyps atratus*) at Calakmul has occurred in concert with increased human presence, doubtless a result of increased food supply in the form of refuse (Jones and Sutter 1992). Baseline data now in hand should allow detection of future changes in the bird communities of several sites.

Applied Contributions of the Maya Project to Conservation in the Selva Maya

From the outset of the Maya Project, we were aware that the information we have just described could best be put to use if made available to the agencies and institutions responsible for protected areas and resource policies. Thus, project results are published yearly as Spanish and English reports, which are distributed within the region. There is strong demand for these reports in Central America, where availability of scientific literature is often limited. Increasingly, reports have been tailored to the needs of Guatemala's Consejo Nacional de Areas Protegidas (CONAP), providing recommendations for management of the Maya Biosphere Reserve. Results are also published in scientific journals.

Aside from disseminating our data, we also established connections to local agencies in charge of conservation activities in our study area. Recently, The Peregrine Fund was enlisted by CONAP and the U.S. Agency for International Development (USAID) to spearhead development of a comprehensive plan for ecological monitoring of the Maya Biosphere Reserve. With input from interested parties, a draft plan has been completed. The product will be a flexible plan for inventory and monitoring of the reserve, at hierarchical levels of simplicity, cost, and human resource availability (Whitacre 1997). The more purely biotic goals are to provide baseline biotic inventory in different areas of the reserve, to reveal impacts of human activities on the biota and determine the ecological integrity of the reserve, and to judge whether management is achieving desired conservation objectives. Other goals are to help ensure sustainability of important economic activities, including logging, collection of nontimber forest products, hunting, and tourism, as well as tracking resource use by reserve residents. Some components of the proposed monitoring scheme are listed in Table 16.1. Many components are already underway through efforts of several nongovernmental organizations, and others will soon be added.

Table 16.1. Proposed content of an ecological monitoring program for the Maya Biosphere Reserve, the Petén, Guatemala.

Item monitored	Methods
Change in forest cover	Remote sensing, image analysis, GIS; park guard patrol reports
Road construction	Same
Habitat fragmentation, connectivity	Remote sensing, GIS, computer modeling
Human population	Periodic census; immigration data collected at entry posts
Livestock population	Same
Sustainability of lifestyles of reserve residents	Periodic census/questionnaires
Sustainability of nontimber forest product industries (chicle, xate, allspice)	Harvest and export data routinely reported to CONAP; studies of plant demography; interviews of collectors, contractors, exporters
Sustainability of commercial logging industry	Harvest data reported to CONAP; demographic studies of target species
Sustainability of hunting	Population trends of game species revealed by "core biotic monitoring program" (see below); hunter surveys in focal villages; age/sex/condition data taken on harvested animals
Tendencies within the tourism industry	Government data; interviews of tourism operators
Core biotic monitoring program	Systematic sampling of bird community, one or more insect groups (butterflies and dung/carrion beetles), and medium and large mammals
Ancillary biotic monitoring program, as resources permit	Systematic sampling of bats, amphibians, permanent vegetation plots, other taxonomically diverse or otherwise appropriate plant or animal groups
Population status of species of special concern	E.g., scarlet macaw, jaguar, harpy eagle

Development of Human Resources

As the Maya Project developed, it became clear that involving local people in biological research was an excellent way to build human capital through training and education. Accordingly, the commitment of project resources to training and education of local people has steadily increased. Among the greatest hallmarks of the project are the level of investment in local individuals and its responsiveness to the concerns of these local partners, aspects that have helped create a measure of true local participation and project "ownership." Indeed, the most important conservation legacy of the Maya Project may well be the creation of a cadre of local people who have received training, experience, and formal education by participating in the project.

Since the project's inception, 115 local people have participated in field work. Eighty individuals have participated for at least one six-month field season, 50 have done so for two years, and 30 for four years or more. At least 36 individuals have become skilled ornithological field technicians. Participants are in the forest nearly every weekday, collecting data on birds or vegetation. They gain familiarity with the scientific method and learn to collect data in a systematic fashion, acquiring hundreds of hours' experience conducting behavioral observations on birds of prey. They gain much experience using radio telemetry to monitor raptor movements (Figure 16.4) and in plot-

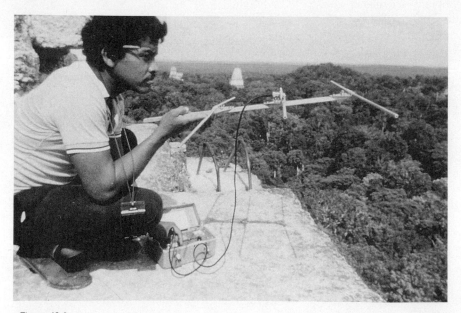

Figure 16.4

Julio Madrid triangulates on radio-tagged ornate hawk-eagle from atop Temple IV, Tikal. (Photo by Craig Flatten.)

ting these and GPS (Global Positioning System) locational data on maps. Many individuals become adept at trapping and handling raptors and in placing radio transmitters on these birds (Figure 16.5), and several have also gained much experience with small songbirds (Figure 16.6). Several long-time project participants are among the most experienced ornithological field workers in Guatemala. Among their ranks are several individuals who have more field experience with certain tropical raptors than anyone else in the world.

Our philosophy has been to invest heavily in the training and education of local participants and to provide opportunities for personal growth by expanding the responsibility vested in individuals. After becoming proficient at necessary skills, participants often become "project chiefs," overseeing teams of two to five field workers in a research project. On a daily basis they program their group's activities, designating tasks, equipment, transportation, and time use. They teach data collection procedures, exert quality control over data collection, and maintain data archives and weekly summaries. At the end of each field season, project leaders summarize data and write a report describing the efforts undertaken and results obtained. They frequently become coauthors of scientific papers, and in several cases have traveled to scientific meetings in Costa Rica, Ecuador, and Mexico to present results. Those individuals

Figure 16.5

Tono Ramos prepares to release an adult ornate hawk-eagle outfitted with a radio transmitter, allowing us to determine its home range. (Photo by D. Whitacre.)

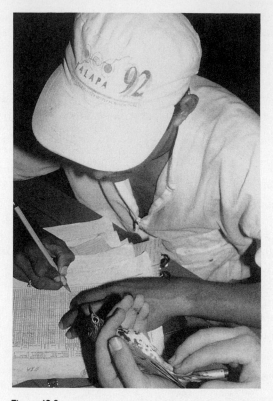

Figure 16.6

Maya Project participants take data on a wood
thrush (*Hylocichla mustelina*), one of the inter-
American migrants most reliant on mature
forest. (Photo by D. Whitacre.)

who proved most diligent and capable often have led field teams in several
different research topics in turn, accumulating an impressive variety of research experience.

Ideally, this ample field experience would be coupled with a college education and even graduate studies in some cases. We are striving to achieve this
outcome, but certain factors prevent us from attaining all that we desire in
this area. The greatest limiting factor is lack of appropriate university programs in the Petén. In the early 1990s, the Universidad de San Carlos de
Guatemala established the Centro Universitario del Petén (CUDEP), a Petén
campus offering three-year technical degrees in conservation and management of tropical forests, agronomy, and tourism.

In addition to providing scholarship support for three students in San Carlos University's biology Licensiatura program, we have provided scholarships to four local Maya Project participants in the CUDEP forestry program mentioned above. While this opportunity is appreciated by the scholarship recipients, they would rather obtain a Licensiatura in Biology—a more advanced degree more closely aligned with their interests. Such a degree program does not exist locally. Because these individuals are all married with families, it is not easy for them to relocate to Guatemala City or some other urban center for the five years a Licensiatura program requires. Hence, the lack of appropriate university programs located near large areas of remaining forest is a limiting factor for Neotropical conservation. Funding agencies could make a major contribution to conservation in Latin America by supporting development of such academic programs in strategic sites. While we strongly endorse the kind of support we have given to local residents, we would recommend to other, similar projects a concerted effort to involve higher-level host country students and scientists in field research; for a variety of reasons, we have not achieved all that we wished along this line.

Training for Government Personnel

The project has provided training for park guards of three government agencies: CONAP, CECON (Centro de Estudios Conservanistas, San Carlos University), and IDAEH (Instituto de Antropología y Historia). Twenty-eight IDAEH resource guards have participated in field research, several for multiple years, while two CONAP resource guards did so for one year. We have conducted research at four of CECON's biotope Reserves for several weeks at a time, during which 23 CECON personnel participated. In addition, we have conducted several training workshops for these agencies on ornithology, ecological research methods, and related topics. In the most recent course, 25 CECON and 17 CONAP employees participated for a total of 98 person-days. In collaboration with CARE, we have taught ornithology to 71 primary and secondary school teachers from the northern Petén in several three-day workshops. All the workshops mentioned above were planned and conducted by the most experienced local project participants.

True Local Participation?

A concern sometimes raised about conservation projects in the region is that although local people may be advised or consulted about projects, true local participation and project ownership is uncommon. We will not claim here that local people entirely own the Maya Project, but many local people participate at a deep level and feel a large measure of ownership. If we have achieved a degree of true local ownership, we have done so mainly by trusting and investing in the individuals who have become involved, and by responding to their concerns and desires. As noted earlier, we have expanded the responsibilities of individuals wherever possible; our faith in these individuals has been amply rewarded. Second, we have invested in individuals, for example, supporting them in formal education and involving them in international scientific meetings. Finally, project leadership has given latitude for locally generated initiatives. When local participants have said, "Why don't we . . . ," the project leadership has listened.

Employment of Project Graduates

To achieve the conservation objectives of the Maya Project, local participants ultimately must "fledge" from the project and use the knowledge they have gained there, ideally in positions where they can spur the progress of conservation in the region. In several instances, project graduates have achieved this goal. One individual has served for three years in the Wildlife Conservation Society's faunal research at Tikal, where he has taught telemetry methods to other personnel. Three project veterans, working as independent contractors, conducted a "rapid ecological assessment" of bird communities of several proposed protected areas in the southern Petén. Two project graduates used radio telemetry to help ARCAS (Asociación de Rescate y Conservación de Vida Silvestre) study the success of reintroduction of confiscated wildlife, and three others were contracted to inventory the birds of a small reserve; their results will be used to promote ecotourism in the area. One project graduate was hired by a company specializing in GPS applications because of the GPS experience he gained through the Maya Project. Most recently, four individuals with ample songbird experience were hired by ProPetén (the Guatemalan branch of Conservation International) to form the core of an avian inventory and monitoring team. It is apparent that the ample experience that Maya Project veterans have in conducting ornithological field research is a valuable commodity within the natural resource management and conservation community in Guatemala.

Environmental Education

Over a three-year period we reached 600 children yearly through an environmental education program in rural schools near Tikal. We have taken children on bird walks and led them in games in which they vicariously experienced the impacts of habitat destruction on birds, as well as the benefits of conservation measures. We have organized art and essay contests and supervised writing assignments, for example, having children catalogue their knowledge of plants used medicinally in their villages. The results were impressive, with one sixth-grade girl listing medicinal uses of 47 plants.

Development of Conservation Policy toward Shifting Cultivation

Conservation research is most effective when it influences policy and results in concrete actions. With regard to shifting agriculture, we have followed up our research by making policy recommendations (Whitacre et al. 1995a) and by developing our own, small-scale action campaign. Milpa farming is not intrinsically incompatible with biotic conservation, and under lower human population densities may actually maximize regional biodiversity, assuming that sizable tracts of mature forest remain. Under prevailing demographic and social conditions, however, additional primary forest is continually brought into the slash-and-burn cycle. Fallow periods today are short, with corn fields in our study area generally returned to farming after a two- to seven-year fallow (Schwartz 1990; Whitacre et al. unpublished data). As a result, newly converted forest will not recover old-growth characteristics during our lifetimes. The vast scale of the slash-and-burn enterprise today results in unacceptable net loss of mature forest.

One thrust of our research has been to examine policy directions that would maximize biotic conservation in the shifting agriculture landscape (Whitacre et al. 1995a). We have considered the potential benefits of (1) lengthening fallow periods, (2) increasing the speed of succession and manipulating tree species composition of second growth, and (3) intensifying agriculture on a subset of currently farmed acreage. Based on our results (see earlier sections), we reject the lengthening of fallow periods as a means of increasing the conservation value of the farming landscape for three reasons. First, our results suggest that even doubling the current two- to seven-year fallow period probably would not significantly benefit those organisms most at risk, that is, species reliant on old-growth forest. Second, lengthening fallow periods while maintaining current harvests would necessitate involving more primary forest in the farming cycle—the very thing conservationists seek to avoid. Finally, lengthening fallow periods is not realistic under current demographic and social conditions.

Some conservation gains doubtless can be made by sparing certain trees during milpa preparation. Fruiting trees can act as magnets for seed-dispersing bats and birds, speeding and diversifying succession after the milpa plot is abandoned. Potential conservation gains from this tactic are limited, however, because obligate old-growth species would receive minimal benefits. To benefit old growth obligates, mature forest must be spared. Many initiatives, including job creation, can help achieve this goal. Within the context of farming methods, the most effective means of reducing pressure on remaining forest appears to be intensification of farming on a subset of the acreage currently farmed to substantially increase per-acre yields, doing away with the need for frequent and prolonged fallow. With sufficient intensification, current overall harvests could be maintained, much land currently involved in the farming cycle could be left to recuperate, and felling of additional forest slowed or prevented, assuming limited population growth and immigration to the agricultural frontier.

Community Outreach: Grassroots Conservation in the Shifting Agriculture Landscape

Based on the above conclusions, we have sought methods by which farmers might increase yields while cultivating the same few acres continually (probably using crop rotation to minimize pest problems) or with much-reduced fallow periods. A promising technology is the use of nitrogen-fixing "green manures" that enhance soil fertility and choke out weeds, decreasing labor inputs and obviating the need for herbicides. The best-known green manure is *frijol abono*, or velvet bean (*Mucuna* sp.).

Since 1994, we have promoted use of frijol abono by farmers south of Tikal. Aided by CARE-Guatemala, we distributed more than 1,200 pounds of seed to some 120 farmers, most of whom planted these seeds during 1994 and 1995. We have dedicated one employee, Gumercindo "Chindo" García, to this effort full-time. Chindo is working with farmers he has known since childhood, which doubtless increases their readiness to receive his message. As of autumn of 1996, some 58 ha of frijol abono plantation had been established. The assiduousness of individuals in caring for the frijol abono has varied: some 25 individuals achieved excellent plantations while many others allowed secondary growth and weeds to overtop their plantations. Six farmers first planted corn in their frijol abono plantations early in 1996, achieving favorable results. Many additional farmers planted corn in their frijol abono plantations in fall and winter of 1996, and the resultant harvest has recently been completed. We measured harvests in ten corn fields that employed frijol abono and ten that did not. This will allow a rigorous evaluation of the effects of frijol abono on corn yields.

While increased opportunities in nonfarm sectors of the economy may decrease reliance on farming and help stem deforestation pressures, one must acknowledge the cultural importance of corn farming in the Maya cultural region, where corn is the premier dietary staple. At a site in Quintana Roo, Murphy (1994) found that corn farming was the most highly esteemed occupation of the majority of adult males, and that profits from other activities may even promote increases of corn acreage by allowing use of hired help. This cultural preference underlines the importance of seeking more environmentally benign technologies for growing corn.

Finally, in advocating agricultural intensification, we are not unaware of the many advantages of shifting cultivation, which include recuperation of soil fertility, weed control through forest succession, and enhancement of hunting opportunities for white-tailed deer (*Odocoileus virginiana*), ocellated turkey (*Agriocharis ocellata*), and other game species. If the number of people engaged in milpa farming were smaller and more stable, we would embrace the traditional milpa system. However, current social and demographic trends demand alternatives if any mature forest is to be spared. Ultimately, solutions to current deforestation patterns hinge on stabilizing the number of people reliant on farming and ranching in the Maya Forest region.

Fire Prevention in the Farming Landscape

Annual burning of slash is a universal feature of shifting cultivation in the Maya Forest. Because burning takes place at the height of the dry season, fire often escapes, degrading mature forest remnants and retarding succession of second growth. Natural fire apparently is rare in the forests of the Petén, and human-caused forest fires may safely be regarded as inimical to conservation interests.

We have developed a fire prevention project, also led by Chindo García, with many of the same farmers who participate in the frijol abono project. Chindo assists farmers in conducting burns and extinguishing hot spots afterward. He has focused on protecting remaining fragments of mature forest by working with farmers who cultivate surrounding areas. Often the spread of fire can be prevented by creating a fire break; during the wetter months, fire prevention is simply a matter of first igniting slash at the downwind side of the field, creating a burned-out area that protects adjacent vegetation when the fire reaches peak intensity. This "black-lining" technique is ideal, as it does not require additional labor of farmers, but the use of fire breaks becomes more important during drought. Convincing farmers to prepare large fire breaks is difficult because this task represents substantial additional labor. Though we have not conducted a rigorous evaluation of the use of fire prevention measures by farmers, our impression is that adoption of such measures has been slow. It would be useful to investigate the possibility that fires serve sociocultural functions of which we are unaware.

Conclusions: An Evaluation of the Maya Project's Accomplishments

We believe that the philosophy and approach of the Maya Project have much to offer as models for projects elsewhere. Ecological research in support of management and conservation is needed throughout the tropics, and involving local people in such research is an excellent means of providing training and developing an appreciation for conservation goals among the general populace. While a pure research program may have advantages in terms of rapid generation of data, the conservation benefits of such a program may be considerably less than those derived through promoting local participation.

The extent to which our research results will affect policy in the Maya Forest and elsewhere remains to be seen. On a local level, though many aspects of our research are theoretically useful to conservation efforts, they may not be of great immediate use to an agency such as CONAP, which is charged with preventing the imminent deforestation of the MBR. For example, we have added greatly to knowledge of the natural history of Neotropical raptors, and this new information can inform efforts to conserve these species. At this juncture, however, the most urgent need is simply to prevent wholesale felling of the forest; this task occupies CONAP personnel fully. Our reports on raptor biology presumably aid them minimally in this monumental task. Still, it would be a mistake to underestimate the long-term contribution of this understanding of raptor species biology to Neotropical conservation. The utility of this information will increase over time as the situation stabilizes and the tasks of tropical conservation become increasingly those of properly managing existing reserves and of restoring degraded ecosystems.

Potential application of our findings in other regions will be somewhat limited by geographical variation in species biology and biotic communities. Hence the population density we have documented for ornate hawk-eagles at Tikal may not provide detailed justification for the size of a new reserve in Brazil or Peru. Still, such data will at least suggest orders of magnitude; they are the best available information of this type to date. Perhaps of greatest immediate utility to conservation are the results of our research on the impacts of prevalent land uses. Because of the sheer magnitude of the slash-and-burn farming endeavor today, our inquiries into the potential for conservation in the farming landscape are a significant contribution, especially because we have followed research by exploration of policy alternatives. By the same token, since forestry will doubtless remain an important land use in the tropics, our explorations of the biotic impacts of selective logging and of regeneration ecology of key timber species will be important contributions. Likewise, our efforts to develop methods for a comprehensive program of ecological monitoring in the Maya Biosphere Reserve are original contributions: though monitoring is a popular concept, examples of active monitoring in protected areas in the tropics are few. Also useful have been our studies of habitat affinities of a large segment of the avifauna of the Maya Forest; these studies have set the stage for using more than 90 bird species as an ecological indicator complex in monitoring.

Most worthy of emulation, however, are not the specific elements of our research agenda. While raptors and songbirds are both useful in conservation planning, the same is true of many faunal and floral groups. New research on probably any component of tropical biota is potentially useful to conservation and management efforts. Rather, the aspects of the Maya Project most worthy of emulation are the project's responsiveness to and investment in local project members and its combination of several elements: biological field research, training and education of local residents, environmental education, and grassroots efforts to conserve habitat by reforming land-use practices. While it is perhaps possible to justify a pure research program the results of which would inform conservation actions, we were not content with such an austere approach amid the multiple challenges of the Maya Forest region. In addition to eventual conservation gains made through application of our research results, we wished to see short-term, tangible results within our sphere of activity.

Though the project began mainly as a research effort, its eventual broadening into grassroots community outreach was a natural outcome of the trusting personal relationships that developed with local people who became long-term field technicians. Through such personal relationships, The Peregrine Fund came to enjoy a high degree of acceptance in the villages where these individuals live. We did not want to squander this trust, and for this reason we began programs of environmental education and promoted agricultural alternatives. These efforts took us well beyond the traditional scope of Peregrine Fund activities, and some might say they diluted our initially narrower research focus to its detriment. If our mission was purely that of research, such a broadened scope would indeed be detrimental; however, our mission includes promoting local conservation, as well as conservation elsewhere, through application of our research results. On balance, we feel there was wisdom in allowing the project to evolve in response to locally perceived needs and in trusting strongly and investing in local individuals who have participated. This evolution, we feel, has led to a well-balanced program and a degree of local ownership that has achieved some of the elusive goals of truly sustainable development. At the very least, we have gathered a great deal of new information about the biology of Neotropical raptors and have changed the lives of a few dozen Peteneros who have worked extensively within the project. We have supported these individuals' innate fascination with the biota of the Petén, and in some cases we have helped to discover and nourish a fierce interest in conducting research. We leave it to the reader to judge whether the main conservation legacy of the Maya Project will be its research results or the changes wrought in the lives of certain local people. Finally, the greatest lesson of the project has been a resounding affirmation of the wisdom of finding good people to work with and then placing substantial confidence in them and investing in their growth.

Acknowledgments

We gratefuly acknowledge the assistance of Edgar Palma, Sofía and Dr. Jorge Paredes and family, and Don Mundo and Pati Solis; we dedicate this chapter to Doña Pati, who is greatly missed. We are grateful to the many Guatemalan government officials who have facilitated our efforts, in particular several directors each of CONAP, IDAEH, and CECON, and the personnel of Tikal National Park, especially Rogel Chí and Rolando Pernillo. The achievements reported here were made possible by the efforts of many local (Petenero) participants. Funding was provided by Ruth Andres, Robert Berry, Crystal Channel Foundation, Evie Donaldson, Fanwood Foundation, Gold Family Foundation, Alfred Jurzykowsi Foundation, KENNETECH/U.S.Windpower, John D. and Catherine T. MacArthur Foundation, Mill Pond Press, National Fish and Wildlife Foundation, Norcross Foundation, Henry and Wendy Paulson, Pew Charitable Trusts, Andrés and Pilar Sada, Bernardo Sada, The Nature Conservancy, U.S. Man and the Biosphere Program, U.S. Agency for International Development, and Frank Weeden Foundation.

References

Angermeier, P. L., and J. R. Karr. 1994. Biological integrity versus biological diversity as policy directives. *BioScience* 44: 690–697.

Askins, R. A., J. F. Lynch, and R. Greenberg. 1990. Population declines in migratory birds in eastern North America. *Current Ornithology* 7: 1–58.

Baker, A. J., P. A. Aguirre-Barrera, W. Morales, and D. F. Whitacre. 1995. Orange-breasted Falcon (*Falco deiroleucus*) breeding biology, nesting sites, and distribution in Guatemala and Belize. *Raptor Research* 29: 52.

Burnham, W. A., J. P. Jenny, and C. W. Turley. 1988. *Progress Report I: Maya Project*. The Peregrine Fund, Boise, Idaho.

Burnham, W. A., J. P. Jenny, and C. W. Turley. 1989. *Progress Report II: Maya Project*. The Peregrine Fund, Boise, Idaho.

Conway, C. J., G. V. N. Powell, and J. D. Nichols. 1995. Overwinter survival of neotropical migratory birds in early-successional and mature tropical forests. *Conservation Biology* 9: 855–864.

Jenny, J. P., and T. J. Cade. 1986. Observations on the biology of the Orange-breasted Falcon (*Falco deiroleucus*). *Birds of Prey Bulletin* 3: 119–123.

Jones, L., and J. Sutter. 1992. Results and comparisons of two years of census efforts at three units of the Maya Biosphere Reserve/Calakmul Biosphere Reserve complex. Pages 63–78 in *Progress Report V, 1992: Maya Project*, D. F. Whitacre and R. K. Thorstrom, eds. The Peregrine Fund, Boise, Idaho.

Lundell, C. L. 1937. *The Vegetation of Petén*. Pub. no. 478, Carnegie Institute of Washington, Washington, D.C.

Lynch, J. 1989. Distribution of overwintering Nearctic migrants in the Yucatán Peninsula, I: General patterns of occurrence. *Condor* 91: 515–544.

———. 1992. Distribution of overwintering Nearctic migrants in the Yucatán Peninsula II: Use of native and human-modified vegetation. Pages 178–196 in *Ecology and Conservation of Neotropical Migrant Landbirds*, J. M. Hagan III and D. W. Johnston, eds. Smithsonian Institution Press, Washington D.C.

Mabey, S. E., and E. S. Morton. 1992. Demography and territorial behavior of wintering Kentucky warblers in Panama. Pages 329–336 in *Ecology and Conservation of Neotropical Migrant Landbirds*, J. M. Hagan III and D. W. Johnston, eds. Smithsonian Institution Press, Washington, D.C.

Madrid, J. A., C. Marroquin V., T. D. Ortiz, M. D. Schulze, J. Hunt, and D. F.

Whitacre. 1995. Monitoring population parameters of a wintering migrant song-bird, the Kentucky Warbler: Persistence pays. Pages 479–483 in *Integrating People and Wildlife for a Sustainable Future*, J. A. Bissonette and P. R. Krausman, eds.The Wildife Society, Bethesda, Md.

Mason, D. 1996. Responses of Venezuelan understory birds to selective logging, enrichment strips, and vine cutting. *Biotropica* 28: 296–309.

Murphy, J. E. 1994. Aprovechamiento forestal y la agricultura de milpa en Ejido X-Maben, zona Maya de Quintana Roo, Mexico. Pages 3–18 in *Madera, Chicle, Caza y Milpa: Contribuciones al Manejo Integral de las Selvas de Quintana Roo, Mexico*, L. K. Snook and A. B. Jorgenson, eds. INIFAP, Mérida, Yucatán, México.

Noss, R. F., and A. Y. Cooperrider. 1994. *Saving Nature's Legacy: Protecting and Restoring Biodiversity*. Island Press, Washington, D.C.

Robinson, S. K. 1994. Habitat selection and foraging ecology of raptors in Amazonian Peru. *Biotropica* 26: 443–458.

Schulze, M. D. 1992. A preliminary description of woody plant communities of Tikal National Park. Pages 53–62 in *Progress Report V, 1992: Maya Project*, D.F. Whitacre and R. K. Thorstrom, eds. The Peregrine Fund, Boise, Idaho.

Schulze, M. D., and D. F. Whitacre. 1996. Effects of logging on Neotropical bird and tree community composition. Technical report to the U.S. Man and the Biosphere Program. The Peregrine Fund, Boise, Idaho.

———. in preparation. classification and ordination of the woody plant communities of Tikal National Park, Guatemala.

Schwartz, N. 1990. *Forest Society: A Social History of Petén, Guatemala*. University of Pennsylvania Press, Philadelphia.

Seavy N. E., D. F. Whitacre, and M. Córdova A. 1995. Yaxhá/Nakum area of the Maya Biosphere Reserve, Guatemala: Baseline ecological assessment, establishment of a framework for ecological monitoring, and training of local personnel. The Peregrine Fund, Boise, Idaho.

Terborgh, J. 1989. *Where Have All the Birds Gone?* Princeton University Press, Princeton, N.J.

———. 1992. Maintenance of diversity in tropical forests. *Biotropica* 24: 283–292.

Thiollay, J. M. 1984. Raptor community structure of a primary rain forest in French Guiana and effect of human hunting pressure. *Raptor Research* 18: 117–122.

———. 1985. Composition of falconiform communities along successional gradients from primary rainforest to secondary habitats. Pages 181–190 in *Conservation Studies of Raptors*, I. Newton and R. D. Chancellor, eds. I.C.B.P. Technical Publication No. 5.

———. 1991. Altitudinal distribution and conservation of raptors in southwestern Colombia. *Journal of Raptor Research* 25: 1–8.

Thorstrom, R. 1993. Breeding ecology of two species of Forest Falcons (*Micrastur*) in northeastern Guatemala. M.S. thesis, Boise State University, Boise, Idaho.

Turley, C. W. 1989. Evaluation of raptor survey techniques. Pages 21–32 in *Progress Report II: Maya Project*, W. A. Burnham, J. P. Jenny, and C. W. Turley, eds. The Peregrine Fund, Boise, Idaho.

Whitacre, D. F. 1997. An ecological monitoring program for the Maya Biosphere Reserve. The Peregrine Fund, Boise, Idaho.

Whitacre, D. F., and C. W. Turley. 1990. Further comparisons of tropical forest raptor census techniques. Pages 71–92 in *Progress Report III: Maya Project*, W. A. Burnham, D. F. Whitacre, and J. P. Jenny, eds. The Peregrine Fund, Boise, Idaho.

Whitacre, D. F., L. E. Jones, and J. Sutter. 1992. Censusing raptors and other birds in tropical forest: Further refinements of methodology. Pages 39–52 in *Progress Report V, 1992: Maya Project*, D. F. Whitacre and R. K. Thorstrom, eds. The Peregrine Fund, Boise, Idaho.

Whitacre, D. F., J. Madrid M., C. Marroquín V., M. Schulze, L. Jones, J. Sutter, and A. J. Baker. 1993. Migrant songbirds, habitat change, and conservation prospects in northern Petén, Guatemala: Some initial results. Pages 339–345 in *Status and Management of Neotropical Migratory Birds*, D. M. Finch and P. W. Stangel, eds. USDA Forest Service, General Technical Report RM-229. Rocky Mountain Forest and Range Experiment Station, Fort Collins, Colo.

Whitacre, D. F., J. Madrid M., C. Marroquín V., T. Dubón O., N. O. Jurado, W. R. Tobar, B. González C., A. Arévalo O., G. García C., M. Schulze, L. Jones S., J. Sutter, and A.J . Baker. 1995a. Slash-and-burn farming and bird conservation in northern Petén, Guatemala. Pages 215–225 in *Conservation of Neotropical Migratory Birds in Mexico*, M. H. Wilson and S. A. Sader, eds. Maine Agricultural and Forest Experiment Station, Misc. Pub. No. 727.

Whitacre, D. F., M. Schulze, and N. Seavy. 1995b. Habitat affinities of a Central American forest avifauna: Implications for conservation in Neotropical slash-and-burn farming landscapes. Technical report to the U.S. Man and the Biosphere Program. The Peregrine Fund, Boise, Idaho.

Winker, K., J. H. Rappole, and M. A. Ramos. 1990. Population dynamics of the Wood Thrush in southern Veracruz, Mexico. *Condor* 92: 444–460.

Chapter 17

Dynamics and Ecology of Natural and Managed Forests in Quintana Roo, Mexico

Dennis F. Whigham, James F. Lynch, and Matthew B. Dickinson

Shaped by both natural and anthropogenic disturbances, the Maya Forest of Belize, Guatemala, and Mexico has changed dramatically over the millennia. The region's floristic composition has become relatively well known to scientists, but many of its ecological processes are still only partially understood. Studying these processes is a long-term project; accordingly, when we first undertook the investigation of the relationship between forest dynamics and migratory bird populations in this region, we intended our research to span many years. An unintended benefit of this strategy was the good fortune of witnessing the effects on the forest of a major natural disturbance: Hurricane Gilbert. As chance would have it, this powerful hurricane struck our study site after we had completed four years of study, offering a rare opportunity to compare the forest's circumstances before and after a massive natural disturbance. Results of this decade-long project provide insights into processes (e.g., annual patterns of precipitation and disturbance, human activities) that influence the structure and function of forests, and how these in turn influence utilization of forest habitats by birds, especially migratory species such as the hooded warbler (*Wilsonia citrina*), wood thrush (*Hylocichla mustelina*), and ovenbird (*Seiurus aurocapillus*), which forage primarily in the forest understory.

Forest Dynamics and Ecology at Rancho San Felipe: Phosphorus Addition, Precipitation, and Hurricane Impacts

In 1984, we initiated an experiment in the northeastern Yucatán Peninsula of Mexico to test Vitousek's (1984) hypothesis that phosphorus limits tree

growth and litterfall production in most tropical forests. Little ecological research had been conducted in dry tropical forests (Murphy and Lugo 1986)
prior to the development of Vitousek's hypothesis, but based on soil characteristics in the northeastern Yucatán (e.g., pH approximately 7.0 and a high
calcium content) we predicted that phosphorus would limit tree growth and
control patterns of nutrient cycling. We also wished to determine whether or
not experimental manipulations of the forest (e.g., removal of leaf litter, addition of phosphorus, etc.) would influence the abundance of resident and
Neotropical migratory birds, especially species that forage in the forest understory.

    Our experiments were conducted at Rancho San Felipe, a privately owned
property approximately 10 km south of the village of Puerto Morelos, Quintana Roo. There was no evidence of recent forest disturbance at Rancho San
Felipe, except for a small area that had been cleared for use in agricultural research. The latter studies revealed that phosphorus was the nutrient that most
limited crop production following clearing of the forest (Felipe Sánchez
Román and Patricia Zugasty Towle, pers. comm.). Details of characteristics of
the dry tropical forest at Rancho San Felipe and the experimental design are
given in Table 17.1 and Table 17.2 and in Whigham et al. (1990).

Table 17.1. Characteristics of dry tropical forests at Rancho San Felipe and
Noh-Bec research sites.

Characteristic	Rancho San Felipe	Noh-Bec
Annual precipitation	~1200 mm with a distinct dry season	~1100–1300 mm with a distinct dry season
Temperature	22–8 degrees C	24–26 degrees C
Soil pH	~7.0	~7.0
Depth	>20 cm	varies w/topography
Soil content	High calcium and high organic matter (~50%)	Organic matter varies from low to >50%
Canopy height	10–20 m	10–30 m
Tree diameter distribution		
10–20 cm	65.6%	66%
20–30 cm	25.6%	17.6%
30–40 cm	5.1%	9.9%
> 40 cm	3.7%	6.6%
Tree density (mean & SE)	768 ± 23 trees/ha	605 ± 5 trees/ha
Tree basal area (mean & SE)	26.9 ± 1.0 m²/ha	25.1 ± 0.2 m²/ha

Growth rates of approximately 1,500 tagged trees were measured yearly from 1984 to 1992. Tagged trees were located in 12 40 x 40 m permanent plots that served either as controls or as sites where one of three manipulations were performed twice each year: (1) all leaf litter was removed, (2) leaf litter was removed and superphosphate fertilizer added, or (3) superphosphate fertilizer was added without removing litter. Monthly collections of litterfall were made from five randomly located 1 x 1 m litter traps in each plot. Litterfall collections were separated into leaves and reproductive parts, then

Table 17.2. Dominant tree species at Noh Bec and Rancho San Felipe. For Noh-Bec, the 13 species listed each have > 50 tagged individuals and they account for 73% of all tagged trees in the 82 permanent plots. Seventy-seven species occur in the 82 plots. For Rancho San Felipe, the ten species listed account for 76% of all tagged trees in 1984 in the 12 permanent plots. Seventy-seven species occur in the 12 plots.

Species	Family	% Total tagged trees
Rancho San Felipe		
Manilkara zapota	Sapotaceae	26.9
Brosimum alicastrum	Moraceae	9.5
Drypetes lateriflora	Euphorbiaceae	9.3
Talisia olivaeformis	Sapindaceae	9.2
Gymnanthes lucida	Euphorbiaceae	7.2
Blomia cupanoides	Sapindaceae	3.9
Beaucarnea pliabilis	Liliaceae	3.7
Myrcianthes fragrans	Myrtaceae	2.4
Coccoloba diversifolia	Polygonaceae	2.3
Bursera simaruba	Burseraceae	1.9
Pouteria unilocularis	Sapotaceae	15.1
Alseis yucatanensis	Rubiaceae	10.2
Sabal mauritiiformis	Arecaceae	8.4
Manilkara zapota	Sapotaceae	7.1
Noh-Bec		
Cosmocalyx spectabilis	Rubiaceae	5.8
Brosimum alicastrum	Moraceae	5.4
Blomia cupanioides	Sapindaceae	4.5
Bursera simaruba	Simarubaceae	3.0
Pouteria campechiana	Sapotaceae	2.8
Drypetes lateriflora	Euphorbiaceae	2.3
Protium copal	Burseraceae	2.2
Simarouba glauca	Simaroubaceae	2.2
Swietenia macrophylla	Meliaceae	2.1

dried, weighed, and analyzed for their phosphorus content. Phosphorus content was also analyzed for litter removed from experimental plots in treatments (1) and (2) described above. Birds were sampled in the 12 plots using two 12 x 2 m nylon mist-nets per plot, operated for three successive mornings in late November 1984 and in February and March during the years 1985 to 1995. Data from the mist-nets in the 12 plots were supplemented by capture data from 15 to 24 mist-nets placed in the same tract of forest but outside of the experimental plots. All captured birds were identified, weighed, sexed, and marked with individually coded plastic leg bands before being released.

Neither litter removal nor phosphorus addition had any detectable influence on tree growth, leaf litterfall, litterfall of reproductive materials, or total nutrients or concentrations of nutrients in litterfall after the first four years of the study (Whigham and Lynch in press), nor were effects observed on the activity of Neotropical migrants or resident bird species (Lynch and Whigham 1995). The most informative results of the first four years of the study were the lack of response to phosphorus additions, the large annual variations in tree growth (Figure 17.1) and leaf litterfall (Figure 17.2), and the relationships of these patterns to annual precipitation (Whigham et al. 1990; Whigham and Lynch in press).

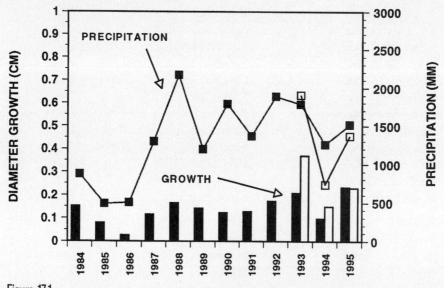

Figure 17.1

Average annual growth (cm) of trees in permanent plots at Rancho San Felipe and Noh-Bec. Rainfall data (mm) are also plotted for both sites. Solid rectangles and columns are data for Rancho San Felipe. Open rectangles and columns are data for Noh-Bec.

In 1988, we decided to modify the original experimental design to simulate the long-term average weekly pattern of precipitation by adding water to half of each of the 12 study plots. Our objective was to continue to test the phosphorus limitation hypothesis, while minimizing the impacts of annual variations in the amount and timing of precipitation. Before we could begin the experimental modifications, however, on September 14, 1988, the site was severely disturbed by Hurricane Gilbert. The emphasis of our project then shifted to an assessment of hurricane impacts (Lynch 1991; Whigham et al. 1991), and we initiated studies to determine how the system responded to the disturbance. All ecological aspects of the initial phase of the study continued, but it was not possible to remove leaf litter from the plots due to the large amount of woody debris generated by the hurricane. We also initiated phenological studies and studies of coarse woody debris (Harmon et al. 1995).

Tree mortality had averaged 0.5% of the tagged trees per year during the four-year pre-hurricane period. The forest was completely defoliated by the hurricane and about 2.5% of the marked trees were killed directly or died over the next five months. By 1993, tree mortality rates had decreased to pre-hurricane levels (Whigham and Lynch in press). The only tree species to experi-

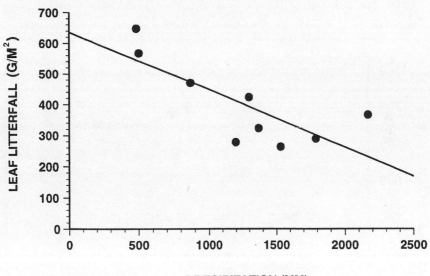

Figure 17.2

Relationship between leaf litterfall (g/m²) and annual precipitation (mm) at Rancho San Felipe between 1984 and 1991. Data for 1988 are included, but the amount of litterfall and precipitation from Hurricane Gilbert has been removed from the annual total. Litterfall associated with Hurricane Gilbert is compared to other years in Figure 17.3.

ence a major long-term detrimental impact due to the hurricane was ramón (*Brosimum alicastrum*), a canopy co-dominant that decreased in the plots from 143 marked trees in 1984 to 4 trees that were barely alive in 1996. In post-hurricane years, absolute and relative tree growth rates of all species but ramón continued to be controlled by annual precipitation patterns rather than any response to hurricane damage (Figure 17.1).

Defoliation of the forest by Hurricane Gilbert resulted in an enormous increase in leaf litterfall (Figure 17.3) and more than a threefold increase in the amount of phosphorus in leaf litterfall, from a mean of 0.25 ± 0.1 g/m^2 for the four pre-hurricane years to 0.7 ± 0.1 g/m^2 generated by the storm (Whigham et al. 1991). The hurricane also had a large impact on the amount of coarse woody debris (downed wood > 10 cm diameter) on the forest floor, which increased from roughly 31 Mg/ha to 47 Mg/ha (Whigham et al. 1991). We estimated that it will take 30 to 150 years for the wood downed by the hurricane to disappear, depending on species-specific differences in decomposition rates (Harmon et al. 1995).

The first post-hurricane mist-netting of birds occurred about five months after the storm. The number of species captured per mist-netting bout increased by approximately 70% and the capture rate (capture rate = 100 x [individuals/net/hr]) doubled (Lynch 1991; Whigham and Lynch in press). Many birds captured following the hurricane were field-associated species such as

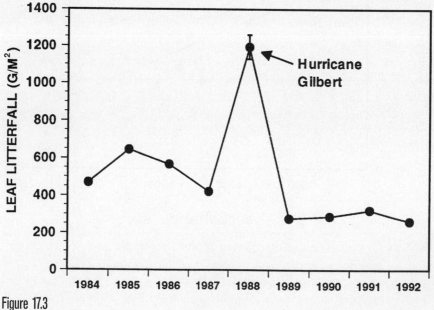

Figure 17.3

Annual leaf litterfall (g/m^2) at Rancho San Felipe between 1984 and 1991.

the indigo bunting (*Passerina cyanea*) and painted bunting (*Passerina ciris*) (Lynch 1992). The species that increased most dramatically was the white-eyed vireo (*Vireo griseus*), a migratory habitat generalist that occurs both in brushy fields and in the forest canopy, but was rarely captured in the understory mist-nets before the hurricane. Its capture rate increased from 0.1 before the hurricane to 3.2 during the first post-hurricane mist-netting bout. The capture rate for the white-eyed vireo began to decline in the second year following the hurricane, but remained higher than the pre-hurricane level through the end of the study in 1995. Other migratory species that typically forage in the forest canopy (e.g., magnolia warbler [*Dendroica magnolia*], black-and-white warbler [*Mniotilta varia*], and American redstart [*Setophaga ruticilla*]) also became more abundant in the dense understory following the hurricane, presumably because the upper canopy was completely defoliated.

The wood thrush (*Hylocichla mustelina*) was the only previously common understory Neotropical migrant that completely disappeared from the forest study plots following the hurricane. This species was not netted in 1989 or 1990, but its capture rate exceeded the mean pre-hurricane capture rate (0.6) in three of the four subsequent years (range = 3.8 in 1991 to 0.2 in 1994). Capture rates were unaffected by the hurricane for the other common understory Neotropical migrants (e.g., hooded warbler [*Wilsonia citrina*], ovenbird [*Seiurus aurocapillus*], Kentucky warbler [*Oporornis formosus*]).

Dynamics and Ecology of a Selectively Logged Forest at Noh-Bec

During the years that we were working at Rancho San Felipe in northeastern Quintana Roo, the Plan Piloto Forestal (PPF), a regional plan for community management of natural forests, was initiated in southern Quintana Roo (Galletti and Argüelles 1987). Most of the PPF's efforts are concentrated on forest-owning ejidos, rural cooperatives established after the Mexican Revolution, roughly 50 to 60 years ago. Two assumptions in the initial forest growth models for the PPF were that the average annual diameter increment of trees varied between 0.5 and 1.0 cm per year, depending on species group, and that natural regeneration was sufficient to sustain economically important species. These assumptions were not based on data for natural forests in the region, however, and it was intended that the management plan would be modified as relevant local data were gathered (Ramírez Segura and Sánchez Román 1992). Our growth data from Puerto Morelos (Figure 17.1) clearly showed that the average annual diameter growth there was much less than 1.0 cm. In addition, little information was available on the regeneration characteristics of either commercial or noncommercial tree species in forests similar to those at Noh-Bec or on their responses to logging disturbance (Negreros 1991; Snook 1993).

   In 1993, we extended our research to the ejido of Noh-Bec with three objectives. First, we wished to determine whether or not tree growth rates at Noh-Bec were similar to those that we had been measuring at Rancho San Felipe. We anticipated that growth rates would be higher at Noh-Bec, where the average annual precipitation is slightly higher than at Puerto Morelos (Table 17.1) and soils generally are deeper. Our second objective was to determine what effects, if any, selective logging had on birds. Based on the generally minor responses of birds to Hurricane Gilbert at Rancho San Felipe, we predicted that selective logging at Noh-Bec would have little impact. Our third objective at Noh-Bec was to characterize the natural disturbance regime within the forest and assess regeneration in the intact forest, in natural treefalls, and in gaps created by selective logging.

   Noh-Bec is located roughly 50 km south of the city of Felipe Carillo Puerto in southeastern Quintana Roo. Forests at Noh-Bec are generally taller than the forest at Rancho San Felipe (Table 17.1), but forests in both areas were considered to be similar in stature and composition according to Miranda's (1958) classification. Information on the forests that we are studying at Noh-Bec can be found in Table 17.1. In 1993, we tagged all trees > 10 cm dbh in 82 circular 0.1 ha plots. The plots were randomly chosen from a set of several hundred 0.1 ha inventory plots that had been established at 100 m intervals along surveyed N–S lines spaced at 250 m intervals from each other.

   Regeneration was studied by sampling seedlings and saplings in closed canopy forest, natural treefall gaps, and logging gaps. We used 40 m wide belt transects and 10 ha plots to sample the distribution, size, and rate of occurrence of natural tree gaps and logging gaps. Sample areas included forest logged about 18 years previously, forest burned 20 years previously, and unlogged forest that had not been burned within the memory of a number of elderly ejidatarios. We predicted that gap size and disturbance type (natural versus logging gaps) would affect the species composition and performance of regenerating trees.

   We sampled birds at Noh-Bec using the same protocol that was applied at Rancho San Felipe. Between 1993 and 1995 we sampled birds during three winters (February through March) and two summers (June and July). Mistnetting, supplemented with point counts (Lynch 1992), was conducted at four forested sites that had been disturbed by selective logging at various times in the past, and at one control site that had never been logged.

   Tree growth rates of all species combined (Figure 17.1) varied over the first three years of the project and, as we found in the forest at Rancho San Felipe, annual differences appeared to be related to variations in annual precipitation. Annual growth of commercially important species, such as mahogany (*Swietenia macrophylla*), varied in the same pattern as was observed for all tree species combined. Between 1993 and 1996, diameter growth of mahogany, one of the fastest-growing commercial species, was 0.65 ± 0.08 cm in the wettest year (1993) and 0.20 ± 0.06 in the driest year (1994). At the other extreme, one of the slowest-growing commercially valuable species, siricote (*Cordia dodecandra* [Boraginaceae]), showed no measurable growth over the four-year period.

Along with adequate growth rates, sufficient regeneration of logged species is necessary if timber harvesting is to be sustainable over the long term. In this forest, canopy openings formed by natural treefall and logging are important sites for regeneration, as are the more intense disturbances caused by fire and hurricanes (Snook 1993). The rates of natural treefall disturbance in Noh-Bec are lower than any reported in the literature for tropical forests (Whigham et al., in press). In wet, lowland tropical forests in the Americas, the natural treefall rate is usually about 1 gap/ha per year, the area opened by treefalls each year is about 1.5% of the forest, and the gap turnover time is around 100 years (Denslow 1987; Yavitt et al. 1995). Gap turnover time, an estimate of the number of years required for the equivalent of 100% of the forest to be opened to gaps, is calculated from the area opened to gaps each year. Over three years, the natural rate of treefall at Noh-Bec was about 0.2 gaps/ha per year, and most gaps were smaller than the minimum size reported for other forests. The area opened to gaps each year was about 0.07% per year, and the gap turnover time was > 6,000 years. Standing gap area (gaps of all ages) is extremely low, at about 0.27% of the forest area. These results hold for even the oldest undisturbed stands we sampled and are consistent among three methods of estimation.

Two nonexclusive explanations for the exceedingly low rate of natural disturbance at Noh-Bec seem promising: first, low rates of treefall disturbance are typical of tropical dry forests generally (Whigham et al., in press), and second, low rates of treefall disturbance are typical of forests that are periodically burned or disturbed by hurricanes. Noh-Bec is by far the driest forest (1,100 to 1,300 mm rainfall per year) for which disturbance rates have been reported. Closest is the forest of Tai National Park in the Ivory Coast (Jans et al. 1993), which receives about 1,800 mm of rainfall per year. In the Tai National Park, the natural treefall rate was approximately 0.7 gaps/ha per year, the area opened to gaps each year was approximately 0.41% per year, and the gap turnover time was 244 years. The rate of disturbance there is lower than that reported for wet lowland forests in the American tropics, but much higher than the drier forest at Noh-Bec, supporting the hypothesis that dry forests are inherently less dynamic than wet forests.

Hurricanes and fires have been an integral part of the disturbance regime at Noh-Bec (Snook 1993), and the low rates of disturbance we measured in Noh-Bec may be explained in large part by the fact that no hurricanes or fires occurred during our four- to five-year study. Because treefall mortality is pulsed in time, long-term monitoring that included major disturbance episodes would likely yield an average rate of disturbance more comparable to the year-to-year rates measured in forests not subjected to major disturbance events. In support of this notion, major disturbance by agricultural clearing (Yavitt et al. 1995), wind storms (Veblen 1985), and fire (Lorimer 1989) have been shown to reduce rates of treefall disturbance many years after the event. Periodic major disturbances thus appear to be of great importance for stand dynamics and regeneration in much of the Maya Forest. These disturbances appear to alternate with long intervals of unusually low rates of treefall disturbance and few opportunities for gap-phase regeneration.

One objective of our regeneration studies at Noh-Bec has been to characterize species in terms of their response to the gradient in canopy openness, which in turn is positively correlated with gap size. Seedlings and saplings growing in closed forest, natural gaps, and felling gap plots were sampled and categorized as either "gap specialists" or "generalists." Gap specialist species occupy only the more open-canopy sites, and large individuals of these species (stem height > 50 m) do not occur below a closed canopy. Conversely, seedlings and saplings of generalist species are distributed broadly across the canopy openness gradient. Using this conservative classification, 32% of the 65 species for which sufficient data are available are gap specialists. This proportion of gap specialists is much higher than occurs in wetter forests at Barro Colorado Island, Panama (6%; Welden et al. 1991) and La Selva, Costa Rica (9%; Lieberman et al. 1995). The majority (68%) of the tree species at Noh-Bec are generalists. It is unclear if drier forests generally have a larger proportion of gap specialists, or whether the higher proportion of gap specialists at Noh-Bec reflects the region's history of major periodic disturbance (Whitmore 1974).

Established understory vegetation appears to inhibit the colonization of gaps by gap specialist species. At Noh-Bec the rubber-tired skidders that are used to remove logs from felling gaps kill or damage small trees and understory vegetation and disturb the litter layer. This disturbance induces an increase in root-sprouting, particularly from a handful of gap specialist species. Physical damage associated with log extraction also results in an increase in the establishment of gap specialists from seed. For these reasons, a typical logging gap has a higher density and proportion of gap specialist individuals than does a natural gap of the same size.

A total of 70 bird species were netted between 1993 and 1994 at Noh-Bec, and 148 species occurred in point counts over the same period. Preliminary analysis of the mist-netting and point count data indicates little impact of selective logging on the occurrence of either migrant or resident bird species. For the ten most commonly netted species (Table 17.3), numbers of individuals and species composition were similar at the unlogged control site and four sites that were logged in 1993, 1992, 1987, and approximately 1950. The only Neotropical migrant among the ten most abundant species was the wood thrush (Hylocichla mustelina). It was also the only common species that showed major differences in capture rates among the five sites: it had an anomalously high capture rate at the unlogged control site in the 1993 winter sample (Table 17.3). However, wood thrush capture rates at this site fell dramatically in the winters of 1994 and 1995, suggesting that the high density in 1993 was only transitory. This species has occasionally been captured in unusually high numbers at other sites in Quintana Roo (J. Lynch, unpublished data), perhaps reflecting local population movements during the overwintering period.

None of the bird species characteristic of heavily disturbed vegetation were encountered in net samples from either the logged sites or the control site at Noh-Bec, although these species were common in nearby fields and regrow-

Table 17.3. Abundance of the ten most commonly netted bird species at five sites at Noh-Bec. Entries are the number of individuals captured in 20 mist-nets over a three-day period. Sites are ordered from most recently disturbed to undisturbed. The wood thrush is a Neotropical migrant. Other species are permanent residents.

| | Year when site was logged | | | | | |
Species	1993	1992	1987	1950	Control	Total
Red-throated ant-tanager *Habia fuscicauda*	41	44	21	31	16	153
Wood thrush *Hylocichla mustelina*	21	14	27	19	58	139
Ruddy woodcreeper *Dendrocincla homochroa*	32	15	27	13	28	115
Tawny-crowned greenlet *Hylophilus ochraceiceps*	24	12	26	25	9	96
Stub-tailed spadebill *Platyrinchus cancrominus*	12	10	21	21	16	80
Red-crowned ant-tanager *Habia rubica*	10	14	19	15	16	74
Thrushlike manakin *Schiffornis turdinus*	12	17	10	12	18	69
White-bellied wood wren *Henicorhina leucosticta*	9	17	20	12	5	63
Tawny-winged woodcreeper *Dendrocincla anabatina*	9	17	11	11	15	63
Olivaceous woodcreeper *Sittasomus griseicapillus*	11	12	11	17	11	62

ing fields. These same species are known to invade forest disturbed by hurricane or wildfire (Lynch 1989, 1991, 1992; Lynch and Whigham 1995). These observations suggest that selective logging as practiced at Noh-Bec causes much less severe disruption of bird populations than do major natural disturbances.

Conclusions

Ten years of data from the Yucatán Peninsula demonstrate that the local dry tropical forests are very dynamic and that they differ in several ways from more humid tropical forests. Annual variations in tree growth are substantial and seem to be driven by annual variation in the total amount and seasonal distribution of precipitation, factors that also appear to control the annual rate of leaf litterfall in both shallow and deep soils (Whigham et al. 1990). The amount of coarse woody debris in Quintana Roo forests appears to be higher than in more humid forests, but this factor is quite dynamic, increasing dramatically after hurricanes while decreasing just as dramatically in areas that burn (Harmon et al. 1995). Rates of natural treefall disturbance in the intervals between major disturbance events are much lower than in wetter forests, suggesting that local forest dynamics may be controlled mostly by periodic disturbances such as hurricanes and wildfire.

Almost all of the habitats that we have examined are important for Neotropical migrant birds. The species that utilize forest habitats appear to be common in both mature and successional forest habitats (Lynch 1989, 1992). Furthermore, the type of selective logging done throughout most of the region appears to have no discernable influence on Neotropical migrant birds or on most resident species. Large-scale disturbances can temporarily influence the dynamics of some bird and plant populations, but recovery tends to be rapid at both the population and ecosystem level. The most lasting damage to dry tropical forest is caused by large-scale conversion to permanent pasture, a land use that displaces most forest-associated birds and slows the rate of recovery of the forest community following pasture abandonment (Lynch 1992).

We are encouraged by the possibility of developing methods for sustainable forestry in portions of the region. Tree growth rates at Noh-Bec may be high enough to sustain timber harvests over the long term even though they are lower than rates assumed in the original management plan. However, observed low regeneration rates of commercially important species may present future problems. Information on natural disturbance and regeneration can be used as a basis for modeling silviculture, but not all types of natural disturbances are equally relevant. At Noh-Bec the majority of commercial timber species (9 out of 13), including mahogany, are gap specialists. Our data suggest that a lack of adequate seed sources and the small size of canopy openings that result from selective logging are leading to commercial elimination of the most important gap specialist species. For regeneration of these gap specialists large-scale natural disturbances such as hurricanes and fires are better silvicultural models than are natural treefalls.

If management for gap specialist tree species is to succeed, larger canopy openings need to be created and colonization rates by desired species must be increased. One proposed solution to the canopy opening problem is to harvest more species and relax the diameter-limit restrictions (Argüelles 1991; Snook 1993). This approach would potentially create larger openings by encouraging the cutting of more trees, assuming that large numbers of smaller-sized commercial trees grow close together. A potential pitfall of this increased harvesting intensity would be an increase in the impact of logging on wildlife and other nontarget species. To overcome the problem of limited seed availability, widespread enrichment planting of mahogany and Spanish cedar (*Cedrela odorata*) has been done, along with casual trials with other species. Although enrichment planting has not been uniformly successful, the potential exists to improve this and other techniques that might make the PPF logging system more sustainable. We are currently working with foresters and the ejidatarios of Noh-Bec to test experimentally enrichment planting techniques, and we will continue to test silvicultural techniques designed to promote natural regeneration of logged species.

Acknowledgments

Our research has been supported by the World Wildlife Fund, Smithsonian Institution (Smithsonian Scholarly Studies Program, International Environmental Sciences Program, Environmental Sciences Program, Research Expeditions Program), U.S. Man and the Biosphere Program, National Science Foundation, Sigma Xi, Tropical Research and Development, International Hardwood Products Association, and the Hardwood Plywood Manufacturers Association. Many individuals helped in the project, but we extend special thanks to Edgar Cabrera Cano, Patricia Zugasty Towle, Felipe Sánchez Román, Ingrid Olmsted, Alan Curtis, Jay O'Neill, Ed Balinsky, Jim Johnson, Paul Wood, Mauro Berlanga, Eduardo Ramirez Sequra, Salvador Gutiérrez, Juan Diego Matias Martinez, Joachin Matias Martinez, Jose Luis Landeros Zurita, Henning Flachsenberg, and Luis Poot Chan.

References

Argüelles Suarez, L. A. 1991. Plan de manejo forestal para el bosque tropical de la empresa ejidal Noh-Bec. Unpublished thesis, UACh, Departamento de Bosques, Texcoco, México.

Denslow, J. S. 1987. Tropical rainforest gaps and tree species diversity. *Annual Review of Ecology and Systematics* 18: 431–451.

Galletti, H. A., and A. Argüelles. 1987. Planificación estratégica para el desarrollo rural: El caso del Plan Piloto Forestal de Quintana Roo. Pages 317–325 in *Proceedings of the International Conference and Workshop on Land and Resource Evaluation for National Planning in the Tropics*. Publication No. GTR WO-39. U.S.D.A. Forest Service/FAO/SARH, Chetumal, Mexico.

Harmon, M. E., D. F. Whigham, J. Sexton, and I. Olmsted. 1995. Decomposition and stores of woody detritus in the dry tropical forests of the Northeastern Yucatán Peninsula, Mexico. *Biotropica* 27: 305–316.

Jans, L., L. Poorter, R. S. A. R. Rompey, and F. Bongers. 1993. Gaps and forest zones in tropical moist forest in Ivory Coast. *Biotropica* 25: 258–269.

Lieberman, M., D. Lieberman, R. Peralta, and G. S. Hartshorn. 1995. Canopy closure and the distribution of tropical forest tree species at La Selva, Costa Rica. *Journal of Tropical Ecology* 11: 161–178.

Lorimer, C. G. 1989. Relative effects of small and large disturbances on temperate hardwood forest structure. *Ecology* 70: 565–567.

Lynch, J. F. 1989. Distribution of overwintering Nearactic migrants in the Yucatán Peninsula, I: General patterns of occurrence. *Condor* 91: 515–544.

———. 1991. Effects of Hurricane Gilbert on birds in a dry tropical forest in the Yucatán Peninsula. *Biotropica* 23: 488–496.

———. 1992. Distribution of overwintering Nearctic migrants in the Yucatán Peninsula, II: Use of native and human-modified vegetation. Pages 178–195 in *Ecology and Conservation of Neotropical Migrant Landbirds*, J. M. Hagan III and D. W. Johnston, eds. Smithsonian Institution Press, Washington, D.C.

Lynch, J. F., and D. F. Whigham. 1995. The role of habitat disturbance in the ecology of overwintering migratory birds in the Yucatán Peninsula. Pages 199–214 in *Conservation of Neotropical Migratory Birds in Mexico*, M. H. Wilson and S. A. Sader, eds. Maine Agricultural and Forest Experiment Station, Miscellaneous Publication 727, Orono, Maine.

Miranda, F. 1958. Estudios acerca de la vegetación. Pages 215–271 in *Recursos Naturales del Sureste y su Aprovechamiento*, E. Beltrán, ed. Los IMERNAR, A.C., México, D.F., México.

Murphy, P. G., and A. E. Lugo. 1986. Ecology of tropical dry forest. *Annual Review of Ecology and Systematics* 17: 67–88.

Negreros, P. 1991. Ecology and management of mahogany (*Swietenia macrophylla* King) regeneration in Quintana Roo, Mexico. Ph.D. dissertation, Iowa State University, Ames.

Olmsted, I. C., A. Lopez Ornat, and G. R. Duran. 1983. Vegetación de Sian Ka'an: Reporte preliminar. CIQRO y SEDUE, Puerto Morelos, Quintana Roo, México.

Ramírez Segura, E., and F. Sánchez Román. 1992. Crecimiento de Arboles de Caoba en el ejido Noh-Bec. Unpublished report. Plan Piloto Forestal, Chetumal, México.

Rico-Gray, V., J. García-Franco, A. Puch, and P. Simá. 1988. Composition and structure of a tropical dry forest in Yucatán, Mexico. *International Journal of Ecology and Environmental Science* 14: 21–29.

Rzedowsky, J., ed. 1978. Vegetación de México. Limusa, México.

Snook, L. K. 1993. Stand dynamics of mahogany (*Swietenia macrophylla* King) and associated species after fire and hurricane in the tropical forests of Quintana Roo, Mexico. Ph.D. dissertation. Yale University, New Haven, Conn.

Standley, P. C. 1930. Flora de Yucatán. *Fieldiana Biologica* 3: 157–429.

Thien, L. B., A. S. Bradburn, and A. L. Welden. 1982. The woody vegetation of Dzibilchaltun: A Maya archaeological site in northwest Yucatán, Mexico. *Middle America Research Institute Occasional Papers* 5: 1–18

Veblen, T. T. 1985. Forest development in tree-fall gaps in the temperate rain forests of Chile. *National Geographic Research* 1: 162–183.

Vitousek, P. M. 1984. Litterfall, nutrient cycling, and nutrient limitation in tropical forests. *Ecology* 65: 285–298.

Welden, C. W., S. W. Hewett, S. P. Hubbell, and R. B. Foster. 1991. Sapling survival, growth, and recruitment: Relationship to canopy height in a neotropical forest. *Ecology* 72: 35–50.

Whigham, D. F., and J. F. Lynch. In press. Responses of plants and birds to hurricane disturbance in a dry tropical forest in Quintana Roo, Mexico. In *Measuring and Monitoring Forest Diversity: Proceedings of the International Network of Biodiversity Plots*, F. Dallmeier, ed. Smithsonian Institution Press, Washington, D.C.

Whigham, D. F., P. Zugasty Towle, E. Cabrera Cano, J. O'Neill, and E. Ley. 1990. The effect of annual variation in precipitation on growth and litter production in a tropical dry forest in the Yucatán of Mexico. *Tropical Ecology* 31: 23–34.

Whigham, D. F., I. Olmsted, E. Cabrera Cano, and M. Harmon. 1991. The impact of Hurricane Gilbert on trees, litterfall, and woody debris in a dry tropical forest in the northeastern Yucatán Peninsula. *Biotropica* 23: 434–441.

Whigham, D. F., M. B. Dickinson, and N. V. L. Brokaw. In press. Background canopy gap and catastrophic wind disturbance in tropical forests. In *Ecosystems of Disturbed Ground*, L. R. Walker, ed. Elsevier, Amsterdam.

White, D. A., and S. P. Darwin. 1995. Woody vegetation of tropical lowland deciduous forests and Maya ruins in the North-central Yucatán Peninsula, Mexico. *Tulane Studies in Zoology and Botany* 30: 1–25.

Whitmore, T. C. 1974. Change with time and the role of cyclones in tropical rain forest on Kolombangara, Solomon Islands. Commonwealth Forestry Institute Paper 46.

Yavitt, J. B., J. J. Battles, G. E. Lang, and D. H. Knight. 1995. The canopy gap regime in a secondary Neotropical forest in Panama. *Journal of Tropical Ecology* 11: 391–402.

Part V

Community Development, Conservation, and Ecotourism

Our final section provides examples of the advances made in community-based conservation and development projects. Some of these articles expand upon community forestry projects discussed from various angles in previous sections, introducing topics such as ecotourism and other ways to harness local resources into sustainable community development projects. Some articles also address the ways that scientists can collaborate with community organizations. This section is the largest, exemplifying the extraordinary diversity of ideas and practices that are being tested, yet it only touches the surface in terms of documenting and analyzing the range of promising ventures currently underway in the Maya Forest.

The two articles that open the section give voice to some of the residents of the Maya Forest. Juan Marroquín is a self-educated peasant leader from ejido Galacia, on the banks of the Lacantún River in the colonization zone of Marqués de Comillas, Chiapas, Mexico. Marroquín directs the efforts of his community and region to conserve and develop their significant stands of tropical rainforest, and his essay demonstrates that peasants understand that those forests benefit both them and the planet. One does not find here the narrow utilitarian vision of forest use frequently ascribed to local inhabitants. Raymundo Terrón, interviewed by editor Hugo Galletti, is one of the founders of the now famous Plan Piloto Forestal community forestry program in Quintana Roo, which is discussed in several other chapters in this volume. The interview shows how local leaders are acutely aware of the need to balance forest conservation with their livelihoods, and must be given the tools that allow them to carry out their vision. Understanding the problems and visions of Marroquín and Terrón is fundamental to creating effective alternative strategies for development and conservation in the region. Next is an article by José Luís Plaza Sánchez on what has emerged as one of the more promising development alternatives for mountainous buffer zones within the Maya Forest. In the Mexican state of Chiapas, in particular, many of the montane regions in and around the Montes Azules Biosphere Reserve provide prime coffee-growing altitude. As Plaza mentions, according to recent research on biodiversity in small coffee farms, so-called shade coffee provides important habitats for migratory birds and other species. This organic strategy offers the added benefits of increasing incomes for small farmers through their participation in high-value gourmet markets in the U.S., Europe, and Japan, and of eliminating an important source of watershed contamination in southern Mexico. But as Plaza makes clear, organic coffee brings with it many challenges and is not a development panacea.

A development strategy that has been heavily promoted in the region is ecotourism. Unfortunately, most of the ecotourism plans involve massive investments and sophisticated tour packages, while communities struggle to find a niche in the market and gain a share of the income from tourism that is not limited to service sector jobs. Several chapters in this section show that the incipient efforts at community-based ecotourism have real promise. Certainly, the Maya Forest has many features that make it an ideal ecotourist destination: unique and varied plants and animals, many of which are endangered or extinct elsewhere in Central America; a coral reef system off the coast of Belize, second only to the Great Barrier Reef in size and species diversity, that is a mecca for diving enthusiasts and deep-sea fishermen; and hundreds of magnificent Maya ruins, including such famous sites as Tikal, Tulum, Lamanai, Caracol, and Palenque. Many other smaller but equally compelling ruins are on or near community lands, and can be developed into markets for the more adventuresome tourist. Arts and crafts, including handwoven Maya textiles that are world-renowned for their intricate patterns and bright colors are important ecotourist attractions. The richest local resources are the indigenous cultures themselves, with their complex variety of languages and customs. The chapter by Reginaldo Chayax Huex, Feliciano Tzul Colli, Carlos Gomez Caal, and Steven P. Gretzinger show the struggle of the only remaining indigenous community with ancestral land claims in the Petén, the Maya Itzá, to craft a sustainable development plan for their community based on forest management, agroforestry, and ecotourism. Ruth Norris, J. Scott Wilbur, and Luís Osvaldo Morales Marín give an overview of community-based ecotourism throughout the Maya Forest region, showing both its promise and its problems. Robert Horwich and Jonathan Lyon present the experience of one of the more successful ecotourism experiences in the region, the Community Baboon Sanctuary based in Bermudian Landing, as well as a newer effort, the Gales Point Manatee Reserve, which is also discussed in the earlier paper by Belsky and Siebert. The final two papers also touch on ecotourism and other efforts to promote local community development and conservation. Conrad Reining and Carlos Sosa Manzanero's article on the ProPetén program is a good window on what a nongovernmental organization with international backing has been able to accomplish and plan under the difficult conditions of the region. ProPetén concentrates on increasing the incomes of local people by improving the methods of extracting, processing, and marketing of both timber and nontimber products. Some of the products were already being taken from the Maya Biosphere Reserve, but were not extracted sustainably or were processed and marketed ineffectively, and new products that can be sustainably harvested have also been found. Finally, Rafael Coc, Laura Marsh, and Elizabeth Platt discuss the grassroots environmental education efforts of the justifiably well-known Belize Zoo.

These chapters collectively show that communities are taking the first steps in learning how to package their attractions without losing their sense of themselves. But they also show that the road is not easy. Ecotourism that is poorly conceived or implemented will fail, leaving communities worse off than when they started. Ecotourism must be approached with care, support, training, and a good sense of appropriate market niches if rewards for the community are to be realized. A major challenge for community-based ecotourism is that the industry must be built from the ground up, since few communities have the facilities for housing and feeding visitors. Other infrastructure for tourism, including roads, airports, and potable water, frequently are not present or well developed in the rural areas that are most in need of tourist income. In addition, creation of a community-based ecotourism industry can require much training and a significant change in mindset on the part of local people who are more accustomed to farming than being service providers.

Yet the knowledge required for successful community conservation activities is even more basic than can be supplied by management training. The people of the region have varying degrees of knowledge of their own environment and history; some have rich indigenous local knowledge, while others are recent colonists who are still learning about their new environment. A more conscious and developed local knowledge can be a commodity for the tourism industry and also engenders a sense of pride and connectedness to the forest that is essential to conservation.

The varied approaches described here are only a few of the possibilities. In conjunction with the research and management strategies described in previous sections, they represent the best hope for preservation of the unique ecosystem and cultural environment that is the Maya Forest.

Chapter 18

The Global Environment and Galacia, the New Ejidal Population Center, Marqués de Comillas Zone, Ocosingo, Chiapas

Juan Marroquín

An open letter to the President of the United States of Mexico; the Constitutional Governor of Chiapas, Mexico; the Secretary of SEMARNAP; Ecologists; National and International Nongovernmental Organizations; and the Society of the Planet Earth.

We, the inhabitants of the new ejidal population center, Galacia, and the Galacia Work Committee of the same ejido, of the Marqués de Comillas zone, in the municipality of Ocosingo, Chiapas, Mexico, would like to discuss the following truth: our planet and its inhabitants are in danger. The Earth and the atmosphere are home to man and other living creatures. We need to care for it; this is the essence of ecology.

Today ecology faces the task of discovering the damage caused by human society and looking for alternative solutions. Clearly this will not be a simple task. We need to be at peace with our planet, to do no further damage. For if we damage one of its elements, we are also damaging its other parts. For each aspect is related to every other aspect. All living beings are tied to the other elements of the universe of the Earth, just as when one part of the human body is sick it affects the entire body.

Now let us talk a bit about the atmosphere and the Earth. The atmosphere is a layer that covers the planet Earth and that extends from the surface of the soil to a height of 80 km in space. It is formed of two separate layers called the troposphere and the stratosphere. The troposphere is approximately 16 km thick; within it the majority of the five trillion tons of air contained in the atmosphere are found. The stratosphere is approximately 64 km thick, and within it is the ozone layer, which acts as a filter to solar radiation and protects us from ultraviolet radiation that causes skin cancer.

The atmosphere is a marvelous and balanced mixture. It is made up of 78% nitrogen, 21% oxygen, and the remaining 1% is formed of other gases such as argon, water vapor, carbon dioxide, neon, helium, krypton, hydrogen, xenon, and ozone. Oxygen is, as we know, the vital gas that we absorb through respiration. The level of oxygen in the atmosphere is required for life, as a decrease in the amount of this important gas would cause us to lose consciousness and life itself. On the other hand, if the levels of oxygen increased dramatically, even green plants would spontaneously catch fire. Nitrogen is the perfect dilution medium for oxygen, but its role is not limited to just that. All living beings rely on nitrogen for building living tissues; as humans we acquire it through the food we eat.

Carbon dioxide normally prevents the cooling of the Earth; however, an excessive quantity of this gas could cause the Earth to heat up to the point that life on Earth would disappear. Ozone is another important gas on which life on Earth also depends. The ozone in the highest layer of the atmosphere, the stratosphere, absorbs the ultraviolet radiation from the sun, thus protecting the inhabitants of the Earth from the damaging effects of this radiation such as cancer. The atmosphere also protects us from meteorites, bodies of rock that come from space, but that disintegrate in the atmosphere, so most never make it to the planet's surface.

Earth, as seen and photographed from space by man, is one unified image, despite the variety of different colors. Truly, Earth is a marvelous jewel in space. It is a marvel because of the diversity of living organisms it contains: microorganisms, insects, fish, birds, animals, forests, plants, water, and humans. The Earth is a vast storehouse of riches that contains all that is necessary to sustain all these forms of life. The more we analyze the atmosphere and the planet Earth, the more miraculous they appear to us. We see clearly the traces of an intelligent mind, a creator who designed a perfect balance, heaven and earth.

Unfortunately, this delicate and perfect balance is being destroyed by the style and way of life of modern man. But is the situation of the atmosphere and planet Earth very serious?

What Man Has Done to the Atmosphere and the Earth

The ozone layer, which protects us from the ultraviolet radiation of the sun, is being destroyed by man with chlorofluorocarbons (CFCs), which are composed of one atom of carbon, two of chloride, and two of fluoride. Scientists estimate that each atom of chloride can destroy thousands of molecules of ozone. In 1992, measurements made via satellites showed a hole in the ozone layer larger than all of North America, and detected decreases in the levels of ozone in Antarctica, Europe, Russia, and Canada.

The atmosphere and the Earth are constantly bombarded by other contaminating agents. Carbon dioxide, for example, is emitted by large industries, cars, and the burning of fossil fuels and wood. To this must be added waste products, radioactive byproducts of nuclear energy plants and agrochemicals. Deforestation continues without control or planning and animal species are going extinct daily. People are ruining the Earth.

The consequences are serious and could be fatal. The hole in and overall decrease in the ozone layer allows more ultraviolet radiation to reach the Earth's surface, and this is producing new cases of skin cancer. The rise in the levels of carbon dioxide is causing the planet to warm up. Droughts are more prolonged in different parts of the Earth. Large areas of agriculture are being lost, and cattle ranching is also being affected by the loss of pasture lands. This has happened and is currently happening. These occurrences are in the news every day. Here in Marques de Comillas in the municipality of Ocosingo, Chiapas, Mexico, in 1986, the drought lasted for six months, and many crops were lost. In 1990 and 1991, again drought affected agricultural production, even though we are in a zone of abundant rainfall due to the tropical forests of the region.

Additionally, the contamination is affecting the most important cities in the world, among them Mexico City, which is covered by a toxic fog produced by the thousands of cars packed into its streets. The air in Mexico City has too much carbon dioxide and not enough oxygen.

Deforestation without any management plan is another cause of the ecological imbalance, resulting in even fewer forests and woodlands, less rain, greater heat, and drought. And when it does rain, rapid flooding is the result. For example, in Marqués de Comillas there was a flood in 1975 and another only 15 years later, in 1990. Then, only five years later, in 1995, there was another. In our analysis, removal of forests along the banks of the rivers, creeks, and natural canals is allowing the water to flow too rapidly, causing these disastrous floods. Before, the trees and the undergrowth slowed the flow of the water. Additionally, the loss of forest cover causes the erosion of fertile soil.

Is There Hope That the Planet Earth and the Atmosphere Can Be Saved?

We think that, yes, there is hope, although it is not within human power to save everything from destruction. But we can and must do something, and contribute to this effort so that we don't continue to damage our home here on Earth. We need to eliminate selfishness, hatred, greed, voracious ambition for wealth, and the excessive exploitation of our natural resources. All of the

Earth and its resources were created for the benefit of humanity, but we must use them well, sensibly, and modestly.

The world leaders are aware of these problems. In 1992, 118 heads of state met at the Earth Summit in Rio de Janeiro, Brazil, where they defined steps to protect the atmosphere and the planet Earth. We hope that these declarations will be translated into actions. But what is the Galacia ejido doing? Is it contributing to the effort so that we stop damaging the atmosphere and the planet Earth?

The property of the Galacia ejido covers 2,600 ha, of which 2,000 are tropical forest that have been conserved for the past 23 years, since 1973. In these forests, and in all of the property, there are many different species of wildlife: jaguars, wild boars, agoutis, armadillos, tapirs, scarlet macaws, toucans, pheasants, ducks, and crocodiles, to name but a few. The 2,000 ha of forest are performing an important role in the environment. They capture large quantities of carbon dioxide and liberate oxygen. The trees are also natural pumps, pulling water up through their roots and respiring it from their leaves in vapor form.

By this the people of Galacia have demonstrated the strength of their conviction and desire to be conservationists. However, through their leaders they have reiterated on several occasions in the past two decades that they don't want a forest that merely stays unchanged. Galacia is convinced that forests are conserved when they are placed under an organized and sustainable management, with the surrounding communities acting as owners of their natural resources.

In the past, the government and its institutions were not convinced of the viability of the idea of simultaneous conservation and rational use of the forest resources, in a balanced and sustainable fashion. Despite signing communal forestry agreements in 1987 and 1989, the government never lent full support to the idea of community forestry. This phase ended when the Patrocinio government annulled the agreement and banned forestry harvests and also banned cattle ranching in Marqués de Comillas.[1]

We, the people of Galacia, did not use the contingency permissions for harvesting granted in 1994, which permitted the harvest of dead wood, because there was none. We considered these permissions as an attempt to push us into committing a crime, because those who issued the permissions knew very well that there was no standing dead wood in the forest and that those who were harvesting were cutting live trees, but the government did nothing to prevent it. Instead, Galacia and its leaders continued to petition for a management plan for their natural resources, similar to the one they had begun in 1987 and similar to ones currently being used in the states of Quintana Roo, Campeche, and Michoacan.

The current federal and state governments, as well as the Secretaries of Natural Resources, Environment and Fisheries, are all convinced that to conserve a resource does not necessarily mean to stop using it. As a result, the government agreed to lift the ban on forest harvest and the restriction on cattle ranching in Marqués de Comillas.[2] We are very appreciative of this new governmental stance on conservation. And through a petition by the Galacia ejido, the Pilot Plan for Regional Development was initiated at the end of 1995 with the goal of sustainable management of the natural resources.

The first step in this plan was initiated on eight ejidos, among them Galacia. This Pilot Plan is directed by SEMARNAP under the general coordination of Deocundo Acopa Lezama,[3] who has a strong foundation of knowledge and experience from his direction of the successful Pilot Plans for the states of Quintana Roo and Campeche. If Sr. Acopa is allowed to continue his work in Chiapas, and he is given the support he needs, then the Pilot Plan in Marqués de Comillas will also be a success. For this reason we asked the government and SEMARNAP that the coordinators and technicians working with Sr. Acopa be knowledgeable people, willing to collaborate for the good of the plan, the communities, and the forest itself. We were prompted to ask this because the economic study of the management is progressing very slowly, which in turn is slowing down the harvest permits. We have also asked SEMARNAP to facilitate the pending forest harvest permits for 1996, before the dry season ends.

To the ecologists and Lacandón Forest surveyors we say: let your criticisms be constructive and don't consider yourselves saviors of the forest. You need to remember that Marqués de Comillas is a buffer zone with communities of people. Have respect for the autonomy of each community regarding its use of natural resources. With respect to lands of the Lacandón Forest, we in Galacia have not touched even one splinter of wood in the 23 years that we have been its neighbors.

We ask the government for funds to finance a portable sawmill as a priority. The National Institute of Indigenous People (INI) has the resources to finance two sawmills. We say to the National Fund of Social Businesses (FONAES): you have cheated us and caused us to lose time and money in all the proposals that we presented in Tuxtla Gutierrez, Chiapas, for one year and eight months. The forest management project that we presented was prepared by a consultant, approved and paid for by FONAES. Because you at FONAES did not wish to give credit for our project, it was easier for you to say, "Your project won't work." You could similarly justify the expense and investment in further bureaucratic processes and developing more petitions. You even recommended another consultant to develop for us a new project for cattle breeding and raising.

FONAES claims to be waiting for us to improve pastures within our property to make them better suited to cattle ranching, yet it extended credit to neighboring ejidos, who have the same pastures of introduced and native species that we have and their cattle are healthy. In the visit they made to

Galacia on March 16 of 1996, we signed a memorandum, thinking that it was because they were going to give us the credit. It turned out to only be justification for their visit to Galacia. FONAES also promised to support the Galacia work committee with a project to improve the pasture grasses, but that promise too was empty.

To the federal and state governments as well as SEMARNAP, we say: don't deceive us with the Pilot Plan as FONAES did and don't ban timber harvest instead of granting permits, as the ex-governor Patrocinio González Garrido did.

We want the pending forest harvest permits so that we can harvest our timber. We want financing for a portable sawmill and equipment for the harvest of timber. We want financing for a project to improve the pasture grasses. We also want credit for a project of cattle ranching and animal husbandry. We want financing to design and execute an ecotourism project.

To the nongovernmental organizations, both national and international, we ask that you support us with economic resources for our projects and we invite you to come visit, to come know Galacia, its forest, and its wildlife.

To all of those addressed by this statement, we say: if you don't take what we have said on this theme seriously and do not assist us in what we ask, then we declare that we are no longer responsible for protecting our forest from our neighbors. We will no longer have the resources or the arguments necessary to stop the destruction, for you give us neither solutions nor alternatives. Let us not forget that our planet Earth and its inhabitants are in danger.

Notes

1. From 1986 to 1989 some communities in the Lacandón rainforest, including Galacia, began experimenting with community management of their forests for timber. These experiments were brought to an abrupt end by the severe restrictions on logging, amounting to a ban, that were promulgated by then Chiapas governor Patrocinio González Garrido in 1989. Some permits were given for harvesting dead wood.

2. The first new permits for community logging in the Marqués de Comillas region since 1989 were authorized in September 1996.

3. See Acopa and Boege, this volume, for a history of the forest management experiences in Calakmul, Campeche.

Chapter 19

....

What Is the Forest to a Small Farmer?
Interview with Raymundo Terrón Santana

Interviewer: Hugo A. Galletti

Raymundo Terrón Santana is a member of the Tres Garantías ejido in southern Quintana Roo. The ejido is a member of the Sociedad de Productores Forestales de Quintana Roo, S.C. (Society of Forest Producers of Quintana Roo). Sr. Terrón is a resin (chicle) tapper, farmer, forest worker, founder of the Forest Pilot Plan, and founder and ex-president of the Sociedad de Productores Forestales de Quintana Roo.

What does the forest mean to me? The forest is a great source of life, there is none greater. Who lives there? The plants, the animals, and the peasants. Who disturbs and intervenes in it? Humans in general, consumers of the products from the forest, and the bureaucrats who set the standards for management of the forests with laws also disturb and intervene in it.

What is going on in the forest and why? It is undeniable that there are problems in the forest. There are problems that we feel (or I feel) require a search for urgent means of solution. We have begun, over the course of more than a decade, a task that is leading toward conservation and at the same time the harvesting of the forest resources found on ejido property. We have defined permanent forest areas, and we have begun rational management in those areas. But this isn't all. We feel that the most important fact is that the peasants, that *we*, are living here. The biggest problem that we have is the economic one, that is to say, the conditions of life for those of us who live in the forested area. The peasant, in order to look for food and sustenance for himself and his children, needs to use whatever he finds, regardless of the cost to the forest. We feel that if these conditions don't change, we will be able to make little progress in what we have been doing. If to this we add the problem of overpopulation (because day by day the rural population is growing), we are going to arrive at a point where the problem is going to become even bigger. On the other hand—and this is a consequence of these needs—we peasants have been losing the culture of our ancestors, which is the means of living in harmony with the forest. I repeat that it is precisely for our needs, because our ancestors didn't live in modern civilization, and there weren't as many outside interests against the peasant.

Benefiting from the forest through the sale of logs or boards gives us an income, but it isn't enough. For the community to move forward there are three points that need to be addressed. The first point is that we need to strengthen the small timber industries of the peasants that have been established in the zone, because these give greater income and are a source of employment. If the timber that is used is the product of a management plan, and if they use the community channels as sources of stock, then they are not going to harm the forestry zone. The other point is that we need to initiate and strengthen other sources of income, outside of the forest, such as agriculture and cattle raising. But this needs to be done in an ordered fashion coordinated with the forest harvests. If we earn an income from these activities, we are not going to go on opening new areas for cultivation at a cost to the forest. Another aspect that needs to be considered to strengthen the local economy is the development of agroforestry. This [change] is made with the goal that working on small, individual plots of land we will be able to have our own forests. Perhaps working on his own plot surrounded by his trees, the peasant will return to the feeling that he is bound to the forest as his ancestors were, and we will once again feel the relationship between the peasant and the forest. We see that the forest is not the only consideration. The forest must produce some income to help improve the well-being of the peasant's family, but money must also come from other sources so that we can conserve the forest.

There are things outside the control of the farmer. With regards to the external aspects, the market and the industry (the large-scale timber industry, not the local industries), the government should take some fairly radical steps. Currently the industry brings to the consumer only the products of the forest that it feels like putting on the market, through control of advertising. But the forest produces many other things that currently aren't sold and don't bring us income. I feel that here is where we need to change things. We need to look for a means to bring to the consumer all that the forests can really produce, and not only the products that bring large profits to the industrialists. If we sell a little of each product, the peasants will be able to increase their incomes without threatening the forest. Certainly, the bureaucrats as well, those who make the laws, need to understand where the problem lies. They need to come to where the peasants are, to be able to adapt the laws so that they govern the management of the forest resources, and at the same time benefit our economy.

I feel that we, the peasants, must be given a greater opportunity to participate so that we can decide how to manage our own resources. I say this because many forget that the forests are ours, and we [must] realize that we peasants are the ones living here 24 hours a day. We are the direct protagonists of what is happening in the forest. If we peasants don't take the agreed-upon steps to protect and rationally benefit from the forest, what will happen is that we will continue to destroy it. But to avoid continuing the destruction, the forest needs to generate an income so that we take interest in preserving it. This is what the people from the outside who are concerned with this issue need to understand: it is not only from a love of nature that the forests will be conserved. If we don't take steps to improve the conditions of life in the rural zone, then the peasants will continue to cut the forest. Whether they like it or not, the authorities cannot stop it, and who knows what the future of these forests will be.

However, there are things that can be done that produce results, and this we know from experience. Previously, more than a decade ago, our forested areas were granted as a concession to a business that removed all the timber. We were simply spectators, we were the true owners of the forest and yet we weren't allowed to touch it. Afterwards, a government program supported us, and we began to harvest the forests for our own benefit. We were able to take over all the aspects of forestry, the work in the forest itself, and the small ejido industries, which are still operating. We were able to participate in the timber market and get better prices for our timber. Currently we are still working in all of this. Fortunately, we can say that in the forested areas, where we began to work more than a decade ago, there are still standing forests, there is still wildlife, and we can say that we have put an end to the destruction. But if we hadn't had this opportunity, surely we would have deforested a large part of these forests.

To stop the destruction of the forest, we defined areas of permanent forest. These areas of permanent forests are zones of the ejido where no activity except forestry is permitted. The ejidal assembly will not allow members to plant there. In the beginning, this decision was not easy. One of the most important issues is that the forest was there, but it served the peasants little because they were not allowed to harvest anything from it, they received almost nothing from the forest; the people focused on extensive cattle ranching and corn farming at great cost to the forest. And the people were accustomed to deforesting where they wished. Thus, when we decided through a majority vote to return to the forest and began to manage it, some peasants couldn't take the pressure and emigrated. They went to other places where they could continue deforesting, where there was no law. It was a problem, since we felt the separation from colleagues alongside of whom we had, for many years, fought for survival.

The work we are doing in the forest is being developed within the area of permanent forest. We divided this area into 25 parcels to work one each year and thus we are advancing year by year. The general assembly of the ejido decides who is going to be in charge of directing each year's work. At the beginning of the season, when the work is about to start, a general assembly is called to name one person responsible for the area that is going to be worked that year. Another person is put in charge of overseeing the sawing of the timber and workers are enlisted: some for the field, as lumberjacks, *brecheros* and *monteros*, others in the sawmill, and still others on the transportation equipment to bring the timber from the forest to the sawmill. Everyone signs up according to his or her abilities, and according to which aspect they want to work in, and thus we begin work for the season. This is repeated every year. At the end of the season, when the rains begin, we transfer our efforts to reforestation. For this we have a nursery where at the beginning of the season seeds of various species, especially mahogany and Spanish cedar as well as fruit species, are planted to be distributed to the peasants. After finishing the harvest, in the area that was harvested that year, the parcel is replanted.

With respect to the market, previously we didn't even know how to determine the volume of a log. We learned all that we needed to know to manage the harvest of timber, and we learned how to gain access to the market to sell our products directly. There are still many things we don't know, but we do know how much our forest is worth and for that we will conserve it. As the forest is the greatest source of life, timber is just one part of this and perhaps only a small part of what the forest is. Currently we are harvesting chicle and honey, and both of these products are exported. Many people live on the income generated by chicle and honey. In the last few years we have been able to greatly improve our production of chicle, and we reorganized the chicle cooperatives. There is great hope for the production of still more products from the forest. There is a great variety of products that can be harvested rationally and that can benefit the peasants' economy. But in this one needs to be realistic: each product has a different market, and because of that, to harvest every product produced by the forest represents an enormous effort. Additionally, in our ejido we have a small camp and tourists come to see the wildlife of the forest.

For this I am very concerned with the opinions of the environmentalists. Well, I haven't personally known an environmentalist, but I do listen to the declarations of environmentalists from all over. Truly, when some mention that the forest should be like a park, and that it should be left untouched so that it can continue to exist, they don't realize their great mistake, nor that they are creating a huge problem for us, the peasants. We have been living in, managing, and harvesting the forest for a long time. And here we will continue. This hasn't ended. In contrast, there are areas where we have been restoring, and which we will incorporate into the permanent forest areas. There are other ecologists who see the situation as we see it, and this is very good for the peasants. I believe that it is better that there are different opinions and that some understand our problem.

One problem that we are seeing is that the community is developing only in forestry. Currently, with the forest management we are doing there are economic gains, but they aren't enough. We need to round out our economy with small-scale agriculture and cattle ranching. For this we have to look for other alternatives, we need to encourage other areas in order to continue conserving what we have. If the problems of the peasant come from deficiencies in economic opportunity, we need to encourage these other avenues of production so that we are not forced to intensify activities in the forest. There is no need to concentrate only on forest management. To people from outside the community it may appear to conflict with conservation of the forest if we have greater income from cattle ranching and agriculture. But it may allow us to ask less of the forest.

But agriculture and cattle ranching are not being practiced in an organized manner now, so they can't serve as a serious boost to the economy. We need to round out our economy with other products from the same area, but not as before with slash-and-burn, but rather with crops that produce high quantities in small areas, including intensive stockraising (*ganadería intensiva*). Only like this will we be able to respect the areas of permanent forest. The economic crisis is a danger to the forest. The prices of the products we need here in the rural areas rise, but the prices of our products don't. Our profits decrease and our wages are worth even less. The people lose hope and there is the danger that they start to invade the forest. The crisis is the enemy of conservation, not the peasant.

The thing to fear the most is the opinion of a famous doctor who speaks on a topic he knows nothing about and who doesn't realize the implications of his recommendations, because just think of the things in which people interfere! I used to think that a national park should be developed in areas where the situation was controllable, but then the biosphere reserve was invented, so large that no one can control it.[1]

I am not a politician, but if they let me make forest policy, I feel I would first try to look at the problems of the people living in the forest, the problems of the peasants. I would begin to work to see how we could develop small projects with these people, because I disagree with the large-scale projects and programs. I feel that this needs to be done in small plots, small groups or with individuals, however it is best managed. But the solutions need to be looked for here at the grassroots level, here where the farms are, where the forestry areas are, where the communities are. From what happens in the communities, we can start to modify the laws so that from the center of the peasant—his way of life, his viewpoint—the standards can be developed. Right now it is the reverse. Things can be directed through management, for as I said in the beginning, those who live in the forest, [among] the plants, the trees, and the animals, are in perfect harmony with nature. What we need to see is how to achieve that harmony for ourselves, humanity.

Note

1. Terrón refers to the opinions of Pedro Vega, a logger and writer from Tenosique, Tabasco, who wrote under the pseudonym Pablo Montañas. Vega recommended the creation of a national park in the highest parts of the Sierras and in the uninhabited watersheds of the Selva Lacandóna. This idea would eventually become the Montes Azules Biosphere Reserve, declared in the Lacandón region in 1978. Although it created a protected area on paper, the decree also included populated areas within it, overlaid pre-existing claims, and later had other claims placed on top of it.

Chapter 20

Organic Coffee Production and the Conservation of Natural Resources in Las Margaritas, Chiapas

José Luís Plaza Sánchez

In 1992, a program was initiated to convert to organic production the coffee farms of 19 rural communities belonging to the ejido unions of La Selva, Juan Sabines, and Maravilla Tenejapa, including the municipalities of Las Margaritas and La Independencia, in the state of Chiapas (see Map 1 in Introduction to this volume). The area is near the Guatemalan border in the southwestern Selva Lacandóna, an area with great importance for conservation because of its proximity to the Montes Azules Biosphere Reserve and to other unprotected areas, such as the Ixcán region, that have great biotic diversity.

The program of organic production—that is, production without herbicides, pesticides, and chemical fertilizers—has been developing in lowland and highland forests inhabited by indigenous peasant farmers, for whom coffee is the sole viable crop for commercial agriculture. During the last two decades, this and other areas of the Selva Lacandóna have been affected by increasing destruction of the original forests, mainly as a result of land opening for cultivation of corn and coffee required by a continual increase in the human population. The initial objective of the program was to convert 1,000 ha of coffee farms to organic production in three years. Realization of this goal was expected to have a positive impact on the income of participating families while promoting conservation of natural resources. Successful establishment of organic coffee farms would also demonstrate that this type of intensive production could be expanded in an area characterized by continually advancing destruction of old-growth forests.

The technology used in the corn farming is shifting (slash-and-burn) agriculture, which is the most frequent method of production in wet tropical

zones. This method requires cultivated lands, or milpas, to be rotated continuously so that agricultural plots can regain their fertility during a fallow period
of two to five years. In contrast, traditional coffee production is semi-intensive and makes use of specialized shade trees, usually species of the genus *Inga*.
Although coffee producers are familiar with chemical fertilizers and insecticides, such products currently are not used in this kind of agricultural production. These products were supplied until 1987 by the Instituto Mexicano
del Café (INMECAFE), a parastatal agency that provided technical assistance and purchased producers' harvests until its liquidation in 1989. Data
from this research project suggest that the main reason coffee producers
stopped using chemical products was that they became too expensive when
the subsidies from INMECAFE ended.

The difficulty of designing and implementing sustainable projects is exem-
plified by the activities of INMECAFE. The agricultural techniques promoted
by this institution over many years did not fit into the established economic
structure of rural family units. Subsidies were essential to make chemical fertilizers and insecticides both affordable and attractive for producers. The disappearance of this institution made continuation of its systems of technical
assistance, harvest subsidies, and marketing of crops impossible. Under the
agricultural, social, and economic conditions characterizing the forested zone
of Las Margaritas—and presumably in many other regions of the wet tropics—
the likelihood that sustainable development projects will be successful in the
long term will depend on one factor: that these projects respect and take into
account the social organization of the communities at which they are directed, while still striving to preserve the natural resource endowment on
which the projects are based.

The abandonment of producers resulting from the termination of IN-
MECAFE set the stage for the beginning of the program of organic production. The ejidos in the border zone had to improve the efficiency and quality
of their production to sustain the income of their members. These producers
also were affected by extremely high levels of world coffee stocks, accompa-
nied by falling international prices between 1989 and 1993. Lack of governmental support made impossible the continuation of a program of production
based on the use of chemical products. Simultaneously, an opportunity arose
to take advantage of the growth experienced by the organic coffee market,
using accumulated experience in the marketing of grain in external markets.
These circumstances led to the initiation of a program of organic production.
In order to make the program sustainable in the long term, it incorporated
two premises: first, that the program should effectively increase the income of
participating families without altering their internal economic equilibrium,
and second, that the program should increase the productivity of coffee farms
while preserving natural resources.

These principles have been followed during four cycles of production, and
during that time the initial goal of 1,000 ha has been surpassed, with 1,287 ha
of organic coffee under production as of late 1996. Although a quantification

of the total impact of the program cannot be made until the final evaluation in 1996 is concluded, some of its effects can be identified now, including measures related to the conservation of natural resources. In this article, I briefly review the ways by which the program of organic production has supported conservation efforts in a zone characterized by environmental fragility.

Characteristics of the Program of Organic Coffee Production

Most of the people registered in the program are Tojolobal Indians; the remainder are Tzotzil Maya and mestizos. At the time of this writing, the program had been extended to 57 communities with 1,304 families. Most of these communities are isolated and lack most public services. Among the participating organizations, the Unión de Ejidos de La Selva (La Selva) is the one most responsible for carrying out the project. This organization has the greatest organizational coherence and possesses the largest amount of resources and experience in the commercial production of coffee.

The structure of the program is organized around a technical team, consisting of six professionals that supervise and permanently train a group of more than 30 technicians coming from the communities. These technicians are producers selected in each community by all the participating members in the program. They are required to attend workshops to learn new cultivation techniques, which they then teach to their peers (see Figure 20.1). Professional agronomists visit the communities to support and advise the commu-

Figure 20.1

Demonstration of new composting methods to coffee farmers in Chiapas.

nities' technicians, and also to record the activities carried out by each producer.

The organic coffee program is an important part of the organizations' strategy to improve their positioning in the international coffee market, in both organic and traditional coffee. In order to get the higher prices that organic coffee commands, international agencies must certify that the coffee produced is authentically organic. The strict control that is maintained over the labor of each producer is aimed at assuring that certification is maintained, and the premium paid for certified organic coffee goes as an incentive precisely to those producers who make the technological transition to organic production. La Selva also has a computerized bar code system to track the exact origin of each sack of coffee that it delivers to its clients. All producers participating in the conversion of coffee farms must follow these recommendations, assisted and supervised by technicians. Changes promoted by the program in the different steps in the production of coffee are shown in Table 20.1.

Organic coffee can increase producers' incomes in two ways: increased price and increased productivity. In the 1995–96 harvest cycle, it is estimated that La Selva provided approximately 5,500 quintales of certified organic coffee and received a premium over market price of 15–20 cents a pound. As for productivity, at the beginning of the program, average yields were below average for the state of Chiapas, but organic production has increased them by 15–20 percent. Until now, La Selva has not confronted any problems in marketing, and it is unlikely to have any for the next several years, since the market for high-quality organic coffee is growing, not only in Europe but also in the United States and Japan.

Traditional Exploitation of Natural Resources

The current natural resource situation is associated directly with the process of settlement and the type of agricultural production established in each micro-region. In the zone of operation of the program, the dominant systems of production are those combining the production of corn and beans—also known as milpa farming, which utilizes shifting agricultural techniques—with the production of coffee and, to a lesser extent, with the keeping of livestock. The existence of these production systems led to some typical forms of replacing original forest cover, generating different degrees of environmental disturbance. In this section, I use data obtained from a four-year longitudinal study to evaluate the impact of the transition to organic coffee production on the natural resource base and the incomes and well-being of the farmers. The data are derived from a survey instrument applied to a sample of 320 producers from 12 locations, providing detailed data at the family level. This information is considered representative of the area where the program of organic production is taking place.

Table 20.1. Changes in cultivation practices introduced by organic coffee production.

Activity		Organic Production	Conventional Production within the Program
Cultivation Practices	Frequency of weeding	Three times per year, leaving vegetation measuring 5 cm in height	Once per year, weeding down to the groundlevel
	Pruning	Careful pruning of all the plants	Disorderly and light pruning
	Removal of leaf shoots	With machete or scissors	
	Agobio (plant doubling to stimulate new shoots)	Only changing the orientation with respect to the sun	Done without consideration of direction
	Shade reduction (removal of branches or trees that create excess shade)	Annually	Not done regularly
Conservation activities	Terraces	Generally, one terrace is created for every plant	Not done
	Creation of living fences	Hundreds of meters of living fences are created with plants in every planting area	Not done
Pest control		Insect-killing agents are used to combat the shoot borer (broca)	Pests and diseases are not combatted. In a few cases, chemical insecticides are used.
Replanting	Nursery production	150 to 200 plants are produced annually.	Nurseries are not used.
	Replanting	Holes 40 cm deep are dug and filled with organic fertilizer.	Shallow holes are dug.

(continues)

Table 20.1. (*Continued*)

Activity		Organic Production	Conventional Production within the Program
Fertilization		Fertilizer is made using coffee residues, forest materials, and cow manure.	Not done. In exceptional cases chemical fertilizer is used.
Harvest	Picking	Fallen beans are not picked up, only ripe beans are picked.	All beans are picked without discrimination.
	Removal of bad beans	Done in all cases	Not done
Processing (*Beneficio húmedo*)	Depulping	Currently the machine is washed before depulping. It is well adjusted so as not to injure the bean. Beans are depulped the same day they are picked.	Cherries are accumulated over various days for a single depulping.
	Fermenting	Done in wooden or cement containers	Done in plastic bags or using *petates* (fiber mats)
	Cleaning	Done only with clean water	Frequently done using dirty water
	Drying	The patio is washed. The beans are not placed on hot patios. Gas dryers cannot be used.	Grains are dried in patios without precautions. On occasion, gas dryers, which transmit odors, are used.
Warehousing		The beans are warehoused separately, away from humidity.	The grains are warehoused regardless of placement.
Packaging		New sacks labeled by each producer are used.	Old and dirty sacks can be used.

The effects of traditional use of the land can be identified from the main activities of production carried out in the area, including clearing for agricultural exploitation or livestock production and exploitation of forested land for nontimber products and wildlife.

Clearing for Agricultural Exploitation

Subsistence Agriculture

As stated earlier, the technique used in subsistence agriculture—milpa farming—is that of slash-and-burn farming, which means that each family must cultivate several plots in a rotation lasting several years. Population growth and the establishment of new families create the necessity for a continuous expansion of the agricultural frontier, felling the tropical vegetation to establish milpas or shortening the rotation of plots by reducing the fallow period, which eventually also creates new pressures on the forest. Milpa production is of fundamental importance to the situation affecting natural resources in the area; 77% of cultivated land in the region is currently used for milpa plots.

Since the 1980s, federal and state authorities have attempted to prohibit the opening of new lands for cultivation, both by halting the parceling out of new agrarian reform units and by imposing sanctions upon those who clear the forest. Further, an agreement was made with the main peasant organizations in the Las Cañadas subregion so that the communities would not allow new clearings on their lands and would stop the accelerated process of colonization. The imposition of restrictions for the clearance of old-growth lands in the area of Las Margaritas—as well as in other areas of Las Cañadas subregion—has decreased the rate of forest colonization in these areas. However, the process is still occurring at a significant speed in other regions close to the Montes Azules Biosphere Reserve, by settlers who were not participants in the agreement.

The difficulty of getting access to new lands has meant that most of the producers in the program cultivate milpa only in *acahuales*, abandoned plots that have been recolonized by fast-growing pioneer species. If left uncultivated, natural succession of species would eventually return the *acahual* plots to the original forest communities. However, the data from this study indicate that at least some producers cleared new plots in primary forest during the last three years, as shown in Table 20.2. The same table shows that the magnitude of clearings has decreased as appropriate sites for cultivation have been depleted. As a result, the mean amount of land opened for cultivation dropped from 6 ha in the 1990s to a little more than 1 ha in the 1990s. The smaller area and extension of clearings made during the last years suggests that marginal sites with poor agricultural conditions have been opened and, as the number of families requiring land grows, human pressure upon the resources in the region is increasing.

Table 20.2. Number and mean area affected by clearings for milpa plots.

Decade	Number of clearings declared by the interviewed producers	Average area of each clearing (ha)
1950s	7	6.14
1960s	2	6.50
1970s	26	4.90
1980s	82	3.30
1990s	11	1.20

Another form of natural resource degradation associated with milpa farming comes from the traditional practice of burning off the vegetation prior to planting. This practice has caused uncontrolled fires for many years. Some memorable fires of great magnitude occurred during 1991. According to some accounts, numerous fires occurred in that year because the dry season was extended and the precautions normally taken to control burning were insufficient. Other accounts suggest that many fires resulted from the negligence of some farmers, identified by the local community. As a result of these acts of carelessness, entire communities were mobilized to fight fires that endured more than ten days; in many cases, efforts were unsuccessful, so the destruction ended only when the rainy season began. Although there is awareness among communities of the enormous losses the fires inflict on their patrimony, local people usually do not impose sanctions upon the responsible individuals. Between 1991 and 1992, entire mountain ranges were devastated in the zone of Las Margaritas; the extent of the destruction was so great that the area will require a minimum of 25 years to recover the original vegetation by natural succession.

Coffee Production

With the establishment of coffee farms, the original vegetation is also altered, either through a gradual process of replacing original trees by others more beneficial for the crops, or by the establishment of farms after practicing slash-and-burn clearing. Under the semi-intensive system carried out in the zone of Las Margaritas, only 10% of the exploited area is used for agricultural practices, even though this surface requires the largest amount of work. Because of the difficulties in establishing and maintaining farms, and the small amount of the territory they require, coffee production is not an important source of environmental disturbance. Furthermore, to some extent the plantation crop maintains a vegetation cover that allows the survival of some animal species. In fact, recent research has suggested that the environmental conditions created by small farmer coffee farms provide suitable habitat for migratory birds and other species.

Livestock Production

The clearing of forest for pasture has been the main cause of the elimination of the original vegetation in a significant portion of the Lacandón Forest. Unlike in other subregions, however, raising livestock has less importance in the program area. Pasturelands correspond to only 13% of the land area used by coffee producers and their families, and fewer than a third of the interviewed producers own animals. The production of yearling calves predominates in the study zone, with a mean number of 7.2 animals per herd. The usual exploitation of livestock consists of rearing calves slightly older than a year. This strategy of production requires producers to assume most of the risks while obtaining very low prices. This method of producing livestock requires extensive pastureland, so the consumption of natural resources per animal is high.

The extensive nature of the production is shown by the formation of herds and insufficient management of pastures. Herds include more breeding males (10 females:1 male) than the generally recommended ratio (20 females:1 male), resulting in an overuse of grazing grounds; these herds consume the largest amount of forage with the lowest productivity. Regarding the management of pasture grounds in the program area, most pastures have native grasses low in nutrients, which requires each animal to graze a larger land area. Table 20.3 shows the composition of these grasslands: 71% of the land area assigned to pasturing is covered by native grasses, 21% has Star of Africa grass

Table 20.3. Grasses used by interviewed families for cattle feed at the beginning of the program.

Type of grass	% of total pasture	Estimated area (ha)
Native species: *Cynodon dactylon, Paspalum orbiculatum*, among others	71	386
Star of Africa (*Cynodon plectostachyum*)	21	116
Other species, principally *Andropogon rufus, Panicum barbinoide,* and *Panicum maximum*	8	42

(an introduced species), and only 8% have other introduced grasses with greater productive potential.

Forest Exploitation

The physiographic conditions in the area where the organic coffee program is located allow the existence of very diverse plant communities. The different climatic and altitudinal conditions of the program area permit the occurrence of lowland and mid-elevation tropical forests, cloud forests, and coniferous forests. These variations occur along an elevational gradient: lowland sites have a warm, humid climate, replaced by an intermediate climate as altitude increases, with a temperate climate at the highest altitudes. A steep altitudinal gradient in short distances produces an overwhelming diversity of plants, resulting from the intermixing of species with northern temperate affinities at altitudes greater than 1,200 m above sea level and species with neotropical affinities at altitudes below 1,200 m above sea level. As mentioned before, a good part of the municipalities of Las Margaritas and La Independencia belong to the Las Cañadas subregion, which some studies have shown is the most complex and richest in species within the whole Lacandona region, even exceeding the Montes Azules Integral Biosphere Reserve.

Forest exploitation at Las Margaritas, as in Las Cañadas, has been less intense than in the rest of Selva Lacandóna, where massive commercial extractions have taken place. This reduced level of forest exploitation was due mainly to great difficulties in transportation. Current extraction practices are small-scale operations that primarily satisfy family needs for household construction materials, manufacture of furniture and fences, and fuel. Only a few species are used, so some—such as mahogany—have been virtually extirpated around villages. Table 20.4 lists the tree species favored by the interviewed communities. No locality has official permits for the commercial extraction of wood, and, according to available information, they have not made any effort to obtain them.

Access to forest resources is not entirely unrestricted. Each family may use those trees inside its property, and if they do not have enough trees, they must ask permission from the local assembly to cut extra trees from community land. Study data indicate that although there is no formal market for timber in the communities, some producers occasionally cut trees to sell for sawn-wood boards, and some others owning chainsaws regularly offer their services for additional income.

Although the Las Margaritas area has not been affected by the large-scale logging seen in other subregions, this fact does not mean that their different forest types are well conserved. On the contrary, during the last decade this region was one of the most greatly damaged areas, losing a large forest area con-

Table 20.4. Main tree species used by the interviewed communities.

Wood for construction	Fuel wood	Wood for furniture manufacture
Canalté (n.i.)	Mahogany (*Swietenia macrophylla*)	Canalté (n.i.)
Cork tree (possibly *Guatteria anomala*)	Cedar (*Cedrela mexicana*)	Chalum (*Inga* spp.)
Zatam (n.i.)	Hormiguillo (*Dalberiga tucurensis* or *Platymiscium dimorphandrum*)	Zatam (n.i.)
Cosanté (*Bernoullia flammea*)	Huanacastle (*Schizolobium parahybum*)	Chacalté (*Sweetia panamensis*)
Mahogany (*Swietenia macrophylla*)	Lengua de vaca (*Cornutia grandifolia*)	
Lengua de vaca (*Cornutia grandifolia*)		
Huanacastle (*Schizolobium parahybum*)		
Palo rayado (probably *Dalbergia granadillo*)		
Pine (*Pinus* spp.)		

n.i. = not identified

sisting mainly of tropical forests to the advance of the agricultural frontier and to fires, as mentioned. Thus, although a government logging ban was established for the entire forest in 1989 in an attempt to halt the destruction of resources, the government's action has had little positive effect in conserving the forests of the program area, as well as those in the rest of Las Cañadas.

The reason that the ban is not an effective policy for forest conservation in areas such as Las Margaritas is because it can only influence the commercial extractions of timber. Because the principal resource of interest to the communities is not the timber but the land itself—either the nutrient-rich substrate of freshly cleared forest soil that is optimal for milpa farming, or the open space required to establish farms or pastures—there is no way to prohibit tree cutting without affecting the subsistence of families. Therefore, any attempt to impose sanctions upon clearing inside territories already granted to the communities has been strongly resisted. Since 1994, when the uprising of the Zapatista Army of National Liberation (EZLN) caused the agricultural au-

thorities to abandon the program area and in some cases weakened the influence of local authorities, clearings have increased significantly.

Nontimber Products

Families turn to the forest occasionally to obtain products other than wood,
especially wild food (berries, leaves, stems, and tubers) as well as fibers and
temporary posts. Most of the interviewed families take advantage of these
types of resources, as indicated by the 92% of individuals who stated that they
use wild plants both to feed farm animals and to supplement their own diet.
The common names of the most used plants are shown in Table 20.5. By comparison, a larger proportion of useful species are found in the lowland tropical
communities than in the highland transitional and temperate communities.
This disparity is likely due to the greater diversity of the tropical forests. In all
communities, the most frequently reported plants are those used as vegetables
(*hierba mora, shiv, hierba dulce,* and *momón*); wild berries, fibers, posts, and
medicinal plants are used less frequently. The frequency distributions suggest
that families resort to the protected forest to collect fruits and medicinal
plants less frequently than has been believed because they probably have
enough products in their orchards and groves nearby.

Exploitation of Fauna

Forest animals constitute an additional resource, one that is particularly important in places where animal populations have not been greatly disturbed
by human settlement. The habitat of the Lacandón Forest harbors one of the
most diverse communities of invertebrates, birds, and terrestrial mammals per
unit of area in the whole country. Nevertheless, the antiquity of settlements
in the study area combined with the intense pressure upon natural resources
produced by a high human population has caused the local extinction of several animal populations. Hunting and fishing constitute two of the most important sources of animal protein, so almost all species extant in the forests
and acahuales are used.

The first species to disappear were those most sensitive to human disturbance, including tapirs, monkeys, and jaguars. Other, more resistant species
have endured until the present, such as peccary, pumas, and crocodiles, which
are hunted in lowland communities of the program that are closer to undisturbed areas. In recent years, large animals have almost disappeared. Only the
most resistant species, such as the tepescuintle (*Agouti paca*), white tail deer
(*Odocoileus virginiana*), armadillo (*Tatusia novemcincta*), squirrels (*Sciurus*
spp.), and various birds, are still used; their populations have increased due to
the removal of their main predators, In fact, when a big predator such as a

Table 20.5. Forest plants used by the interviewed communities (frequencies).

Lowland* (196 informants)		Highland** (123 informants)	
Name	Frequency	Name	Frequency
Hierba mora (*Solanum nigrum*)	54	Hierba mora (*Solanum nigrum*)	41
Pacaya (*Chamaedorea aguilariana*)	44	Pacaya (*Chamaedorea aguilariana*)	24
Shiv or chapaya (*Astrocayum mexicanum*)	54	Shiv or chapaya (*Astrocayum mexicanum*)	19
Hierba dulce (*Lippia dulcis*)	13	Momón (*Piper sanctum*)	13
Momón (*Piper sanctum*)	12	Bushnay (*Spathiphyllum friedrishthali*)	7
Zapote (1) (*Achras zapota*)	7	Culish (n.i.)	5
Zapote (2) (*A. zapota*) and (*Diospyros blepharophylla*)	4	Tzul (*Bauhinia divaricata*)	4
Palmito (*Chamaedorea* spp)	6	Xoma (*Govania lupuloides*)	3
Paterna (*Inga paterno*)	4		
Cuxuxito (n.i.)	4		
Quina (*Coutarea latiflora*)	3		
Uva cimarrona (*Vitis tilifolia*)	3		
Xoma (*Govania lupuloides*)	3		

Notes: *Twenty-one other plants were recorded but excluded from the table because the frequency was less than 3. ** Ten other plants were recorded but excluded from the table because the frequency was less than 3. (1) Plants named by informants were securely identified as *A. zapota*. (2) Plants named by informants could be either of the two species named. n.i. = not identified.

jaguar enters the area, local people have an incentive to kill it, as it competes with them for prey.

Undoubtedly, wild animals represent one of the most important elements in the families' diet. More intense use of animal resources is made in lowland communities and those close to unlogged areas. According to current information, hunting and fishing are not regulated by the communities, so each individual may hunt any species during any time of the year without restraint. This situation has caused some animals with high market value, such as peccary, monkeys, and parrots, to be increasingly rare. As a result, it would be highly beneficial for the communities themselves to establish minimum regulations to control exploitation and ensure that the resources are not depleted.

Fishing is another source of animal protein in the families' diets, particularly in the lowland communities, which have greater access to rivers and lakes (although in some areas, fishing is seasonal, taking place primarily during the rainy season). In addition to fish, frequent consumption of turtles, snails, and crabs could be verified in villages close to rivers and lakes, although the proportion of these items consumed could not be estimated.

Influence of the Organic Coffee Program on the Conservation of Natural Resources

As stated earlier, it is very difficult to carry out conservation efforts under conditions of high demographic pressure. In lowland tropical zones, conservation of resources is particularly difficult as a result of the impact of migratory agriculture and hunting on the subsistence economy. For this reason, there is strong pressure to expand the agricultural border. Even in mountainous areas, where vegetation is intact because the land cannot support agricultural production, only a few of the most resistant animal species can survive alongside the human population. In this context, the organic production program has opportunities to contribute, in theory at least, to the conservation of natural resources. First, organic production results in a more intensive use of the family work force, up to 92% more labor than traditional production. This additional use of family labor can be recognized and paid by the market through the premium paid to organic coffee, especially in the solidarity markets. As well, the more intensive use of family labor may reduce pressures to expand the agricultural frontier. If they prove successful, organic techniques may be applied to other crops, particularly corn and bean farming, and may raise their productivity, thus reducing the need for milpa clearing. Unfortunately, even when these techniques work on behalf of conservation, the size of the program area is still too small to have an appreciable influence on the rest of the region. As well, the notion that organic production works on behalf of natural resource conservation is based on the assumption that these products will command a higher price in the market. Obtaining such high prices is not an easy task, because the price of any product depends on market conditions. Even if the identification of a high revenue product is possible—for instance, as occurred with rubber during some periods—this business opportunity is likely to disappear over time due to either a larger number of producers or the development of alternative products, which will cause the prices received by producers to decrease. In the case of organic products, the disappearance of premiums paid to producers would discourage dramatically the continuation of organic practices.

But even the current market premium is insufficient. The experience of the La Selva organic coffee program shows that the premium obtained has not completely compensated for production costs. This has been particularly true when traditional coffee prices go up, meaning that the amount of the premium declines in relative terms. For example, during the period of the program the price of organic coffee over traditional coffee declined to as little as 5%, during a period of very high prices. In these cases, the organization has had to invest a lot of time convincing producers to keep practicing in organic methods. One of the principal arguments for continuing is that even if organic production does not currently result in much higher prices, the price of organic will resist falls in the market more readily, giving some protection against market fluctuations. It will also be necessary to search for consumers or donors who are willing to pay for the positive externalities of organic production: soil retention, uncontaminated watersheds, and migratory bird habitat, among other benefits.

Principal Conservation Measures Promoted by the Program

As mentioned above, the conservation effects of organic coffee production are several. First, it ends the use of chemical products. In their place, materials from the environment are used for fertilization, and mechanical practices and biological agents are used to control pests and diseases. Second, the program has helped to install small-scale terraces and other structures to enhance the formation and conservation of soil. Third, the program conserves and increases existing vegetational cover, both herbaceous ground covers that protect the soils and trees that provide shade for the crops. Fourth, the program sponsors educational campaigns among producers to control hunting and prevent the local extinction of some animal species. Fifth, the program extends organic techniques to other crops, such as corn, beans, and other vegetables. Sixth, the program educates farmers on the advantages of not burning, a message that has been particularly absorbed by the community of Maravilla Tenejapa.

Other positive results from organic practices are evident in the farms. All producers have observed improvements in the foliage and size of plants, as well as in the amount and quality of fruits. Evident changes in the richness of soil organic matter can also be appreciated. This demonstrable improvement in the plants has had a powerful effect, convincing many producers—initially reluctant to participate in the program—to register. However, natural resource conservation and recuperation have not been as effective outside the farms. Efforts to control hunting have not produced good results because this activity is still fundamental to family subsistence. Nor have many significant advances been made outside of the program in halting the practice of burning land for milpa farming, because it so deeply rooted in tradition. Further, program outcomes were limited by the EZLN uprising in the region. This conflict has isolated many communities since 1994; during this time, many demonstration plots were lost, and producers were not in any condition to change their production techniques.

In matters of resource conservation, the impact of the program depends also on what is meant by "organic" production. For some agencies, certification is limited to assuring that consumers receive a product free of chemical contaminants, with no broader measures of environmental conservation considered. Other agencies have a wider scope, requiring the incorporation of specific soil conservation and reforestation practices, to ensure that the consumers receive a product that also promotes general environmental improvement. Although the last approach may enhance conservation, the current lower price for organic coffee means that producers must shoulder the increasingly onerous costs of these conservation practices, increasing their percentage of unpaid family labor. As a consequence, their level of well-being and their incentive to continue with organic production declines. This situation raises again the question of who pays the costs of conservation: the inhabitants of tropical forests or foreign consumers. Also, this situation suggests the existence of some limits to the long-term sustainability of organic coffee production.

Some Lessons Learned from the Program of Organic Coffee Production

Despite the shortcomings and problems discussed above, the initial analysis of La Selva's program of organic coffee production can be judged successful both in technical terms—given the rapid pace with which the transition to organic took place—and in managerial terms, given the success in marketing the product and the rapid growth in international markets. The strong technical and commercial performances were partly due to the fact that La Selva and the other ejido unions had their own technical staffs, giving them autonomy in this area. Although the grassroots organizations participating in the program are still maturing, important project results can be recognized. Thus, it is interesting to point out some of the lessons they themselves draw from the conception, promotion, and execution of the program.

The main lesson is that natural resource conservation is most clearly attained in the coffee-growing areas themselves because here producers receive tangible economic benefits. In milpa and livestock production areas, it will be difficult for families to carry out conservation efforts without being rewarded by the market. Nonetheless, the dissemination of organic production techniques in the program area is an important first step toward a more rational and sustained use of existing resources.

Another important lesson of the program is that initiatives like this must be undertaken as part of a global strategy to use existing grassroots organizations to improve the positioning and increase the quality of organic products in the markets. It was also necessary for the ejido unions to consolidate themselves organizationally before they could begin implementing the program, which points out the necessity for any conservation and development program to begin by building and strengthening grassroots organizations. Furthermore, the project was influenced by other organizations who were the pioneers in Mexico in the production of organic coffee, such as the Union of Indigeous Communities of the Isthmus Region (UCIRI) and Indigenous Peoples of the Sierra Madre of Motozintla (ISMAM). Since La Selva could study their experiences, the cost of learning decreased significantly, in both technical and commercial terms. The project was also able to take advantage of traditional community structures (for example, producers' committees), that were used as the basis for training community members to become paraprofessional agronomists. Based on a "farmer-to-farmer" methodology, the training allowed for the ejido members to be instructed primarily by their community peers. However, decisions about production and marketing were made with the support of professional staff. They were able to suggest and implement the system of strict quality control of collected coffee, aided by the development of a computerized bar code system supported by foreign funders, and the pursuit of clear and credible policies of purchasing member's crops and export. Thus, particular market prices and technical assistance for members are announced only when they are securely attainable. At the same time, the organizations' market credibility in terms of quality and organic production must be maintained at any cost.

Participation in the program must be voluntary, without religious or social restrictions or pressure. This implies that no producer can be forced to register, and resources are not granted merely as an incentive to join. The principle used is that members obtain benefits only as they invest time in working, and a high standard is used to evaluate their performance. Financial support is crucial during the beginning of the organic production program. In particular, a market premium for this grade of coffee must be assured. At the same time, it must be taken into account that certifying agencies can be very stringent during the first cycle of production, limiting immediate sales. Participating farmers must be provided some form of subsidy during this initial period, or they may be forced to abandon it.

Chapter 21

The Bio-Itzá Reserve: History of an Indigenous Effort to Conserve the Maya Itzá Community of San José, El Petén, Guatemala

Reginaldo Chayax Huex, Feliciano Tzul Colli,
Carlos Gomez Caal, and Steven P. Gretzinger

We the Itzá, the last descendants of the Maya lineage in the Petén forest, are watching the forest vanish, its herbs and trees, the animals of its land and water. Our Mayan language is disappearing too, and the traditions of our great fathers. The forest is dying, the animals are dying, and we are dying also. To live, we need the forest, and the forest needs us. We must take care of the forest, and the forest must care for us, because we are partners of the jaguar, owner of the forest; partners of the scarlet macaw, ornament of the Mayas; partners of the tapir, animal of seven skins; partners of the mahogany, tree of our canoes; partners of the ramón tree, the food of our ancestors; partners of the smoke of the copal tree, the spirit of our great ancestors. United together, we make our home in a piece of jungle, land of the Maya Itzás, on the shore of the great Lake Itzá in San José, where once lived Kan Ek, the last Maya king.

In 1697, prior to the Spanish conquest of the Itzá Empire, at least eight villages were located on the northern and eastern shores of Lake Petén Itzá (see Map 1 in Introduction to this volume). Among these villages, governed by the lord Cobox, were communities called Chuc, Okot, Tibox, Calagua, Acheetz, Chetin, Xatencuh, and Ixpetén (Means 1917; Villagutierre Soto-Mayor 1983). The communities were dominated by the Itzá, a culture of non-Maya origin that had moved south from what is now Yucatán, Mexico, to modern-day El Petén, Guatemala, where they mixed with indigenous Maya groups, adapting many traits of the people among whom they settled. Today, these villages have either vanished or been transformed; inhabitants either abandoned them during the years of strife against the conquistadors, or the villages were changed to suit the needs of the Spanish. For example, Schwartz (1990) proposes that the municipality of San José may be an old pre-conquest village. Although little documentation exists, San José appears to have been officially founded by the Catholic monks, the lords Martin de Urzua and Arismendi, after 1697. It is impossible to determine the original name of the town of San José, as the early monks changed the name upon their arrival. San José was only formally recognized by governmental decree in 1851, but it may have ancient roots.

The Petén as a whole is a very different place than in the time before the conquest, and it is still changing due to population growth and immigration. According to the National Institute of Statistics (INE), 2,567 inhabitants were counted in the San José Municipality during the Tenth National Population Census conducted in 1995 (CIEDES 1995). Although population increases in the town of San José per se are low, population growth in the neighboring community of Nuevo San José has been dramatic. The entry of immigrants from areas outside of the Petén has had negative impacts on the forest resource (Atran 1993). Besides traditional agriculture, the native inhabitants of San José commonly use nontimber forest products such as *Chamaedorea* sp. (xate), *Pimienta dioica* (allspice), and latex from the *Manilkara zapota* tree (chicozapote) as sources of income and subsistence (Cowgill 1961; Schwartz 1990). Moreover, San José has more than ten carpenters who produce furniture for local use and for the central area of the Petén department. For local people, the forest is a source of natural resources that contribute significantly to their livelihood. In contrast, most of the immigrants do not view the forest as a source of income, but rather as an obstacle that must be eliminated to promote agriculture and livestock production (Palma 1995).

Formation of the Bio-Itzá Committee

During the late 1980s, residents of San José began witnessing an increase in the destruction of municipal forests by loggers from outside the community. An increasing number of new immigrants from other parts of Guatemala contributed to continued deforestation (Schwartz 1990). In response to these threats, San José residents decided to organize a nonprofit committee to conserve a small area of relatively untouched forest remaining in the municipal lands. The idea to establish this private reserve came from an article published in the local newspaper stating that the Guatemalan Protected Areas Law (Decree 4-89) allowed the formation of such areas by town governments and their residents.

Soon afterward, the residents of San José welcomed into their midst foreign scientists who would aid in their efforts. In 1990, Dr. Scott Atran, a linguist from the University of Michigan, arrived at San José to learn the Maya Itzá language. During this time, Dr. Atran became familiar with the threats facing the forests of San José. To provide the community with a better orientation on how to avoid further destruction, Dr. Atran invited other professionals to visit the community. In 1991, an Austrian botanist, Richard Fritsch, arrived to study the ethnobotanical uses of the local vegetation. As part of his research, Fritsch was introduced to a large area of primary forest that was considered deserving of special protection. During the same year, a local effort called the Project to Rescue the Maya Itzá Language (PRIMI) was created to develop educational materials and promote bilingual teaching. A novel aspect of this project was that elderly Maya were paid to teach younger people how to speak and write the Maya Itzá language. Also in 1991, Dr. Anthony Stocks, formerly of the nonprofit organization Cultural Survival, came to meet the Maya Itzá. A meeting was organized to propose to Sr. Graviel Oliva, the town mayor, that the town establish a protected zone on municipal lands. The major orally agreed and suggested the creation of a voluntary committee of interested people to write a background document that would describe the purpose of the reserve.

On November 28, 1991, committee members of the Itzá Biosphere Project were legally nominated. As residents of the region, they felt it was their duty to defend the natural resources and protect the fauna and flora in danger of extinction. The San José Board of Directors, the town mayor and his advisory board, and members of the recently formed committee all signed an official proclamation to this effect, duly noted in the San José book of acts (Number 16, Folio 307, Act 45-91). The committee is currently composed of 55 heads of families in San José. The committee is directed and represented by a president and vice president (Reginaldo Chayax Huex and Feliciano Tzul Colli, respectively). Committee decisions are made during meetings of the board of directors. Representatives of the committee are elected or reelected every two years during a meeting with all the members.

Establishment of the Bio-Itzá Reserve

Upon legalization of the aforementioned committee, a proceeding was initiated to obtain a concession allowing the exclusive use of the reserve for conservation purposes. Initially, some community members thought that the foreign advisors were making a secret business deal to gain access to the municipal lands. Public discussions explained to the general populace that the only purpose for the reserve was to benefit the local community.

The main objective of the Bio-Itzá Reserve is to conserve and defend the remaining primary forest of the Maya Itzá in the San José community as the heritage left by their Maya ancestors and necessary for the community's continued existence within the forest. An important aspect of this goal is to conserve the culture and language of the Itzá, who are among the last native inhabitants of the Petén's forests, because the Itzá possess a thousand-year-old tradition of forest management, agriculture, and hunting.

After surveying the proposed forest reserve and carrying out a series of somewhat tedious bureaucratic proceedings, a 50-year lease was signed that granted exclusive access to 3,600 ha of forest to the local committee (CATIE 1995). The Bio-Itzá Reserve is on municipal property approximately 24 km from the town of San José, a location chosen to prevent the reserve from overlapping with any adjacent community's property. The entire area is located within the buffer zone of the Maya Biosphere Reserve (CATIE 1995) and is bordered by the Biotopo El Zotz protected area to the north, the municipality of Flores to the east, and other municipal lands to the south and west. The physical limits of the reserve were established in 1993 with assistance from The Nature Conservancy and CONAP, Guatemala's park management agency.

Characteristics of the Bio-Itzá Reserve

The general area of the reserve is characterized by a hot climate with a mean annual temperature of 23.9 C and rainfall of 1,324 mm. The period with the lowest amount of precipitation occurs between February and May; the *canicula* (a short period of wet-season drought) occurs in July or August. No permanent water sources or rivers are found within the zone (Guillen et al. 1993). Two distinct forest types can be clearly recognized in the Bio-Itzá Reserve. Approximately 290 ha of the reserve consists of lowland forest dominated by the corozo palm (*Orbignya cohune*). The rest of the reserve (3,310 ha) is a relatively homogenous forest, two-thirds of which were selectively logged in 1979 for mahogany (*Swietenia macrophylla*) and Spanish cedar (*Cedrela odorata*). In 1981, a portion of the area was burned and in 1989, another logging operation extracted canxán (*Terminalia amazonia*), and Santa Maria (*Calophyllum brasiliense*), as well as more cedar and mahogany (Stanley and Gretzinger 1996). Aside from these timber species, the reserve harbors most of the plant species common to the warm and humid climate in the Petén region (Lundell 1937).

The diverse vegetation is used by the Maya Itzás for medicine, ornamentation, construction, artisanry, and the like (Atran 1993). Some of the plants most commonly used by the Maya Itzás include the species listed in Table 21.1. There is also a large number of animal species that make the reserve their home; however, uncontrolled hunting as well as the destruction of natural habitat has caused a reduction in the number of these animals, which look for shelter in areas with ample food and few predators. The animal species most commonly used or affected by the Maya Itzá are listed in Table 21.2.

Table 21.1. Tree species found in the Bio-Itzá Reserve commonly used by the Itzá.

Common name	Maya name	Scientific name
Cedar or cedro	K'uch'e	*Cedrela* spp.
Mahogany or caoba	Ch'kilte'	*Swietenia macrophylla* King
Malerio or mylady	Zuxuyux	*Aspidosperma megalocarpon*
Pimienta or allspice	Navakuk	*Pimenta dioica*
Siricote	Ko'te	*Cordia dodecandra*
Hormigo	Chpax	*Platymischium dimorphandrum*
Guaya	Guayum	*Talisia olivaeformis*
Guarumo or trumpet tree	Xicooch	*Cecropia peltata*
Majagua	Kampak	*Mortoniodendron* sp.
Huano or botan palm	Xa'an	*Sabal* sp.
Nargusta	Canx·n	*Terminalia amazonia*

Table 21.2. Animal and bird species found in the Bio-Itzá Reserve commonly used by the Itzá.

Common name	Maya name	Scientific name
Tepezcuintle, paca, or gibnut	Jale'	*Agouti paca*
Deer	Kej	*Odocoileus virginianus*
Coche de monte	Kitann	*Tayassu tajacu*
Jaguar or tigre	B'alam	*Felis onca*
Pheasant	K'ambul	*Crax rubra*
Cojolita	K'ox	*Penelope purputarances*
Parrot	Tu'ut'	*Amazona* sp.
White turtle	A'ak	*Dermatemys mawei*
Rattlesnake	Zab'	*Crotalus durissus*
Petén turkey	Kutz itza	*Porphyrula martirica*

Achievements of the Bio-Itzá Committee

Once the committee and the reserve had been officially established in 1992, a question was raised: How could people from the community maintain vigilance over the reserve? Given its distant location and large size, the most practical protection strategy was to hire local citizens to work as park rangers within the reserve. Dr. Atran helped the committee write a proposal that was funded by Cultural Survival to cover the living expenses of the first four park rangers. These rangers were selected from villagers who had shown the most initiative and spirit by working without compensation during the reserve's initial development. A jungle camp called Limón was established as a base for the park guards to initiate control activities. Their presence stopped the arrival of landless immigrants, who were already destroying the surrounding forest, essentially rescuing the reserve from imminent deforestation. Furthermore, two local sawmills had obtained municipal permits for timber extraction in the reserve. These permits were later rescinded through the efforts of the Bio-Itzá committee with assistance provided by employees of the U.S. Agency for International Development (USAID in Guatemala).

Subsequent funding for the reserve from the Austrian government allowed the continuation of patrols by park guards through 1995. By this point, the number of rangers had doubled from four to eight. The park guards and volunteers from the community carried out long working days under harsh conditions to fulfill the basic protection and management tasks in the reserve, such as constructing by hand 16 km of trails inside the reserve. Several nongovernmental organizations also have supported the committee's efforts to preserve the community's natural resources. The Centro Agronomico Tropical de Enseñanza e Investigación (CATIE), a Central American University in Costa Rica, began working jointly with the Bio-Itzá Committee in 1992 to provide technical advice on community forest management. CATIE has attempted to combine the local knowledge of the Maya Itzás with the technical criteria of biologists and managers to develop an appropriate resource management system. Several activities have been completed, including a forest inventory, low-impact timber harvesting, visits to neighboring countries and other community-managed forests for educational purposes, field visits in the reserve for the whole community, public meetings to decide the course of management, and creation of a forest management plan (CATIE 1995).

Ecotourism is considered an appropriate complement to the reserve's goals. The Maya Itzás are becoming increasingly active in this area as a way to obtain additional income while protecting the forest. Two conservation organizations, The Nature Conservancy and ProPetén, have aided the community in this area (Beavers 1995). Anticipating tourist development in the reserve, the committee recently completed the construction of two rustic dormitories, built large enough to lodge up to 12 visitors, and a kitchen. The camp will be managed by the committee; though the facilities are spartan, a basic level of comfort will be provided to those interested in learning how to live harmoniously with the forest. Simultaneously, information about culture, history, ethnobotany, ethnozoology, natural medicine, and traditional Maya religion is being gathered and taught to visitors. Groups from several different countries have already been hosted by the committee.

An international conservation organization called "Eco-Logic" and the University of Michigan have promoted the protection and development of archaeological sites, as well as the initiation of cultural, linguistic, and ethno-botanical projects. Eco-Logic funded the restoration of the Guineo archaeo-logical site, composed of five large mounds forming a square, and trail con-struction. Up to the present, the committee has not received technical assistance for the management of nontimber forest products, but such projects are certainly possible in the near future.

All of these changes have not been entirely without problems. It is inter-esting to note that some NGOs were rejected by the residents of San José be-cause residents' autonomy, knowledge, and traditions were not respected dur-ing the project design. In fact, residents suspected that representatives of some NGOs may have intended to deceive members of the Bio-Itzá committee. On one occasion, a foreign technical advisor attempted to obstruct the activities of another NGO in the community, with the purpose of exploiting the situa-tion for his particular benefit. This individual isolated and dominated the committee by writing proposals in his own language—one that the commit-tee members did not understand. The advisor even attempted to block com-munication between the committee and other people. When the committee finally realized that the foreign advisor was mismanaging funds destined for the reserve, they spoke directly with the funding source and forced the indi-vidual to leave the community. Although this experience was a bitter one in-deed, it matured the committee and taught community members to defend their own interests.

Problems Affecting the Future of the Bio-Itzá Reserve

A major problem for the reserve has been the lack of moral and economic re-solve by the municipal mayor's office with respect to the need to protect the reserve and save the Maya Itzá language. There are continuous internal power struggles among different community members, and the reserve's future is therefore far from secure. It is ironic that within five years after the reserve was established many of the external threats have been reduced, but internal management and political issues still pose a great danger to the biological legacy left by the ancestors of the modern-day Maya Itzá people.

One particularly difficult issue is the confusing legal status of the land own-ership. Although the reserve was granted to the committee in usufruct for a 50- year period starting in 1991, the agreement was contingent upon the pay-ment of an annual fee. This fee was paid only in the first year. Lack of funds has prevented subsequent payments, thus putting in question the right of the committee to manage the reserve.

The existence of only one dirt road from San José to the Bio-Itzá becomes an obstacle during the rainy season when it floods and restricts access. This road is necessary to patrol the reserve because other communities continue to extract forest resources from within the reserve or own agricultural lands ad-

jacent to it. Adjoining agricultural fields can be a problem for the reserve because the common practice of slash-and-burn agriculture commonly causes
forest fires in Petén forests, and has been responsible for several fires within
the reserve.

Finally, the reserve is threatened by the fact that the Bio-Itzá committee
does not have sufficient capital to buy basic equipment or maintain qualified
personnel to carry out management and protection tasks. Maintaining park
rangers to patrol the area regularly is essential for the reasons stated earlier,
but patrol activities should be complemented by educational activities among
neighboring communities. Other activities that must be carried out in the
near future are the construction of watering stations for both native fauna and
outside visitors, and electrical energy generation to improve living conditions
for park rangers and visitors. The committee would like to construct a low-
cost, solar-power system that does not generate contaminants. Finally, the
transportation of people and materials from the municipal capital of San José
to the working area (24 km) is a major difficulty. Because this area is uninhabited, there is no public transportation, and a four-wheel-drive pickup truck
is required.

Conclusion

To date, the Bio-Itzá committee has been dedicated mainly to the basic protection of the forested area, with an increasing involvement in management
activities, revolving around forestry, bee keeping, and ecotourism. The committee's achievements are impressive and have been obtained with minimal
and variable outside technical and financial assistance. These achievements
include acquiring a long-term concession for the exclusive use of 6 km^2 inside
the reserve for conservation purposes coordinated by a local committee; reforestation of old skid trails using native tree species such as siricote, Spanish
cedar, and mahogany; construction of basic buildings and trails; completion of
a forest inventory and management plan; hiring and training of a staff of local
park rangers; successful use of community volunteers to perform management
tasks; and construction of a committee office in the San José area. The project has also raised funds from supporting organizations, including several
major nongovernmental conservation foundations.

The conservation strategy adopted in the Bio-Itzá Reserve should guarantee the existence of a special area that protects the primary forest structure
and biodiversity of a classic Petén forest type. This forest will provide the indigenous community with not only the intrinsic functions of a natural forest
but also an opportunity to continue harvesting traditional products. However,
increased community involvement in reserve management and extension regarding the reserve's objectives are necessary to resolve some of the internal
issues that currently threaten the future of the Bio-Itzá. Well-intentioned in-

ternational support would be useful in helping the process along, but without the interest, involvement, and resolution of the San José community, this grassroots effort cannot be expected to withstand the tremendous pressures it faces.

References

Atran, S. 1993. Itzá Maya tropical agro-forestry. *Current Anthropology* 34: 633–789.

Beavers, J. 1995. *Community-Based Ecotourism in the Maya Forest: Six Case Studies from Communities in Mexico, Guatemala, and Belize.* The Nature Conservancy, Flores, Guatemala.

Centro Agronómico Tropical de Investigación y Ensenanza (CATIE). 1995. *Plan de Manejo Forestal Integrado de la Reserva Bio-Itzá, San José, El Petén.* Proyecto CATIE/CONAP, Flores, Guatemala.

CIEDES. 1995. *Apoyo al Desarrollo y Manejo Sostenible de la Reserva de la Biósfera Itzá, Municipio de San José, Petén.* MAGA, Santa Elena, Guatemala.

Cowgill, U. M. 1961. Soil fertility and the early Maya. *Transactions of the Connecticut Academy of Arts and Sciences,* Vol. 42. New Haven, Conn.

Guillen, A., C. Goméz, C. Flores, C. Matus, M. A. Manzanero, y O. Navas. 1993. Propuesta de Plan de Manejo de Bosques de la Reserva Bio-Itzá, San José, Petén, Guatemala. Paper presented at the Workshop for the 6th International Intensive Course of Silviculture and Management of Natural Tropical Forests. CATIE, Turrialba, Costa Rica.

Lundell, C. L. 1937. *The Vegetation of Petén.* Publication No. 478 of the Carnegie Institute, Washington, D.C.

Means, P. A. 1917. *History of the Spanish Conquest of Yucatán and the Itzás.* Peabody Museum of Archaeology and Ethnology of Harvard University Occasional Papers, No. 7, 142. Harvard University Press, Cambridge, Mass.

Palma, E. 1995. *El Manejo Forestal Comunitario en la Selva Maya-Version Campesina.* CATIE, Turrialba, Costa Rica.

Schwartz, N. B. 1990. *Forest Society: A Social History of Petén, Guatemala.* University of Pennsylvania Press, Philadelphia.

Stanley, S. A., and S. Gretzinger. 1996. Timber management of forest patches in Guatemala. Pages 343–365 in *Forest Patches in Tropical Landscapes,* J. Schelhas and R. Greenberg, eds. Island Press, Washington, D.C.

Villagutierre Soto-Mayor, J. 1983. *History of the Conquest of the Province of the Itzá.* Translated by R. D. Wood, with notes by F. E. Comparato. Labyrintos Publishers, Culver City, Calif.

Chapter 22

Community-Based Ecotourism in the Maya Forest: Problems and Potentials

Ruth Norris, J. Scott Wilber,
and Luís Oswaldo Morales Marín

The Maya Forest is the largest block of humid, subtropical forest remaining in Central America. Rich in both natural and cultural resources, it is nonetheless no different from any other large natural area in the tropics in one respect: considerable pressures exist from both local people and outside economic interests to exploit the region's natural wealth. Poorly controlled, unsustainable use of the natural resource base, especially the extraction of mahogany and cedar, has done much to degrade the standing forest. With its perceived value diminished, the forest has been viewed as nothing more than a hindrance to agriculture and ranching that completes its conversion. Slash-and-burn agriculture and unsustainable extraction of forest products are two of the few means of survival for many of the region's residents. Pressure on forest areas is compounded by an ongoing influx of people from other parts of Central America into the region looking for land and opportunities that the natural resource base may offer. The lack of economic alternatives and insufficient support for basic human needs, such as in health and education, contribute to the instability of the lives of the inhabitants of the region. Under this situation, many residents have no time to consider the long-term use of their natural resources when they have to use them immediately to ensure their daily survival.

Governments and nongovernmental organizations (NGOs) have emphasized development of protected areas as a standard conservation measure. As shown in Map 1 (see Introduction to this volume), an unusual abundance of parks and reserves exists in the Maya Forest region. Within these reserves, governments have restricted logging and other economic activities to guarantee the survival of fragile and unique ecosystems. This practice has created a debate on how to conserve nature while allowing local residents to use the natural resource base at the same time. Conflicts, unauthorized farming and logging, and the inability to successfully manage and police parks have demonstrated that the needs of local populations must be taken into consideration in order to protect natural areas. Clearly, conservation is not possible without development—yet development that is not approached with a strongly conservationist ethic will almost certainly destroy the forest resources.

How, then, can development and conservation be intertwined? Economic alternatives that increase the value of standing forests—such as natural forest management, which provides for the sustainable production of wood and nonwood products, microenterprise development, agroforestry, and ecotourism—are supported in various communities by NGOs and government projects. These sources of income combined with traditional economic activities may help to maintain an equilibrium between humans and nature. However, the communities must be actively involved in these enterprises if they are to succeed. Key steps include the following: assure that communities and their leaders actively participate in programs and realize economic benefits; develop environmental education programs to reinforce the linkage between conservation and development; and integrate programs to complement one another and generate the greatest economic benefits while conserving natural resources. These integrated programs must be promoted by the most charismatic members of each community, who will continue to involve their communities in a resource-conserving overall development strategy.

Background: The Maya Forest

The Maya Forest has been occupied by humans for millennia. Ancient Maya cities dating as far back as 1200 B.C.E. are found throughout the forest. Those dating to the Classic Period, ca. 200 B.C.E. to ca. A.D. 900, testify to an astonishing density of human population—by some estimates, almost 4 million people at the height of Classic Maya civilization (Culbert 1973). Maya ruins represent one of the primary attractions for tourists visiting the region. They also may represent an ominous warning to modern residents, as some experts have speculated that overintensive use of natural resources in the region led to famine, warfare, and ultimately the disintegration of Classic Maya civilization (Culbert 1973). Though the modern population of the Maya Forest is nowhere near as large as the ancient population at its height, twentieth-century technology permits a much more rapid and thorough extraction of resources, which means that conversion and degradation of the Maya Forest is occurring far more rapidly than in ancient times. The biological and cultural richness of the Maya Forest is threatened by a variety of forces, including but not limited to the conversion of forests to agriculture; the plundering of archaeological sites; legal and illegal trade in wildlife, wildlife products, and cultural artifacts; logging; and extraction of other renewable and nonrenewable resources, including oil and mineral wealth.

The two most notable problems in the Maya Forest region are its diminishing forest areas and poverty. These problems occur in varying degrees from country to country. In Mexico, degradation of forest lands is so severe in places that loggers have been known to cross into Guatemala and Belize to steal trees of the valuable species, such as mahogany and cedar. Satellite photography of the border between Mexico and Guatemala's Petén region shows a perfectly straight delineation between deforested Mexican territory and forested Guatemalan lands (Garrett 1989). However, the rate of deforestation in Guatemala has been accelerating as farmers from the Guatemalan highlands, forced to leave by overcrowding, poverty, or political unrest, have moved into the Maya Forest seeking farmland. In Belize, the rate of deforestation has been somewhat slower because Belize historically has had a small population and low industrial development. In recent years, however, expansion of farms, sugar plantations, and cattle ranches—industries requiring open land—as well as population growth related to immigration from other parts of Central America, have taken a toll on Belizean forests.

The economies of all three countries composing the Maya Forest rely to some extent on extractive industries, but tourism is a strong source of income for each one. In Guatemala, tourism is the second-largest source of foreign exchange and employs over 45,000 people. Mexico also has a strong tourist industry, nearly half of which is devoted to visitors to protected areas and archaeological remains. Tourism in Belize is not as strong as in the other two countries, but this partly reflects the fact that the industry has begun to develop only recently. Once the secret haven of bird-watchers and diving enthusiasts (Belize has the second-largest barrier reef in the world), in the past decade Belize has begun to popularize its natural attractions to a much greater extent. As a consequence, tourism is now the largest sector in the economy, yet it is still among the most rapidly growing industries.

Ecotourism may prove to be a particularly promising opportunity in the Maya Forest because of the unique combination of natural and cultural attractions in the region. Natural attractions are contained primarily within protected areas such as the Calakmul and Montes Azules Biosphere Reserves in Mexico (723,000 ha and 331,000 ha, respectively); the Río Bravo Conservation Area (228,000 ha) and the Maya Mountains (about 405,000 ha of protected areas) in Belize; and the Maya Biosphere Reserve (1.6 million ha) in Guatemala. Ancient Maya ruins such as Tikal, Dos Pilas, Bonampak, Yaxchilán, Calakmul, and Caracol attract tourists from all over the world. Well-preserved tracts of forest, most of which surround ancient ruins, contain flora and fauna that are threatened or extinct in other parts of Central America. These include animals such as the jaguar, tapir, and cayman; birds such as the quetzal, toucan, and macaw; and numerous rare plants and trees, many of which may not even have been described yet by scientists. The region is also home to indigenous Maya cultures such as the Lacandónes, Choles, Tzeltales, Yucatecs, Itzás, Kekchis, and Mopans. Traditional crafts produced by these cultures, particularly weaving and pottery, are sold worldwide. The increasing popularity of these attractions contributes to the continued prominence and growth of tourism in the region.

Ecotourism for Conservation: Concepts, Possibilities, and Pitfalls

Nature-based tourism, or "ecotourism," does not have one clear definition and may have different meanings for different people. Western (1993) proposes one definition that fits into the context of how ecotourism could be developed in the Maya Forest region: "Ecotourism is about creating and satisfying a hunger for nature, about exploiting tourism's potential for conservation and development, and about averting its negative impact on ecology, culture, and aesthetics." This definition includes two points that are important in the effort to promote economic development in the Maya Forest region while trying to conserve its natural resources: (1) ecotourism is a style of tourism that can be used as a tool for conservation of natural areas, and (2) ecotourism is a development tool that can be ecologically, economically, and socially sustainable. The theory behind it is simple: because most of the destruction of forests and other habitats is driven by people's need to grow crops or earn income to support their families, such destruction can best be prevented if continuing sources of employment and income are created *that depend upon keeping the resource intact.* Tourism is an excellent means of fostering this circumstance: a *campesino* who captures a bird to sell to the pet trade will earn money once, but a person or organization that protects local nesting areas and provides food, lodging, and guide services to bird-watchers can earn income many times over. However, for the effects to be felt in communities, local residents must become involved in the tourism market. This aspect further defines one type of tourism addressed in this chapter: "community-based" ecotourism, which refers to ecotourism developed and managed by local people for their own benefit.

Ecotourism is an alternative industry that many conservation organizations consider promising. Tourism is the largest industry in the world, and it continues to grow. By the year 2005, it will have doubled its present size if it continues to grow at current rates (World Travel and Tourism Council 1992). Yet even tourism is potentially an enormous threat to the Maya Forest, if the number of visitors exceeds the carrying capacity of the area, if visitors knowingly or unknowingly engage in habitat destruction or illegal trade, or if the infrastructure developed to attract and serve the tourist trade is created at the expense of delicate habitats. Ecotourism, which emphasizes natural and cultural attractions as the basis for tourism development, thus promoting a less destructive brand of tourism, may be a force to slow or stop such destruction. By its very nature, ecotourism depends upon maintaining biological and cultural integrity; in promoting the industry, ecotourism projects of necessity must promote conservation of pristine natural and cultural sites. One example of this is the Mundo Maya project, a five-country effort by Mexico, Belize, Guatemala, Honduras, and El Salvador to develop the tourism potential of the region by creating linked areas in which the conservation of natural and cultural attractions is paramount. Ecotourism is not, however, a panacea, but must become a valuable element in a diversified, stable development program.

Ecotourism in the Maya Forest

Ecotourism represents a direct link between conservation and economic development. Although it can have a profound impact upon community development, an aspect that will be further discussed below, ecotourism can also be a source of funding to protect natural resources. Nongovernmental organizations in Mexico, Guatemala, and Belize regularly support their conservation programs by selling tours, guide services, maps, publications, and souvenirs to tourists. Many tourists voluntarily contribute amounts above and beyond the actual costs of their trips to support conservation programs in the areas they visit. However, in order to successfully safeguard natural resources, ecotourism must necessarily adhere to certain rules. All tourism has an impact upon the natural environment; ecotourist outfits cannot eliminate that impact, but they can minimize it by instructing tourists and enforcing fairly strict codes of conduct. These may include asking tourists to stay on trails and other designated areas away from particularly sensitive habitats such as nesting grounds; keeping groups small in size; avoiding disturbances such as feeding wildlife or loud noises; and discouraging littering or souvenir collecting, particularly of sensitive or rare species.

Tourism is one of the largest industries in the respective economies of Guatemala, Belize, and Mexico—the three nations that compose the Maya Forest—in terms of the level of income generated. In Guatemala, tourism ranks second behind coffee export in the generation of foreign exchange (INGUAT 1993). Tourism accounts for 25% of the Gross Domestic Product of Belize (Lindberg and Enriquez 1994), and in Mexico it accounts for about 25% of all nonpetroleum foreign income (Boo 1990). Because it has such a positive economic impact on their national economies, all three countries composing the Maya Forest region are placing greater emphasis on tourism by investing in the development and promotion of their attractions, particularly ecological and archaeological features. The government of Guatemala, for example, has adopted a Plan for the Development of Sustainable Tourism to the year 2005, including as part of its general policies the development of basic infrastructure, tourist products, and facilities standards, particularly in the Petén, where the majority of the intact forest is located. The plan explicitly requires that expansion of facilities for tourism be done in proportion to the carrying capacity of the local environment, and it also proposes increased conservation of natural and cultural heritage. In Mexico, reserves and protected areas attract almost half of all foreign visitors. Famous archaeological sites such as Bonampak, Yaxchilán, and Calakmul lie within or near biosphere reserves, yet are within relatively easy reach of major urban centers such as Chetumal, Campeche, and San Cristobal de las Casas. A well-established infrastructure (airports, roads, hotels, guide services, etc.) already exists for many of the principal attractions in Mexico. Belize, on the other hand, lacks many infrastructural elements, but is highly competitive in specialized services such as guides for natural history and diving. Though much of the current tourist development is concentrated on the coastal islands, the Belize Tourism Bureau and Ministry of the Environment and Tourism are developing policies to promote "eco-cultural" tourism, defined as "tourism with an environmental conciousness, which respects local cultures and traditions, and which provides economic benefits for both rural and urban communities." Conservation and tourism in Belize are directly related; nearly 35% of the country's land has been designated as protected areas, and these sanctuaries represent a significant potential tourist draw.

Impact of Ecotourism on Environment and Society

Tourism has the potential to create both positive and negative impacts for the Maya Forest. Because of the natural and archaeological richness of the area, a high volume of tourism may be created that could have a significant positive economic impact on local economies. However, both the natural areas and the archaeological sites are fragile and may be damaged by too many visitors. The presence of foreign tourists can also have a strong negative impact on local cultures, which in turn can lessen the attraction of an area, thus making tourism a short-term boom that does not contribute to long-term economic development. In order to use ecotourism as an effective conservation strategy, a balance must be found among tourism, development, and nature. Such a balance, though difficult to achieve, may be possible. Many people are interested in visiting natural areas such as the Maya Forest through tourism that permits visitors to enjoy nature while minimizing the negative impacts that their presence may cause. Likewise, local people in businesses associated with tourism and recreation—hotels, restaurants, diving outfitters, etc.—realize that knowledge of local flora, fauna, and archaeological sites can be helpful in promoting their businesses. By emphasizing the educational aspects of tourism, many businesses and organizations actively promote a less damaging brand of tourism and recreation. In Belize, for instance, conservation education goes hand in hand with recreation: signs, pamphlets, posters, and T-shirts advise visitors to the Belize Zoo against disturbance and destruction of wild species and habitat, while visitors to the barrier reef are enjoined by local divemasters to avoid harming the delicate coral formations that are a significant source of income for the Belizean tourist industry.

Conservation organizations and government agencies have begun to encourage initiatives focusing on ecotourism. For instance, a small grants program created by The Nature Conservancy (TNC), in conjunction with the MAYAFOR project sponsored by the U.S. Agency for International Development (USAID), has received a strong response from groups seeking to establish ecotourism initiatives (Wilber 1995). Of the 18 projects financed by TNC, nine are ecotourism related. A survey undertaken in 1995 that examined existing ecotourism projects funded by TNC showed that many such ventures are too new to have reached full self-sufficiency (Beavers 1995). Most ecotourism projects in this survey still rely on aid and support from outside of their communities. The survey, which was conducted in the form of a mobile seminar, was also intended to provide an opportunity to community representatives from Mexico, Guatemala, and Belize to witness firsthand different examples of community-based ecotourism projects in the Peten in Guatemala and in Belize. The primary value of the study tour was that it enabled the participants to determine whether ecotourism might be a viable option for their own communities and to exchange information, experiences, and ideas with their peers in neighboring countries. The majority of the projects visited, described in general terms in Table 22.1, were at a critical stage at the time of the survey in which they had to establish themselves and compete in the market. The exceptions to this rule were the Community Baboon Sanctuary (CBS) and the Toledo Ecotourism Association (TEA), both of which have five or more years of ecotourism experience and are located in Belize.

It should be noted that some so-called ecotourism projects in the Maya Forest are not solely or even principally focused upon either nature or tourism. Most groups interested in developing tourism as a source of income for the community seek to use all of the potential attractions in the area, which allows them to appeal to as diversified an audience as possible. As shown in Table 22.1, many groups in the TNC survey complemented the natural attractions by promoting archaeology and indigenous culture; in some instances, however, cultural attractions were the initial focus of the tourism business, but natural features were included in order to broaden the project's appeal. Three projects—the Guatemalan Bio-Itzá Reserve, the Ixchel ethnobotanical preserve in Belize, and the Community Baboon Sanctuary (CBS), also in Belize—began as conservation-based projects and later devel-

Table 22.1. Principal characteristics of community-based projects visited in the mobile seminar (from Beavers 1995).

Project / founding date	Years working	Years in ecotourism	Ecotourism activities[a]	Attractions promoted[b]	Infrastructure[c]
Ixlú, Dec. 1994*	1	1	C	CR, AR, N	CS, GS
Zocotzal, 1994*	1	1	PA	N, AR	A, GS
Uaxactún, Feb. 1993	2	2	PA	N, AR	A, GS
Eco-Escuela, 1993	2	2	PA	C, N	Language school
Ixchel S.C., 1990	5	1	C	N, C	A, GS, F
Bio-Itzá, 1991	4	1	C	N, AR	A, GS, F
Amigos de El Pilar, 1993	2	1	PA	AR, CR, N	A, GS, CS
Community Baboon Sanctuary, 1985	10	10	C	N	A, GS, F
Maya Centre (Cockscomb), 1989	6	6	PA	CR	CS
Toledo Ecotourism Assoc., 1990	5	5	PA	N, C, AR, CR	A, GS, F, CS

* In planning or construction stage; had not begun to function as of Dec. 1995

[a]Component (C) or principal activity (PA) of the project

[b]Nature (N), Archaeology (AR), Culture (C), Crafts (CR)

[c]Accommodations (A), Guide Services (GS), Food (F), Craft Sales (CS)

oped ecotourism as a sideline to subsidize their conservation activities. In turn, the original natural features that prompted the conservation projects became part of the tourist attraction. Other initiatives—the Ixlú Eco-artisan Project in Guatemala and the Maya Centre in Belize—promoted crafts as their principal attraction, but included aspects relating to conservation and thus became "ecotourist" programs.

Ecotourism As a Community Development Strategy

Although tourism is growing rapidly in the region, communities will not have an opportunity to participate in the market without sufficient backing. In order to participate in ecotourism and compete in the market, communities need financial and technical assistance. Infrastructure, training, and other types of support are critical if communities are to successfully run ecotourism enterprises. Support from governments and NGOs is required to ensure that these projects develop to their potential and have the chance to survive over the long term. Without this support, the potential positive impact on local economies and the natural resource base that ecotourism could bring may be lost. The majority of the communities involved in ecotourism in the Maya Forest region are just initiating their activities (Beavers 1995).

One matter complicating the establishment of community-based ecotourism is the issue of user rights governing the natural resource base, especially with regard to protected areas. As shown in Table 22.2, all of the ecotourism projects surveyed were located inside or near protected areas. This factor can be both an advantage and a disadvantage for communities because protected areas imply restrictions in the use of natural resources that may limit their economic development. However, protected areas may provide an opportunity for communities to generate income from nature because nature attracts tourists. Tourism income in turn may have positive implications for communities' economic development and the conservation of the protected areas. These issues can directly affect the manner in which ecotourism projects operate. Many ecotourism projects' installations (such as accommodations, etc.) are located on owned or rented property, whereas the majority of the natural attractions (forests, rivers, lakes, caves, etc.) and/or archaeological sites are located on government property. Therefore, access to the resources/attractions depends on the rights granted to communities by the government, some of which are listed in Table 22.2 for specific cases. In the case of the CBS, the people of the community were the owners of the sanctuary and were protecting it directly. Other projects must lease the land; for instance, the Bio-Itzá Reserve has a 50-year lease, and the Ixchel ethnobotanical reserve a 30-year lease, enabling them to directly protect these lands, but for a limited time. Other projects surveyed by TNC did not own or lease the surrounding natural resources; tourists were entering and leaving protected areas according to the regulations governing the reserves. In some areas, the

Table 22.2. Socioeconomic aspects of the community-based projects (from Beavers 1995).

Project	NGO and/or government support	Located in/near parks/protected areas	Land and resource use rights: Installations/attractions	Group size and characteristics
Ixlú	Yes	Archaeological site of Ixlú	60-year lease from village/undefined	11 men
Zocotzal	Yes	Entrance to Tikal	Own/undefined	8 women and youth
Uaxactún	Yes	Archaeological site of Uaxactún	Own and donation/Undefined	14 men, women, youth
Eco-Escuela	Yes	No	Rented/NA	Not a group
Ixchel S.C.	Yes	Archaeological site and Bio-Itza[a]	Rented/rented	12 women, not a group
Bio-Itzá	Yes	El Zotz Biotope[b]	Rented/rented	30 men
Amigos de El Pilar	No	Archaeological site of El Pilar	Not determined/usufruct rights	50 men
CBS	Yes	No[c]	Own/private parcels	70 landowners
Maya Centre	Yes	Entrance to Cockscomb Basin Sanctuary	Donated/usufruct rights	37 women from 90% of families in community
TEA	Yes	Archaeological sites and protected areas[d]	7-year lease/undefined	7 families from each of 5 communities

[a]Installations located on 13 ha of land leased from municipality for 30 years for reforestation.
[b]Community group leasing 3,600 ha of municipal land for 50 years for conservation and sustainable use.
[c]Community sanctuary; see Horwich and Lyon, this volume, for details.
[d]Communities plan to develop their own protected areas (Village Protected Area, VPA).

entities in charge of the resource recognized the needs of the communities and were working with them (Maya Centre, Amigos de El Pilar). In other cases the communities were still trying to define their rights and relationships with the areas (Uaxactún, Zocotzal, TEA).

A final and important characteristic concerning the development of ecotourism in communities is the organizational aspect. Organization and investment in ecotourism in the communities visited was accomplished through groups and committees that represented the tourism interests of the population, or at least a sector of the population (Beavers 1995). Because the communities did not have the resources—mainly financial—for individual investment and development of ecotourism, they received support from NGOs or governments. This circumstance promoted the idea that development should be group-based in order to impact as many people as possible. Therefore, these initiatives had to take into account communities as a whole in the development of their projects. This fact meant that these groups had to focus upon community relations and community opinion, something about which private organizations do not have to be as concerned.

Strategies for Success in Community-Based Ecotourism

Put simply, the difference between community-based ecotourism and ecotourism sponsored by private conservation organizations is this: privately sponsored ecotourism seeks to preserve the resource by benefiting the local people, whereas community-based ecotourism seeks to benefit the local people by preserving the resource. Communities are willing to conserve nature, but only in a manner that permits them to continue to develop and improve their quality of life. This perspective is clearly seen in the Uaxactún and Maya Centre projects, where protected areas and communities attempt to coexist and work together so that conservation and development can coincide. Local people generally are aware of the fact that ecotourism will not replace their traditional economic activities. However, they often feel that it has the potential to generate additional income for them, so they frequently approach conservation projects from an entrepreneurial perspective. From their point of view, the first and most important step toward conservation is to ensure that community-based ecotourism initiatives are competitive and profitable. This distinction does not mean that community groups are any less concerned with conservation of resources than outside, private organizations; it simply means that their priorities are slightly different from those of private organizations.

Objectives of Community-Based Ecotourism

Ideally, ecotourism operated by communities should both satisfy tourists' desire for adventure and comfort and contribute toward satisfying the basic economic needs of the community by employing natural and cultural resources in local development. The standard of living should improve, and the value attributed to natural and cultural resources should likewise increase. Specifically, ecotourism should motivate local people to value and conserve resources—including not only natural resources but also local culture and language. It should also encourage participation in community groups, create opportunities for training and technical assistance, develop communities' ability to manage financial resources or establish community development funds, and lead the establishment of well-managed reserves, educational facilities (such as museums or botanical gardens), and other attractions.

In general, communication, group image, relationships with the community, and the efficient operation of groups and their activities are the key elements required to manage and administer these community-based ecotourism businesses. However, one disadvantage of businesses managed by groups is that no single person retains ultimate authority or responsibility. Groups generally must come to an agreement in order to make decisions, a process that often takes more time. This manner of functioning can be inefficient in comparison with private ecotourism enterprises; thus, ensuring efficient and cohesive organization of the group becomes an important part of the foundation of a project. This strategy requires that all group members be involved, take some initiative, and accept responsibilities—a goal more easily achieved when all involved perceive that they will benefit from their association with the group, particularly once the project is functioning.

Keys to Success

Many factors that can impede the success of newly operational ecotourist services are simple, avoidable problems: latrines that are not properly maintained (i.e., those with odors, nonfunctional doors, etc.), inadequate or poorly maintained bathing facilities (e.g, poor drainage, poor design, and lack of cleanliness), and menus that lack variety, are not well prepared, and are overpriced. Other problems include guide services that employ guides who do not know enough about archaeological sites, local flora and fauna, or local customs, or whose knowledge is poorly presented. The attractions available to community groups and the development and promotion of these attractions are important considerations that can contribute to or impede the success of a tourism operation (Table 22.3). Communities that are just beginning to develop an ecotourism industry are often unsure how to promote themselves in order to create a niche in the tourist market. Marketing tools such as pamphlets and advertisements in local hotels and other establishments and promotion by word of mouth are commonly the means of publicity that new projects utilize. In some cases, the project may begin operation with too little planning or forethought. Projects located at a distance from principal attrac-

Table 22.3. General problems and deficiencies identified by the participants on the Mobile Seminar (from Beavers 1995).

Organization	Training/Education	Infrastructure	Services	Promotion
Lack of equal participation among members; not all sectors of the community are represented.	More training needed in management, administration and implementation. Also, safety and first aid training is especially important.	Facilities substandard for tourist services.	Lack of quality control.	Insufficient information about promotion methods outside local community.
Poor communication between group and community. Expected benefits and distribution should be outlined more clearly to avoid misunderstandings.	More training needed for guides: archaeology, nature, group management, and tourist expectations.	Facilities should match tourist expectations.	Lack of knowledge about tourists' expectations.	Lack of liaison with other communities and tourism enterprises.
Poor delegation of functions.	Greater information exchange among projects is needed.	Financial aid needed to improve infrastructure.	Inefficient organization and operation of services.	Communities promote too few attractions, usually only one.

tions and that lack sufficient transportation for visitors, for instance, will be unlikely to succeed in promoting those attractions.

To be successful in promoting ecotourism projects, a community should have certain characteristics. These include:

- Natural and physical attributes such as potable water, attractive views and landscapes, cultural resources, and access roads. The community should have an inventory and map of these attributes and attractions, and should be able to provide this information in several languages.

- Community organization that emphasizes participation by men and women, young and old. It is particularly important that young people be involved, because ecotourists themselves tend to be young people, and their peers are more likely to understand the types of adventures and experiences that they seek. It is also important that the organization taking the leadership role of the venture have an understanding and acceptance of business practices, including the basis of quality services and effective means of competition with other businesses. The managing entity must constantly evaluate its performance, be open to change, seek out and emphasize the most beneficial activities, and be willing to reduce or abandon efforts that do not achieve the desired results.

- Relationships with NGOs that can provide assistance. In many cases, NGOs have been the source of start-up funding, training, and technical assistance. NGOs often have members who are both potential visitors and sources of advice. The best NGOs provide diagnostics, feasibility studies, and assistance from planning to implementation to evaluation, but are careful to let the community take a leadership role and avoid creating dependency.

- Ability to work with the local tourism industry, including chambers of commerce or tourism operators, to develop and enhance the tourism market.

According to the experiences of participants in the TNC survey of ecotourism projects, organization and the involvement of the community in their initiatives appeared to be the foundation for building successful community enterprises (Beavers 1995). Good organization in this sense refers to coordination, communication, management, and administration to help ensure the business aspects of ecotourism are strong enough to compete in the market. Issues of leadership, lack of active and complete participation by group members (including the lack of delegation of functions and authority), and poor relationships or communication between these initiatives and their respective communities were mentioned as problems that could be barriers for the success of the projects.

An important observation of some survey participants who had dealt with organizational problems was that the objectives, benefits, and distribution of the benefits from the project should be clearly defined in order to avoid misunderstandings and problems. The community group involved in a project must ensure that the community in general understands and accepts the effort that the group is making in order to minimize conflicts that impede the success of community ecotourism projects. Groups must take care not to create false expectations, and must therefore be more sensitive to community relations than private businesses typically are. It was noted in the survey that some groups were not very large in relation to the size of the community, or that they were not inclusive of all sectors of the community (i.e., they excluded women, youth, etc.). However, some projects appeared to have the potential to affect much wider sectors of the community than others (see Table 22.2 for group sizes). Many of the projects attempt to reach beyond the membership of the groups in terms of providing benefits to the communities. For example, the TEA set up a system of rotations between service providers so that everyone had a chance to participate and gain income. Also, with some of the income generated by ecotourism, a fund was established in order to provide money for health care and education in the TEA communities. Likewise, Uaxactún rotated its visitors among the restaurants in the village to guarantee that a greater proportion of community members received the benefits from tourism. The Maya Centre women's group represented almost all of the families in the community, and the crafts business they had established at the entrance to the Cockscomb Basin Wildlife Sanctuary appeared to be providing a level of benefit for all of them. Other projects were more focused on immediate members, but even these had plans to either expand membership or to provide greater distribution of the benefits from ecotourism within the community.

Conclusion

The Maya Forest has an abundance of wildlife, scenic areas, and archaeological ruins that are attracting an increasing number of tourists. The income from these ecotourists can provide the financial justification for protecting the biological communities. Yet ecotourism presents two challenges to the conservation of the region. First, the activities of the tourists and the facilities that they use must not accelerate the damage to the forest. The number of tourists and their wealth have the potential to strongly influence the local environment. Second, the tourist industry must provide benefits to rural communities so that they can become advocates for conservation. Many communities are accepting this opportunity and are developing ecotourist facilities and programs. The best outcome of this approach is that communities preserve both their environment and their own culture in the process. Finding the right balance between development that is profitable and long-term conservation represents a challenge for the ecotourism industry.

Acknowledgments

This chapter represents a synthesis of draft papers submitted on the topic of eco-tourism at a workshop in Chetumal, Mexico in November 1995, drawing exten-sively on an unpublished paper by John Beavers. Elizabeth Platt was responsible for the editing and reworking.

References

Beavers, J. 1995. Ecotoursim and communities in the Maya Forest region: A tri-na-tional mobile seminar on community-based ecotourism. The Nature Conser-vancy/USAID/MAYAFOR, unpublished report.

Boo, E. 1990. *Ecoturismo: Potenciales y Escollos*. World Wildlife Fund/Conservation Foundation/USAID, Washington, D.C.

———. 1995. Introduction to ecotourism. In *Compatible Economic Development: Tourism*, Northrup Brad and Jerry Touval, eds. Workbook prepared for The Nature Conservancy's Conservation Training Week, Quito, Ecuador, May 21–27, 1995.

Culbert, T. P., ed. 1973. *The Classic Maya Collapse*. University of New Mexico Press, Albuquerque.

Garrett, W. E. 1989. La Ruta Maya. *National Geographic* 176: 424–479.

Instituto Guatemalteco de Turismo (INGUAT). 1993. *Cifras de la Industria Turistica*. Guatemala City, Guatemala.

Lindberg, K., and J. Enriquez. 1994. *An Analysis of Ecotourism's Economic Contribution to Conservation and Development in Belize*, Volumes 1 and 2. World Wildlife Fund and Ministry of Tourism and the Environment, Belize.

Lindberg K., and D. E. Hawkins, eds. 1993. *Ecotourism: A Guide for Planners and Man-agers*. The Ecotourism Society, North Bennington, Vt.

Northrup, B., and J. Touval, eds. 1995. *Compatible Economic Development: Tourism*. Workbook prepared for The Nature Conservancy's Conservation Training Week, Quito, Ecuador, May 21–27, 1995.

Wilber, J. S. 1995. Small grants as a tool for conservation and community develop-ment in the Maya Forest: A focus on the Maya Biosphere in Guatemala. The Na-ture Conservancy, unpublished.

World Travel and Tourism Council. 1992. *The WTTC Report: Travel and Tourism in the World Economy*. WTTC, Brussels, Belgium.

Chapter 23

Community-Based Development As a Conservation Tool: The Community Baboon Sanctuary and the Gales Point Manatee Project

Robert H. Horwich and Jonathan Lyon

Ecotourism has been touted as a viable new strategy for nature conservation and sustainable local development, and developing nations have been encouraged to embrace this fast-growing industry (Ceballos-Lascurain 1991). However, there often is a gap between the promise and the reality of ecotourism development. Ecotourism can have negative consequences for local people and the environment, including overvisitation and damage to natural resources (de Groot 1983; Alderman 1990), local inflation, and exacerbation of a cultural and economic gap between local people and affluent travelers. These negative consequences can lead to local opposition to many ecotourism activities (Johnston 1990). Despite these drawbacks, effective ecotourism remains as a viable tool that can interest and motivate rural people to protect the wildlands where they work and live. Given attainable economic incentives, true local involvement in the management of lands, and a proper framework, many rural people have shown that they will take responsibility to protect their lands (Western et al. 1994). In this chapter, we report on two conservation efforts that have produced positive results by employing community-based development as a conservation tool: the Community Baboon Sanctuary and the Gales Point Manatee Project.

The Community Baboon Sanctuary (CBS) represents a pioneering experiment in community-based conservation for the protection of black howler monkey (*Alouatta pigra*) habitat on private lands. The Gales Point Manatee Project (GPMP) reflects an attempt to expand and improve on the CBS experiment. The goals of the GPMP were to create a protected area much larger than the CBS that included both private and public lands but remained locally managed. Belize's history of ecotourism activities shaped these projects, but the projects themselves have also influenced subsequent developments in the ecotourism industry. As the success of these projects demonstrates, ecotourism projects can function as interim protection for wild areas that would otherwise be utilized for more destructive industries. Regarding these experimental projects or any potentially damaging technique for conservation, we believe that a simple question needs to be asked: Is the proposed solution potentially better than the environmental degradation likely to result from continuing trends? Examination of the specific successes and challenges in the implementation of the two projects helps to address the gap that is often found between the promise of rural ecotourism and the reality of its day-to-day operation.

History of Tourism and Conservation in Belize

Between 1980 and 1990, Belize became an increasingly popular ecotourism destination (Boo 1990). In the 1980s, conservationists convinced Belizean politicians of the potential of ecotourism for attracting foreign capital into the country. They argued that these funds could be obtained with only small expenditures by the government and limited infrastructure development, yet the industry would have minimal environmental impact. Thus ecotourism provided economic and political justification for the protection of certain national areas, including the relatively high-profile Cockscomb Basin Wildlife Sanctuary (Boo 1990). Belizean ecotourism generated strong conservation interest from both the national government and local communities (Boo 1990; Lindberg and Enriquez 1994; Horwich and Lyon 1996). However, differences arose between these two groups in how Belize's ecotourism efforts and infrastructure should develop. These differences ultimately have accentuated the economic and sociological divisions between these two groups.

Most of the income generated by early ecotourism was centered in the large cities that supported the necessary facilities to attract tourists. Early ecotourism consisted primarily of brief day-outings from the cities. This first wave of ecotourism development influenced foreigners and wealthy Belizeans to create private reserves and convinced politicians, affluent investors, and politically powerful persons of the economic importance and value of preserving the natural resources (Horwich and Lyon 1996). The government of Belize rapidly embraced the wave of affluent tourism, providing new services and ultimately creating the Ministry of Tourism and the Environment (Boo 1990). Concomitant with this wave of ecotourism was the development of the first community-based conservation/ecotourism program in the country, the Community Baboon Sanctuary. However, the government's interest in rural, community-based ecotourism developed at a much slower pace (Godfrey 1990). During the initial development of ecotourism in Belize, rural people saw the economic possibilities of ecotourism. However, many individuals and communities lacked both the materials and capital needed to participate in the ecotourism industry. With the initiation and subsequent development of the CBS, rural Belizeans now had a foot in the door of the ecotourism industry.

History and Development
of the Community Baboon Sanctuary

The history and development of the Community Baboon Sanctuary is well documented. We will highlight just a few aspects of the project here (readers interested in detailed accounts should see Horwich and Lyon 1988, 1990, 1995). The CBS, a pioneering experimental approach to the conservation of private lands, was centered in an area that contains one of the largest existing populations of black howler monkeys (*Alouatta pigra*) in Central America ("baboon" is the word for black howler monkey in the local Creole dialect). The conservation area mostly consists of semideciduous riparian forests along the Belize River. These forests are highly disturbed secondary growth containing few economically valuable species. The CBS was founded in 1985 by the authors and community members in the village of Bermudian Landing, initially including 820 ha owned by 12 landowners. In 1986, under the auspices of the Belize Audubon Society and with funding from World Wildlife Fund–U.S. (WWF), the sanctuary was expanded to include approximately 4,800 ha of land owned by residents of the villages of Flowers Bank, Isabella Bank, Scotland Halfmoon, Double Head Cabbage, Willows Bank, and St. Paul's Bank/Big Falls.

Creation of the CBS proceeded in seven discernible steps (Horwich 1990; Horwich and Lyon 1988): (1) identifying the area for conservation based on the viability of the black howler population; (2) contacting local people to garner interest in howler conservation; (3) formalizing a conservation strategy through education to increase villagers' awareness of the plan and contacting local and area politicians; (4) initially developing the sanctuary, including property and vegetation mapping, howler censusing, development of tourism plans, initiation of an education program, preparation of land management plans, and voluntary pledges from landowners; (5) publicizing the sanctuary through various media, including newspapers, magazines, radio, and TV; (6) expanding the sanctuary to include additional landowners; and (7) formalizing a sustainable infrastructure to include permanent staff as well as programs in education, conservation, research, and locally controlled ecotourism development.

The heart of the howler conservation effort is centered on individual land management plans for each landowner designed to protect the riparian habitat of the black howler. Landowner participation in the CBS is completely voluntary; each landowner participant has signed a witnessed, voluntary pledge to abide by a specific management plan. The land management plans ask individual landowners to pursue simple, low-cost management guidelines that include maintaining a 21 m (66 ft) riparian forest corridor along the river, leaving a forest buffer strip along property boundaries, leaving a strip of forest across large cleared areas, and leaving specific howler food trees in large clearings. In short, the management plan incorporates basic nature reserve designs (Lyon and Horwich 1996). If all the forested lands were developed for

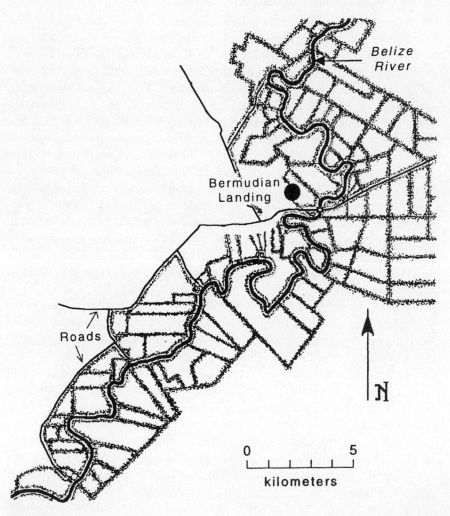

Figure 23.1

Map of the Community Baboon Sanctuary exhibiting hypothetical remaining skeletal forest if all lands were utilized and management pledges were adhered to.

pasture or agricultural clearings and the pledges were adhered to, the CBS would maintain a minimal, continuous, skeletal forest from which the howlers would be able to forage in the regenerating forests (Fig. 23.1). Although the CBS has taken a focal species approach, the conservation effort has the end result of promoting general forest protection.

The CBS presently includes over 120 landowners and has the potential to expand to include additional landowners. One important long-term management goal of the CBS is to connect it with the nearby Crooked Tree Wildlife Sanctuary to the north and Mussel Creek area to the east, both of which support howler populations. During its formation period, the CBS was placed under the auspices of the Belize Audubon Society, which helped guide its development. Since 1994, the CBS has been managed by a management committee composed of an elected member from each of the villages in the sanctuary. Current CBS employees include an office manager, a guide manager, and two guides who work on a commission basis. Other community members work for the CBS as part-time guides on weekends.

In addition to its howler conservation program, the CBS has programs in education, research, and ecotourism (Horwich and Lyon 1995). The CBS office is housed in a small museum built in 1989 (Belize's first) that is the focus of the CBS education and tourism program (Figure 23.2). An extensive book

Figure 23.2

Schoolchildren learn about howler monkeys in the CBS museum.

on the natural history of the area has been published (Horwich and Lyon 1990) and an extensive trail system has been developed that is used for tourism, education, and research. The research program has focused primarily on the black howler monkeys, with studies on their ecology, social behavior, population changes, genetics, and morphology. The results of these studies guided a 1992–1994 howler translocation effort. Sixty-two howlers were moved successfully from the CBS to the Cockscomb Basin Wildlife Sanctuary in order to form a new viable population in a region where they previously had been hunted to extinction. Other animal studies in the CBS include population studies of the bird community, studies of the Central American river turtle (Polisar and Horwich 1994), and studies on forest regeneration and tree phenology (Lyon and Horwich 1996) as well as studies of the CBS program (Hartup 1994).

The CBS conservation program was originally designed to protect and enhance howler habitat (Figure 23.3). However, with a conspicuous abundance of monkeys within the CBS, favorable and increasing publicity about the pro-

Figure 23.3

One method of enhancing howler habitat was to create bridges over man-made gaps in the forest such as roads. These bridges not only allow the monkeys to move between forest patches in relative safety, they allow visitors to see the monkeys in the open.

ject, and a growing awareness of ecotourism in Belize, the linkage between the CBS and ecotourism potential seemed inevitable. Ecotourism development in the CBS was suggested by members of the Bermudian Landing community. It was decided in a series of meetings with landowners (Figure 23.4) that ecotourism would take the form of a locally operated bed-and-breakfast program where visitors would stay overnight and take meals in villagers' homes. Local guides would then take visitors onto participating landowners' lands to view the howlers. All income would go directly to the local participants. In 1987, students from the University of California, Santa Cruz, constituted the first organized group of ecotourists to test how villagers would respond and whether the approach was feasible. Tourism gradually increased from a handful of tourists in 1985 to 1,600 in 1989 (Hartup 1994), increasing fourfold to over 6,000 in 1990, of which 3,000 were schoolchildren. Over 4,000 foreign visitors were recorded in 1995–96. In order to create a tangible focal point for the sanctuary's unique conservation program, a small natural history museum that doubles as a visitor's center was built in 1989. To further enhance infrastructure in the CBS, a grant was obtained in 1989 from the Inter-American Foundation to give loans to villagers to remodel their houses to accommodate tourists.

Figure 23.4

Community members meet to discuss the disposition of land for the sanctuary.

Development of the Gales Point Manatee Project

While the CBS was initiated without any government participation, the Gales Point Manatee Project (GPMP) was started with a broad base of support both within the community and within the government (Boardman 1994; Lindberg and Enriquez 1994; Horwich and Lyon 1996). The lands in the Gales Point region support a variety of communities and ecosystems, including coastal beaches, mangrove forests, littoral forests, pine forest and savanna, brackish lagoons, saline marshes, transitional broadleaf forest, cohune palm forests, karst hill forests, and riparian forests. This variety of communities, habitats, and ecosystems is superimposed on a mosaic of public and privately owned lands. The main population center in the area is Gales Point Village, located on the Southern Lagoon. Since 1968, the lands encompassing the GPMP have been proposed as a protected area several times (Zisman 1989).

The GPMP was begun by a proposal to the government of Belize in February 1991 by Community Conservation Consultants. The proposal utilized lessons from the CBS experience to facilitate development of a community-based conservation program for this ecologically complex region. In developing the proposal, Rob Horwich and Chris Augusta (a long-term part-time resident of the area) worked in cooperation with Gales Point villagers to gather ideas and secure a signed petition of endorsement. Upon submission of the proposal to the government, both the Ministers of Natural Resources and Tourism and the Environment expressed interest in the concept and eventually agreed to organize a meeting at Gales Point to discuss the proposal. This meeting also included politicians and staff of the Departments of Forestry and Archaeology as well as members of the tourism community and villagers.

Based on the above-described meetings, a follow-up proposal for the GPMP was submitted by Horwich and Lyon that called for the creation of a multiple-land-use plan for the region that incorporated aspects of the philosophy put forth by UNESCO's Man and the Biosphere (MAB) Program (Figure 23.5). Core areas were proposed for formal protection of specific selected ecosystems, namely (1) the Manatee River drainage, (2) the Peccary Hills and adjacent pine ridge, and (3) the mangrove forest between the Southern Lagoon and the Caribbean Sea with the nearby beach, which is an important hawksbill turtle nesting site. Two main buffer areas were set aside for potential sustainable use: the southern Manatee forest was designated for selective logging and the Bocatura Pine Ridge was designated for limited hunting, with the stipulation that, to prevent erosion of the topsoils, no vehicular traffic would be allowed. Much of the area surrounding Northern Lagoon and west of Southern Lagoon, including Gales Point, was designated as a transition area where most human activity would take place. Additional areas where citrus groves were being planted along the Sibun

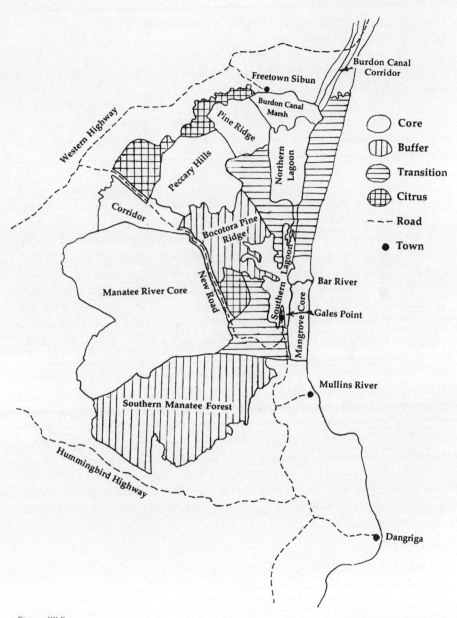

Legend:
- Core
- Buffer
- Transition
- Citrus
- Road
- Town

Map labels: Burdon Canal Corridor, Freetown Sibun, Burdon Canal Marsh, Western Highway, Pine Ridge, Peccary Hills, Northern Lagoon, Corridor, Bocotora Pine Ridge, New Road, Manatee River Core, Southern Lagoon, Bar River, Mangrove Core, Gales Point, Southern Manatee Forest, Mullins River, Hummingbird Highway, Dangriga

Figure 23.5

Map exhibiting the initial Management Plan for the Manatee Area in 1991 with core, buffer, and transition zones.

River were designated for agriculture, as well as an area along the New Road to be used for villagers' farms.

The government responded to Horwich and Lyon's proposal by creating the Manatee Special Development Area (MSDA) in November 1991. In January 1992, the villagers of Gales Point formed the Gales Point Progressive Cooperative (GPPC) to promote sustainable economic development and to conserve the natural environment of the region. A number of associations were created under the GPPC, including a bed-and-breakfast association, a tour operators' association, a farmers' association, and a local products association. Early on, the GPPC had strong village support, with over 50% of the adult community getting involved in at least one of the cooperative's programs. With help from the Belize Tourist Board and the Cooperative Department, the GPPC held a number of training programs for its residents to develop leadership and organizational skills as well as business training. By March 1992 a Trickle-Up Program grant had been obtained for cooperative members. The GPPC used the money for small grants to individuals who wanted to get involved in the ecotourism program. A zoning plan was created for the area that included a plan for a corridor along the Manatee River between the Manatee West SDA and Five Blues National Park, which was accepted by the government. At that time, the Gales Point project was coordinated by the Belize Enterprise for Sustainable Technology (BEST). Additional information was gathered to direct management recommendations for the Southern Lagoon Watershed and for specific protection of the manatee (*Trichechus manatus*) (Augusta et al. 1993).

With the help of Community Conservation Consultants, BEST received USAID and United Nations Development Program Global Environmental Fund grants for a biodiversity study and village improvements. The biodiversity grant included a survey of species in the area, vegetation mapping, and research programs, including studies on tree phenology, forest composition, and hunting and fishing surveys. Additional information was drawn from a prior primate survey of the area.

Linking Community Conservation, Ecotourism, and Land Management

The CBS was one of the first experiments in community-based conservation and ecotourism (Horwich and Lyon 1988, 1990). The CBS project spawned a small revolution in thinking among rural communities in Belize; since its inception, over 30 rural communities have initiated community-based ecotourism and resource management programs (Figure 23.6) (Horwich and Lyon 1996). These community programs encompass diverse management systems developed for a variety of land tenure systems ranging from entirely private

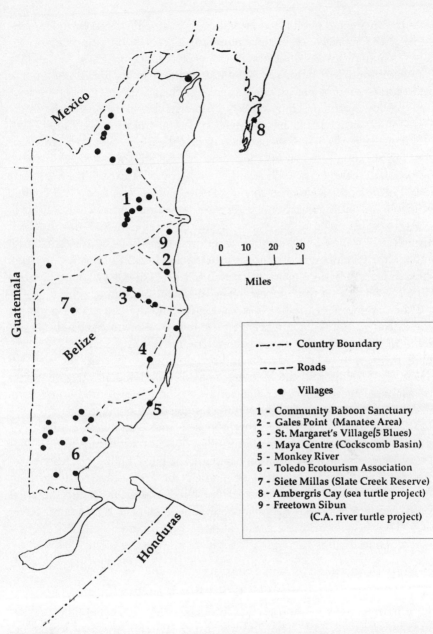

Figure 23.6

Belize map showing the location of communities interested in ecotourism/conservation programs in 1995.

lands to private and public land mosaics (e.g., the GPMP) to entirely public lands. These management systems represent a progression of interaction between communities and government (Horwich and Lyon 1996).

In addition to generating rural community interest, implementation of the CBS ecotourism program spawned interest at the government level. Because the CBS ecotourism program was established in cooperation with the Belize Audubon Society (BAS), an organization that at the time was running Belize's national parks, a linkage between national park development, management, and community conservation was forged. Evidence of these linkages can be found between the CBS and the Cockscomb Basin Wildlife Sanctuary (Boo 1990). Both sanctuaries shared methods of development and created analogous initial organizational structures and community economic programs. In addition, both sanctuaries promoted local economic development through community-based ecotourism efforts, including the hiring of local trail guides, development of crafts industries, and bed-and-breakfast tourism. The Cockscomb Basin is managed by staff from a local village (Maya Centre) under the auspices of the BAS for the government of Belize.

Other examples of the linkages among community conservation efforts, ecotourism, and land planning can also be found in Belize. Special Development Areas (SDAs) were created as interim protected areas by the government in response to conservation and development concerns. As has been shown, the formation of the Manatee Special Development Area (MSDA) and Manatee West SDA can be traced to a proposal presented jointly by a local community group, the Gales Point Progressive Cooperative (representing the only community within the proposed SDA), and Community Conservation Consultants. The community-based organization known as Friends of Five Blues Association, from St. Margaret's Village, Belize, has reached an agreement with the government to manage the Five Blues National Park (Werner 1994; Horwich and Lyon 1996). The Association for the Preservation of Monkey River has a similar agreement to manage the Monkey River SDA. The seeds of all these collaborations were planted with the government–community linkage originally set in motion in the CBS.

Successes and Challenges in Community Development

The initiation and evolution of the CBS and GPMP were very different, despite their common goals. The CBS was initiated with no preconceived blueprint; no directly appropriate models or specific techniques existed for use as a template. In short, the CBS was created as an experimental endeavor, whereas the GPMP was a common-sense extension of the CBS. The CBS was developed solely within existing communities, while the GPMP required networking a whole variety of government and nongovernmental agencies and individuals. Furthermore, because the GPMP deals with public and private lands, the challenges of effectively promoting community conservation are much more complex than in the CBS. Both projects are in interim stages of development; their complexity and the difficulty in securing adequate funds makes any critical evaluation premature at this point. However, we have learned some lessons from both projects that can be applied to other community-based projects. The successes have thus far outweighed the challenges and give sufficient hope that these and other community based projects may be continued, and their lessons used to mold future projects.

Successes: Ecotourism As an Effective Tool

Influence of the CBS on other community-based conservation initiatives. An additional offshoot of the CBS program centered on the economically important endangered Central American river turtle (*Dermatemys mawii*). Based on CBS support and partial sponsorship, the turtles were targeted for study and protection (Polisar and Horwich 1994). This study ultimately led the government to strengthen laws restricting hunting of the species. This activity also stimulated the Community of Freetown Sibun in central Belize to initiate a program for river turtle protection. In another instance, staff from the CBS, along with members of the BAS and the Belize Tourism Industry Association, stimulated local community interest in creating a reserve along the Monkey River.

Two final examples illustrate how the CBS model was used to direct other Belizean conservation programs. Greg Smith, a turtle biologist, used the CBS approach to create a sea turtle conservation program. He later began working with Gales Point villagers to protect the nesting areas of the endangered hawksbill sea turtle (*Eretmochelys imbricata*) within the Manatee SDA. This program, which now releases 12,000 hawksbill hatchlings per year, is attempting to achieve long-term sustainability through tourist participation in the research. A second conservation program in Cayo District for lands along Slate Creek used the CBS landowner contact method as a model.

Impact on local economies. The level of local ecotourism in many rural communities in Belize has increased in recent years, contributing to the incomes of local people through the creation of service jobs, including provision of room, board, guiding, and transportation as well as jobs created by museums and sanctuaries. For example, in the CBS in 1989, Hartup (1994) estimated that some US$30,000–$40,000 per year had been brought into the area by 3,000 foreign tourists. During 1995–96, 4,000 recorded foreign tourist visits further increased income entering the village economy. An active research and student volunteer program typically brings another $5,000–$10,000 per year. The initial wave was led by a foreign student program run through the Monkey Bay Biological Station in Belize. In both the CBS and the GPMP, students were the first paying tourists for both of the modest bed-and-breakfast programs, based in part on their willingness to live within the milieu of the local communities. Overall, much of the income generated through ecotourism and research in both projects has stayed in the community.

Cost effectiveness and sustainability of conservation programs. The two projects have been cost effective and relatively inexpensive both to initiate and to maintain in the early stages (Horwich and Lyon 1996). Both the CBS and GPMP were developed within the socioeconomic norms of the existing community, required minimal infrastructure development, and involved no capital outlay by participants. Furthermore, no guarantees of economic returns were suggested and no unrealistic expectations were promised from ecotourism development. Given these premises, and the willingness of foreign facilitators and partners to live and work within the village economic structure (i.e., comparable salaries, work schedules, and living conditions), both projects were operated on relatively small budgets (averages under US$10,000/year).

The structures of the CBS ecotourism and conservation programs have reached the point where they are at or near sustainability, given proper financial management. A continual pool of funds has been generated through a flat $5 U.S. tour fee. Guides, in turn, are paid a percentage of the overall tourist income. CBS staff also sell goods to tourists and take a percentage of services and sales facilitated for villagers. Unfortunately, initial problems created by inexperience in setting up financial accountability among CBS staff have been difficult to overcome, and all the financial possibilities for sustainability are not being pursued. Nonetheless, based on a decade of ecotourism development, the CBS has the potential to financially sustain current operations based on present levels of tourism visitation.

The promise of sustainability in the GPMP has been more elusive. Ecotourism revenues have made a substantial impact on the community, but their continuity and sustainability have been problematic. However, the government gave the cooperative in Gales Point a grant to build a hotel. Unfortunately, the fund dispersal by the government was not sufficient and the hotel remains unfinished. Its completion would result in a positive step toward creating a sustainable program for the GPMP that could maintain a permanent staff and ecotourism infrastructure.

Engendering local pride in natural resources. Local pride in the CBS has centered on protection of howler monkeys and on a spirit of volunteerism that respects the needs and decision-making ability of the rural landowner. In the GPMP, local pride has centered on villager conservation efforts to protect the manatee and the extensive ecological diversity in the local landscape. In both projects, pride and a sense of recognition have increased through the process of local empowerment and via popular support for the goals of the projects. The projects have awakened a sense of achievement and have stirred a widespread ecological consciousness and stewardship ethic. Furthermore, both projects have evolved in the public eye, which, among nonrural people and foreign tourists alike, has resulted in renewed interest and respect in rural culture, including crafts, music, and stories, and the role of rural peoples in preserving the nation's natural heritage. The perceived success of these projects has developed its own momentum in the country, and, in many cases, rural villages have initiated grassroots conservation efforts centered on the unique attributes of their own local natural resources. Rural people in the CBS and the GPMP have provided a model of private land ownership that has benefits for community conservation and development programs worldwide.

Community conservation programs not only integrate local people in the pursuit of conservation objectives, but they also directly involve rural residents in real conservation situations and research efforts. The capacity of rural people to participate in and manage resource-monitoring efforts and the implementation of conservation programs on the ground represents a vast untapped human resource. Furthermore, conservation jobs create conservation-minded villagers within the community. This integration fosters discussions of conservation issues by villagers with tourists, students, and researchers and promotes an ongoing dialogue about natural resource concerns.

The creation and opening of the CBS museum, the first in Belize, marked the beginning of a yearly occasion for a festival and celebration. This celebration, in addition to noting the conservation aspects of the CBS, also has refocused community attention on the cultural heritage and tradition of the local Creole villagers. Due in large part to museum exhibits highlighting local Creole culture and history and the yearly festival, there has been a rise in ethnic consciousness, which has sparked a renaissance in Creole folk singing, storytelling, and traditional bush crafts. In this vein, the community of St. Paul's Bank, an outlying village in the CBS, is creating a small museum focusing on the cultural uses of the forest.

The cultural revival at Gales Point has been less expansive but nonetheless significant. Due to growing interest in the project both within and outside Belize, there has been renewed interest in exploring the cultural heritage of the village and its recent history. This interest has manifested in a resurgence of traditional basket-making as well as newer crafts, a growing focus on drum-making and drumming by local villagers, and continued interest in the boat-making heritage in the coastal village.

Challenges: Pitfalls and Problems in Community-Based Conservation

Organizational and structural problems. For all the successes experienced by the founders of the CBS and GPMP, there have also been difficulties, most of which are clearly apparent in hindsight. Organizational problems have been a recurring theme, especially in the early stages of these experimental projects. In the CBS, a local management committee should have been established at the outset, as was done in the GPMP and later projects. The current management structure of the CBS is based on a weak management committee that is not dealing effectively with personnel and historical power struggles. The result has been a continual battle for control of the CBS and its financial benefits. Personnel problems previously had led to mismanagement of funds, lack of record keeping and financial accountability, and poor management. These difficulties have been partially remedied with the recent establishment of a new staff structure created by the local management committee, which has encouraged better financial accountability.

The lack of a cohesive management structure in the CBS was due partially to historical events. The CBS initially was organized under the Belize Audubon Society, at the time the only Belizean-managed-and-controlled conservation organization in Belize. The BAS had a full-time executive director and staff and was supported by funding from a U.S. conservation organization. When finances were withdrawn prematurely by the U.S. organization in 1986, the BAS executive director's position was discontinued. CBS staff were left without direct supervision. For two years CBS staff were supervised only by the BAS volunteer board of directors. Because no local management committee was in place at the time in the CBS, an inordinate burden and responsibility was placed on the CBS manager. A management committee was installed later; consequently, the management committee has never exercised its full powers because it was formed after the initial staff had run the sanctuary under the BAS without a management committee for over five years. In retrospect, a formal and legal oversight committee of village landowners should have been formed prior to the initiation and promotion of the CBS. The establishment of a legal committee or cooperative would have increased community participation in the ground-level process of planning and implementation and might have reduced some of the intra- and inter-village conflicts that have subsequently arisen.

Because of the problems and difficulties described above, we guided the formation and management of the GPMP early in the project's development. We involved as many community members as possible in early meetings and public discussions about the project. This approach resulted in a broad base of community support early on in the project. Furthermore, we encouraged the formation of a local cooperative to oversee management of the proposed project prior to any ecotourism development. In contrast, in the CBS, management training was concentrated on a single individual. Although the GPMP has not been as economically successful as the CBS, the establishment of an equitable management structure at the outset has promoted continued interest in the goals of the projects, has shared the economic benefits of the ecotourism program in a fair manner, and has preserved the integrity of the project.

Problems generated by development. Existing socioeconomic, social, and cultural antagonisms within a given community can be exacerbated by increased income in the community (Boo 1990). In the CBS, inequitable distribution of tourism income among and between community members is creating a competitive atmosphere between both villages and participants. Also, the increased money coming into the village from ecotourism and increased rural/urban travel has facilitated some major urban problems within the rural community. The primary problems are centered on substance abuse, primarily crack cocaine and alcohol. The increase in crack and alcohol abuse has also increased the activity of non-CBS related persons bothering tourists for money. These persons, some of whom work or have worked for the CBS, sometimes circumvent the established CBS rules to prevent the CBS from receiving income from the tourists. If this practice should increase, it has the potential of crippling both the CBS ecotourism and conservation programs. These same problems have the potential to develop in Gales Point and other community projects depending on several factors, including the ease of travel between rural villages and urban areas, ready availability of low-cost drugs, and the use of ecotourism income for direct purchase of drugs. Crack cocaine stands as a major potential obstacle in the future success of some community conservation programs in rural villages.

Affluent tourism outcompetes local tourism. A common problem in the evolution of rural conservation development projects is the threat that nonvillagers or foreigners will purchase lands in or adjacent to a conservation project and open up tourism facilities that compete directly with the locally based ecotourism industry. Competing ecotourism operations run by nonvillagers have sprouted up in both the CBS and the GPMP. One ecotourism operation has fraudulently claimed that they were active participants in the CBS while never encouraging their clientele to participate in sanctuary programs or paying fees to the CBS management structure. One obvious result of this activity is a decrease in the income feeding directly into the village economy. In Gales Point, foreign business concerns have been purchasing private lands adjacent to the lagoons. Although foreign and Belize City entrepreneurs have expressed conservation intentions, an inevitable result of their presence will be a gradual dismantling of the community/cooperative management structure and strong competition from noncommunity-based tourism endeavors.

Affluent ecotourism not linked to the socioeconomic concerns and cultural fabric of the surrounding local community will diminish the very community and cultural attributes that the external programs are attempting to exploit. Such tourism projects outside the control of local peoples will thus destroy one of the main tourism attractions. In Belize, ecotourism competition is occurring throughout the country and will continue to increase unless steps are taken to limit such ventures. Some possible solutions include community members forming land partnerships to reduce pressures to sell properties, implementation of zoning regulations, legislation to protect the viability of rural conservation programs, and pressure from internal and external conservation organizations on operations attempting to infiltrate and exploit community conservation programs.

Discussion and Conclusions

Risk is an inevitable component of community-based projects due to the changing dynamics of any given community in response to unpredictable internal and external forces. Risk is especially prevalent in experimental projects such as the CBS. Our initial inexperience in creating a management structure for the CBS and the lack of adequate ecotourism planning hampered the smooth development and evolution of the CBS. Ecotourism efforts were focused on increasing tourist interest in the area rather than on creating a local infrastructure to accommodate the ecotourists. In retrospect, it would have been wiser to attract resources to build a small hotel operated by a village or CBS cooperative as was attempted in Gales Point. Instead, outside interests have attempted to capitalize on and exploit the reputation and success of the CBS. However, in the initiation of any untried technique for conservation, a simple question needs to be addressed: Is the proposed solution potentially better than the environmental degradation likely to result from continuing trends? In the case of the CBS and GPMP, the partial success of these projects and their continued endurance should be viewed and critically appraised as stepping stones and mileposts for continued experimentation in community conservation.

Community-based conservation projects demand a long-term commitment by initiators and concerned participants. However, the required human, financial, and material support to maintain such commitments is often at odds with the short time frames associated with many granting, funding, and human support agencies. Difficulty in securing funding, for these projects is due partly to the experimental nature of many of them, the unpredictability of outcomes, and the changing ecological matrix in which the projects are immersed. For example, despite widespread community interest and enthusiasm in the GPMP and despite interest in the program as a model for study, the project has had difficulty in attracting long-term funding. However, because of the low budgetary demands and cost effectiveness of programs such as the CBS and GPMP, even minimal levels of long-term financial commitment have real potential to ensure program stability.

The influence of the CBS and GPMP projects has extended beyond Belize's borders. These projects represent a unique situation where rural residents in a developing country have been setting a conservation precedent for both more affluent countries and other countries in various stages of development. Some of the experimental ideas and techniques used by the rural residents of Belize are now being used in a variety of projects in the United States, Mexico, and Russia (Horwich and Lyon 1996). The Community Baboon Sanctuary (CBS) introduced the potential for ecotourism to other rural Belizeans and inspired rural people to become involved in the industry. The CBS also stressed the difference between local management and empowerment versus locals working for outside tourism concerns. Such large outside agencies develop their own infrastructures for bringing tourists to a given site, allowing locals little control over tourism in their area. Given more responsibility, people respond with more involvement. Villagers initially perceived the wildlife and forests as an economic resource for tourism but conservation attitudes in the CBS are linked closely to the intrinsic value of the howler monkeys as well.

Initially, the tourism industry ignored the Community Baboon Sanctuary structure while flocking to the resource (Horwich and Lyon 1996). The travelers themselves embraced the conservation concepts but were rarely encouraged to contribute to the sanctuary; instead, local tourism efforts were often in competition with other national and international groups represented by the tours. This situation must change if the industry is to play a beneficial role in promoting conservation efforts. The industry must contribute some of its profits back into direct conservation efforts and community development; ecotourism programs should add a donation for each project visited in the total tour package and encourage additional contributions from their clients to the projects and encourage them to purchase goods and services from local people.

The influence and expansion of community-based conservation projects in the last decade recently has been explored (Western et al. 1994). However, there are still too few established projects; far more energy is spent on reviewing existing projects than is spent creating new ones. While we are encouraged by community participation in these ecotourism/conservation projects, we are disappointed that many in the ecotourism industry, its clients, and those engaged in academic research are not doing enough to support the ground-level conservation efforts. Despite glossy brochures and the preponderance of "ecotourism" companies, too few benefits from ecotourism go to local people, communities, or the protection of the environment, as the goals of ecotourism dictate. Rather, ecotourism often accentuates the economic disparity between the tourists and the local communities, sometimes with the consequent loss of the natural resources to the community. Any truly conservation-guided ecotourism company must be based on sustainability and the involvement and empowerment of the local people in rural areas where the ecotours occur.

References

Alderman, C. L. 1990. A study of the role of privately owned lands used for nature tourism, education and conservation. Conservation International, Washington, D.C.

Anon., 1995. *Guide to Community-Based Ecotourism in Belize*. The Ministry of Tourism and Environment and the Belize Enterprise for Sustained Technology, Belmopan, Belize.

Augusta, C., B. Boardman, and R. H. Horwich. 1993. Land use considerations for the Southern Lagoon watershed. Community Conservation Consultants, Gays Mills, Wis.

Boo, E. 1990. *Ecotourism: The Potentials and Pitfalls*. Vols. 1 and 2. World Wildlife Fund, Washington, D.C.

Boardman, B. 1994. Gales Point Manatee. *Belize Currents* 14: 4–6.

Ceballos-Lascurian, H. 1991. Tourism, ecotourism, and protected areas. Pages 24–30 in *Ecotourism and Resource Conservation*, volume 1. J. A. Kusler, ed. Omnipress, Madison, Wis.

de Groot, R. S. 1983. Tourism and conservation in the Galapagos Islands. *Biological Conservation* 26: 291–300.

Godfrey, G. 1990. Tourism development should involve Belizeans at every level. *Belize Today* 4: 9–11.

Government Information Service. 1994. *Belize Today* (video on community-based tourism). Ministry of Tourism and the Environment, Government of Belize, Belmopan, Belize.

Hartup, B. K. 1994. Community conservation in Belize: Demography, resource use, and attitudes of participating landowners. *Biological Conservation* 69: 235–241.

Horwich, R. H., and J. Lyon. 1988. Experimental technique for the conservation of private lands. *Journal of Medical Primatology* 17: 169–176.

———. 1990. *A Belizean Rainforest—the Community Baboon Sanctuary*. Orangutan Press, Gays Mills, Wis.

———. 1995. Multilevel conservation and education at the Community Baboon Sanctuary, Belize. Pages 235–253 in *Conserving Wildlife: International Education and Communication Approaches*, S. K. Jacobson, ed. Columbia University Press, New York.

————. 1996. Rural ecotourism as a conservation tool. In *Development of Tourism in Critical Environments*, T. V. Singh, ed. Centre for Tourism Research and Development, Lucknow, India.

Johnston, B. R. 1990. 'Save Our Beach Dem and Our Land Too!' The problems of tourism in 'America's Paradise.' *Cultural Survival Quarterly* 14: 31–37.

Lindberg, K., and J. Enriquez. 1994. *An Analysis of Ecotourism's Economic Contribution to Conservation and Development in Belize*. Vols. 1 and 2. World Wildlife Fund, Washington, D.C.

Lyon, J., and R. H. Horwich. 1996. Modification of tropical forest patches for wildlife protection and community conservation in Belize. Pages 213–229 in *Forest Patches in Tropical Landscapes*, J. Schelhas and R. Greenburg, eds. Island Press, Washington, D.C.

McGill, J. N. A. 1994. *Special Development Areas*. Consultancy Report No. 13 of the Rural Physical Planner, Ministry of Natural Resources, Belmopan, Belize.

Polisar, J., and R. H. Horwich. 1994. Conservation of the large economically important river turtle *Dermatemys mawii* in Belize. *Conservation Biology* 8: 338–342.

Werner, L. 1994. Pondering "Parks vs. People" in Belize. *Americas* (March/April).

Western, D., R. M. Wright, and S. C. Strum. 1994. *Natural Connections*. Island Press, Washington, D.C.

Zisman, S. 1989. *The Directory of Protected Areas and Sites of Nature Conservation Interest in Belize*. Occasional Publication No. 10, Department of Geography, University of Edinburgh, Scotland.

Chapter 24

Illuminating the Petén's Throne of Gold: The ProPetén Experiment in Conservation-Based Development

Conrad Reining and Carlos Soza Manzanero

There are so many people talking about the planet and how to save it, and so few taking action to make sure that happens. Talking or acting? That is the challenge.
—Wangari Maathai, The Greenbelt Movement, Kenya

Environmentalists and development professionals once regarded conservation and development as antithetical. However, there has been a growing understanding in recent years that conservation and development are not mutually exclusive, but, in fact, are mutually interconnected through the concept of sustainable development, defined by the World Commission on the Environment (The Brundtland Commission) in 1987 as development that "meets the needs of the present generation without compromising the needs of future generations" (Serageldin 1993). Considering that most "hotspots" of biodiversity lie within developing countries, it is important to understand the intimate connection between poverty and environmental degradation, because "rainforest parks are destroyed by need as well as greed" (Nations 1990). Developing countries simply do not have the luxury, as developed countries do, of "preserving" forests by putting fences around them with signs saying, "Settlers, stay out of this national park!" Instead, conservationists interested in saving tropical forests need to find alternative management approaches that move beyond a false "trees versus people" dichotomy. We need to create a new paradigm of sustainable development that considers both the health of ecosystems and the needs of the people living within and around them.

In recent years, an innovative model for this kind of sustainable development has emerged: biosphere reserves. In accordance with UNESCO guidelines, biosphere reserves are zoned into different levels of protection that blend wilderness areas with other zones intended for scientific research, tourism, education, and the economic activities of surrounding communities. This fluid, mosaic-like design is intended to incorporate the needs of local people living in the outer zone while giving them a vested interest in the protection of the reserve. As such, biosphere reserves would become "models of an ecologically balanced relationship between humans and their environments where, contrary to conventional wisdom, it would be possible to pursue higher economic standards of living while simultaneously ensuring the protection of critical environmental areas" (Wargo 1990). Yet, despite all the pleasant talk in academic circles about sustainable development and biosphere reserves, it is important to consider critically whether conservation and development can work together in the real world.

In this paper, we examine the case of the Maya Biosphere Reserve, established in 1990 in the Department of El Petén, Guatemala. This region is an important place for research and conservation work because for centuries it was a relatively isolated frontier land, untouched by modernity. The mixed-race peoples who settled in the Petén after the Spanish conquest in 1697 developed a "forest society" through methods of cash and subsistence production that were sustainable both economically and ecologically (Schwartz 1990). Today, many native Peténeros still base their subsistence on these extractive activities, showing that it is possible to use the forests without destroying them. These traditional Peténeros live by a value system of ecological reciprocity: what one takes from the forest, one must return in some fashion—a simple yet powerful concept that is consistent with modern conservation strategies (Schwartz 1995).

Within the past few decades, however, modernization and growth have occurred so quickly that they threaten to break down this forest society. The Petén's population has grown from roughly 20,000 people in 1960 (Schwartz 1990) to over 400,000 in the mid-1990s; the annual rate of growth in the region is currently at 9.8%, of which 6.6% stems from migration (M. A. Palacios, pers. comm. 1996). From 1960 to the present, nearly half of all the Petén's forests have been lost due to outside economic, political, and demographic factors. Also in this period, land tenure and political problems in other parts of Guatemala have forced landless peasants to migrate north in search of agricultural land. Most of these immigrants first settled in the southern Petén, but as resources there grow scarce, many continue to migrate to the northernmost forests of the department. Settling along roads initially opened for timber and oil exploitation, these new immigrants cut down large tracts of forest for extensive monocultivation of corn and cattle ranching because they are unfamiliar with the traditional livelihood strategies of the old forest society, and have little access to technical assistance, credit, and markets for products other than corn, beans, and beef.

Whether or not conservationists can slow present rates of deforestation in the Petén and save the Maya Biosphere Reserve while still meeting the needs of local people remains to be seen. This case study provides an overview of one nongovernmental organization's (NGO's) experiment in conservation-based development. With funding from the U.S. Agency for International Development (USAID), Conservation International established a local nongovernmental organization called ProPetén in 1991. This project seeks to strengthen the Guatemalan government's National Council for Protected Areas (CONAP), demarcate clearly the reserve's boundaries, intensify the use of already cleared lands in the buffer and multiple-use zones, build environmental awareness, and develop alternative economic activities that promote the conservation of standing forests. In doing so, ProPetén seeks to ally itself with the Peténero forest society.

ProPetén is very much a project of Conservation International (CI), a nonprofit organization dedicated to saving endangered tropical ecosystems in more than 20 countries in Asia, Africa, and Latin America. CI's mission is to conserve global biodiversity and demonstrate that human societies are able to live harmoniously with nature. In order to balance conservation goals with local needs, CI's ecosystem conservation approach integrates science, economics, and community development. ProPetén, CI's Guatemala program, employs this interdisciplinary approach, using scientific, socioeconomic, and political tools to develop solutions to complex ecological problems.

Based in Flores, the departmental capital and economic hub of the Petén, ProPetén works in communities in the central and western regions of the reserve. Given that most forest destruction occurs around access routes into the reserve, such as roads, rivers, and oil pipelines (Sader et al. 1994 and 1996), ProPetén decided to focus its energies along two important and endangered corridors (see Map 1 in Introduction to this volume): (1) the road from San Andrés to Carmelita and (2) the region surrounding the San Pedro and Chocop Rivers. ProPetén currently works with six key communities in these two zones: Carmelita, San Andrés, and San José (three older communities that retain strong Peténero values), and El Cruce a Dos Aguadas, Centro Campesino, and El Corozal (young communities settled within the last two decades with fewer ties to the traditional forest society). Despite their different settlement histories and value systems, these six communities have one important thing in common: they are permanent settlements whose residents will not leave the reserve. Given this reality, ProPetén's mission is to slow or stop deforestation around these communities by helping the residents design and implement integrated resource management strategies and develop economic alternatives to monocultural farming, cattle ranching, and unsustainable logging.

In addition to its community-based projects, ProPetén also works with government conservation agencies, local communities and municipalities, and other NGOs to improve the overall protection and management of the reserve. What follows is an in-depth report of ProPetén's ongoing work in promoting conservation-based development in the region. An equally detailed analysis of why these and other projects have or have not succeeded is beyond the scope of this paper. Nevertheless, in the conclusion of this chapter, we mention at least a few of the lessons we have learned and outline some of the challenges ahead. In future publications, we hope to share more information and critical perspectives on ProPetén's experiences in the field.

Natural Forest Management

ProPetén works with several communities in the reserve to develop plans for integrated resource management. The overall goal of these plans is to help communities maximize the economic return from their lands while maintaining healthy and diverse ecosystems. ProPetén helps communities manage multiple resources within their jurisdiction, including timber, nontimber forest products, ecotourism attractions, wildlife, archaeological sites, and agricultural and grazing lands. ProPetén also helps communities determine sites that, for ecological or cultural reasons, should be off-limits to any kind of intensive use. By doing so, a community can tailor its resource management plans to suit its socioeconomic profile and the biophysical characteristics of its landholdings. ProPetén uses several methods to implement this strategy, such as helping communities to gain legally recognized access rights to forest lands, developing the technical and institutional capacity within those communities to manage their forests, and building markets for new and existing forest products.

Integrated Forestry in Carmelita

Situated deep within the multiple-use zone of the reserve, Carmelita is home to 65 families. This community is an excellent example of the forest society because its residents have depended for decades on the extraction of forest products for their livelihoods (Reining et al. 1992). According to the laws that established the reserve, residents of Carmelita have a right to carry out carefully controlled extraction of timber and nontimber forest products around the community (CATIE 1996). In August 1996, ProPetén helped Carmelita to obtain from CONAP legally recognized access rights to about 53,000 ha of land in the multiple-use zone. In return, the residents have promised to protect the forest from outsiders who would use it for unsustainable activities such as cattle ranching. This community concession will also help protect the nearby national park of El Mirador from colonization by settlers.

In addition to legal advice, ProPetén provides training and technical assistance to the community to improve forest extraction activities in the concession area. With input from the community, ProPetén developed a comprehensive management plan based on broad-scale resource surveys of the entire concession area, detailed ecological and silvicultural studies of smaller areas to be used for extractive activities and tourism, marketing and economic analyses, and a formal environmental assessment. To further evaluate the ecological impact of the management plan, ProPetén and the communities monitor populations of key economic species and overall changes in biodiversity.

Because this project seeks to strengthen the community's tradition of harvesting different forest products, timber extraction plays a relatively minor role in the management plan. Indeed, only 8,000 of the 53,000 ha in the concession will be subject to timber extraction. Two species with existing markets, mahogany (*Swietenia macrophylla*) and Spanish cedar (*Cedrela odorata*), plus up to five more secondary species, will be selectively extracted on a 40-year cutting cycle. The community will also harvest xate, chicle, and allspice on these same 8,000 ha. The remaining 45,000 ha will either be set aside for protection or used for harvesting nontimber forest products, economic and ecological factors permitting.

Agroforestry, Tree Nurseries, and Reforestation

Many long-time residents of the Petén have developed their own agroforestry systems, combining both native and imported species. New migrants to the Petén, however, often adopt methods of unsustainable, monocultural farming because they are unfamiliar with integrated cropping techniques suited to the thin soils of the Petén (Figure 24.1). New migrants also have little access to credit, technical assistance, and markets for projects other than corn, beans, and beef. To address this problem, ProPetén trains farmers in alternative agricultural methods that combine old Peténero farming traditions with recent innovations. Led by Zacarías Quixchán of San Andrés, a local, self-taught expert in agroforestry, ProPetén initiated a series of workshops and established agroforestry demonstration plots with families in the communities of El Cruce a Dos Aguadas, Carmelita, and Centro Campesino in 1995.

Complementing this work, ProPetén helps communities to enrich the surrounding forests with key economic species, including mahogany, Spanish cedar, chicle (*Manilkara zapota*), allspice (*Pimenta dioica*), and siricote (*Cordia dodecandra*). ProPetén currently supports nurseries in four communities that

Figure 24.1

Dwellings of colonists along the road to El Naranjo. (Photo by James D. Nations.)

provide tree seedlings to local families and schools to reforest fallow agricultural plots. In a special project in Carmelita, ProPetén has reforested a plot with chicle to research and monitor regeneration of this species.

Environmental Enterprises

In addition to helping communities manage their forests better, ProPetén works to help local people find alternative livelihoods through the development of micro-enterprises based on value-added forest products and low-impact tourism. ProPetén provides a wide range of support services to these enterprises in areas such as product development and marketing, business training, low-cost credit, and appropriate technology. Finally, through its monitoring and evaluation program, ProPetén ensures that all these micro-enterprises are economically, ecologically, and socially responsible and sustainable.

Value-Added Forest Products

The people of the Petén have long traditions in harvesting and marketing forest products, some of which date back to pre-Columbian times. Within the reserve lie high densities of economically valuable timber and nontimber forest species—densities so high, in fact, that scientists hypothesize that they might be the result of ancient Maya selection (Brokaw 1990). The extraction of gums, ornamental plants, spices, resins, oils, waxes, honey, medicinal plants, and construction materials from the forest continues to provide a substantial source of income for the rural people of the Petén. In some cases, these resources can provide a local family with three times the average daily wage in the Petén—far more than the return from clearing forests to plant corn or raise cattle (Reining et al. 1992). Building on these harvesting traditions, ProPetén has developed the value-added forest products described below.

Potpourri. In the village of El Cruce a Dos Aguadas, ProPetén has assisted local people to produce a potpourri, Gatherings™, made from forest botanicals. Early in 1993, ProPetén helped the community build a processing facility for the potpourri and other nontimber forest products (Figure 24.2). Workers collect assorted forest botanical products such as dried leaves, seeds, hulls, flowers, and bark. The hand-collected botanicals are then sun-dried, colored with vegetable dyes, scented with fragrant natural oils, and packaged in hand-painted gourds or biodegradable cellophane. CI's Conservation Enterprise Department helps to market the potpourri at local, national, and international levels, working, for instance, with two U.S.-based distributors who sell Gatherings™ to a variety of retail stores and catalogues. By 1995, annual production of this potpourri had reached 12,000 units, and today the processing facility has the capacity to produce at least 25,000 units a year. The enterprise currently employs three people full-time, approximately five more people part-time, and more than one hundred harvesters during the collection season. Community participants like the project because the full-time employees earn more than they would in subsistence agriculture, and the part-time workers earn cash to supplement other subsistence activities.

Xate, chicle, and allspice. Historically, the three most important nontimber forest products in the Petén have been xate, chicle, and allspice. Xate (*Chamaedorea* spp.) is an ornamental palm exported for use as a green backdrop in flower arrangements. Allspice is the immature fruit of *Pimenta dioica*, which, when dried, is used in cooking worldwide and for curing fish in some parts of Europe and Russia. Chicle, a white latex harvested from *Manilkara zapota*, serves as the base for natural chewing gum. Although synthetics have largely replaced chicle in the U.S. and European gum industry, Japanese companies still export the natural ingredient to other Asian gum companies.

Between 5,000 and 7,000 families in the Petén earn income from the harvest of these products, which bring $4 to $6 million to Guatemala's economy each year. Full- and part-time harvesters collect these products throughout the reserve, with production concentrated in the towns of Carmelita and Uaxactún (Reining et al. 1992). ProPetén seeks to strengthen participation in

Figure 24.2

Processing materials at the potpourri facility at
the village of El Cruce a Dos Aguadas. (Photo ©
Syms/Boyton.)

these activities and ensure that harvesting techniques and quantities are ecologically sustainable.

To improve the xate industry, ProPetén seeks to address two principal problems: first, harvesters are paid by the quantity, not the quality, of the leaves
they collect, which tends to encourage overharvesting. Second, facilities for
selecting and packaging the leaves are located in the urban areas of San Ben-
ito and Santa Elena, as well as Guatemala City. The high cost of transporting
the harvest to these selection and packing facilities far from the source means
that profits typically go to the middlemen, rather than to the harvesters themselves. In response to these problems, ProPetén is working with a cooperative
of ten women in Carmelita to establish a processing facility directly in the village by late 1996. This cooperative will pay more for high quality xate leaves,
which will keep more of the final product value in the community and should
discourage harvesters from cutting unmarketable plants.

ProPetén also works with several communities, including Carmelita, Uaxactún, and El Cruce a Dos Aguadas, to improve techniques for harvesting allspice berries and leaves. The goal of this project is to establish an oil production facility that will be owned and operated by members of a community, much like the xate processing cooperative in Carmelita. This business has the potential to be quite lucrative because appropriate distillation systems can produce an essential allspice oil that sells for nearly U.S. $50/lb on the New York commodities market. ProPetén has completed marketing analyses, studies on appropriate technology, and community business training for this project, and production will probably begin in mid-1997.

Ingredients for personal care products: Corozo palm oil and jaboncillo. In May 1994, Conservation International launched the Renewable Rainforest Resources project with Croda Inc., a leading supplier of raw materials such as vegetable oils, essential oils, and waxes to makers of personal care products and cosmetics. This collaboration enables CI to introduce sustainably harvested products into the mainstream personal care market. As of late 1996, three of the five products being traded under the Croda/CI partnership come from the Petén, including oil extracted from the nuts of the corozo palm (*Orbignya cohune*), extracts of jaboncillo or "soap berry" (*Sapindus saponaria*), and allspice extract.

In particular, corozo oil has great marketing potential because it can be used as a substitute for palm oil, a common ingredient in personal care products. In contrast to plantation-produced palm oil, corozo grows naturally in the Petén and is one of the most common species in the reserve. Taking advantage of corozo's natural abundance, ProPetén initiated the production of corozo oil in 1994 and is currently selling four to six tons per year to Croda Inc. In addition to these international sales, the national market for corozo oil looks favorable, according to studies by CI staff. For logistical and technological reasons, ProPetén initially established a production facility in the Petén's central urban area. However, the organization soon hopes to transfer this facility with appropriate technology to a community called La Máquina in the buffer zone of the reserve. Like the women's xate cooperative in Carmelita, this business would be locally owned and operated.

Enchanted gold leaves. In conjunction with a U.S.-based gift manufacturer called Enchanted Gold, ProPetén is coordinating a project with residents of El Cruce a Dos Aguadas to collect bulk quantities of leaves with interesting shapes or vein patterns, which come mainly from secondary forests around the community. Local workers press the leaves for shipment to the U.S., where they are dipped in gold to make jewelry, Christmas ornaments, and bookmarks. The project employs three people full-time during the dry season, plus dozens of part-time collectors. Coupled with the potpourri production center located in the same village, this enterprise has helped create a local constituency with a vested economic interest in the survival of the surrounding forest.

Low-Impact Nature and Adventure Tourism

There is great potential in the Petén to develop low-impact nature and adventure tourism (or "ecotourism") in ways that benefit local people and help protect the integrity of the reserve. Tourism is already an important part of Guatemala's national economy, generating more than $250 million annually. Moreover, ecotourism is the fastest-growing segment of Guatemala's tourism industry, and the Petén is the fastest-growing ecotourism destination in the country (INGUAT 1995a, 1995b). The ecotourism market from the U.S. and Canada is quite large; recent studies indicate that the Petén is an ideal destination for such tourists (HLA and ARA 1995). Roughly 15% of all tourists to Guatemala travel to the Petén to see the extensive Maya ruins of Tikal, which drew over 100,000 visitors in 1994 (INGUAT 1995a). Despite these promising statistics, few tourists venture outside of Tikal to explore the dozens of significant Maya ruins located across the region. ProPetén, therefore, seeks to promote ecotourism to alternative sites in the Petén through the projects described below. In addition to these field programs, ProPetén is working with local communities, private tour operators, government agencies, and other NGOs to determine carrying capacities and other guidelines for tourism in the reserve.

Tour routes. ProPetén promotes alternative tourism routes to archaeologically and ecologically important areas of the reserve, which can benefit regional conservation efforts in two complementary ways. First, these tourism initiatives create jobs and income for rural villages in hostelry, guiding, and logistical support. Through these opportunities, local people become economically invested in maintaining the ecological and cultural integrity of the sites. Second, strong evidence also suggests that an increased tourist presence in remote areas can help limit illegal commercial logging, wildlife poaching, and looting of archaeological sites, which are significant problems in the reserve.

To help develop these routes, ProPetén provides financial and technical assistance in four areas:

(1) *Development of tourism products*: ProPetén works with local communities to design the routes and obtain financing to build any necessary infrastructure, such as trails, rustic lodges, camping grounds, and sanitation services.

(2) *Community organization and training*: ProPetén has established local tourism committees in the three participating communities of Carmelita, Centro Campesino, and El Cruce. Through these committees, community members receive training in business, foreign languages, and general tourism

services such as hostelry, guiding, and food preparation.

(3) *Marketing and promotion*: With support from CI's Conservation Enterprise Department, ProPetén promotes and markets the ecotourism routes on both national and international levels. Staff members also facilitate links between private tour operators and the communities.

(4) *Monitoring and evaluation*: ProPetén's scientific research team evaluates the short- and long-term impacts of increased tourism in the reserve. Based on community input, they have developed a unique monitoring program in which both guides and tourists will collect information on the presence of macrofauna, the condition of the trails, camping grounds, and sites, and human settlement along the routes.

By involving community members in all stages of development of the routes, ProPetén hopes to maximize the economic benefits and employment opportunities for local people.

So far, ProPetén has established three ecotourism routes along strategic corridors of the reserve, which are called the Scarlet Macaw Trail, El Mirador Trail, and Bio-Itzá–El Zotz Trail. Of the three, the six-day tour of the Scarlet Macaw Trail is the best developed. Departing from the island of Flores, the first destination is Centro Campesino, a typical agricultural community in the buffer zone south of the reserve, which provides overnight lodging, guides, horses, and food. The route continues to the archaeological site of El Perú, situated within dense tropical forest. Although the site has been neither thoroughly excavated nor interpreted, it serves as a striking example of the rampant looting of the Petén's archaeological treasures because black-marketeers have sawed off the faces of many of El Perú's spectacular stelae (stone monoliths) for sale to private collectors and museums in the U.S. and Europe (Graham 1988). The site is also home to nesting grounds of the scarlet macaw, which is highly endangered because poachers steal month-old chicks for sale in the illegal pet trade. Since the initiation of the route, however, archaeological looting and nest poaching have decreased, according to ProPetén staff.

The route continues east along the Río San Pedro, passing ProPetén's biological station and the community of Paso Caballos. Traveling by boat and then on foot, tourists arrive to the panoramic cliffs of Buena Vista, which provide an excellent view of the floodplains below. After overnight camping at the bluffs, the next destination along the route is the potpourri production center in El Cruce a Dos Aguadas. From there, tourists drive to San Andrés for relaxation and swimming in Lake Petén Itzá. A day-long visit to the ruins of Tikal at the end of the excursion is optional. As this description indicates, the Scarlet Macaw Trail employs varied transportation methods (horseback, boat, foot, and car) and highlights different ecological, geographical, archaeological, and social attractions.

All told, between six and ten people in each community receive direct economic benefits as guides and cooks for the ecotourism routes. In May 1996, ProPetén organized a successful trip along the Scarlet Macaw Trail with well-known and reputable tour operators. At the moment, ten of these international operators have committed to promoting the trip to their clients in 1997, and the communities hope to host at least 15 trips in the upcoming year.

Center for Information on the Nature, Culture, and Arts of the Petén

Located in the main square of Flores, the Center for Information on the Nature, Culture and Arts of the Petén (CINCAP) is a hub for regional tourism initiatives. Since its opening in 1994, several thousand people have visited the center. In addition to providing visitors with information and promotional materials on ecotourism in the Petén, the center holds exhibitions concerning the natural and social history of the region's ancient and modern cultures, and it also houses a self-sufficient cooperative store that sells local handicrafts and ecological products. CINCAP also serves as a center for regional environmental education and training in tourism and has facilities to host conferences and meetings for community groups, NGOs, and government agencies.

Eco-Escuela de Español

The Eco-Escuela is located in the town of San Andrés, across the lake from the island of Flores. This Spanish school provides tourists with an ecologically oriented language program and homestays with local families. In addition to daily, one-on-one language instruction, students may participate in a variety of environmental activities, including interpretive nature walks, volunteer work, field trips, and weekend excursions into the reserve. Involving both language students and local residents in sustainable tourism initiatives, the Eco-Escuela has built an educational nature trail for the community, begun outreach programs to local schools, and started a fund for community improvements. The school also links its students to ProPetén's other regional initiatives in ecotourism, such as the alternative tour routes described above.

Because all the teachers, administrators, and hosts are from San Andrés, the school generates significant revenue for the community. As of October 1996, the Eco-Escuela was providing direct economic benefits to nearly 60 families in San Andrés, equal to the number once employed by a large sawmill in town, which closed in the early 1990s. Since its inception in 1993, the school has provided thousands of student-weeks of language training. Over 20 students on average attend the school each week, and more than 600 students study at the school each year. Since opening its doors in 1993, the school has worked toward financial and managerial independence from ProPetén, and in

October 1996, ownership and management were completely transferred to the teachers and host families.

Monitoring and Evaluation

As the aforementioned projects evolved, it became clear that ProPetén needed to establish complementary projects in monitoring and evaluation. In 1994, the organization solidified its ecological and social investigations into a cross-cutting program that seeks to establish a better understanding of the complex anthropogenic impacts on forest cover and biodiversity in the reserve. Based on this information, ProPetén, along with other governmental and nongovernmental organizations, can more effectively prioritize its conservation work. Some monitoring projects are aimed at evaluating the effects—both positive and negative—of ProPetén's activities, while others address factors beyond the scope of the project's work. ProPetén's monitoring and evaluation program operates at three levels of resolution, as outlined in the next few paragraphs.

At the first and broadest level of monitoring, ProPetén monitors the biological integrity of the entire reserve and its buffer zone, totaling over 2 million ha. Using a time-series change detection process, a team from the University of Maine, NASA, and ProPetén analyzed LANDSAT satellite imagery from 1986, 1990, 1993, and 1995. This analysis showed that between 1990 and 1993, annual rates of forest clearing in the buffer zone were about 2.2%. From 1993 to 1995, the annual rate increased to 2.7% in the buffer zone. During that same period, annual deforestation also increased within the core and multiple-use zones, averaging about 0.2% change during the 1990–93 period and 0.4% from 1993 to 1995 (Sader et al. 1996). Broad-scale satellite studies such as this one will be carried out every two to three years to enable governmental and nongovernmental organizations to assess the impact of their regional conservation programs on land use in the reserve.

At the second level of monitoring, ProPetén focuses on its three priority zones, which range from 85,000 to 125,000 ha each: (1) the eastern side of the Laguna del Tigre National Park, (2) the El Cruce a Dos Aguadas–El Zotz Biotope complex, and (3) the Carmelita–El Mirador National Park complex. At this level, ProPetén carries out several ecological monitoring activities, which include classifying and evaluating changes in vegetative communities using remotely sensed data, verifying remotely sensed data via on-the-ground surveys, and mapping and monitoring harvester camps, road networks, and water sources used by forest harvesters. Socioeconomic monitoring at this level focuses on changes in land-use patterns and the large-scale activities of forest harvesters and communities.

The third level of monitoring focuses on individual ecological and human communities. At this scale, ProPetén carries out ecological studies to measure the sustainability of its projects in natural forest management, the extraction of nontimber forest products, and the development of ecotourism within the reserve. Ecological topics include studies on phenology of trees of ecological importance, characterization of flora and fauna, and population monitoring of endangered wildlife, timber species, and species used in nontimber forest products (Gould and Rodríguez 1996). ProPetén also carries out socioeconomic research on the community level to evaluate various anthropogenic impacts on the reserve. For example, researchers conduct regular surveys of communities within the reserve and "control" communities outside the reserve to assess levels of education, poverty, and environmental awareness and behavior. In these socioeconomic investigations, researchers pay close attention to variables of class, ethnicity, gender, and age.

All monitoring data are integrated into ProPetén's Geographic Information System (GIS). By integrating spatial data (such as roads, rivers, and political boundaries) with descriptive data (such as topography and forest inventories), GIS technology allows local researchers to assemble, display, and analyze diverse sets of data to develop better management plans for forestry, tourism, and so on. For example, ProPetén's forest management team combines resource inventories and topographical data on the GIS to determine which areas are most suitable for selective timber extraction in Carmelita. Using additional software, ProPetén's staff can use satellite images to map out changes in forest cover throughout the reserve. The GIS is also capable of integrating socioeconomic data such as census figures with physical, biological, and ecological data. ProPetén shares this information with other NGOs and governmental decisionmakers to help them make better conservation policies for the reserve.

Policy and Legal Issues

To complement and support its conservation projects, ProPetén has launched a series of initiatives on local, national, and international levels to analyze and reform laws and policies regulating petroleum development, the harvesting of timber and nontimber forest products, tourism, and migration/settlement in the reserve. ProPetén also plays a role in catalyzing and coordinating the proper enforcement of those policies by the appropriate institutions. This policy work requires constant and close consultation with CONAP and other government agencies, USAID, local communities, municipalities, the business sector, forest harvester groups, and other NGOs. With an office in Guatemala City, ProPetén's policy department serves, in effect, as a "watchdog" for the reserve by investigating and monitoring decisions made by government and business leaders in Guatemala City, Washington, D.C., and even in the distant offices of multinational corporations. In other words, the

policy department establishes a critical link between political centers of decision making and the areas and people affected by those decisions. Recent policy projects are described below.

User Rights for Traditional Harvesters

One of ProPetén's policy priorities is to help harvester groups and communities obtain legally recognized rights to carry out sustainable, extractive activities in the multiple-use zone of the Reserve. As described earlier in this chapter, residents of Carmelita have earned their living for many decades through
the sustainable extraction of forest products. With support from ProPetén's
legal team, leaders of Carmelita recently completed negotiations with
CONAP to receive a community forest concession of 53,000 ha. In June
1997, the community completed its first wood harvest under the contract negotiated with CONAP. By formalizing their right to the resources in the surrounding forest, this community concession gives Carmelita residents a stake
in protecting their forests from outside agriculturists, ranchers, and industrial
loggers.

Management of Nontimber Forest Products, Tourism, and Oil and Gas in the Maya Biosphere Reserve

In collaboration with various governmental, nongovernmental, business, and
community groups, ProPetén is developing guidelines for the management of
nontimber resources, tourism, and petroleum in the reserve. In the case of
nontimber products, important issues include the size of harvest concessions,
licensing and revenue systems, and monitoring and evaluation techniques
(Sobenes 1995). For tourism, key issues include the roles of CONAP and the
Guatemalan National Institute for Tourism (INGUAT) in the management
of tourism in the reserve, if and how tourism concessions will be granted, and
fee structures for protected areas (Godoy 1996). Important topics in the proposed guidelines for oil and gas development include performance bonds,
restoration standards, and the siting of pipelines, roads, and waste pits (Gordon et al. 1996). With working papers already completed for each of these
topics, ProPetén will initiate a process of consultation and consensus-building
with relevant parties on these guidelines, which it hopes to complete by the
end of 1997.

ProPetén established itself as an effective and powerful negotiator through
more than two years of policy work to protect one of the core zones of the reserve, Laguna del Tigre National Park, which holds Central America's largest
freshwater wetlands and, unfortunately, also contains the region's largest oil
field. In 1994, Basic Resources, the transnational petroleum company operat-

ing the field, received a $20 million loan from the World Bank's International Finance Corporation (IFC) to build a pipeline through the Reserve (Figure 24.3). In 1995, Basic approached the IFC for an additional $24 million for oil field expansion and the construction of another pipeline outside the park. In response, ProPetén's policy staff worked with CONAP and CONAMA to increase their regulatory oversight of these activities. After two years of difficult negotiations, CI achieved a significant victory in July 1996 when Basic agreed to strengthen its own environmental management practices and receive biannual monitoring visits from the IFC's environmental staff. The oil company also agreed to contribute $130,000 annually until at least 2010 for general management and protection of the Laguna del Tigre National Park, in addition to expanding their budget for environmental management in the contract area. ProPetén's policy staff is now helping to determine conservation priorities for the region and will suggest how these funds can be most effectively administered and spent. Also, the policy staff will maintain a vigilant watch over the oil company's work and will file formal written complaints to the proper authorities if Basic fails to comply with the negotiated agreements.

Figure 24.3

Forest clearing along a pipeline route in the Petén.
(Photo © Conrad C. S. Reining.)

Core Zone Protection

In the second phase of USAID's Maya Biosphere Reserve project, which began in 1996, ProPetén assumed responsibility for facilitating core zone protection and management in three areas of the central reserve: Laguna del Tigre National Park, El Mirador National Park, and the El Zotz Biotope. Until 1996, ProPetén had primarily focused on forest management, sustainable economic alternatives, and applied research—in other words, activities suited to the multiple-use and buffer zones of the reserve. Core zone protection and management is quite different work, including activities such as demarcating boundaries; training, managing, and housing park guards; and working with nearby communities to respect and protect the integrity of core zones. ProPetén is not responsible for the actual implementation of all this work; implementation is the responsibility of CONAP and CECON (the Center for Conservation Studies at the University of San Carlos). Rather, ProPetén's role is that of a catalyst that ensures that the work gets done in a timely fashion with the involvement of all appropriate parties. Demarcation will be completed for El Zotz and will be underway for eastern Laguna del Tigre by the end of 1996, and demarcation of El Mirador will be completed in 1997.

To date, most of ProPeten's core-zone protection work has focused on the eastern side of Laguna del Tigre. These activities are centered around the Scarlet Macaw Biological Station, located at the confluence of the Sacluc and San Pedro Rivers. The surrounding ecosystems include primary and secondary upland forest, floodplain forest, grass-sedge wetlands, and recently abandoned farms. The station has two main purposes: to provide a space where scientists may conduct research under relatively controlled conditions and monitor changes in biodiversity, and to establish a joint presence with CONAP aimed at discouraging colonization of the river corridors. With the collaboration of CONAP and the municipality of San Andrés, the station was completed in early 1997. Built on the site of an old hunting and logging camp, the station had cabins and bunkhouses for workers and researchers, electrical power, radio communications, a laboratory, and a network of trails on the old logging roads.

With a commanding view of both rivers and the surrounding floodplains, the biological station serves to discourage colonization of the national park. In fact, 11 families have relocated outside the reserve as a direct result of the station, and illegal logging and hunting have virtually ceased in the immediate vicinity. ProPetén hopes to expand the station's zone of influence to cover about 80,000 ha of the national park through the establishment of several satellite stations guarded by CONAP or the San Andrés municipality. However, the station's strategic location is also a liability. In March 1997, the station was completely destroyed by a well-organized group of settlers, and 13 of the station's workers were taken hostage for two days. ProPetén has reoccupied the site, begun reconstruction, and negotiated with nearby settlements. Nevertheless, this event serves to illustrate the great challenges facing the reserve.

Community Organization and Training

One of the main goals of ProPetén is to ensure that all the aforementioned conservation-based development projects become self-sufficient and run by local communities. To achieve this kind of sustainability, a truly interdisciplinary and participatory approach is necessary. With that in mind, ProPetén established a cross-cutting program in community organization and training in February 1993. This program seeks to foster self-sufficiency in the communities and to improve the capacity of local people to explore a broad range of long-term conservation choices.

ProPetén's extension workers constitute the heart of the community organization and training program. They are typically young teachers or high school graduates who are hired by ProPetén to live and work in rural communities of the reserve with ongoing conservation projects. These extensionists coordinate ProPetén's projects with local groups and work to ensure that the communities are sufficiently well organized socially and politically to take on ownership of the projects in the long term.

In some cases, ProPetén's extensionists work with established groups such as the communities' civic improvement committees (*comités de promejoramiento*). In other cases, the extension team helps to establish ad hoc committees dedicated to a specific activity such as tourism or forest management. The extensionists work closely with these local groups to coordinate all training sessions and workshops held by ProPetén's forest management, environmental enterprise, and policy programs. The extension team also helps find instructors and teachers for these training sessions, mainly selecting individuals from other NGOs and government agencies. Finally, as needs arise, the extensionists provide support for local groups such as dispute mediation among local leaders, advice on petitioning government agencies for better community services, and training in business and accounting skills.

Given the realities of poverty, it would be difficult for ProPetén to work in rural communities on conservation issues without also addressing basic human needs. Hence, ProPetén's extensionists seek to address the general development needs of communities whenever possible. In the past, they have sponsored projects to build latrines and energy-efficient stoves, coordinate community clean-ups, establish family gardens with local women, seek medical supplies for health clinics, and so on.

Because women in the Petén are socially connected to family and community in ways that men often are not, the involvement and empowerment of women is crucial to sustainable development (Grandia 1996). Therefore,

ProPetén seeks to create conditions to stimulate women's equality in society and improve the ability of local women to make a broader range of economic and life choices in childbearing, health care, education, and natural resource management for themselves and their children. Indeed, women are very involved with ProPetén's environmental enterprise programs; for example, a majority of the owners and managers of the Eco-Escuela are women, and all of the participants in the newly formed xate cooperative in Carmelita are women.

Also, because many villagers in the Petén have little schooling, they require training not only for specific conservation projects, but also for basic skills such as reading, writing, and simple arithmetic. In fact, in rural communities of the reserve, at least half of the residents are illiterate and most others have only attended primary school for a few years and read with minimal literacy. To help raise education levels in these communities, ProPetén's extension team facilitates the work of CONALFA, a government literacy program, and IGER, a nongovernmental program that provides adult education by correspondence. The ProPetén extensionists also incorporate environmental themes into the curricula of these two programs and, in some communities, actually teach the classes.

In addition to these two programs, ProPetén's extensionists give weekly and sometimes even daily lessons about conservation in the primary schools. They also work with local teachers to develop educational activities for children that might include guest lectures, arts and crafts with ecological themes, field trips to the forest, tree plantings, and school gardens. To support these educational programs, ProPetén has established "ecological libraries" in two communities, El Cruce a Dos Aguadas and Carmelita, which have reading materials relevant to rural life in the Petén.

Conclusions

Gustavo Valenzuela, an artist and intellectual who has lived in the Petén most of his life, once remarked to one of the authors of this chapter, "*Somos mendigos en un trono de oro*" ("We are beggars on a throne of gold"). He believes that immediate poverty prevents the local people of the Petén from seeing the great sustainable wealth of the forest environment they inhabit. Out of economic necessity, they are forced to cut down the forest for swidden agriculture. Still others cut down the forest for short-term profits in cattle ranching and logging. In response to this destruction, conservationists in the NGO community are trying to develop alternative economic activities for local people that will give value to a standing forest.

The choices for the future of the Petén are difficult and, like beggars sitting on a throne of gold, we may not always have a clear vision about which path to take. Is "sustainable development" possible or realistic for the Petén? As

Norman Schwartz (1990) writes, the "Petén is no longer an isolated hinterland. The frontier has been settled, and the society has become unsettled." Indeed, in recent history the Petén has been characterized by unsettling and anarchic economic development. Over half of the Petén's forests have been cut down for the benefit of a small group of loggers, cattle ranchers, and military generals. On paper, the cash generated from this deforestation has contributed to national "growth." Yet, the destruction of the Petén's rich biological wealth has not resulted in any real improvements in the well-being of the thousands of people who have migrated to the Petén in search of a better life. They remain poor, still beggars, as the throne of gold disappears beneath them.

Schwartz (1990) observes, "Peténeros argue that there is still time to save the forests. There may also be time to rebuild a more humane, stable way of life in the lowlands." With the faith that there is still time to protect the reserve while meeting local people's needs, ProPetén has developed the five-pronged approach to conservation-based development discussed in this chapter: (1) integrated resource management; (2) environmental enterprise development; (3) monitoring and evaluation; (4) natural resource policy analysis and reform; and (5) community organization and training. While we have thus far emphasized the achievements of ProPetén and hope they may serve as models for future conservation-based development initiatives, we also acknowledge that ProPetén has made mistakes. Moreover, the organization has not fully resolved some fundamental tensions that exist between its conservation goals and regional development needs. We present these unresolved issues below as a series of questions that outline some of the challenges ahead for ProPetén.

Will communities take on ownership of these projects in the long term? Are ProPetén's projects socially sustainable? Based on a fundamental belief that conservation and development programs must be people-centered, ProPetén has tried to promote local participation at every step of the process. However, given limited resources and time constraints, we sometimes find ourselves reverting to old "top-down" methods of development work. If ProPetén's projects are to be truly participatory and democratic, it may take years, even decades, to begin witnessing concrete changes. Yet, because donors are anxious to see results, ProPetén may be rushing into communities too fast and cutting short the slow, participatory methods needed to plan projects properly. ProPetén works quickly, however, because we are keenly aware of the rapid rates of deforestation in the region. As such, we fear that by the time local people fully perceive themselves as stakeholders in the conservation of the reserve, there may not be any forests left.

How can ProPetén best work with migrant settlements that lack unified community organizations? ProPetén works with many heterogeneous communities with different political structures. Older villages like Carmelita have strong local leaders who support conservation initiatives. Other recently settled villages, like El Cruce a Dos Aguadas, are strongly divided by ethnicity and class, and some leaders are opposed to conservation initiatives. As an "outsider," ProPetén sometimes finds itself unwittingly embroiled in local political struggles and uncomfortably allied with particular factions in these divided communities. Our challenge is to find ways of avoiding such alliances and/or redirecting them for the benefit of conservation.

Is ProPetén reaching the poorest of the poor, or is it inadvertently magnifying social and economic inequalities? In ProPetén's community-based projects, the people most likely to participate are the "middle poor"—in other words, those who are a little better off economically and can take the risk of investing time and energy into conservation projects. Even as ProPetén helps the middle poor to improve their economic well-being, we cannot be certain that we are achieving our conservation goals, because the organization cannot control how local people spend their earnings. For example, there is no guarantee that a person working for the potpourri production center in El Cruce will not invest his or her earnings in agricultural expansion, especially if this person does not have a secure food base. Hence, we must constantly be aware of the roles that "greed" and "need" play in deforestation—and consciously expand our efforts to reach the poorest of the poor. Indeed, it is often the neediest or the very poor (i.e., the newest immigrants to the region) who carry out the most unsustainable livelihood strategies.

Does ProPetén spread its energies too thinly when carrying out interdisciplinary work? Is the organization trying to do too much, too fast? In this ever-challenging work, ProPetén staff members find themselves having to be experts on so many things—forest management, law, business, anthropology, agriculture, community organizing, public health, and so on. Because deforestation is happening so quickly, it is tempting to adopt new projects even though they may diffuse the organization's energy too much. Perhaps a more productive approach would be to share the work by building coalitions among NGOs who have different kinds of expertise.

Are community development needs necessarily compatible with conservation? We must acknowledge that some conservation and development goals may be irreconcilable. For instance, local people have petitioned ProPetén's help in repairing, even paving, roads into the reserve. However, such a project would be incompatible with the organization's conservation goals because it would attract new settlers into forested areas. Yet, how do conservationists—who travel in four-wheel-drive trucks across the reserve—explain (unhypocritically) to a local farmer that the road to the market should not be paved or improved?

Will ProPetén's work be "drowned out" by external factors? Despite widespread attention by the international environmental community, the reserve continues to be threatened by economic, political, and demographic trends—many of which are beyond the power of any single NGO to change. Whitacre (1996) argues that too many conservation groups concentrate their efforts *within* the reserve, when the greatest threat to the reserve is the expansion of the agricultural frontier. He argues, therefore that governmental and non-governmental conservation groups ought to focus more on the "ultimate" factors of deforestation such as migration and population growth, which originate outside the reserve.

Other significant threats to the reserve today include oil development, industrial logging, and repatriation of refugees from Mexico. Even as we "act locally" to establish economic alternatives to deforestation, we must "act globally" as well to address these and other external factors that threaten the reserve. This leads us to our next and final question: *Is there political will to support conservation-based development and resolve external threats to the reserve?* The long-term success of NGOs will depend not only on their own programs, but also on the ability of governmental institutions to function effectively. CONAP, the most important public institution working for conservation in the Petén, lacks political and financial support from the national government. With the recent election of President Alvaro Arzú, CONAP has reorganized itself with several positive results. Overall, the organization is more professional; it has increased its interaction with the NGOs and other branches of government and has finally filled many posts that had been chronically vacant since the creation of the reserve. However, CONAP continues to be the subject of much criticism, both from NGOs and from local communities, for its excessively centralized bureaucracy, inadequate financial management, poor public relations, and the like. Yet, in criticizing CONAP, we actually weaken our own conservation cause. Therefore, a major challenge for ProPetén and other NGOs is to strengthen CONAP politically, technically, and socially at the local and national levels.

As these questions show, there are many unknown variables and challenges ahead for ProPetén as it works for conservation-based development in the Maya Biosphere Reserve. There are encouraging signs, nevertheless, that ProPetén and others involved in the Maya Biosphere Reserve project may be having a positive effect. Recent satellite images show that deforestation in the corridor from El Cruce a Dos Aguadas to Carmelita has slowed considerably since project activities began in 1993. Barring major policy shifts by the Guatemalan government, it should be possible to further slow, or stop entirely, deforestation in this corridor. This outcome should be possible if we continue building on the experiences gained and lessons learned by ProPetén and other NGOs, the Guatemalan government, and the communities themselves in this ongoing experiment in conservation-based development. With creativity, determination, and a little bit of luck, we may be able to build a modern forest society for the twenty-first century.

Acknowledgments

The authors wish to thank several people—Juan Pablo Ávalos Choc, José Contreras, Sharon Flynn, Kevin Gould, Dan Irwin, Kathleen Judd, Fred Meyerson, Jim Nations, Ingrid Neubauer, Chris Rader, Gustavo Rodríguez Ortíz, Norman Schwartz, and Michelle Sister—for their thoughtful comments and contributions to this chapter. We are also indebted to our many compañeros in ProPetén who have given their talents and energies to the conservation of the Maya Biosphere Reserve. Without them, this paper would never have been written.

References

Brokaw, N., E. Mallory, and P. Alcorn. 1990. *Trees of Rio Bravo: A Guide to Trees of the Rio Bravo Conservation and Management Area, Belize.* Manomet Bird Observatory, Manomet, Mass.

CATIE (Centro Agronómico Tropical de Investigación y Enseñanza). 1996. *Plan Maestro: Reserva de la Biósfera Maya.* Consejo Nacional de Áreas Protegidas (CONAP), Turrialba, Costa Rica.

Godoy, R. 1996. *Políticas Mínimas de Turísmo Para la Reserva de la Biósfera Maya.* Draft Report. Conservation International, Guatemala.

Gordon, D., M. Guerin-McManus, and A. B. Rosenfeld. 1996. *A New Model for Oil Development in the Tropics.* Draft Report. Conservation International, Washington, D.C.

Gould, K., and G. Rodríguez. 1996. *Evaluation of the Ecological Sustainability of Natural Dye Extraction in the Forests of El Cruce Dos Aguadas, San Andrés, Petén.* Conservation International, Petén, Guatemala.

Graham, I. 1988. Homeless hieroglyphs. *Antiquity* 62: 122–126.

Grandia, L. 1996. From dawn 'til dawn: Valuing women's work in the Petén, Guatemala. Senior Thesis, Yale University, New Haven, Conn.

HLA Consultants and the ARA Consulting Group, Inc. 1995. *Ecotourism Nature/Adventure/Culture: Alberta and British Columbia: Market Demand Assessment.* Prepared for Canadian Heritage and others. Edmonton, Alberta, and Vancouver, British Columbia.

Instituto Guatemalteco de Turismo (Guatemalan Tourism Institute—INGUAT). 1995a. *Estadísticas de Turismo 1994.* Bulletin No. 23. Guatemala City.

INGUAT. 1995b. *Desarrollo Turístico Sustentable Hacia el Año 2005.* Published Report, Guatemala City.

Nations, J. D. 1990. Protected areas in tropical rainforests. Pages 208–216 in *Lessons of the Rainforest,* S. Head and R. Heinzman, eds. Sierra Club Books, San Francisco.

ProPetén. 1996. *Plan Integrado de Manejo de Recursos: Resumen Ejecutivo.* Concesion Forestal Comunitaria de Carmelita, San Andrés Petén. Unpublished report. Conservation International, Petén, Guatemala.

Reining, C., R. M. Heinzman, M. C. Madrid, S. López, and A. Solórzano. 1992. *Nontimber Forest Products of the Maya Biosphere Reserve, Petén, Guatemala.* Conservation International, Washington, D.C.

Sader, S. A., T. Sever, J. C. Smoot, and M. Richards. 1994. Forest change estimates for the northern Petén region of Guatemala—1986–1990. *Human Ecology* 22: 317–332.

Sader, S. A., T. Sever, and J. C. Smoot. 1996. Time-series tropical forest change detection: A visual and quantitative approach. In *Multispectral Imaging for Terrestrial Applications*, B. Huberty, J. B. Lurie, C. A. Caylor, P. Coppin, and P. C. Robert, eds.

Schwartz, Norman. 1990. *Forest Society: A Social History of the Petén, Guatemala.* University of Pennsylvania Press, Philadelphia.

———. 1995. An anthropological view of the forest culture of Petén, Guatemala. Paper presented at the American Association for the Advancement of Science (AAAS) Annual Meeting. Panel on Five Ways of Looking at a Tropical Forest, February 17, Atlanta, Ga.

Serageldin, Ismael. 1993. Making development sustainable. *Finance and Development.* (December): 7.

Sobenes, A. 1995. *Propuesta de Políticas Para El Manejo de Los Recursos Forestales No Maderables en Guatemala (Especialmente Xate, Chicle y Pimienta Gorda).* Conservation International, Guatemala City.

Wargo, John. 1990. *Reconciling Conservation and Development in Biosphere Reserve: The Role of Incentives.* Yale School of Forestry and Environmental Studies, New Haven, Conn.

Whitacre, David. 1996. *Main Factors and Processes Threatening Biological Diversity and Integrity of the Maya Biosphere Reserve and Recommendations for Reducing and/or Mitigating These Impacts.* A Report to the Consejo Nacional de Áreas Protegidas (CONAP) and USAID. The Peregrine Fund, Boise, Idaho.

Chapter 25

The Belize Zoo: Grassroots Efforts in Education and Outreach

Rafael Coc, Laura Marsh, and Elizabeth Platt

In recent decades, zoos the world over have embraced a new role in educating the public about conservation. No longer simply repositories of exotic and unusual creatures, zoos have taken an active role in expanding public awareness of threats to biodiversity. Yet few zoos anywhere in the world have accomplished so much starting with so little, and found such innovative methods to spread the conservation message, as the Belize Zoo and Tropical Education Center. In many ways, this once-modest organization has developed an ideal of how a zoo should interact with the viewing public to create a greater understanding of the natural world and promote harmony between nature and humanity.

From its beginnings in 1983, the Belize Zoo has developed along a path unlike most modern zoos. It began almost by accident, when a documentary filmmaker working in Belize left behind a collection of captive animals, including jaguars, margay cats, great curassows, and peccaries, that could not be returned to the wild. The film's animal handler, Sharon Matola, resolved the matter of the homeless animals by opening a small, makeshift facility; from this tiny collection has evolved a well-known, highly respected zoo and tropical education center that differs from most zoos in many respects. The principal difference lies in the fact that the animals housed in the zoo are exclusively animals native to Belize. Whereas most other zoos collect an exotic array of animals from all regions of the earth, the Belize Zoo is dedicated first and foremost to educating both foreign visitors and Belizean natives alike about the country's natural resources. Understanding and conserving those resources are its primary goals. In keeping with this message, none of the animals on display have been deliberately collected from the wild; all were found either orphaned or injured, or had been kept as pets prior to coming to the zoo.

Though the zoo's existence was spread principally through word-of-mouth at first, its popularity increased very rapidly. The discovery that most Belizeans, adults and children alike, were seeing many of the birds, mammals, and reptiles characteristic of their country for the first time at the zoo, inspired the creation of outreach programs aimed at educating schoolchildren about Belizean wildlife. School visits, slide show presentations, and short discussions with students and teachers paved the way for an introduction to zoo environmental programs. Encouraging teachers to participate in teacher workshops held at the zoo was another effective way of disseminating environmental education in the country. The Belize Zoo filled an important gap by providing an exciting educational center where students, the public, and visitors to Belize could view the wildlife of Belize and learn the importance of conserving these natural resources. As a direct result of the programs developed by the Belize Zoo, interest in local wildlife has grown tremendously over the past decade, and attendance at the Belize Zoo has steadily increased. A further result has been a notable increase in both public and political awareness for the need to preserve and sustain Belize's natural resources. Environmental education has proven to be a powerful tool in raising the level of national environmental awareness.

The original haphazard cages have been transformed over the years into a collection of naturalistic habitat enclosures, which became the basis of the zoo's conservation education program. The Tropical Education Center (TEC) is a separate facility run by the Belize Zoo specifically for outdoor education programs. The Center has a large lecture hall, lab area, library, bird observation deck, and 84 acres of savanna, wetland, and broadleaf forest corridors with a network of trails. From this framework, environmental education programs reach out to various target groups in the country (Figure 25.1). An important method used by the zoo's staff—originally a staff of one, Matola herself, but now including more than 20 full-time workers—was to create a sense of identification with the zoo's animals among the Belizean visitors. To accomplish this, the zoo popularized the individual animals' "personalities": April the Baird's tapir, Rambo the toucan, and Balboa the boa constrictor became familiar friends to many of Belize's schoolchildren courtesy of zoo outreach programs. With respect to April and Rambo, presentations at the zoo emphasized the position of the tapir and toucan as the national animal and bird to teach visitors to take pride in native wildlife. In order to encourage the protection of the tapir, for instance, each year the Belize Zoo education staff holds a birthday party for April, an original member of the menagerie. The celebration is highlighted by the presentation of a "cake" made from April's favorite food items. Hundreds of children celebrate the event at the zoo,

Figure 25.1

Students learn about pond ecology in a course run by the Belize Zoo and Tropical Education Center.

where they participate in educational games. The more portable Balboa, on the other hand, has been a frequent "show-and-tell" visitor to schools, an exciting event for children who rarely see live snakes due to the common Belizean attitude toward these creatures—kill them before they bite you, an understandable reaction given the presence of several extremely dangerous varieties (including coral snakes, rattlesnakes, and the deadly, aggressive fer-de-lances) in Belizean forests. For other animals, the sense of familiarity and friendship was established by the ingenious handpainted signs placed at each exhibit. Unlike the standard zoo sign—printed in small, neat type, written in language that is informative, factual, inevitably somewhat dry, and clearly intended for adult readers—the signs at the Belize Zoo are messages painted in bold, colored letters, written as if each animal was communicating directly to the visitor in the Creole commonly spoken by many Belizeans (Figure 25.2). The signs are simple, direct, and occasionally humorous although quite serious in their message—and as a result, they are far more likely to make an impression on readers, particularly children.

The Belize Zoo's success dramatically illustrates the importance of the conservation outreach programs it sponsors. Environmental education programs target schools and communities nationwide (Figure 25.3). In Belize, "nationwide" programs are a challenging prospect: many communities are virtually

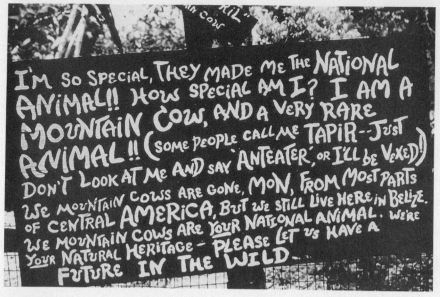

Figure 25.2

Signs at the Belize Zoo are written in the style of local dialects and have a strong conservation theme.

Figure 25.3

The zoo's outreach program brings conservation materials to rural schools.

inaccessible by road, so the zoo staff must find alternative methods of bringing the information to rural locations. When communities are inaccessible by vehicle, equipment is loaded on a mule; a three-hour hike through the forest is not unusual to reach remote areas. Some villages are located along waterways, so local boats become the preferred mode of transportation to these sites. In communities that do not have electricity, the zoo's portable generator provides the necessary power for slide presentation. The attention and excitement shown by the children in schools and by local people greatly outweigh any hardships encountered reaching the sites.

Yet many of the most valuable experiences can only be found at the zoo itself. Recognizing the value of these programs, the Belizean government's Education Department sponsors a Rural School Scholarship, which brings students in from surrounding villages to the zoo for a day of interactive education. This program has been very successful in educating an audience that would otherwise be unable to participate. In addition, hundreds of primary schoolchildren gather at the zoo to display their projects at the annual Environmental Science Fair. This event encourages the participation of primary schools countrywide to develop projects that teach children the value of natural resources. Projects have included illustrating the sustainable use of natural resources, the depiction of natural resource management strategies, and solution-oriented pilot projects for communities. Another program drawing students who do not normally come to the zoo on their own is the High School Work Experience Program, in which students participate in animal management, husbandry, and environmental education courses taught at the zoo.

Zoo environmental education programs are directed toward different groups with different lifestyles, attitudes, knowledge, and interests. In recognizing these differences, the programs provide useful information to the various communities. At a national level, the message is spread via radio programs created by the zoo's director. Radio Belize and British Forces Radio are the predominant media for reaching Belize's rural communities; popular weekly shows such as *Rambo Says* and brief but effective *Walk on the Wild Side* spots discuss conservation and wildlife issues. Posters about the environment and conservation issues, as well as the zoo education newsletters, are circulated nationwide. To broaden their impact in this multi-ethnic nation, the zoo's environmental message is disseminated in several languages. Posters illustrating details of the wildlife laws of Belize, for example, are written in English, Spanish, Creole, and Chinese, four of the many languages peculiar to this small nation. As most Belizeans speak at least one of these—in addition to German, Garifuna, and several Mayan dialects—the multilingual efforts are likely to reach the vast majority of this highly literate population.

The Belize Zoo has also been successful in collaborating with other organizations to promote conservation. One of the most popular and successful outreach programs is the Conservation Carnival, a collaborative effort between the Belize Audubon Society and the Center for Environmental Studies. The program aims to raise awareness and promote the wise use of natural resources among Toledo and Corozal residents, introducing not only schoolchildren but entire communities to the concepts behind protected areas and wildlife conservation. Another example is a successful pilot project, Maya Growth Industries, initiated by the zoo and PACA project (Proyecto Ambiental Para Centro America). This project worked with the Maya of Toledo to encourage the sustainable use of natural resources through the production of local handicrafts such as baskets, embroidery, and slate carvings.

The Belize Zoo has been instrumental in promoting regional environmental education in part through its publications. Its premier publications are children's books, *Hoodwink the Owl* and its companion, *The Further Adventures of Hoodwink the Owl*, both written to bring complex conservation issues to an elementary level of comprehension. Elementary-level science curricula in the country now include concepts and messages from the Hoodwink books. For more advanced students, Environmental Education Manuals were developed in collaboration with the Ministry of Education and local environmental nongovernmental organizations. No other publications of this kind existed in the country prior to their development. The environmental manuals and corresponding lesson plans, which covered marine life, wildlife, land use, and pollution, are still used extensively in classrooms throughout the country.

The staff of the Belize Zoo and Tropical Education Center also have created publications designed to address both specific conservation issues in Belize and gaps in general natural history information. For example, a book entitled *A Field Guide to the Snakes of Belize*, by General Curator Tony Garel and Director Sharon Matola, was created primarily to change negative attitudes about snakes in Belize, but also to address a woeful lack of information on the varied species present in Belizean forests. Other publications developed and compiled by the zoo staff as resources for the Natural History Workshops held at the TEC include *Soils of Belize*; *Geology of Belize*; *Life and Times of a Belizean Blue*; *A Checklist of the Birds of Belize*; *Meet and Color Iguana Belle*; *A Handbook of the Mammals of Belize*; *A Handbook of the Birds of Belize*; *The ABC's to the Vegetation of Belize*; *Wetlands Education Program*; and audiocassette summaries on the soils, geology, and birds of Belize. Finally, *The Belize Zooletter*, a newsletter with contributions from the Education Department, keeper staff, and TEC staff and management, is published quarterly. It has an international distribution to members abroad as well as a large local audience. The zoo is an ever-evolving institution, and a regular information forum highlights its progress.

The Tropical Education Center has grown in both programming and use in recent years. TEC hosts a number of zoo-coordinated camps and workshops, as well as operates its own programs. The Belize Zoo Summer Youth Camp promotes youth involvement in environmentally related activities within their respective school and community. The Teacher Training Workshop developed by the Belize Zoo provides an ideal opportunity for teachers to come together, share their knowledge, and learn to incorporate outdoor activities in the classroom. Most recently, the Belize Zoo has initiated a course on the natural history of Belize. Because of the tremendous growth in ecotourism in recent years, tour guides were chosen as a target group to participate in the Natural History Workshop through a collaborative effort with the Belize Tourist Board (BTB) and the Belize Tourist Industry Association (BTIA). As the Natural History Workshop continues to be offered by the Belize Zoo, other potential participants will be invited, such as Forestry Department staff, environmental nongovernmental organizations, and other educational institutions. Finally, program development at the Tropical Education Center is expanding for school groups. A wetlands curriculum that combines a zoo visit with wetlands discovery at TEC is currently being drafted by the Zoo Education Department. Site-specific programs are underway to teach numerous concepts, such as ecological connections, ecosystem processes, plant identification, and interactive conservation methods.

As much as any other facility of its kind in the world, the Belize Zoo and Tropical Education Center has demonstrated the true potential of conservation education. Nowhere has a grassroots organization created such a varied, successful enterprise so quickly, starting with so little. Through its varied and innovative approaches, the Belize Zoo has made itself an indispensable part of Belize's conservation movement, yet it is also among the most popular institutions available to the public.

Acknowledgments

Thanks are due to several anonymous reviewers for comments on the original paper and especially to Richard Primack for his guidance in reworking the paper. Special thanks to Sharon Matola for comments on the draft manuscript and for kindly supplying photos.

References

Coe, R., and L. Marsh. 1995. The Belize Zoo and Tropical Education Center: Environmental Education: A Multi-Faceted Approach. Paper presented at the Workshop on Conservation and Community Development in the Selva Maya of Belize, Guatemala, and Mexico, Chetumal, Mexico, November 8–10, 1995.

Current Biography. 1983. Biographic profile of Belize Zoo founder Sharon Matola.

Common Terms and Names

....

baboon Belizean Creole name for the black howler monkey (*Alouatta pigra*).

bajo Lowland swamp forest.

bayleaf See *huano*.

botan See *huano*.

breadnut Common name for a tree species, *Brosimum alicastrum*, also called *ramón*, that occurs throughout the Maya Forest and is often found in close association with Maya ruins. The tree's nut-like fruits are edible and are a source of food for various animal species; they are also sometimes collected by local people and ground into flour.

buffer zones Areas around biosphere reserve core areas where carefully monitored economic activities are permitted. Ideally, by permitting use of these less sensitive portions of the reserve, more fragile ecosystems in the core areas will be left undisturbed.

canicula Local name for a short period of wet-season drought in the Petén, usually occurring in July or August.

caoba Common name for mahogany (*Swietenia macrophylla*). A highly valued timber tree.

cedro Common name for Spanish cedar (*Cedrela mexicana* or *C. odorata*). A highly valued timber tree.

chicle Resinous sap collected by chicle tappers (*chicleros*) from the tree species *Manilkara zapota*, used in the manufacture of chewing gum. The name "chicle" may also refer to the tree itself, although the species is more commonly called sapodilla or chicozapote.

chicozapote See *chicle*.

chiquibúl Inferior-quality chicle resin. As a proper name, *Chiquibul* applies to protected forests in both southern Belize and the southeastern corner of the Petén, as well as to the river that flows between these two reserves.

cohune Common name for the palm species *Orbigyna cohune*, also known as corozo. The species, a tall, easily recognized palm, is characteristic of a floristic community bearing its name ("cohune ridge") that occurs on rich, well-drained soil.

concessions Formal agreement between a government and a private organization to allow the latter to extract resources from public lands. Concessions usually limit the methods of extraction and amount of resource removed in the time specified by the concession.

corozo See *cohune*.

dbh Diameter at breast height. In forestry, a tree's girth is measured at "breast height," roughly four feet six inches (135 cm) off the ground.

ejido A cooperative landholding system used in Mexico. Cooperative members (*ejidatarios*) are granted usufruct rights to the land through the Agrarian Reform program. Ejidatarios reside on the land and make decisions as to its use in a general assembly.

high-grading A logging practice in which the timber outfit extracts only the timber with high market value, leaving the remaining trees behind. This practice seems less harmful than clear-cutting, but in fact it can greatly reduce the regeneration capabilities of the targeted species.

huano Common name for the botan or bayleaf palm (*Sabal mauritiiformis*); the word also refers to the fronds of this species, which are preferred over the fronds of other species for construction of thatch roofs.

Kekchi One of many groups that make up the Maya linguistic family, the Kekchi originate in highland Guatemala, primarily in the Department of Alta Verapaz. Many Kekchi families have migrated into the Petén and southern Belize in search of farmland or work as chicle tappers.

Ladino A person of mixed Indian and Spanish descent. See also *mestizo*.

logyards Areas in the forest cleared by loggers for the purpose of stacking cut timber and loading it for transport to processing plants or markets. These areas can be important sites for regeneration of valuable sun-loving species such as mahogany.

Maya Mountains An area of uplifted limestone mountains in southern Belize and the southern Petén, Guatemala.

Mesoamerica Literally, "Middle America." The term is generally used to refer to the section of Central America from central Mexico south to Honduras and northern El Salvador. The area roughly corresponds to the ancient civilizations of the Olmec, Maya, Zapotec, Mixtec, and Aztec, as well as the regions now inhabited by these peoples' modern descendants.

mestizo See *ladino*.

milpa Small plots for subsistence agriculture, traditionally planted with corn, beans, squash, and other common local crops. "Milpa" is often used synonymously with "shifting cultivation" or "slash-and-burn cultivation," as the plots are not used for long-term farming, but true milpa farming is rotational. As a plot's fertility declines, usually after two or three years of farming, the farmer (*milpero*) clears another section of forested land and allows the older plot to return to forest. The older plots are brought back into cultivation after a period of about 7 years, at which time enough regrowth has occurred to suppress weedy species.

paper parks A park for which legal authorization has been granted, but which has no means of enforcing its boundaries. Typically, such parks are created with the intention of preventing or ending unsustainable or harmful activities such as logging or shifting agriculture, but with no capabilities to enforce the restrictions, park managers are unable to fulfill the original mission.

pimienta gorda Common name for the allspice tree (*Pimenta dioeca*). The berries of this tree are collected for use as a spice.

quintal A unit of measure for produce. 1 quintal (qq) = 100 lbs.

Ruta Maya Ecotourism strategy linking Mexico, Guatemala, Belize, Honduras, and El Salvador. Publicized in *National Geographic*, the Ruta Maya concept advocates a conservation strategy based upon the notion that the forests must become a source of income. This income theoretically would come from increased tourism attracted by the culture, archaeology, and ecology of the region.

xate (pronounced shah-tay) A fern of the genus *Chamadorea*, native to Central America, which is commonly harvested for shipment overseas for use in floral arrangements.

Common Acronyms

CBS   Community Baboon Sanctuary (Belize). Grassroots organization for protection of howler monkey habitat. See Horwich and Lyons for extended discussion.

CECON   Centro de Estudios Conservacionistas, San Carlos University (Guatemala). University center specializing in conservation studies.

CI   Conservation International (U.S.). A U.S.-based nongovernmental organization focusing on species and habitat conservation. Its Guatemalan branch, ProPetén, works out of Flores, Petén.

CONAP   Consejo Nacional de Areas Protegidas (Guatemala). Government agency responsible for management of reserves and protected areas in Guatemala.

CUDEP   Centro Universitario del Petén (Guatemala). A branch of the Universidad de San Carlos de Guatemala located in the Petén that offers courses in conservation and management, agronomy, and tourism for local residents.

DIGEBOS   Directorado General de Bosques (Guatemala). Government agency in charge of forest resources.

FAO   Food and Agriculture Organization (United Nations).

FYDEP   Empresa Nacional de Fomento y Desarrollo Económico del Petén (Guatemala). Defunct government agency created to oversee development in the Department of El Petén. Replaced by CONAP.

IDAEH   Instituto de Antropología y Historia (Guatemala). Government branch that maintains cultural heritage sites and monuments.

INAFOR   Instituto Nacional Forestal (Guatemala). Defunct government agency in charge of forestry. Replaced by DIGEBOS.

INAH   Instituto Nacional de Antropología y Historia (México). Government institution in charge of monuments, archaeological remains, and cultural heritage.

INFOP   Instituto Nacional de Fomento de Producción (Guatemala). De-
             funct government agency intended to encourage production in the
             Petén. Replaced by FYDEP.

INGUAT   Instituto Guatemaliteco de Turismo (Guatemala). Government
             agency in charge of tourism.

INMECAFE Instituto Mexicano del Café (México). Defunct government
             agency mandated to support coffee growers.

MAB   Man and the Biosphere Program. A program striving for sustainable
             use of biological communities, developed and sponsored by UN-
             ESCO (United Nations Educational Scientific and Cultural Orga-
             nization). This program is distinct from the United States program
             of the same name (USMAB).

MBR   Maya Biosphere Reserve (Guatemala). The largest single protected
             area in the Maya Forest, inaugurated in 1993 under the UNESCO
             Man and the Biosphere Program.

MIQRO   Maderas Industrializadas de Quintana Roo (México). An agency
             authorized in the 1950s by presidential decree to govern the timber
             industry in Quintana Roo, Mexico.

ODA   Overseas Development Agency (U.K.). Government agency that
             sponsors research and development projects aimed at encouraging
             responsible economic growth in developing nations.

PFB   Program for Belize (Belize). A nongovernmental organization that
             supports sustainable development research in Belize. PFB's largest
             program is the operation of the Río Bravo Conservation and Man-
             agement Area in northwestern Belize.

PPCh   Plan Piloto Chiclero (México). A community forestry initiative in-
             tended to rebuild chicle industry community cooperatives as pro-
             duction and marketing organizations.

PPF   Plan Piloto Forestal (México). A community forestry initiative in
             Quintana Roo designed to govern forestry activities in ejido lands.

RBCMA   Río Bravo Conservation and Management Area (Belize). Private
             protected area run by the Program for Belize.

SARH   Secretario de Agricultura y Recursos Hydraulicos (México). De-
             funct Mexican federal agency in charge of agriculture and water re-
             sources.

SEDESOL   Secretaría de Desarrollo Social. Mexican government agency es-
             tablished in 1992, focusing on social welfare programs.

SEDUE   Secretaría de Desarrollo Urban y Ecologia. Mexican government
             agency that handled urban and environmental affairs; dissolved in
             1992.

TNC   The Nature Conservancy (U.S.). A U.S.-based nongovernmental organization that encourages habitat conservation through land purchases, debt swaps, and sustainable development initiatives.

USAID   U.S. Agency for International Development. Government agency that sponsors programs to encourage responsible economic growth in developing nations.

USMAB   The U.S. State Department's program aimed at encouraging sustainable use of biological communities. Modeled after the UNESCO MAB program.

Contributors

Deocundo Acopa Avenida 12 de Octubre, Esq. 2o Poniente Norte, Palenque, Chiapas 29960, Mexico

James R. Barborak The Wildlife Conservation Society, 4424 NW 13th Street, Suite A-2, Gainesville, FL 32609 *email:* wcsfl@afn.org

Jill Belsky Associate Professor, Department of Sociology, University of Montana, Missoula, MT 59812-1047 *email:* sojmb@selway.umt.edu

Neil Bird Forest Planning and Management Project, Forest Department, Ministry of Natural Resources, Belmopan, Belize.

Eckart Boege INAH Veracruz, Apartado Postal 305, 91000, Xalapa, Veracruz, Mexico

David Barton Bray Chair, Department of Environmental Studies, Florida International University, Miami, FL 33185 *email:* dbbray@aol.com

Nicholas V. Brokaw Manomet Observatory, P. O. Box 1770, Manomet, MA 02345 *email:* nbrokaw@aol.com

Exceslau Reginaldo Chayax Huex Presidente, Comite Bio-Itzá, San Jose, Peten, Guatemala

Rafael Coc Tropical Education Center Station Manager, The Belize Zoo, 29 Miles Western Highway, P. O. Box 1787, Belize City, Belize

Mathew B. Dickinson Department of Biological Sciences, Florida State University, Tallahassee, FL 32306-2043

Barbara L. Dugelby The Nature Conservancy, 1815 North Lynn Street, Arlington, VA 22209 *email:* bdugelby@tnc.org

Henning Flachsenberg Instituto de Foresteria Mundial, Leuschner Str. 91, Hamburg 22031, Germany

Hugo A. Galletti Reforma No. 21, CP 77000, Chetumal, Quintana Roo, Mexico

Carlos Enrique Gomez Caal Tecnico Forestal, CATIE/CONAP, Flores, Peten, Guatemala

Steven P. Gretzinger Rogue Institute for Ecology and Economy, 762 A Street, Ashland, OR 97520 *email:* sgretz@mind.net

John M. Hagan Manomet Observatory, P. O. Box 1770, Manomet, MA 02345 *email:* jmhagan@ime.net

Robert H. Horwich Director, Community Conservation Consultants, RD 1, Box 96, Gays Mills, WI 54631

Jeffrey Paul Jorgenson Professor, Departemento de Biologia, Pontificia Universidad Javeriana, A. A. 56487, Santa fe de Bogota, Colombia *email:* jjorgens@javercol.javeriana.edu.co

Elizabeth Losos Center for Tropical Forest Science, Smithsonian Tropical Research Institute, 900 Jefferson Drive, Suite 2207, Washington, DC 20560

James F. Lynch Smithsonian, Environmental Research Center, P. O. Box 28, Edgewater, MD 21037

Jonathan Lyon Edgewood College, 855 Woodrow Street, Madison, WI 53711 *email:* jlyon@edgewood.edu

Elizabeth P. Mallory Manomet Observatory, P. O. Box 1770, Manomet, MA 02345

Juan Marroquín Avenida 12 de Octubre, Esq. 2o Poniente Norte, C.P. 29960, Palenque, Chiapas, Mexico

Laura Marsh Department of Anthropology, Washington University, Box 1114, St. Louis, MO 63110

Paul J. Martins Proyecto Catie/Remarm, CATIE, 7170 Turrialba, Costa Rica

Sharon Matola Director, The Belize Zoo and Tropical Education Center, P. O. Box 1787, Belize City, Belize

Luís Oswaldo Morales Marín Tecnico, Recursos Naturales, ProPeten/CI, Casa Ingeniero Asturias, Flores, Peten, Guatemala

James D. Nations Vice President, Latin American Programs, Conservation International, 2501 M Street, N.W., Suite 200, Washington, DC *email:* jnations@conservation.org

Ruth Norris 1310 South Carolina, S.E., Washington, DC 20003

Darrell Novelo Programme for Belize, 2 South Park Street, Belize City, Belize

Jennifer L. O'Hara Yale School of Forestry, 370 Prospect Street, New Haven, CT 06511 *email:* jennifer.ohara@yale.edu

Silvio Olivieri Conservation International, 2501 M Street, N.W., Suite 200, Washington, DC 20037 *email:* s.olivieri@conservation.org

Elizabeth Platt   76 Quint Avenue, #6, Allston, MA 02134

José Luís Plaza Sánchez   AICA Consultores, S.C., Cerrada La Palma 32-C, Colonia La Joya, C.P. 14090, Tlalpan, D.F. Mexico

Ismael Ponciano   Director, CECON, Avenida de la Reforma 0-63, Zona 10, Guatemala, Guatemala

Richard B. Primack   Professor of Biology, Biology Department, Boston University, 5 Cummington Street, Boston, MA 02215 *email:* primack@bio.bu.edu

Conrad Reining   Director, Guatemala Program, Conservation International, 2501 M Street, N.W., Suite 200, Washington, DC 20037 *email:* c.reining@conservation.org

Chris Rodstrom   Coordinator, Regional Conservation Analysis, Conservation International, 2501 M Street, N.W., Suite 200, Washington, DC 20037 *email:* c.rodstrom@conservation.org

Stephen F. Siebert   Associate Professor, School of Forestry, University of Montana, Missoula, MT 59812 *email:* siebert@selway.umt.edu

Laura K. Snook   Nicholas School of the Environment, Box 90328, Duke University, Durham, NC 27708 *email:* lsnook@env.duke.edu

Carlos Soza Manzanero   ProPeten, Casa Ingeniero, Flores, Peten, Guatemala

Laura Tangley   2853 Ontario Road, N.W., #218, Washington, DC 20009

Feliciano Tzul Colli   Vice Presidente, Comite Bio-Itzá, San Jose, Peten, Guatemala

Dennis F. Whigham   Smithsonian Environmental Research Center, P. O. Box 28, Edgewater, MD 21037

David Whitacre   Research Scientist, Director, "Proyecoto Maya," The Peregrine Fund, Inc., 5666 West Flying Hawk Lane, Boise, ID 83709 *email:* wcbp@aol.com

Dominic White   World Wide Land Conservation Trust, Blyth House, Bridge House, Halesworth, Suffolk IP19 8AB, United Kingdom

Andrew A. Whitman   Manomet Observatory, P. O. Box 1770, Manomet, MA 02345 *email:* awhitman@prodigy.com

J. Scott Wilber   The Nature Conservancy, 1815 North Lynn Street, Arlington, VA 22209 *email:* swilber@tnc.org

Roger Wilson   Programme for Belize, 2 South Park Street, Belize City, Belize

Name Index

Subject Index